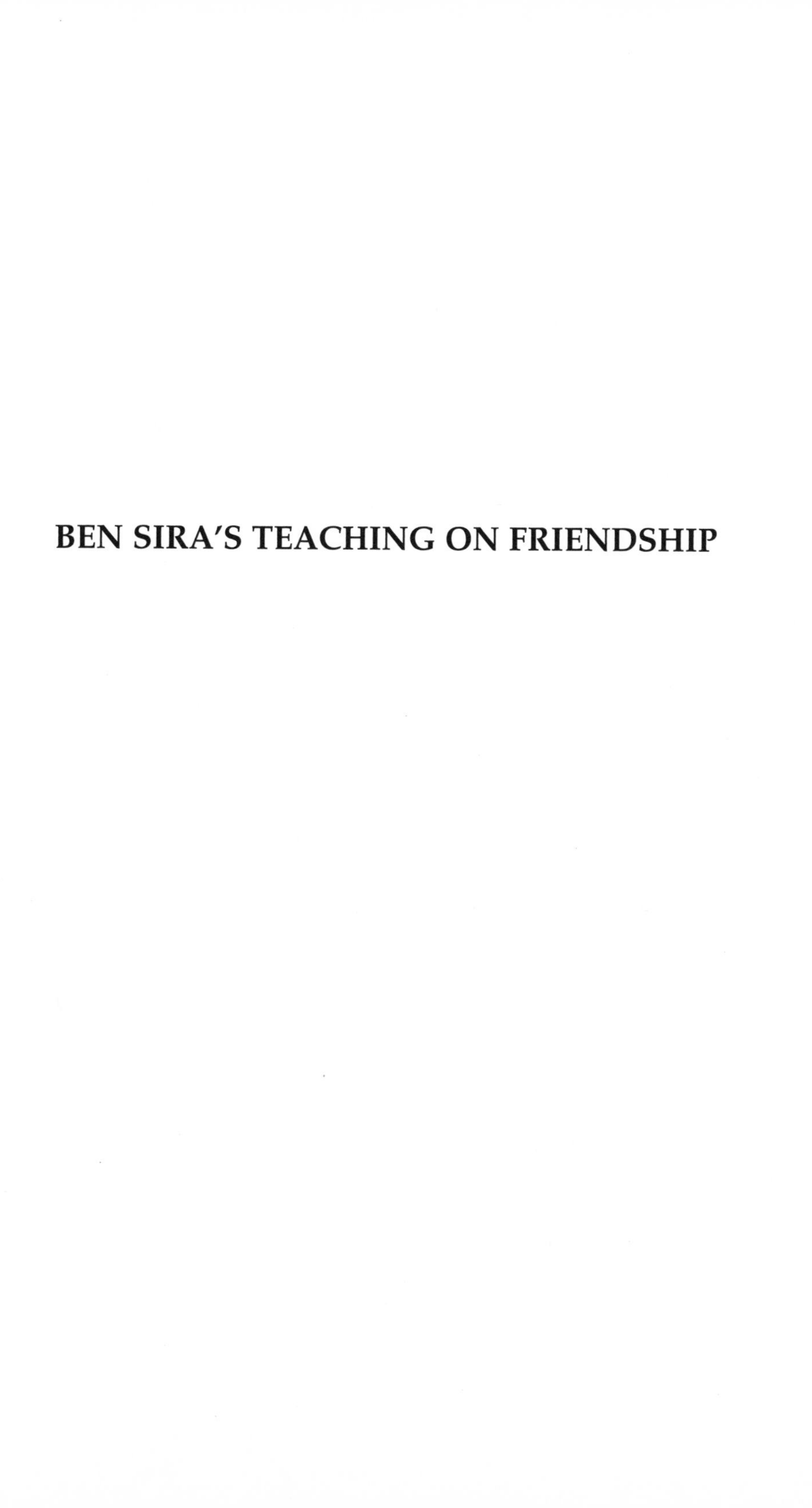

BEN SIRA'S TEACHING ON FRIENDSHIP

Program in Judaic Studies
Brown University
Box 1826
Providence, RI 02912

BROWN JUDAIC STUDIES

Number 316

BEN SIRA'S TEACHING ON FRIENDSHIP

by
Jeremy Corley

BEN SIRA'S TEACHING ON FRIENDSHIP

by
Jeremy Corley

Brown Judaic Studies
Providence

Library of Congress Cataloging-in-Publication Data
Corley, Jeremy.
Ben Sira's teaching on friendship / by Jeremy Corley.
p. cm. —(Brown Judaic Studies ; no. 316)
Includes bibliographical references and index.
ISBN 1-930675-09-7 (cloth : alk. paper)
1. Bible. O.T. Apocrypha. Ecclesiasticus—Criticism, interpretation, etc. 2. Friendship—Biblical teaching. I . Title. II. Series.

BS1765.6.F73 C67 2001
229'.4'06—dc21 2001052405
10 09 08 07 06 05 04 03 02 5 4 3 2 1

Printed in the United States of America
on acid-free paper

Contents

Foreword

This study of Ben Sira's teaching on friendship is a revision and updating of my doctoral dissertation, accepted in spring 1996 at the Catholic University of America in Washington, D.C. The updating has taken note of many important works relevant to the topic published in the last five years.

It was during Trinity Term 1980, in an undergraduate class with Professor James Barr at Oxford University, that I first read Sir 6:5–17 in Hebrew. Little did I imagine that a decade and a half later, that pericope, and six others by Ben Sira on friendship, would occupy me full-time for two years. I thank my bishop, Rt. Rev. Crispian Hollis, for giving me the opportunity of doing graduate work in Biblical Studies at the Catholic University of America. In addition, I offer my grateful thanks to Rt. Rev. Aidan Shea and the community of St. Anselm's Abbey for their hospitality to me during my time at Catholic University. I also thank the university's Board of Trustees for remitting the tuition fees for my doctoral studies.

I am grateful to the Biblical Studies faculty at Catholic University for all they have taught me. First and foremost, I thank Professor Alexander A. Di Lella, O.F.M., my dissertation director, for sharing from his unrivaled knowledge of Ben Sira, as well as for his incisive criticism and his patient guidance. Second, I thank Professor Christopher T. Begg, my first reader, for his generous assistance and timely comments. Third, I thank Professor Joseph Jensen, O.S.B., my second reader, for his personal kindness and help. I also thank fellow doctoral students for their friendship, especially Michael Duggan, Patrick Madden, Carol Dempsey, Vincent Skemp, and Joseph E. Jensen. I am grateful, too, for the help of the staff at Catholic University's Mullen Library, especially Bruce Miller and Monica Blanchard. Thanks are also due to those who enabled me to see Cairo Genizah manuscripts of Ben Sira, especially Professor Stefan Reif in Cambridge and Dr. Seth Schwartz in New York. In addition, I thank Laura Millman for reading my manuscript and suggesting many stylistic improvements.

During the period when I was revising my work for publication, I received help from many people. First, I am grateful for the support of the parishioners at St. Joseph's Church in Newbury, as well as the community of Douai Abbey in Berkshire. Second, I am thankful for the assistance of the community at Ushaw College in Durham, particularly

Rev. James O'Keefe, the President, and my biblical colleagues Rev. Timothy Swinglehurst and Rev. Michael Winstanley, S.D.B. Third, I am indebted to the Ben Sira Research Institute in Salzburg for bibliographic help, especially to its Director, Professor Friedrich Reiterer, and to Dr. Renate Egger-Wenzel.

I also wish to express my gratitude to the editors of Brown Judaic Studies, particularly Professor Shaye Cohen, who read the first draft and made some good suggestions, and Professor Saul Olyan, who accepted the final manuscript. Additional thanks are due to Bob Buller, who enabled a difficult manuscript to be published in the format of the series.

Finally, I pay tribute to my family, who have taught me both fidelity and the fear of God. In particular, I dedicate this work to my father and to the memory of my mother.

Ushaw College, Durham
July 2001

Abbreviations

Primary Sources

Aristotle	
Eth. eud.	*Ethica eudemia*
Eth. nic.	*Ethica nicomachea*
Rhet.	*Rhetorica*
[*Rhet. Alex.*]	*Rhetorica ad Alexandrum*
b.	Babylonian Talmud
B. Qam.	*Baba Qamma*
Cicero	
Amic.	*De amicitia*
Der. Er. Rab.	*Derek Ereṣ Rabbah*
ʿEd.	*ʿEduyyot*
1 En.	*1 Enoch*
Euripides	
Orest.	*Orestes*
Ḥag.	*Ḥagigah*
Hesiod	
Op.	*Opera et dies*
Homer	
Il.	*Iliad*
Od.	*Odyssey*
Isocrates	
Ad Nic.	*Ad Nicoclem* (*Or.* 2)
Antid.	*Antidosis* (*Or.* 15)
Demon.	*Ad Demonicum* (*Or.* 1)
Josephus	
Ag. Ap.	*Against Apion*
Ant.	*Jewish Antiquities*
J.W.	*Jewish War*
m.	Mishnah
Philo	
Hypoth.	*Hypothetica*
Plato	
Apol.	*Apologia*
Gorg.	*Gorgias*

Leg.	*Leges*
Resp.	*Respublica*
Symp.	*Symposium*
Plautus	
Cas.	*Casina*
Qoh. Rab.	*Qohelet Rabbah*
Šabb.	*Šabbat*
Sophocles	
Aj.	*Ajax*
Phil.	*Philoctetes*
Xenophon	
Cyr.	*Cyropaedia*
Mem.	*Memorabilia*

Secondary Sources

AB	Anchor Bible
ABD	*Anchor Bible Dictionary*. Edited by D. N. Freedman. 6 vols. New York: Doubleday, 1992.
AEL	*Ancient Egyptian Literature*. M. Lichtheim. 3 vols. Berkeley and Los Angeles: University of California Press, 1971–1980.
AGJU	Arbeiten zur Geschichte des antiken Judentums und des Urchristentums
AJP	*American Journal of Philology*
AnBib	Analecta biblica
ANET	*Ancient Near Eastern Texts Relating to the Old Testament*. Edited by J. B. Pritchard. 3d ed. Princeton, N.J.: Princeton University Press, 1969.
AOAT	Alter Orient und Altes Testament
APOT	*The Apocrypha and Pseudepigrapha of the Old Testament*. Edited by R. H. Charles. 2 vols. Oxford: Clarendon, 1913.
ATD	Das Alte Testament Deutsch
BASOR	*Bulletin of the American Schools of Oriental Research*
BBB	Bonner biblische Beiträge
BBET	Beiträge zur biblischen Exegese und Theologie
BDB	Brown, F., S. R. Driver, and C. A. Briggs. *A Hebrew and English Lexicon of the Old Testament*. Oxford: Oxford University Press, 1907.
BEATAJ	Beiträge zur Erforschung des Alten Testaments und des antiken Judentums
Bib	*Biblica*

BibOr	Biblica et orientalia
Bijdr	*Bijdragen*
BJS	Brown Judaic Studies
BN	*Biblische Notizen*
BZ	*Biblische Zeitschrift*
BZAW	Beihefte zur Zeitschrift für die alttestamentliche Wissenschaft
BZNW	Beihefte zur Zeitschrift für die neutestamentliche Wissenschaft
CBQ	*Catholic Biblical Quarterly*
CBQMS	Catholic Biblical Quarterly Monograph Series
CHJ	*Cambridge History of Judaism.* Edited by W. D. Davies and Louis Finkelstein. Cambridge: Cambridge University Press, 1984–.
ConBOT	Coniectanea biblica: Old Testament Series
CRINT	Compendia rerum Iudaicarum ad Novum Testamentum
CSHJ	Chicago Studies in the History of Judaism
CurBS	*Currents in Research: Biblical Studies*
DBSup	*Dictionnaire de la Bible: Supplément.* Edited by L. Pirot and A. Robert. Paris: Letouzey et Ané, 1928–.
DJD	Discoveries in the Judaean Desert
EHAT	Exegetisches Handbuch zum Alten Testament
EncJud	*Encyclopaedia Judaica.* 16 vols. Jerusalem: Keter, 1972.
EstBib	*Estudios bíblicos*
GKC	*Gesenius' Hebrew Grammar.* Edited by E. Kautzsch. Translated by A. E. Cowley. 2d ed. Oxford: Oxford University Press, 1910.
HAR	*Hebrew Annual Review*
HTR	*Harvard Theological Review*
HUCA	*Hebrew Union College Annual*
JANESCU	*Journal of the Ancient Near Eastern Society of Columbia University*
JBL	*Journal of Biblical Literature*
JJS	*Journal of Jewish Studies*
JNSL	*Journal of Northwest Semitic Languages*
Joüon	Joüon, P. *A Grammar of Biblical Hebrew.* Translated and revised by T. Muraoka. 2 vols. Subsidia biblica 14/1–2. Rome: Pontifical Biblical Institute, 1991.
JQR	*Jewish Quarterly Review*
JSHRZ	*Jüdische Schriften aus hellenistisch-römischer Zeit*
JSJSup	Supplements to the Journal for the Study of Judaism
JSNTSup	Journal for the Study of the New Testament: Supplement Series

JSOT	*Journal for the Study of the Old Testament*
JSOTSup	Journal for the Study of the Old Testament: Supplement Series
JSPSup	Journal for the Study of the Pseudepigrapha: Supplement Series
JTS	*Journal of Theological Studies*
LCL	Loeb Classical Library
LD	Lectio divina
LEC	Library of Early Christianity
MilS	*Milltown Studies*
NAB	New American Bible
NJB	New Jerusalem Bible
NJBC	*New Jerome Biblical Commentary*
NovTSup	Supplements to Novum Testamentum
NRSV	New Revised Standard Version
OBO	Orbis biblicus et orientalis
OTE	*Old Testament Essays*
OTL	Old Testament Library
OTP	*Old Testament Pseudepigrapha.* Edited by J. H. Charlesworth. 2 vols. New York: Doubleday, 1983–1985.
PzB	*Protokolle zur Bibel*
RAC	*Reallexikon für Antike und Christentum.* Edited by T. Klauser et al. Stuttgart: Hiersemann, 1950–.
RB	*Revue biblique*
REJ	*Revue des études juives*
RHPR	*Revue d'histoire et de philosophie religieuses*
RivB	*Rivista biblica italiana*
RTL	*Revue théologique de Louvain*
SBFLA	*Studii biblici franciscani liber annuus*
SBJ	La Sainte Bible ("Bible de Jérusalem")
SBLDS	Society of Biblical Literature Dissertation Series
SBLEJL	Society of Biblical Literature, Early Judaism and Its Literature
SBLMS	Society of Biblical Literature Monograph Series
SBLRBS	Society of Biblical Literature Resources for Biblical Study
SBLSCS	Society of Biblical Literature Septuagint and Cognate Studies
ScEs	*Science et esprit*
ScrB	*Scripture Bulletin*
SJLA	Studies in Judaism in Late Antiquity
SJOT	*Scandinavian Journal of the Old Testament*
SSS	Semitic Study Series
STDJ	Studies on the Texts of the Desert of Judah

SubBi	Subsidia biblica
SVTP	Studia in Veteris Testamenti pseudepigrapha
TBT	*The Bible Today*
TDNT	*Theological Dictionary of the New Testament.* Edited by G. Kittel and G. Friedrich. Translated by G. W. Bromiley. 10 vols. Grand Rapids, Mich.: Eerdmans, 1964–1976.
TDOT	*Theological Dictionary of the Old Testament.* Edited by G. J. Botterweck and H. Ringgren. Translated by J. T. Willis et al. Grand Rapids, Mich.: Eerdmans, 1974–.
ThViat	*Theologia viatorum*
ThWAT	*Theologisches Wörterbuch zum Alten Testament.* Edited by G. J. Botterweck and H. Ringgren. Stuttgart: Kohlhammer, 1970–.
TLNT	*Theological Lexicon of the New Testament.* C. Spicq. Translated and edited by J. D. Ernest. 3 vols. Peabody, Mass.: Hendrickson, 1994.
TThSt	Trierer theologische Studien
TTZ	*Trierer theologische Zeitschrift*
TU	Texte und Untersuchungen
UF	*Ugarit-Forschungen*
VT	*Vetus Testamentum*
VTSup	Supplements to Vetus Testamentum
WHJP	World History of the Jewish People
WUNT	Wissenschaftliche Untersuchungen zum Neuen Testament
ZAW	*Zeitschrift für die alttestamentliche Wissenschaft*
ZKG	*Zeitschrift für Kirchengeschichte*

Texts and Manuscripts

G	Greek text
G^{AB}	Greek manuscripts Alexandrinus and Vaticanus
G^{SV}	Greek manuscripts Sinaiticus and Venetus
G^{248}	Greek manuscript 248
H	Hebrew text
H^{ABmg}	(Cairo Genizah) Hebrew manuscripts A and B-margin
H^{2Q11Q}	Hebrew manuscripts from Qumran Caves 2 and 11
H^{M}	Hebrew manuscript from Masada
L	Latin text
LXX	Septuagint
MS(S)	manuscript(s)
MT	Masoretic Text (with Hebrew verse numbering)

P.	Papyrus
S	Syriac text
S^{AW}	Syriac text of Ambrosian Codex and Walton Polyglot
S^{LM}	Syriac text of Lagarde and Mosul editions

Chronology of Ben Sira's Age

538 B.C.E.	Decree of Cyrus allowing Jews to return from exile
515	Dedication of Second Temple in Jerusalem
ca. 348	Death of Plato, author of *Lysis*
332	Alexander the Great's conquest of Palestine
322	Death of Aristotle, author of *Nicomachean Ethics*
301	Ptolemy I inaugurates Ptolemaic rule over Palestine
ca. 245	Approximate date of Ben Sira's birth
ca. 219	Accession of high priest Simeon II
ca. 200	Battle of Panium and victory of Antiochus III
ca. 196	Death of high priest Simeon II; Rosetta Stone in Egypt
ca. 195	Hephzibah inscription in Galilee
ca. 180	Completion of Ben Sira's book
ca. 175	Approximate date of Ben Sira's death
175	Accession of Antiochus IV Epiphanes
167	Desecration of Jerusalem temple by Antiochus IV
164	Rededication of Jerusalem temple by Maccabees; death of Antiochus IV
132	Arrival of Ben Sira's grandson in Egypt
ca. 115	Grandson's Greek publication of Ben Sira's book
ca. 75	Writing of Masada Ben Sira scroll
63	Pompey's conquest of Palestine for the Romans
43	Death of Cicero, author of *De amicitia*
ca. 25	Writing of Qumran Cave 2 Ben Sira text
ca. 25 C.E.	Writing of Qumran Cave 11 Psalter with Sirach 51
70 C.E.	Roman destruction of Second Temple in Jerusalem

1

Introduction

The purpose of this study is to elucidate Ben Sira's teaching on friendship[1] within the religious and cultural context of his time, in view of the Hellenistic emphasis on φιλία ("friendship").

While friendship is of contemporary interest in the realms of theology, philosophy, psychology, and general culture,[2] until recently there has been little research into the understanding of friendship in Second Temple Judaism. This study aims to fill the lacuna by focusing on the apocryphal/deuterocanonical Wisdom of Ben Sira. In fact, no book of the Hebrew Bible says as much about friendship as does the Wisdom of Ben Sira.[3]

---

[1] Here I borrow D. Konstan's working definition of friendship as "a mutually intimate, loyal, and loving bond between two or a few persons" who are unrelated by blood; see his *Friendship in the Classical World* (Cambridge: Cambridge University Press, 1997), 1.

[2] On the theology of friendship, see, e.g., G. Meilaender, *Friendship, a Study in Theological Ethics* (Notre Dame, Ind.: University of Notre Dame Press, 1981); B. P. McGuire, *Friendship and Community: The Monastic Experience 350–1250* (Cistercian Studies 95; Kalamazoo, Mich.: Cistercian Publications, 1988); P. J. Wadell, *Friendship and the Moral Life* (Notre Dame, Ind.: University of Notre Dame Press, 1989); C. White, *Christian Friendship in the Fourth Century* (Cambridge: Cambridge University Press, 1992); E. Moltmann-Wendel, *Rediscovering Friendship* (London: SCM, 2000). On the philosophy of friendship, see, e.g., N. K. Badhwar, *Friendship: A Philosophical Reader* (Ithaca, N.Y.: Cornell University Press, 1993); L. A. Blum, *Friendship, Altruism, and Morality* (London: Routledge & Kegan Paul, 1980); M. Pakaluk, ed., *Other Selves: Philosophers on Friendship* (Indianapolis: Hackett, 1991); O. Leaman, ed., *Friendship East and West: Philosophical Perspectives* (Richmond, Surrey: Curzon, 1996). On the psychology of friendship, see M. Argyle, *The Psychology of Interpersonal Behavior* (Harmondsworth: Penguin, 1967); S. Duck, *Friends, For Life: The Psychology of Close Relationships* (New York: St. Martin's, 1983); L. B. Rubin, *Just Friends: The Role of Friendship in Our Lives* (New York: Harper & Row, 1985). On friendship in general culture, see A. Bloom, *Love and Friendship* (New York: Simon & Schuster, 1993); D. J. Enright and D. Rawlinson, *The Oxford Book of Friendship* (Oxford: Oxford University Press, 1991).

[3] Cf. P. W. Skehan and A. A. Di Lella, *The Wisdom of Ben Sira* (AB 39; New York: Doubleday, 1987), 187. Note that the Greek manuscript Vaticanus (henceforth G^B)

The present chapter deals with previous research on friendship in Ben Sira, friendship in the ancient world, the historical setting of Ben Sira, authorship and social setting, the sage's theology, his social ethics, literary aspects of his work, textual questions, and my method in this study. Chapters 2–6 consider the seven major pericopes in which Ben Sira treats friendship: 6:5–17; 9:10–16; 13:15–23; 19:13–17; 22:19–26; 27:16–21; 37:1–6. Chapter 7 offers a concluding summary, while the appendix offers a brief survey of the book's incidental references to friendship outside the seven major pericopes.[4]

1. Previous Studies of Friendship in Ben Sira

English-language treatments of the topic of friendship in Ben Sira have hitherto been concise thematic studies.[5] D. J. Harrington's 1994 survey of the topic briefly treats the theme under three headings: making friends, being friends, and losing friends.[6] In addition, W. H. Irwin's 1995 article examines Ben Sira's analogy between God's relationship with those who fear him and a person's relationship with one's friends.[7] Moreover, in his study of parallels between Ben Sira and other ancient

uses the word φίλος ("friend") forty-eight times in Ben Sira; hence, 30 percent of the Septuagint's 160 instances of the term occur in Ben Sira.

[4] In the seven major pericopes G^B uses the word φίλος thirty times, while the incidental references employ φίλος eighteen times (see table 1 in the appendix).

[5] There are no treatments of friendship among the twenty-nine books on Ben Sira (all published 1965–1992) listed in D. J. Harrington's survey, "Sirach Research since 1965: Progress and Questions," in *Pursuing the Text: Studies in Honor of Ben Zion Wacholder on the Occasion of His Seventieth Birthday* (ed. J. C. Reeves and J. Kampen; JSOTSup 184; Sheffield: JSOT Press, 1994), 164–76. Note that Ben Sira's book is sometimes known by the Greek name Sirach or the Latin title Ecclesiasticus.

[6] D. J. Harrington, "Sage Advice about Friendship," *TBT* 32 (1994): 79–83. Harrington comments on Ben Sira's approach: "He was not much concerned with the definition of friendship, or why people need friends, or what constitutes friendship. Rather, he offers practical wisdom about making friends, being a faithful friend, and threats to friendship" (80). See also J. Corley, "Friendship according to Ben Sira," in *Der Einzelne und seine Gemeinschaft bei Ben Sira* (ed. R. Egger-Wenzel and I. Krammer; BZAW 270; Berlin: de Gruyter, 1998), 65–72.

[7] W. H. Irwin, "Fear of God, the Analogy of Friendship and Ben Sira's Theodicy," *Bib* 76 (1995): 551–59. Irwin states: "Ben Sira sees a similarity between friendship and the fear of God and the theme of testing in each" (552).

literature, J. T. Sanders notes the sage's affinities with Theognis's view of friendship, as well as with the teaching found in a demotic Egyptian sapiential work preserved in Papyrus Insinger.[8] In French, H. Duesberg's brief summary on friendship in Ben Sira observes a number of parallels between the sage's words and the insights of Theognis or the teachings of ancient Near Eastern wisdom literature.[9]

The only German publication before 1996 devoted to the theme of friendship in Ben Sira is a detailed tradition-critical study of Sir 6:5–17 by G. Krinetzki.[10] Krinetzki explains the poem's use of expressions, motifs, and idioms drawn from the Hebrew Bible and then discusses the sage's creative handling of these traditional materials.[11] In her study of Ben Sira's cultural environment, O. Wischmeyer also briefly considers friendship within her discussion of the family.[12] Furthermore, M. Paeslack treats Ben Sira's vocabulary of friendship (in the grandson's Greek translation) within the context of the LXX and the New Testament.[13]

---

[8] J. T. Sanders, *Ben Sira and Demotic Wisdom* (SBLMS 28; Chico, Calif.: Scholars Press, 1983), 30–32, 64–65, 70–71. Ben Sira's connection with Theognis was already noted by T. Middendorp (*Die Stellung Jesu ben Siras zwischen Judentum und Hellenismus* [Leiden: Brill, 1973], 15), while its similarity with Papyrus Insinger is mentioned by P. Humbert (*Recherches sur les sources égyptiennes de la littérature sapientiale d'Israël* [Mémoires de l'Université de Neuchatel 7; Neuchatel: Secrétariat de l'Université, 1929], 134).

[9] H. Duesberg, *Les scribes inspirés: Introduction aux livres sapientiaux de la Bible* (2 vols.; Paris: Maredsous; Tournai: Desclée, 1966), 2:625–28. Duesberg observes that the friendship concept in Ben Sira covers not only private friendship but also business relationships, as well as general social courtesy (2:625).

[10] G. Krinetzki, "Die Freundschaftsperikope Sir 6,5–17 in traditionsgeschichtlicher Sicht," *BZ* 23 (1979): 212–33.

[11] Krinetzki (ibid., 231) concludes by emphasizing the sage's creativity: "Es ist sicher nicht zu viel behauptet, wenn wir abschließend feststellen, daß Sirach bei aller Anlehnung an vorgeprägtes Traditionsgut zumeist sehr originelle Formulierungen und Gedanken ausgebildet hat."

[12] O. Wischmeyer, *Die Kultur des Buches Jesus Sirach* (BZNW 77; Berlin: de Gruyter, 1995), 33–34. She asserts that Ben Sira has in view individual rather than group friendships: "Sirach betrachtet also 'den Freund' von vornherein als individuellen, privaten Partner des familiären Lebenskreises, nicht aber als Teil eines öffentlichen Freundeskreises" (33).

[13] M. Paeslack, "Zur Bedeutungsgeschichte der Wörter φιλεῖν 'lieben,' φιλία 'Liebe,' 'Freundschaft,' φίλος 'Freund' in der LXX und im NT," *ThViat* 5 (1953–1955): 51–142, esp. 78–79; see also G. Stählin, " φίλος, φίλη, φιλία," *TDNT* 9:146–71, esp. 156–57.

In 1996 F. V. Reiterer published the papers presented in German at a symposium on friendship in Ben Sira, held in 1995 at the University of Salzburg.[14] The papers treated seven of Ben Sira's friendship pericopes (Sir 6:5–17; 12:8–12; 19:6–19; 22:19–26; 25:1–11; 27:16–21; 37:1–6).[15] As the only book published on the theme of friendship in Ben Sira, its textual, poetic, and thematic studies are fundamental for any future discussion of the topic. The diversity of viewpoints adopted by individual scholars offers a variety of insights but leads perhaps to a certain disunity in approach.[16]

Also helpful to my study were the major commentaries on Ben Sira. The most important recent commentary is the work of P. W. Skehan and A. A. Di Lella.[17] Of great significance, too, are the older commentaries of R. Smend, N. Peters, and M. Z. Segal.[18]

---

[14] F. V. Reiterer, ed., *Freundschaft bei Ben Sira: Beiträge des Symposions zu Ben Sira, Salzburg 1995* (BZAW 244; Berlin: de Gruyter, 1996).

[15] The Salzburg volume includes the seven symposium papers and two thematic studies: P. C. Beentjes, "'Ein Mensch ohne Freund ist wie eine linke Hand ohne die Rechte': Prolegomena zur Kommentierung der Freundschaftsperikope Sir 6,5–17" (pp. 1–18); L. Schrader, "Unzuverlässige Freundschaft und verläßliche Feindschaft: Überlegungen zu Sir 12,8–12" (pp. 19–59); H. V. Kieweler, "Freundschaft und böse Nachrede: Exegetische Anmerkungen zu Sir 19,6–19" (pp. 61–85); J. Marböck, "Gefährdung und Bewährung: Kontexte zur Freundschaftsperikope Sir 22,19–26" (pp. 87–106); O. Kaiser, "Was ein Freund nicht tun darf: Eine Auslegung von Sir 27,16–21" (pp. 107–22); G. Sauer, "Freundschaft nach Ben Sira 37,1–6" (pp. 123–31); F. V. Reiterer, "Gelungene Freundschaft als tragende Säule einer Gesellschaft: Exegetische Untersuchung von Sir 25,1–11" (pp. 133–69); I. Krammer, "Scham im Zusammenhang mit Freundschaft" (pp. 171–201); R. Egger-Wenzel, "Der Gebrauch von תמם bei Ijob und Ben Sira: Ein Vergleich zweier Weisheitsbücher" (pp. 203–38); followed by a useful bibliography (pp. 241–51). Unlike the Salzburg volume, my study does not discuss 12:8–12 or 25:1–11, except for a brief treatment of 12:8–9 and 25:1, 9 in the appendix. However, I do consider 9:10–16 and 13:15–23, two passages that are not discussed in the Salzburg volume.

[16] For instance, Greek parallels to Ben Sira's teaching receive some attention on pp. 36–38 and 67–68 but are regarded critically on pp. 15–16. Also, a retroverted Hebrew text contributes to the discussion on pp. 65–81 and 112, whereas retroversion is regarded as questionable on p. 88. In addition, illustrations of Ben Sira's teaching from the Hebrew Bible (e.g., from the narratives about David) receive consideration on p. 130 but are largely dismissed on pp. 13–15.

[17] Skehan and Di Lella, *Wisdom of Ben Sira.* Particularly useful is the extensive bibliography (93–127); see also the supplementary listing in A. A. Di Lella, "The Wisdom of Ben Sira: Resources and Recent Research," *CurBS* 4 (1996): 161–81. Bibliographic help is also provided in F. V. Reiterer, ed., *Bibliographie zu Ben Sira* (BZAW 266; Berlin: de Gruyter, 1998); and F. García Martínez, "Ben Sira: A

2. Friendship in the Ancient World

a. Introduction

Ben Sira writes his poems on friendship within a cultural tradition linked most closely with Israel's heritage but also having some contacts with the cultures of ancient Greece, Egypt, and Mesopotamia. Here I survey writings on friendship from ancient Israel, Greece, Egypt, and Mesopotamia; the main focus is on texts that serve as possible antecedents or parallels for Ben Sira's teaching.

b. Israel

Rather than providing an elaborate theology of friendship, the Hebrew Bible conveys its insights through both narratives and proverbial sayings, while certain biblical texts also attest to a political sense of friendship (= "alliance").[19]

Many of the friendship narratives in the Hebrew Bible center around the figure of David. The classic example is David's friendship with Jonathan, sealed with a covenant (1 Sam 18:1–3; 20:3, 8, 17; cf. the phraseology of Sir 6:17a; 37:2b); another case is the king's friendship with Barzillai (1 Sam 17:27–29; 19:32–40). In addition, 1 Sam 25:18–35 tells of

---

Bibliography of Studies, 1965–1997," *Masada VI: The Yigael Yadin Excavations 1963–1965: Final Report* (ed. S. Talmon; Jerusalem: Israel Exploration Society, 1999), 233–52.

[18] R. Smend, *Die Weisheit des Jesus Sirach, erklärt* (Berlin: Reimer, 1906) [henceforth: *Sirach, erklärt*]; N. Peters, *Das Buch Jesus Sirach oder Ecclesiasticus* (EHAT 25; Münster i.W.: Aschendorff, 1913); M. Z. Segal, ספר בן־סירא השלם (3d ed.; Jerusalem: Bialik Institute, 1972). For a recent summary of scholarship on Ben Sira, see M. Gilbert, "Siracide," *DBSup* 12:1389–1437.

[19] For a general survey of the Hebrew root אהב ("love," "be a friend"), see A. T. H. Luc, "The Meaning of ʾHB in the Hebrew Bible" (Ph. D. diss., University of Wisconsin, Madison, 1982); cf. J. Bergman, A. O. Haldar, and G. Wallis, "אהב," *TDOT* 1:99–118. Here I leave out of consideration the idea of friendship with God, on which subject see E. Peterson, "Der Gottesfreund: Beiträge zur Geschichte eines religiösen Terminus," *ZKG* 42 (1923): 161–202; and Konstan, *Friendship in the Classical World,* 167–70. Although Israel's tradition calls Abraham the "friend of God" (Isa 41:8; 2 Chr 20:7; CD 3.2; *Jub.* 17:18; Jas 2:23), Ben Sira does not develop the concept of "friendship toward God" (Wis 7:14) as something distinct from the love of God (Sir 1:10 G; cf. Deut 6:5). I also leave aside the love of neighbor (Lev 19:18), on which see H. P. Mathys, *Liebe deinen Nächsten wie dich selbst: Untersuchungen zum alttestamentlichen Gebot der Nächstenliebe (Lev 19,18)* (OBO 71; Göttingen: Vandenhoeck & Ruprecht, 1986); cf. T. Söding, "Nächstenliebe bei Jesus Sirach: Eine Notiz zur weisheitlichen Ethik," *BZ* 42 (1998): 239–47.

Abigail's friendly attitude toward David, which led to their marriage after Nabal's death (1 Sam 25:39–42).[20]

Other friendship stories in the Hebrew Bible concern Ruth and Job. The successful international friendship between Ruth and Naomi (Ruth 1:6–18; 2:19–3:5; 4:13–17) occurs within the relationship of mother-in-law and daughter-in-law.[21] By contrast, although Job's friends remain with him at his time of suffering (Job 2:11–13), they fail as comforters (Job 13:4–5; 16:2–5; 19:2–3).

Within the prophetic and sapiential texts of the Hebrew Bible, there are several laments over the faithlessness of false friends. After warning of the slander of neighbors (Jer 9:4–5), Jeremiah says that his former friends now watch for his downfall (Jer 20:10). Similarly, Ps 41:10 laments a betrayal by a close friend (a motif occurring in Sir 37:2), just as Job mourns that his quondam friends have turned against him (Job 19:14, 19; cf. 6:14–17; 12:4; 16:20).

The book of Proverbs also warns that, whereas prosperity causes one to acquire friends, poverty generally leads one to lose them (Prov 14:20; 19:4, 6–7; cf. Sir 6:11–12; 12:8–9; 13:21–23). Even though a faithful person is rare (Prov 20:6), Proverbs does refer to a friend who sticks closer than a brother (Prov 18:24). Nevertheless, although Israel's protocanonical wisdom books (Proverbs, Job, Qoheleth) speak of friendship in various places, Ben Sira's book is the earliest extant Jewish wisdom text to deal extensively with the subject.

In addition, friendship in the Hebrew Bible can have a political sense. Especially in the preexilic era, "friendship" can refer to an international treaty; for instance, 1 Kgs 5:15 describes King Hiram of Tyre as a "friend" (אֹהֵב, i.e., "ally") of David.[22] Some of the historical books of the Bible also refer to "friends of the king," that is, royal advisors. Thus, 1 Kgs 4:5 designates Solomon's advisor Zabud as "the companion of the king" (רֵעֶה הַמֶּלֶךְ), while 2 Sam 15:37 and 16:16 call Hushai

---

[20] For my proposal that 1 Sam 25 underlies Sir 6:5–17, see my exegesis of 6:5b, 9b, 16a, 17b in ch. 2 below.

[21] See G. S. Jackson, "Naomi, Ruth, and Orpah," *TBT* 32 (1994): 68–73. On Job's experience, see briefly Marböck, "Gefährdung und Bewährung," 97–98. On Qoh 4:9–12, see T. M. Hart, "Qoheleth Looks at Friendship," *TBT* 32 (1994): 74–78.

[22] In referring to the MT, I have followed Hebrew verse numberings throughout; thus, 1 Kgs 5:15 MT = 1 Kgs 5:1 in English translations. On the political sense of friendship language, see W. L. Moran, "The Ancient Near Eastern Background of the Love of God in Deuteronomy," *CBQ* 25 (1963): 77–87, esp. 78–82; J. A. Thompson, "The Significance of the Verb *Love* in the David-Jonathan Narratives in 1 Samuel," *VT* 24 (1974): 34–38.

"the companion of David" (רֵעֶה דָוִד).[23] In the Hellenistic era, the phrase "friends of the king" appears frequently in 1 Maccabees (e.g., 1 Macc 2:18; 3:38; 10:20; 11:57), while the term "first friends" also occurs in 1 Macc 10:65; 11:27; 2 Macc 8:9.[24]

In his allusions to the Hebrew Bible Ben Sira refers to both narrative and sapiential material on friendship. Although he is aware of the Hellenistic imperial government, his cautious instinct warns against political friendship with those in authority (cf. Sir 9:11–13; 13:9–13).

Although friendship is not a major theme in most of the Qumran texts, it receives some treatment in sapiential writings such as 4QInstruction and 4Q424 (though their fragmentary nature makes exact interpretation uncertain).[25] For instance, 4Q417 2 i 7 (part of 4QInstruction) apparently matches Sir 9:11–13 in its advice to be wary of evil and hostile persons, while 4Q424 1.6 seems to share with Sir 27:16–21 a concern that a friend keep one's secrets.

c. Greece

Homer, the father of Greek poetry, speaks of friendship, such as that between Achilles and Patroclus.[26] Although Sir 13:17a resembles Homer's saying on the hostility between wolves and lambs (*Il.*

---

[23] Cf. T. N. D. Mettinger, *Solomonic State Officials: A Study of the Civil Government Officials of the Israelite Monarchy* (ConBOT 5; Lund: Gleerup, 1971), 63–69. In my study all biblical translations are mine, unless noted otherwise.

[24] On these categories in the Seleucid administrative system, see E. Bikerman, *Institutions des Séleucides* (Service des Antiquités: Bibliothèque archéologique et historique 26; Paris: Geuthner, 1938), 40–50; on the Greco-Roman context, see C. Spicq, "φίλος τοῦ Καίσαρος," *TLNT* 3:458–61; Konstan, *Friendship in the Classical World*, 95–98, 105–8.

[25] For a brief introduction to these works, see D. J. Harrington, *Wisdom Texts from Qumran* (New York: Routledge, 1996), 40–63.

[26] On friendship in the Greco-Roman world, see the survey provided by Konstan, *Friendship in the Classical World*, which includes one reference to Ben Sira (p. 150, quoting St. Ambrose); idem, "Greek Friendship," *AJP* 117 (1996): 71–94. See also L. Dugas, *L'amitié antique d'après les moeurs populaires et les théories des philosophes* (2 vols.; Paris: Alcan, 1894; rev. ed., 1914); K. Treu, "Freundschaft," *RAC* 8:418–34; J. C. Fraisse, *Philia: la notion d'amitié dans la philosophie antique: essai sur un problème perdu et retrouvé* (Paris: Vrin, 1974); P. Marshall, *Enmity in Corinth* (WUNT 2/23; Tübingen: Mohr, 1987), 1–34; L. F. Pizzolato, *L'idea di amicizia nel mondo antico classico e cristiano* (Filosofia 238; Turin: Einaudi, 1993); J. T. Fitzgerald, ed., *Friendship, Flattery, and Frankness of Speech: Studies on Friendship in the New Testament World* (NovTSup 82; Leiden: Brill, 1996); idem, ed., *Greco-Roman Perspectives on Friendship* (SBLRBS 34; Atlanta: Scholars Press, 1997).

22.262–265), it is unlikely that Ben Sira took the motif directly from him.[27]

Much of the poetry of the sixth-century B.C.E. Greek elegiac writer Theognis consists of sayings concerning friendship, especially warnings about the fickleness of supposed friends (e.g., Theognis 115–116; 643–644; 697–698).[28] The number of parallels between Theognis and Ben Sira on this and other topics leads Sanders to claim: "It would appear that Ben Sira did, indeed, read and use the elegiac poems of Theognis, at least Book 1."[29]

The tragedian Euripides (480–406 B.C.E.) portrays the friendship of Orestes and Pylades in his play *Orestes.* He employs financial imagery to speak of the value of friendship (*Orest.* 1155–1156; cf. Sir 6:14–15) and speaks of the importance of fidelity in friendship (*Orest.* 725–727; cf. Sir 6:14–16). Moreover, the tragedian differentiates true friends from those who have merely the "name" of friends (*Orest.* 454–455; cf. Sir 37:1) and speaks of the duty of assisting one's friends in their time of need (*Orest.* 665; cf. Sir 37:4–5).[30]

---

[27] On the parallel, see my exegesis of Sir 13:17a in ch. 4 below. Note also that Sir 14:18 uses a motif similar to *Il.* 6.148–149; cf. Sanders, *Ben Sira and Demotic Wisdom,* 39. On friendship in Homer, see Konstan, *Friendship in the Classical World,* 24–42; and J. T. Fitzgerald, "Friendship in the Greek World Prior to Aristotle," in Fitzgerald, ed., *Greco-Roman Perspectives on Friendship,* 13–34, esp. 15–26.

[28] On Theognis's view of friendship, see W. Donlan, "*Pistos Philos Hetairos,*" in *Theognis of Megara: Poetry and the Polis* (ed. T. J. Figueira and G. Nagy; Baltimore: Johns Hopkins University Press, 1985), 223–44; Konstan, *Friendship in the Classical World,* 49–52; Fitzgerald, "Friendship in the Greek World Prior to Aristotle," 29–33. Whereas some of the poems in Theognis's book 2 (1231–1388) express homosexual themes, these are lacking in Ben Sira. By contrast with the Hellenistic environment where homosexual practice was common, the sage teaches that "he who acquires a wife gains the best acquisition, a helper like himself and a pillar of support" (36:29 G), and asserts the superiority of a wife over all other friends (40:23).

[29] Sanders, *Ben Sira and Demotic Wisdom,* 29. Sanders asserts that Ben Sira "uses Theognis material to expand themes which he inherits from the Judaic proverbial tradition; this is true especially of his use of Theognis' observations about friendship" (55). For a more critical examination of the proposed parallels between Ben Sira and Theognis, see H.-V. Kieweler, *Ben Sira zwischen Judentum und Hellenismus: Eine Auseinandersetzung mit Th. Middendorp* (BEATAJ 30; Frankfurt a.M.: Lang, 1992), esp. 129–95.

[30] On Euripides' view of friendship, see J. Tyler, "Philia and Echthra in Euripides" (Ph. D. diss., Cornell University, 1969); U. Schmidt-Berger, "Philia: Typologie der Freundschaft und Verwandtschaft bei Euripides" (Ph. D. diss., University of Tübingen, 1973); and briefly Konstan, *Friendship in the Classical World,* 58–63.

The figure of Socrates (469–399 B.C.E.) is prominent in the works of both Plato and Xenophon. Plato (427–348 B.C.E.) recounts Socrates' discussion of friendship in the *Lysis*,[31] where he applies the maxim of "like to like" to friendship between good persons.[32] Plato's contemporary Xenophon (430–356 B.C.E.) treats friendship particularly in his defense of Socrates, entitled *Memorabilia*. Socrates' teaching on friendship, as recorded by Xenophon, emphasizes the need both to test potential friends and to value faithful friends, who should be few in number.[33]

The Greek orator Isocrates (436–338 B.C.E.) also speaks of friendship in his oration *To Demonicus*.[34] He admonishes, "Be pleasant to all, but cultivate the best" (*Demon.* 20; cf. Sir 6:6), and teaches, "Prove your friends by means of the misfortunes of life.... We come to know our friends when we are in misfortune" (*Demon.* 25; cf. Sir 6:7–10; 12:8–9). In addition, he insists on the duty of guarding secrets (*Demon.* 22; cf. Sir 27:16–21).

The classic Greek treatment of friendship occurs in books 8 and 9 of the *Nicomachean Ethics* of Aristotle (384–322 B.C.E.).[35] In discussing the nature of friendship, the philosopher says: "Some define it as a matter of similarity; they say that we love those who are like ourselves: whence the

---

[31] On Plato's view of friendship, see D. Bolotin, *Plato's Dialogue on Friendship: An Interpretation of the Lysis, with a New Translation* (Ithaca, N.Y.: Cornell University Press, 1979); A. W. Price, *Love and Friendship in Plato and Aristotle* (Oxford: Clarendon, 1989); O. Kaiser, "Lysis oder von der Freundschaft," in *Der Mensch unter dem Schicksal: Studien zur Geschichte, Theologie und Gegenwartsbedeutung der Weisheit* (BZAW 161; Berlin: de Gruyter, 1985), 206–31.

[32] *Lysis* 214d asserts: "There is a hidden meaning, dear friend, intended by those who say that like is friend to like, namely that the good alone is friend to the good alone"; cf. W. R. M. Lamb, trans., *Plato: Lysis, Symposium, Gorgias* (LCL; New York: Putnam, 1925), 43. See Sir 13:15–17 for a similar sentiment.

[33] Cf. *Mem.* 2.6.1 (testing; cf. Sir 6:7); 2.4.1 (fidelity; cf. Sir 6:14–16); 2.6.27 (fewness; cf. Sir 6:6). On Xenophon's view of friendship, see Konstan, *Friendship in the Classical World*, 79–86.

[34] G. Norlin and L. van Hook, trans., *Isocrates* (LCL; 3 vols.; New York: Putnam, 1928–1945), 1:5–35; the two quotations of Isocrates are from 1:15, 19. On Isocrates' view of friendship, see Konstan, *Friendship in the Classical World*, 93–97.

[35] See S. Stern-Gillet, *Aristotle's Philosophy of Friendship* (Albany: State University of New York Press, 1995); P. Schollmeier, *Other Selves: Aristotle on Personal and Political Friendship* (Albany: State University of New York Press, 1994); J. Steinberger, *Begriff und Wesen der Freundschaft bei Aristoteles und Cicero* (Erlangen: privately published, 1955); Price, *Love and Friendship in Plato and Aristotle*. More briefly, see Konstan, *Friendship in the Classical World*, 67–78; F. M. Schroeder, "Friendship in Aristotle and Some Peripatetic Philosophers," in Fitzgerald, ed., *Greco-Roman Perspectives on Friendship*, 35–57, esp. 35–45.

proverbs 'Like finds his like,' 'Birds of a feather flock together,' and so on" (*Eth. nic.* 8.1.6 §1155a).[36] He also asserts that "the happy man requires friends" (*Eth. nic.* 9.9.3 §1169b).[37] In addition, he divides friendships into three categories: those for utility, those for pleasure, and those for virtue (*Eth. nic.* 8.3.1–8.4.6 §1156a–1157b).[38] Although it is unlikely that Ben Sira knew Aristotle's works, the Greek philosopher expresses some ideas that also appear in the Hebrew sage's writing.

d. Egypt

Egypt's early wisdom literature makes some reference to friendship; for example, the third-millennium B.C.E. Instruction of Ptahhotep (sections 33–35) urges the testing of a potential friend, as well as a generous attitude toward friends.[39]

From the mid-second millennium B.C.E. the Instruction of Any 5.7–8 offers teaching similar to Ben Sira's (cf. Sir 9:13, 16; 6:17):

> Keep away from a hostile man,
> Do not let him be your comrade;
> Befriend one who is straight and true,
> One whose actions you have seen.
> If your rightness matches his,
> The friendship will be balanced.

The closest similarities to Ben Sira's friendship instructions occur, however, in two demotic works from the late Ptolemaic era, the Instruction of Ankhsheshonq and Papyrus Insinger.[40] Ankhsheshonq

---

[36] H. Rackham, trans., *Aristotle: The Nicomachean Ethics* (LCL; New York: Putnam, 1926), 453. This widespread idea appears in Sir 6:11, 17; 13:15–16.

[37] Ibid., 559. Likewise, Ben Sira includes "friend and comrade" among his list of good things (40:23) and declares: "Happy is the one who finds a true friend" (25:9a L); see my brief discussion in the appendix.

[38] Ben Sira, by contrast, divides friendship into two basic categories: fickle, self-centered friendships of mere utility (6:8–12; 37:4), and lasting, unselfish friendships of the wise and God-fearing (6:14–17; 9:10, 14–16; 37:5–6). Note that whereas Aristotle engages in systematic philosophical discourse, Ben Sira speaks in the concise poetic style of proverbial wisdom.

[39] For a translation, see *AEL* 1:72–73. On testing, compare Sir 6:7; on generosity, compare Sir 14:13. For the following quotation from the Instruction of Any, see *AEL* 2:138.

[40] Though the manuscript of Ankhsheshonq is late Ptolemaic (probably second or first century B.C.E.), its composition may be earlier (cf. *AEL* 3:159). Equally, whereas the handwriting of P. Insinger is from the first century C.E., the

14.8, for instance, urges caution toward potential friends (cf. Sir 6:7): "If you become the companion of a wise man whose heart you do not know, do not open your heart to him."[41] Moreover, Ankhsheshonq 13.6 notes the effect of the company one keeps (cf. Sir 9:14): "The friend of a fool is a fool; the friend of a wise man is a wise man."

Papyrus Insinger also has many affinities with the Wisdom of Ben Sira, particularly in the area of friendship.[42] A section concerning social relationships (P. Insinger 11.23–12.18) exhibits some resemblances to Ben Sira. Like Ben Sira, P. Insinger 12.15 insists on testing potential friends (cf. P. Insinger 11.23; Sir 6:7): "One does not discover the heart of a wise man if one has not tested him in a matter."[43] In addition, P. Insinger 12.18 teaches that adversity provides the real test of friendship (cf. Sir 6:8; 12:8): "One does not discover the heart of a friend if one has not consulted him in anxiety."

e. Mesopotamia

The Wisdom of Ahiqar, found in a late fifth-century B.C.E. Aramaic papyrus, counsels vigilance in social relationships. Besides advising the complete keeping of confidences, Ahiqar employs animal imagery to urge caution in one's friendships.[44]

f. Conclusion

This survey of friendship in the ancient world has drawn out various ideas current in ancient Israel, Greece, Egypt, and Mesopotamia. While it

---

composition is probably late Ptolemaic (*AEL* 3:184). Even if the latter work originated after Ben Sira's death, the Hebrew sage may have known an earlier model on which it is based.

[41] For this quotation of Ankhsheshonq and the following one, see *AEL* 3:169–70. Other sayings of Ankhsheshonq concerning friends and companions include 13.2, 7–8, 24; 14.3; 16.4; 21.6, 10; 26.13, 22; 28.4. For further similarities between Ankhsheshonq and Ben Sira, see Sanders, *Ben Sira and Demotic Wisdom,* 103–5.

[42] The resemblances have been noted by Humbert, *Recherches sur les sources,* 134; W. Fuß, "Tradition und Komposition im Buche Jesus Sirach" (Th.D. diss., University of Tübingen, 1962), 64; Sanders, *Ben Sira and Demotic Wisdom,* 64–65, 70–71.

[43] This quotation from P. Insinger and the next one are both from *AEL* 3:195. Other sayings of P. Insinger on friends and companions include 6.21; 13.13, 18; 16.8.

[44] Keeping confidences: Ahiqar Saying 15; cf. Sir 27:16–21. Animal imagery: Ahiqar Sayings 9–10; 28; 36; cf. Sir 13:17–19. See the editions of J. M. Lindenberger, *The Aramaic Proverbs of Ahiqar* (Baltimore: Johns Hopkins University Press, 1983); I. Kottsieper, *Die Sprache der Ahiqarsprüche* (BZAW 194; Berlin: de Gruyter, 1990).

is certain that Ben Sira knew Israelite wisdom texts such as the book of Proverbs, it is unlikely that he was acquainted with Aristotle's *Nicomachean Ethics.* However, the many parallels suggest the possibility that he had some direct or indirect knowledge of the poetry of Theognis and knew some form of the demotic sapiential tradition contained in Papyrus Insinger.[45]

3. Historical Setting

a. Dating of Ben Sira's Book

Scholars agree that Ben Sira's book dates from 195–175 B.C.E.[46] The panegyric on Simeon II (Sir 50:1–24) indicates its earliest possible date to be approximately 196 B.C.E., when this high priest died.[47] The absence of any reference to the religious turmoil that followed the accession of the Seleucid king Antiochus IV Epiphanes (175–164) suggests 175 B.C.E. as the latest possible date.[48] A date between 195–175 B.C.E. is also indicated by

---

[45] So Skehan and Di Lella, *Wisdom of Ben Sira,* 49: "The dependence of Ben Sira on several non-Jewish writings seems beyond question.... He probably even read, in whole or in part, the works of Theognis and Phibis [= P. Insinger]"; cf. Sanders, *Ben Sira and Demotic Wisdom,* 54–55, 96–100. However, Middendorp's suggestions of parallels between Ben Sira and Greek literature on the theme of friendship (*Die Stellung Jesu ben Siras,* 9, 14–16, 18, 21, 23) receive a cautious assessment from Kieweler, *Ben Sira zwischen Judentum und Hellenismus,* 84, 94–95, 100–101, 120–25, 127–28, 145–48, 150–52, 175–76, 204, 206.

[46] Cf. Skehan and Di Lella, *Wisdom of Ben Sira,* 10 (ca. 180 B.C.E.); M. Hengel, *Judaism and Hellenism* (2 vols.; Philadelphia: Fortress, 1974), 1:131 (190–175 B.C.E.); M. Gilbert, "Wisdom Literature," in *Jewish Writings of the Second Temple Period* (ed. M. E. Stone; CRINT 2/2; Assen: Van Gorcum, 1984), 291 (190 B.C.E.); Segal, ספר בן־סירא השלם, 6 (ca. 180 B.C.E.); H. Jagersma, *A History of Israel from Alexander the Great to Bar Kochba* (Philadelphia: Fortress, 1986), 42 (ca. 190 B.C.E.); D. S. W. Williams, "The Date of Ecclesiasticus," *VT* 44 (1994): 563–66 (ca. 175 B.C.E.).

[47] Skehan and Di Lella, *Wisdom of Ben Sira,* 9. The phrases "in his generation" (בְּדוֹרוֹ) and "in his days" (בְּיָמָיו) in 50:1–3 suggest that the high priest was no longer alive when Ben Sira wrote (ibid., 550). The date of Simeon II's death is not entirely certain; see O. Mulder, *Simon de hogepriester in Sirach 50* (Almelo: privately published, 2000), esp. 410. Most scholars identify Simeon II with "Simeon the Just" (cf. Skehan and Di Lella, *Wisdom of Ben Sira,* 550). However, J. C. VanderKam considers the title as belonging to Simeon I; see "Simon the Just: Simon I or Simon II?" in his *From Revelation to Canon* (JSJSup 62; Leiden: Brill, 2000), 224–40.

[48] Shortly after his accession, Antiochus Epiphanes began his program of enforced hellenization by appointing Jason as high priest (2 Macc 4:7–15). The

the grandson's prologue to his Greek translation of Ben Sira's book, since he speaks of himself as "having arrived in Egypt in the thirty-eighth year of the reign of [ἐπί] the king Euergetes [= 132 B.C.E.] and having been there at the same time [συγχρονίσας]" (Prologue 27–28).[49] Thus, if Ben Sira published his work between 195–175 B.C.E., he may have been born around 245 B.C.E. and died around 175 B.C.E.

b. Historical Evidence

The generation living after Ben Sira's death underwent the crisis of Antiochus Epiphanes' persecution of the Jews and the Maccabean reaction; as sources for this history we have the two books of Maccabees and the book of Daniel, as well as Josephus's *Antiquities.* For Ben Sira's own lifetime, however, there is a dearth of historical sources. Archaeology has yielded the Zeno papyri, which provide evidence for the Ptolemaic administration of Transjordan in the mid-third century B.C.E., and also the Hephzibah inscription of about 195 B.C.E., commanding the Seleucid soldiers to protect the local villagers.[50] In addition, Josephus's *Antiquities* preserves the "Tobiad romance" (*Ant.* 12.4.1–11 §§154–236) as well as Antiochus III's decree (*Ant.* 12.3.3–4 §§138–146) remitting certain taxes in Jerusalem and acknowledging the sacredness of the temple for the Jews (ca. 198 B.C.E.).[51]

---

king's hellenizing program culminated in his plunder of the Jerusalem temple in 169 B.C.E. (1 Macc 1:20–24; cf. Dan 11:28) and his profanation of the sanctuary in 167 B.C.E. (1 Macc 1:44–63; 2 Macc 6:1–11; cf. Dan 11:31–36).

[49] Although the thirty-eighth year of King Ptolemy VII Physkon Euergetes II (170–164 and 146–117 B.C.E.) was 132 B.C.E., the aorist participle συγχρονίσας implies that the grandson was writing after the king's death in 117 B.C.E.; cf. Skehan and Di Lella, *Wisdom of Ben Sira,* 9. Thus, if the grandson published his translation ca. 115 B.C.E., his grandfather could have written two generations earlier, not long before 175 B.C.E.

[50] On the Zeno papyri, see Hengel, *Judaism and Hellenism,* 1:21–22, 39–43, 47–48; on the Hephzibah (Scythopolis) inscription, see J. E. Taylor, "Seleucid Rule in Palestine" (Ph. D. diss., Duke University, 1979), 108–68. On the historical background to Ben Sira's life, see L. L. Grabbe, "Jewish Historiography and Scripture in the Hellenistic Period," in *Did Moses Speak Attic? Jewish Historiography and Scripture in the Hellenistic Period* (ed. L. L. Grabbe; JSOTSup 317; Sheffield: Sheffield Academic Press, 2001), 129–55.

[51] On the "Tobiad romance," see Hengel, *Judaism and Hellenism,* 1:268–70; he notes that it contains "gross errors" as well as "exact information" (1:269). For a detailed analysis of Antiochus III's decree, see Taylor, "Seleucid Rule in Palestine," 51–107.

c. The Ptolemaic and Seleucid Empires

In the third and early second centuries B.C.E. Palestine was under the control of Hellenistic rulers, first the Ptolemies of Egypt (301–200 B.C.E.) and thereafter the Seleucids of Syria. Whereas during the Fourth Syrian War Antiochus III failed to conquer Palestine for the Seleucid Empire, being defeated at Raphia in 217 B.C.E., he was victorious at the Battle of Panium around 200 B.C.E.[52] The people of Jerusalem initially welcomed the Seleucids (Josephus, *Ant.* 12.3.3 §136; cf. Dan 11:14) and were doubtless pleased when Antiochus III issued a decree reducing the city's taxation (Josephus, *Ant.* 12.3.3 §§138–144). However, needing money for reparations to the Romans after the Peace of Apamea (188 B.C.E.), the Seleucids levied further taxes (Dan 11:20), while the finance minister Heliodorus sought to plunder the treasury of the Jerusalem temple (according to 2 Macc 3:4–40). In view of the violence and greed of Israel's Ptolemaic and Seleucid rulers, Ben Sira offers sober warnings to his students not to befriend those with civil authority (Sir 9:13).

d. Hellenization in Palestine

The process of the hellenization of Palestine began with Alexander the Great's conquest of Palestine from the Persian Empire in 332 B.C.E.[53] Thereafter, Hellenistic culture gained importance in Palestine. It is likely that under the influence of Greek cultural patterns, esteem for friendship (φιλία) increased. Although after Ben Sira's death the Maccabees were successful in defeating Antiochus Epiphanes, they could not escape the dominance of the Greek language. Whereas Ben Sira, a resolute but moderate opponent of Hellenism,[54] writes entirely in a Hebrew free of Greek

---

[52] For a sketch of the history of the period, see Hengel, *Judaism and Hellenism,* 1:1–12; Jagersma, *History of Israel,* 22–43; Skehan and Di Lella, *Wisdom of Ben Sira,* 13–16; L. L. Grabbe, *Judaism from Cyrus to Hadrian* (2 vols.; Minneapolis: Augsburg Fortress, 1992), 1:212–20; J. K. Aitken, "Biblical Interpretation As Political Manifesto: Ben Sira in His Seleucid Setting," *JJS* 51 (2000): 191–208, esp. 202–5.

[53] See Hengel, *Judaism and Hellenism,* 1:58–106; and the critical response of L. H. Feldman, *Jew and Gentile in the Ancient World* (Princeton, N.J.: Princeton University Press, 1993), esp. 6–18. O. Kaiser sees the importance of friendship in Ben Sira's day as a response to the increasing isolation of the individual in a time of change; see "Gottesgewißheit und Weltbewußtsein in der frühhellenistischen jüdischen Weisheit," in *Der Mensch unter dem Schicksal,* 122–34, esp. 128–30.

[54] While the sage resolutely opposes the radical hellenizers who desert the law of the Most High (41:8), his writings exhibit traces of Hellenistic culture (his esteem for friendship, his mention of symposia, his echoes of the sentiments of Theognis, his similarities with Stoic thought). "Ben Sira borrowed Gentile

loanwords, the story of the Maccabean resistance to enforced hellenization is (ironically) preserved in Greek in the two books of Maccabees.

e. The Tobiads and the Oniads

In the mid-third century B.C.E. the high priest Onias III lost the civil leadership (προστασία) of his people, as a result of his refusal to continue paying taxes to the Ptolemies. In his place Joseph son of Tobias was appointed to the office. By promising the Ptolemies higher tax revenues, he gained not only the official leadership of the Jewish people but also the position of tax farmer (διοικητής) for the whole of "Syria and Phoenicia."[55]

During the twenty-two years that this Tobiad held power (Josephus, *Ant.* 12.4.6 §186),[56] Jerusalem became a prosperous city. According to Josephus's source, Joseph son of Tobias "brought the Jewish people from poverty and a state of weakness to more splendid opportunities of life" (*Ant.* 12.4.10 §224).[57] However, this Tobiad was notorious for his cruelty toward those who refused to pay taxes to him (*Ant.* 12.4.5 §§180–185), and his respect for the Torah was scant. Although the high priest seems to have regained the προστασία with the decree of Antiochus III around 198 B.C.E., the Tobiad family remained powerful. Hence, when Ben Sira criticizes the blind pursuit of riches (Sir 31:5–7) and the disregard of the poor (13:17–23) on the part of Israel's wealthy class, it is quite possible that he is referring to the Tobiads and their circle.[58]

f. Demographic Trends

During the third century B.C.E. immigration from Greece and improved farming methods led to an increase in the population of Palestine,[59] resulting in the foundation of new cities. The influx of foreigners and the process of urbanization, combined with the economic hardship due to the high level of taxation, doubtless contributed to a weakening of family bonds among the Judean population. In this context,

---

thoughts and expressions as long as these could be reconciled with the Judaism of his day" (Skehan and Di Lella, *Wisdom of Ben Sira,* 16).

[55] Josephus, *Ant.* 12.4.1–4 §§158–179; cf. Hengel, *Judaism and Hellenism,* 1:27.

[56] Josephus's dating of those twenty-two years after the Seleucid conquest of Palestine seems anachronistic. Joseph son of Tobias may have held power between 239–217 B.C.E.; cf. Hengel, *Judaism and Hellenism,* 1:269.

[57] H. St. J. Thackeray et al., trans., *Josephus* (LCL; 10 vols.; New York: Putnam; Cambridge, Mass.: Harvard University Press, 1926–1965), 7:113.

[58] Cf. V. Tcherikover, *Hellenistic Civilization and the Jews* (Philadelphia: Jewish Publication Society of America, 1959), 148–51.

[59] Cf. Hengel, *Judaism and Hellenism,* 1:39–47.

it is likely that friendship became more important in Jewish culture, as Ben Sira's ample treatment of the topic suggests.

4. Authorship and Social Setting

a. Place of composition

All indications point to Jerusalem as the place where Ben Sira composed his work,[60] since the city plays a central role in the book. The author's praise of the high priest Simeon II (50:1–24) not only describes his repairs to the temple and fortification of the city (50:1–4) but also gives what seems to be an eyewitness account of the temple liturgy (50:5–21). In addition, the sage beseeches God's mercy on the holy city of Jerusalem (36:18–19) in a prayer that begins: "Save *us*" (36:1).[61] Furthermore, the wisdom that he praises in 24:1–29 comes to dwell in Jerusalem (24:10–11). All these observations imply that the sage composed his book in Jerusalem.

b. Identity of the Author

The sage's full name was probably Yeshua ben Eleazar ben Sira, but I will use the name by which he is commonly known, Ben Sira.[62] The fifty-one chapters of his didactic poetry indicate that he was a teacher. He directs his words to young men (cf. Sir 9:1–9; 36:26–31; 42:9–14), whom, following an ancient sapiential tradition (e.g., Prov 1:10; 2:1; 3:1), he often addresses individually as בְּנִי ("my son"; e.g., Sir 3:12, 17; 4:1). He probably ran an educational establishment, since in 51:23 G he urges the unlearned to lodge in the "house of instruction."[63] Moreover, his praise of

---

[60] Although 50:27c G calls the author ὁ Ἱεροσολυμίτης ("the Jerusalemite"), this designation is lacking in H^B and S and may be secondary.

[61] Emphasis added. In favor of Ben Sira's authorship of 36:1–22, see J. Marböck, "Das Gebet um die Rettung Zions in Sir 36,1–22 (G: 33,1–13a; 36:16b–22) im Zusammenhang der Geschichtsschau Ben Siras," in *Gottes Weisheit unter Uns* (Herders Biblische Studien 6; Freiburg i.B.: Herder, 1995), 149–66, esp. 157–58. Unless otherwise indicated, all Ben Sira references are to H, where extant, or else to G.

[62] While Sir 50:27c G calls him Ἰησοῦς υἱὸς Σιραχ Ελεαζαρ ("Jesus son of Sira [son of] Eleazar"), 50:27b and 51:30gh H^B name him שִׁמְעוֹן בֶּן יֵשׁוּעַ בֶּן אֶלְעָזָר בֶּן סִירָא ("Simeon son of Yeshua son of Eleazar son of Sira"); cf. Skehan and Di Lella, *Wisdom of Ben Sira*, 3.

[63] Scholars dispute when schools began in ancient Israel; cf. Hengel, *Judaism and Hellenism,* 1:78–83; A. Lemaire, "The Sage in School and Temple," in *The Sage in Israel and the Ancient Near East* (ed. J. G. Gammie and L. G. Perdue; Winona

the scribal profession (39:1–11) in comparison with manual occupations (38:24–34) echoes a long educational tradition deriving from Egypt, where a similar "Satire on the Trades" (ca. 1900 B.C.E.) occurs in several papyri.[64] Indeed, Ben Sira may have been one of the "scribes of the Temple" mentioned by Josephus (*Ant.* 12.3.3 §142).[65]

A somewhat aristocratic tone pervades the sage's writing. His widespread traveling (Sir 34:9–13) may indicate that he was a diplomat or counselor (38:33; 39:4). His students were probably from the upper class,[66] although he cautions them against the unbridled pursuit of wealth (31:5–7) and urges them to care for the poor (4:1–10). His poetry mentions certain Hellenistic customs, such as the symposium (31:12–32:13).[67]

5. Theological Themes in Ben Sira's Teaching

a. The Fear of God, Wisdom, and the Law

Three interconnected themes in Ben Sira's theology are the fear of God, wisdom, and the law, which together provide guidance for right living and a happy life (cf. Sir 9:14–16; 19:20; 21:11).

Lake, Ind.: Eisenbrauns, 1990), 165–81; J. L. Crenshaw, "Education in Ancient Israel," *JBL* 104 (1985): 601–15; J. P. J. Olivier, "Schools and Wisdom Literature," *JNSL* 4 (1975): 49–60; Wischmeyer, *Die Kultur des Buches Jesus Sirach,* 175–77; J. J. Collins, *Jewish Wisdom in the Hellenistic Age* (OTL; Louisville: Westminster/John Knox, 1997), 36–38.

[64] For a translation, see *AEL* 1:184–92; cf. Skehan and Di Lella, *Wisdom of Ben Sira,* 449. See also C. A. Rollston, "Ben Sira 38:24–39:11 and the Egyptian Satire of the Trades: A Reconsideration," *JBL* 120 (2001): 131–39, where Rollston sets the "Satire" within a broader literary tradition in Egypt.

[65] Compare the tentative suggestion of Hengel, *Judaism and Hellenism,* 1:133. On the importance of the temple cult and the priestly class in Ben Sira's thought, see S. M. Olyan, "Ben Sira's Relationship to the Priesthood," *HTR* 80 (1987): 261–86.

[66] Cf. R. Gordis, "The Social Background of Wisdom Literature," *HUCA* 18 (1943–1944): 77–118; compare the sage's advice on the treatment of slaves (Sir 7:20–21; 33:25–30). According to Collins (*Jewish Wisdom in the Hellenistic Age,* 30), "Ben Sira made his living by instructing the well-to-do." B. G. Wright suggests that "Ben Sira would have belonged to a retainer class that acted as mediators between the rulers, primarily priests in ancient Judea, and ordinary Jews"; see his "'Fear the Lord and Honor the Priest': Ben Sira As Defender of the Jerusalem Priesthood," in *The Book of Ben Sira in Modern Research* (ed. P. C. Beentjes; BZAW 255; Berlin: de Gruyter, 1997), 189–222; quotation from p. 195.

[67] See Wischmeyer, *Die Kultur des Buches Jesus Sirach,* 106–9, as well as my exegesis of Sir 9:10 in ch. 3 below.

One of the most prominent themes in Ben Sira's work is the fear of God, which appears more than fifty-five times in his book.[68] The sage uses this theme, derived from the earlier biblical books, to bring various aspects of social ethics, seemingly secular, into the sphere of Yahwist religion.[69]

From the opening poem of the book (Sir 1:1–10) to its final acrostic (51:13–30), wisdom is also a major theme in Ben Sira.[70] Accordingly, in 9:14b the sage advises making friends with wise persons.

Furthermore, keeping the law is an important element in Ben Sira's teaching.[71] He recommends that God's law should guide one's friendships (9:15b G), including the manner of reproving a friend (19:17b G).

b. Creation and Retribution

Creation is still another significant theme in the sage's theology.[72] It underlies the sage's formulation of the axiom "like to like"

---

[68] For a thorough survey, see J. Haspecker, *Gottesfurcht bei Jesus Sirach: Ihre religiöse Struktur und ihre literarische und doktrinäre Bedeutung* (AnBib 30; Rome: Pontifical Biblical Institute, 1967); cf. his list of occurrences of the phrase (48–50). On the connection between fear of the Lord, wisdom, and the law, see Skehan and Di Lella, *Wisdom of Ben Sira*, 75–80, as well as A. A. Di Lella, "Fear of the Lord As Wisdom: Ben Sira 1,11–30," in Beentjes, ed., *Book of Ben Sira in Modern Research*, 113–33.

[69] Thus, Ben Sira introduces the theme of the fear of God at the end of pericopes in 6:16b; 9:16b; 25:10–11; 40:26–27. On the same theme in earlier biblical tradition, see L. Derousseaux, *La Crainte de Dieu dans l'Ancien Testament* (LD 63; Paris: Cerf, 1970).

[70] See esp. J. Marböck, *Weisheit im Wandel: Untersuchungen zur Weisheitstheologie bei Ben Sira* (BBB 37; Bonn: Hanstein, 1971; repr., BZAW 272; Berlin: de Gruyter, 1999); O. Rickenbacher, *Weisheitsperikopen bei Ben Sira* (OBO 1; Göttingen: Vandenhoeck & Ruprecht, 1973). For a brief survey, see A. A. Di Lella, "The Meaning of Wisdom in Ben Sira," in *In Search of Wisdom: Essays in Memory of John G. Gammie* (ed. L. G. Perdue et al.; Louisville: Westminster/John Knox, 1993), 133–48.

[71] On this topic, see M. Jolley, "The Function of Torah in Sirach (Wisdom Literature)" (Ph. D. diss., Southern Baptist Theological Seminary, 1993); E. J. Schnabel, *Law and Wisdom from Ben Sira to Paul: A Tradition-Historical Enquiry into the Relation of Law, Wisdom, and Ethics* (WUNT 2/16; Tübingen: Mohr, 1985), 8–92; S. Burkes, "Wisdom and Law: Choosing Life in Ben Sira and Baruch," *JSJ* 30 (1999): 253–76.

[72] See K. W. Burton, "Sirach and the Judaic Doctrine of Creation" (Ph. D. diss., University of Glasgow, 1987); R. A. Argall, *1 Enoch and Sirach: A Comparative Literary and Conceptual Analysis of the Themes of Revelation, Creation and Judgment* (SBLEJL 8; Atlanta: Scholars Press, 1995), 135–64; S. Goan, "Creation in Ben Sira,"

(13:15–16), his appreciation for the goodness of friendship (25:9; 40:23), and his use of the root יצר ("form") in 37:3.

The concept of divine retribution, a further important element in the theology of Ben Sira,[73] may underlie his thought in 22:23. However, wider questions of theodicy and free will have little place in the sage's instruction on friendship.[74]

c. Life and Death

Life and death are significant concepts in Ben Sira's theology (see 11:14; 15:17; 37:18; cf. Deut 30:15).[75] The approach of death can easily come about, whether as a result of befriending someone powerful (Sir 9:13) or through betrayal by a friend (37:2). Although the later versions insert mention of life after death, in Ben Sira's original text there is no afterlife in which humans may receive rewards or punishments (cf. 7:17; 14:16; 17:27–28).[76] Instead, death is the "decree for all flesh" (41:4 G).[77]

MilS 36 (1995): 75–85; F. V. Reiterer, "Die immateriellen Ebenen der Schöpfung bei Ben Sira," in *Treasures of Wisdom: Studies in Ben Sira and the Book of Wisdom: Festschrift M. Gilbert* (ed. N. Calduch-Benages and J. Vermeylen; BETL 143; Leuven: Peeters, 1999), 91–127.

[73] See A. A. Di Lella, "Conservative and Progressive Theology: Sirach and Wisdom," *CBQ* 28 (1966): 139–54, esp. 143–46; W. Dommershausen, "Zum Vergeltungsdenken des Ben Sira," in *Wort und Geschichte* (ed. H. Gese and H.-P. Rüger; AOAT 18; Kevelaer: Butzon & Bercker, 1973), 37–43; Argall, *1 Enoch and Sirach*, 211–47; Skehan and Di Lella, *Wisdom of Ben Sira*, 83–87.

[74] On the sage's theodicy, see G. L. Prato, *Il problema della teodicea in Ben Sira* (AnBib 65; Rome: Pontifical Biblical Institute, 1975); U. Wicke-Reuter, *Göttliche Providenz und menschliche Verantwortung bei Ben Sira und in der Frühen Stoa* (BZAW 298; Berlin: de Gruyter, 2000); L. Schrader, *Leiden und Gerechtigkeit: Studien zu Theologie und Textgeschichte des Sirachbuches* (BBET 27; Frankfurt a.M.: Lang, 1994), esp. 205–32. On free will, see J. Hadot, *Penchant mauvais et volonté libre dans la sagesse de Ben Sira (L'Ecclésiastique)* (Brussels: Presses Universitaires, 1970).

[75] Cf. M. Milani, "La correlazione tra morte e vita in Ben Sira: Dimensione antropologica, cosmica e teologica dell'antitesi" (S.S.D. diss., Pontifical Biblical Institute, Rome, 1995).

[76] Cf. V. Hamp, "Zukunft und Jenseits im Buche Sirach," in *Alttestamentliche Studien: Friedrich Nötscher zum Sechzigsten Geburtstag, 19, Juli 1950, Gewidmet von Kollegen, Freunden und Schülern* (ed. H. Junker and J. Botterweck; BBB 1; Bonn: Hanstein, 1950), 86–97; Collins, *Jewish Wisdom in the Hellenistic Age*, 92–96.

[77] On Sir 41:1–4, see F. V. Reiterer, "Deutung und Wertung des Todes durch Ben Sira," in *Die alttestamentliche Botschaft als Wegweisung: Festschrift für Heinz Reinelt* (ed. J. Zmijewski; Stuttgart: Katholisches Bibelwerk, 1990), 203–36;

6. Social Ethics

a. Caution, Honor, and Shame

Extreme caution characterizes Ben Sira's teaching on behavior in society.[78] Hence, caution is a hallmark of the sage's teaching on friendship. One must test a potential friend (6:7), be wary of friends (6:13), and realize that not every self-proclaimed friend actually is one (37:1). Moreover, the sage encourages his students not to neglect a needy friend, in case they themselves suffer as a result of the caution of others (22:25–26).

Closely allied to Ben Sira's cautious outlook is the importance for him of gaining honor and avoiding shame (cf. Sir 41:14a; 41:16–42:8).[79] Whereas false shame may lead a person to make unnecessary promises, thereby causing the end of friendship (20:23), true shame is the appropriate response to one's use of insulting words (41:22c). The sage also sees revealing a confidence as something shameful (22:22c).

b. Women

In recent years Ben Sira's outlook toward women has been a focus of scholarly attention.[80] The fact that the sage's teaching on friendship (9:10–16; 37:1–6) twice follows an instruction on relations with women (9:1–9; 36:26–31) suggests that the friendship passages refer principally to

---

Schrader, *Leiden und Gerechtigkeit*, 233–52 (pp. 252–301 consider the sage's other passages on death).

[78] See J. T. Sanders, "Ben Sira's Ethics of Caution," *HUCA* 50 (1979): 73–106; he notes the similarity with the cautious outlook of Papyrus Insinger (103–6).

[79] Ibid., 83–86; cf. Krammer, "Scham im Zusammenhang mit Freundschaft"; D. A. deSilva, "The Wisdom of Ben Sira: Honor, Shame, and the Maintenance of the Values of a Minority Culture," *CBQ* 58 (1996): 433–55; C. V. Camp, "Understanding a Patriarchy: Women in Second Century Judaism through the Eyes of Ben Sira," in *"Women Like This": New Perspectives on Jewish Women in the Greco-Roman World* (ed. A. J. Levine; SBLEJL 1; Atlanta: Scholars Press, 1991), 1–39; idem, "Honor and Shame in Ben Sira: Anthropological and Theological Reflections," in Beentjes, ed., *Book of Ben Sira in Modern Research*, 171–87; P. J. Botha, "The Ideology of Shame in the Wisdom of Ben Sira: Ecclesiasticus 41:14–42:8," *OTE* 9 (1996): 353–71.

[80] Cf. W. C. Trenchard, *Ben Sira's View of Women: A Literary Analysis* (BJS 38; Chico, Calif.: Scholars Press, 1982); M. Gilbert, "Ben Sira et la femme," *RTL* 7 (1976): 426–42; Skehan and Di Lella, *Wisdom of Ben Sira*, 90–92; Camp, "Understanding a Patriarchy"; S. Schroer, *Die Weisheit hat ihr Haus gebaut: Studien zur Gestalt der Sophia in den biblischen Schriften* (Mainz: Grünewald, 1996), 96–109.

relations with male friends.[81] This accords with the fact that the sage's students were young males. Nevertheless, the allusions underlying Sir 6:5–17 present a female character (Abigail) as a model of friendship, while the male figure (Nabal) is a counterexample of boorishness.[82]

c. Social Justice

In line with biblical teaching, found in the law codes, the prophets, and the wisdom literature, Ben Sira insists on the need for social justice (cf. 4:1–10; 34:21–35:22).[83] This aspect is prominent in Sir 13:15–23, which graphically delineates the mistreatment of the poor by the rich. The sage's use of animal imagery in 13:17–19 derives particularly from prophetic critiques of Israel's leaders.

d. Speech

Like other sages, Ben Sira considers control of speech an important part of wise social behavior.[84] Sirach 27:16–21 teaches that the betrayal of confidences spells the end of friendship. Similarly, Sir 22:22 contrasts the forgivable offense of a rash word against a friend with the unpardonable fault of betraying a secret behind his back. As a counterpart, Sir 19:13–17 discusses a beneficial use of the tongue, namely, to reprove a misbehaving friend.

---

[81] Cf. the titles "Les femmes" for 9:1–9 and "Rapports avec les hommes" for 9:10–18 in H. Duesberg and P. Auvray, *Le livre de l'Ecclésiastique* (SBJ; Paris: Cerf, 1953), 53–54. See also P. J. Botha, "Through the Figure of a Woman Many Have Perished: Ben Sira's View of Women," *OTE* 9 (1996): 20–34, esp. 30–32.

[82] See further my exegesis of Sir 6:5–17 in ch. 2.

[83] Cf. Skehan and Di Lella, *Wisdom of Ben Sira,* 88–90; Marböck, "Macht und Mächtige im Buche Jesus Sirach," in *Gottes Weisheit unter Uns,* 185–94; J. Corley, "Social Responsibility in Proverbs and Ben Sira," *ScrB* 30 (2000): 2–14; B. Baldauf, "Arme und Armut im Buch Ben Sira: Eine philologisch-exegetische Untersuchung" (M.Th. diss., University of Salzburg, 1983); V. Morla Asensio, "Poverty and Wealth: Ben Sira's View of Possessions," in R. Egger-Wenzel and I. Krammer, eds., *Der Einzelne und seine Gemeinschaft bei Ben Sira,* 151–78.

[84] Cf. J. I. Okoye, *Speech in Ben Sira with Special Reference to 5,9–6,1* (European University Studies 23/535; Frankfurt a.M.: Lang, 1995); G. Krinetzki, "Die Sprüche über das Reden und Schweigen in Sir 20 in traditionskritischer Sicht," in *"Diener in eurer Mitte": Festschrift für Dr. Antonius Hofmann, Bischof von Passau zum 75. Geburtstag* (ed. R. Beer et al.; Passau: Passavia Universitätsverlag, 1984), 64–81; A. A. Di Lella, "Use and Abuse of the Tongue: Ben Sira 5,9–6,1," in *"Jedes Ding hat seine Zeit…": Studien zur israelitischen und altorientalischen Weisheit: Diethelm Michel zum 65. Geburtstag* (ed. A. A. Diesel et al.; BZAW 241; Berlin: de Gruyter, 1996), 33–48.

7. Ben Sira's Poetry[85]

a. Literary Forms[86]

Although Ben Sira sometimes uses hymns, prayers, and a long encomium, most of his book consists of didactic poems.[87] All seven pericopes discussed in my study belong to the category of the didactic poem.[88] While incorporating traditional proverbs and biblical phrases, the sage molds his poems into neat literary constructions.

b. Structure of Ben Sira's Book

Ben Sira's book may be divided into eight parts (each starting with a sapiential poem) plus the appendices (which end with a wisdom poem).[89]

---

[85] On Ben Sira's poetry, see Skehan and Di Lella, *Wisdom of Ben Sira,* 63–74; on poetic techniques in biblical Hebrew, see esp. W. G. E. Watson, *Classical Hebrew Poetry* (JSOTSup 26; Sheffield: JSOT Press, 1984); as well as L. Alonso Schökel, *A Manual of Hebrew Poetics* (SubBi 11; Rome: Pontifical Biblical Institute, 1988).

[86] On the literary genres employed by Ben Sira, see W. Baumgartner, "Die literarischen Gattungen in der Weisheit des Jesus Sirach," *ZAW* 34 (1914): 161–98; Skehan and Di Lella, *Wisdom of Ben Sira,* 21–30; cf. also P. J. Nel, *The Structure and Ethos of the Wisdom Admonitions in Proverbs* (BZAW 158; Berlin: de Gruyter, 1982), 9–17. Hymns include Sir 18:1–7; 39:16–35; 42:15–43:33; 51:1–12; prayers include 22:27–23:6; 36:1–22. The "Praise of the Ancestors" in 44:1–50:24 uses the form of an encomium, according to T. R. Lee, *Studies in the Form of Sirach 44–50* (SBLDS 75; Atlanta: Scholars Press, 1986), esp. 206–39.

[87] Baumgartner applies the term *Lehrgedicht* ("didactic poem") to Sir 6:5–17 ("Die literarischen Gattungen," 164); so also Beentjes, "Ein Mensch ohne Freund," 8. Rather than just assembling maxims, the sage generally creates thematic poems. Haspecker (*Gottesfurcht bei Jesus Sirach,* 121) asserts that Ben Sira's book includes genuine redactional units intended by the author. Similarly, in Egyptian wisdom literature the *sebayit* consists of integrated units of instruction on sapiential themes, rather than mere lists of individual proverbs.

[88] The primary setting of the friendship pericopes is thus the schoolroom (cf. Sir 51:23), where perhaps they served as writing exercises. It is also possible that, like the elegiac poetry of Theognis, some of Ben Sira's friendship poems (e.g., 6:5–17; 9:10–16) were recited at banquets and symposia (cf. 32:3–8). For an examination of the Hebrew sage's use of earlier material, see Fuß, "Tradition und Komposition."

[89] I have adapted the following structure from Skehan and Di Lella, *Wisdom of Ben Sira,* xiii–xvi. See also J. D. Harvey, "Toward a Degree of Order in Ben Sira's Book," *ZAW* 105 (1993): 52–62, whence I have taken the titles of parts 1–4, 6–7 (61); Harvey calls 32:14–33:18 a wisdom poem (53). See further the discussion in J. Marböck, "Structure and Redaction History of the Book of Ben Sira: Review and

Part 1, 1:1–4:10: "Understanding Wisdom"
begun by wisdom poem (1:1–10)
Part 2, 4:11–6:17: "Applying Wisdom Personally"
begun by wisdom poem (4:11–19)
Part 3, 6:18–14:19: "Applying Wisdom Socially"
begun by wisdom poem (6:18–37)
Part 4, 14:20–23:27: "Applying Wisdom to Speech and Thought"
begun by wisdom poem (14:20–15:10)
Part 5, 24:1–32:13: "Applying Wisdom to Domestic Life"
begun by wisdom poem (24:1–34)
Part 6, 32:14–38:23: "Using Wisdom to Make Good Decisions"
begun by wisdom poem (32:14–33:18)
Part 7, 38:24–42:14: "Demonstrating the Results of Wisdom"
begun by wisdom poem (38:24–39:11)
Part 8, 42:15–50:24: "Wisdom in Creation and History"
begun by wisdom poem (42:15–43:33)
Appendices, 50:25–51:30
ended by wisdom poem (51:13–30)

Attention to this overall structure reveals that the friendship pericopes do not occur randomly in Ben Sira's book but rather fit in with their wider context. Thus, part 2 ("Applying Wisdom Personally") contains the first friendship poem (6:5–17), concerning wise personal conduct in relation to potential friends. Because part 3 deals with "Applying Wisdom Socially," it naturally has much to say on friendship (7:12, 18; 9:10–16; 12:8–9; 13:15–23; 14:13). In its treatment of "Applying Wisdom to Speech and Thought," part 4 discusses both one form of speech that benefits friendship, namely, reproof (19:13–17), and the damage to friendship caused by other kinds of speech, namely, insults and breaches of confidentiality (22:19–26). Since part 5 deals with "Applying Wisdom to Domestic Life," Sir 27:16–21 considers the harm done to friendship by the disclosure of secrets, which typically occurs behind the closed doors of one's home. Finally, because part 6 concerns "Using Wisdom to Make Good Decisions," Sir 37:1–6 treats distinguishing between good and bad friends.

Prospects," in Beentjes, ed., *Book of Ben Sira in Modern Research,* 61–79; H.-W. Jüngling, "Der Bauplan des Buches Jesus Sirach," in *"Den Armen eine frohe Botschaft": Festschrift für Bischof Franz Kamphaus zum 65. Geburtstag* (ed. J. Hainz et al.; Frankfurt a.M.: Knecht, 1997), 89–105; G. Sauer, "Gedanken über den thematischen Aufbau des Buches Ben Sira," in Calduch-Benages and Vermeylen, eds., *Treasures of Wisdom,* 51–61; O. Mulder, *Simon de hogepriester in Sirach 50,* 41–60.

c. Delimitation

Delimiting pericopes in Ben Sira can be a complex task because of textual problems and the aphoristic nature of the book. One may use both internal criteria (genre,[90] subject matter, and style) and external factors (the context). I have found seven stylistic criteria helpful in delimitating Ben Sira's pericopes: repetition of key words, *inclusio*, nonalphabetic acrostics, opening and closing rhyme, chiasm, a closing refrain, and favorite concluding themes.[91] A brief treatment of these seven points follows.

First, repetition of a key word often indicates the subject matter of a pericope; thus, Sir 6:5–17 G employs φίλος ("friend") nine times, while 22:19–26 G uses it five times. Second, *inclusio* marks the opening and closing cola of 27:16–21, which both employ the phrase מְגַלֶּה סוֹד ("one who reveals a confidence").[92] Third, a nonalphabetic acrostic of twenty-two or twenty-three bicola frequently indicates a unified poem or cluster of poems; for instance, 36:26–37:11 is a twenty-three-line poem on the choice of associates (wife, friends, and advisors), within which 37:1–6 forms a subunit on friendship.[93] Fourth, opening and closing rhyme often marks the start of a new pericope or its conclusion.[94] Fifth,

[90] Thus, the prayer in 36:1–22 is distinct from the teaching that begins in 36:23. However, since much of Ben Sira comprises didactic poems, frequently no difference of genre may exist between adjacent units.

[91] On these stylistic features, see Watson, *Classical Hebrew Poetry*, 287–95 (key words); 282–87 (*inclusio*); 199 (nonalphabetic acrostics); 229–34 (rhyme); 201–8 (chiasm); 295–99 (refrains); 65 (thematic closure).

[92] See my reconstructed text in ch. 5 below. For a twofold *inclusio* delimiting 13:15–23, see the delimitation section of ch. 4; for a list of Ben Sira's *inclusiones*, see Skehan and Di Lella, *Wisdom of Ben Sira*, 73–74.

[93] Recognition of a nonalphabetic acrostic in the surrounding material may also help demarcate a pericope; thus, a twenty-two-line poem (5:1–6:4) precedes the sage's first friendship passage (6:5–17), while a twenty-two-line sapiential poem (6:18–37) follows. Skehan and Di Lella provide a list of Ben Sira's nonalphabetic acrostics (ibid., 74). On the analogy of the alphabetic acrostic (e.g. Sir 51:13–30; Pss 111; 112; Prov 31:10–31), I define a "nonalphabetic acrostic" as a Hebrew poem in which the number of lines (22 or 23) imitates the number of letters in the Hebrew alphabet. Skehan and Di Lella offer an explanation of the twenty-third line in such poems (ibid., 576). In his brief discussion of biblical twenty-two-line poems (*Classical Hebrew Poetry*, 199), Watson asserts that such compositions "were obviously modelled on alphabetic acrostics, the restrictive feature of alphabetic sequence being lifted."

[94] Examples of opening rhyme include 6:5a (internal rhyme); 9:10bd; 13:15ab, 16a. Instances of concluding rhyme include 6:17a (internal rhyme); 9:16ab;

a chiastic pattern (combined with an *inclusio*) unifies one pericope (27:16–21).[95] Sixth, Ben Sira sometimes employs a closing refrain to mark the end of a passage.[96] Seventh, the sage sometimes uses a favorite theme, such as the fear of God or the law or death, to conclude a pericope.[97]

d. Stanzaic Patterns

In my study I divide Ben Sira's poems into stanzas.[98] On a smaller scale, key words often serve to delimit stanzas; thus, the threefold repetition of one phrase in 6:8–10 and of another in 6:14–16 shows the stanzaic pattern in 6:5–17. An *inclusio* may also delimit a stanza; thus, the resemblance of 6:8b and 6:10b suggests that 6:8–10 is a stanza. Sometimes, too, opening and closing rhyme occurs; thus, in 13:15–23 the first stanza uses internal rhyme in its last bicolon (13:20a), while the second has rhyme in its opening bicolon (13:21ab).

e. Sound Patterns: Rhyme, Alliteration, and Assonance

Sirach 44:1–8 provides the clearest example of end-rhyme in the sage's book.[99] Besides the examples of opening and closing rhyme listed

---

13:23abcd. For further discussion of opening and closing rhyme, see the poetic analyses of Sir 6:5–17 (ch. 2); 9:10–16 (ch. 3); and 13:15–23 (ch. 4) below. Of interest is Watson's observation: "In Akkadian poetry, rhyme … serves to mark strophic structure" (ibid., 231).

[95] On the chiasm in Sir 27:16–21, see my poetic analysis in ch. 5 below. For a list of shorter chiastic patterns in Ben Sira's book (including 6:5–6a, 14; 9:10), see Skehan and Di Lella, *Wisdom of Ben Sira*, 67–73.

[96] One closing refrain occurs in 6:4a H^A = 19:3b H^C; another in 20:30–31 G = 41:14–15 G; another in 31:11b H^B = 44:15b H^{BM}. Compare the refrain in Isa 9:11, 16, 20 and 10:4; or Cant 2:7; 3:5; 5:8.

[97] For the fear of God, see 6:16b (concluding 6:5–17); 9:16b (ending 9:10–16); 25:10–11 (concluding 25:7–11); 40:26–27 (ending 40:18–27); cf. Haspecker, *Gottesfurcht bei Jesus Sirach*, 136 n. 30. For the law, see 9:15 G (concluding 9:10–16); 19:17 G (ending 19:13–17). Poems ending with mention of death (or the grave or worms) include 7:1–17, 18–36; 9:1–9; 11:7–28; 13:24–14:19; 18:30–19:3; 27:22–28:7; 39:1–11; 44:1–15.

[98] Stanzaic divisions are also noted in Skehan and Di Lella, *Wisdom of Ben Sira*, passim. On stanzaic patterns in biblical poetry, see Watson, *Classical Hebrew Poetry*, 163–65.

[99] On Sir 44:1–8, see P. W. Skehan, "Staves, Nails and Scribal Slips (Ben Sira 44:2–5)," *BASOR* 200 (1970): 66–71; for the reading בְּמִכְתָּם ("in song," 44:5b), see pp. 69–70. On rhyme in Sir 5:6; 10:27; 11:3; 13:1, 24; 36:18–19, see Skehan and Di Lella, *Wisdom of Ben Sira*, 64–67. On biblical Hebrew rhyme, see Watson, *Classical Hebrew Poetry*, 229–34.

above, many bicola exhibit rhyme (e.g., 6:11; 7:18). In addition, Ben Sira often uses alliteration (e.g., 6:5ab, 14b, 15ab, 17ab) and assonance (e.g., 6:5ab, 8a, 11–12a, 12b–13).[100]

8. Texts, Editions, and Textual Criticism

a. Texts and Text Editions[101]

The earliest Hebrew Ben Sira MSS come from between 100 B.C.E. and 73 C.E.[102] However, the six Cairo Genizah MSS from the tenth to twelfth centuries C.E., comprising about two-thirds of the sage's book, constitute the majority of the extant Hebrew texts.[103]

---

[100] See the listing in Skehan and Di Lella, *Wisdom of Ben Sira*, 64–67. On Hebrew alliteration and assonance, see Watson, *Classical Hebrew Poetry*, 222–29. On alliteration and assonance in Sir 6:5–17, see the poetic analysis of the pericope in ch. 2 below.

[101] For a listing of the Hebrew MSS, see Skehan and Di Lella, *Wisdom of Ben Sira*, 52–53 (texts), 93–94 (publications); G. Sauer, *Jesus Sirach (Ben Sira)* (JSHRZ 3/5; Gütersloh: Mohn, 1981), 485–86; A. Minissale, *La versione greca del Siracide: Confronto con il testo ebraico alla luce dell'attività midrascica e del metodo targumico* (AnBib 133; Rome: Pontifical Biblical Institute, 1995), 29–30. For the new critical edition, see P. C. Beentjes, *The Book of Ben Sira in Hebrew: A Text Edition of All Extant Hebrew MSS and a Synopsis of All Parallel Hebrew Ben Sira Texts* (VTSup 68; Leiden: Brill, 1997); note that Beentjes sometimes departs from the standard verse numeration (e.g., on pp. 27–28 he prints 6:5–17 as 6:4–16). For the Hebrew MSS discovered before 1968 (i.e., excluding H^{F}), two hand editions are readily available: the publication (with parallel Greek, Syriac, and Latin texts) of F. Vattioni, *Ecclesiastico: Testo ebraico con apparato critico e versioni greca, latina e siriaca* (Pubblicazioni del Seminario di Semitistica, Testi 1; Naples: Istituto Orientale di Napoli, 1968); and the Hebrew edition (with an English introduction) of Z. Ben-Ḥayyim, *The Book of Ben Sira: Text, Concordance and an Analysis of the Vocabulary* (Jerusalem: Academy of the Hebrew Language/Shrine of the Book, 1973).

[102] The Masada scroll, containing portions of Sir 39:27b–44:17b (henceforth H^{M}), dates from the early first century B.C.E. The two fragments (2Q18) from Qumran Cave 2, consisting of a few words of Sir 6:14–31 (henceforth H^{2Q}), come from the latter half of the first century B.C.E., while the Cave 11 Psalms Scroll (11QPs^{a}), containing Sir 51:13a–20c, 30b (henceforth H^{11Q}), dates from the early first century C.E. Cf. Skehan and Di Lella, *Wisdom of Ben Sira*, 53. Part of Sir 18:33 occurs in the Qumran Beatitudes text 4Q525 25.4, according to E. Puech, *Textes Hebreux (4Q521–4Q528, 4Q576–4Q579): Qumran Cave 4.18* (DJD 25; Oxford: Clarendon, 1998), 164–65.

[103] Cf. Skehan and Di Lella, *Wisdom of Ben Sira*, 52–53. The six MSS are H^{A}, H^{B}, H^{C}, H^{D}, H^{E}, and H^{F}. For details of the first publications of these MSS, see (besides the following footnotes) the bibliography at the end of this study.

Out of the seven pericopes discussed in detail in chapters 2–6 below, three (Sir 6:5–17; 9:10–16; 13:15–23) are attested in H^A, an eleventh-century MS from the Cairo Genizah. Both 6:5–17 and 13:15–23 occur in MS leaves (T-S 12.864) housed at Cambridge University Library,[104] while the Genizah MS of 9:10–16 (ENA 2536) is kept at the Jewish Theological Seminary of America in New York.[105] Sirach 37:1–6 is extant in two Cairo Genizah MSS, namely, among portions of H^B housed at the British Library in London,[106] and among the leaves of H^D kept at the Bibliothèque de l'Alliance Israélite Universelle in Paris.[107] For the remaining three pericopes (Sir 19:13–17; 22:19–26; 27:16–21) no Hebrew MSS are extant.[108]

The three major ancient versions (in descending order of importance) are the Greek (G), the Syriac (S), and the Latin (L). For the Greek text I have used J. Ziegler's critical edition in the Göttingen Septuagint series.[109] All extant Greek MSS interchange 30:25–33:13a with 33:13b–36:16a; however, for these portions Ziegler has restored

---

[104] For Sir 3:6b–7:29a; 11:34b; 12:2a–16:26b, see S. Schechter and C. Taylor, *The Wisdom of Ben Sira: Portions of the Book Ecclesiasticus from Hebrew Manuscripts in the Cairo Genizah Collection Presented to the University of Cambridge by the Editors* (Cambridge: Cambridge University Press, 1899), 3–10. For photographs, see *Facsimiles of the Fragments Hitherto Recovered of the Book of Ecclesiasticus in Hebrew* (Oxford: Oxford University Press; Cambridge: Cambridge University Press, 1901).

[105] For 7:29a–11:33d; 12:1; 11:34a, see E. N. Adler, "Some Missing Chapters of Ben Sira," *JQR* 12 (1899–1900): 466–80, esp. 468–71 (with photographs).

[106] For 31:12–31; 36:24–37:26, see G. Margoliouth, "The Original Hebrew of Ecclesiasticus XXXI.12–31, and XXXVI.22–XXXVII.26," *JQR* 12 (1899–1900): 1–33, esp. 4–12.

[107] For 36:29a–38:1a, see I. Lévi, "Fragments de deux nouveaux manuscrits hébreux de l'Ecclésiastique," *REJ* 40 (1900): 1–30, esp. 3–4; note that Lévi designates this MS H^C.

[108] I suggest, however, that the previously unexplained word נסה ("test") that follows Sir 36:31 in the anthological H^C belongs to 27:17a (cf. S); see further ch. 5 below. A gloss after 31:2ab H^B exhibits loose similarities with 27:16; see the footnote on 41:18c in the appendix. For discussion of a Cairo Genizah prosodic poem based on Sir 22:22cd–23:9, see ch. 6 below. In the following section on method, I explain my reasons for reconstructing a Hebrew text for 19:13–17; 22:19–26; 27:16–21.

[109] J. Ziegler, *Sapientia Iesu Filii Sirach* (2d ed.; Septuaginta 12/2; Göttingen: Vandenhoeck & Ruprecht, 1980); I have followed his verse numbering throughout. I have also consulted H. B. Swete, *The Old Testament in Greek* (3d ed.; 3 vols.; Cambridge: Cambridge University Press, 1907), 2:644–754, as well as (for G^{248}) J. H. A. Hart, *Ecclesiasticus: The Greek Text of Codex 248* (Cambridge: Cambridge University Press, 1909).

the correct verse numeration (in parentheses) in his publication of the Greek text. In the absence of a critical edition of the Syriac text, I have referred to A. M. Ceriani's facsimile edition of the Ambrosian Codex (S^A) and to P. A. de Lagarde's publication of the British Library Codex 12142 (S^L).[110] For the Old Latin text found in the Vulgate MSS I have employed the Rome critical edition of San Girolamo.[111]

b. Textual Criticism

Whereas the whole question of the textual criticism of Ben Sira is vast and complex, the present discussion is necessarily brief.[112] Following Di Lella's 1966 study, most scholars now accept the general authenticity of the Cairo Genizah Hebrew MSS, while acknowledging that they contain corruptions acquired in the course of transmission.[113] The corruptions are of various kinds: scribal errors, retroversions, theological editings, and expansions or omissions.

i. Scribal Errors. Orthographic errors and corruptions abound in the Hebrew MSS of Ben Sira, although scribes have corrected some mistakes by means of marginal notes. Comparison with another Hebrew MS or with the versions often brings to light such errors. For instance, in 37:4 comparison with H^B reveals two mistakes in H^D: the reading שֻׁלְחָן

[110] A. M. Ceriani, *Translatio Syra Pescitto Veteris Testamenti ex codice Ambrosiano sec. fere VI photolithographice edita,* 2/4 (Milan: Pogliani, 1878); P. A. de Lagarde, *Libri veteris testamenti apocryphi syriace* (Leipzig: Brockhaus; London: Williams & Norgate, 1861). I have also used the Polyglot of B. Walton (S^W), *Biblia sacra polyglotta,* 4 (London: Roycroft, 1657), and the Mosul edition (S^M), *Biblia sacra juxta versionem simplicem quae dicitur Pschitta,* 2 (Beirut: Imprimerie Catholique, 1951).

[111] *Biblia Sacra iuxta latinam vulgatam versionem, 12: Sapientia Salomonis, Liber Hiesu filii Sirach* (Rome: Typis Polyglottis Vaticanis, 1964); see also the (as yet incomplete) Beuron edition of W. Thiele, *Vetus Latina: Die Reste der altlateinischen Bibel 11/2: Sirach (Ecclesiasticus)* (Freiburg i.B.: Herder, 1987–), of which by 1998 seven fascicles were published, covering Sir 1:1–19:28.

[112] On the textual criticism of Ben Sira, see briefly Skehan and Di Lella, *Wisdom of Ben Sira,* 55–60; and Gilbert, "Siracide," 12:1390–1402. Fuller treatments appear in A. A. Di Lella, *The Hebrew Text of Sirach: A Text-Critical and Historical Study* (Studies in Classical Literature 1; The Hague: Mouton, 1966); H.-P. Rüger, *Text und Textform im hebräischen Sirach: Untersuchungen zur Textgeschichte und Textkritik der hebräischen Sirachfragmente aus der Kairoer Geniza* (BZAW 112; Berlin: de Gruyter, 1970); Schrader, *Leiden und Gerechtigkeit,* 13–57; Minissale, *La versione greca del Siracide.*

[113] See Di Lella, *Hebrew Text of Sirach,* esp. 47–77. For a table listing corruptions in the Hebrew MSS, see Minissale, *La versione greca del Siracide,* 153–71.

("table," H^B) is supported by S against the reading שַׁחַת ("the pit," H^D), while the reading מִנּוֹב ("from fruit"/"from Nob," H^D) is evidently an error for מִנֶּגֶד ("aloof," H^B; cf. G, S).[114]

ii. Retroversions. Di Lella suggests that the Cairo Genizah MSS contain some retroversions from S, while Ziegler proposes that they preserve some retroversions from G.[115]

iii. Theological Adaptations. Translators or scribes have made theological adaptations to the text during the course of its transmission. S tends to omit references to the law; thus, whereas Sir 19:17b G says, "And give place to the law of the Most High," 19:17b S merely repeats the thought of 19:15b S.[116] In addition, S deletes what it perceives as unfavorable mentions of the poor; for instance, it omits the whole of 13:20, which is present in H^A and G. The versions also alter Ben Sira's sayings to incorporate references to the afterlife. Thus, whereas 7:17b H^A asserts, "A mortal's hope is worms," 7:17b G declares, "An impious person's punishment is fire and worms."[117]

iv. Other Expansions or Doublets, and Omissions. Occasionally the textual witnesses omit single verses or longer passages; for example, S passes over most of Ben Sira's discussion of true and false shame (41:14–42:8), retaining only parts of 41:19–20.[118] More often, the texts contain expansions. After 13:17b, for instance, H^A adds a gloss lacking in G, S, and L:

---

[114] Minissale (*La versione greca del Siracide,* 165–68) provides a classified list of scribal errors in H.

[115] On retroversions from S, see Di Lella, *Hebrew Text of Sirach,* 106–47. On retroversions from G, see J. Ziegler, "Zwei Beiträge zu Sirach," *BZ* 8 (1964): 277–84; idem, "Ursprüngliche Lesarten im griechischen Sirach," in *Mélanges Eugène Tisserant* (7 vols.; Studi e testi 231; Vatican City: Biblioteca Apostolica Vaticana, 1964), 1:461–87.

[116] Cf. M. M. Winter, "The Origins of Ben Sira in Syriac," *VT* 27 (1977): 237–53, 494–507, esp. 498 (a list of eight passages where S removes or alters a reference to the law found in G). On the tendency in S to favor the poor, see 245–49.

[117] See further C. Kearns, "The Expanded Text of Ecclesiasticus: Its Teaching on the Future Life As a Clue to Its Origin" (S.S.D. diss., Pontifical Biblical Institute, Rome, 1951); cf. Minissale, *La versione greca del Siracide,* 225–26. For the tendency of S to eliminate passages contrary to belief in the afterlife, see M. D. Nelson, *The Syriac Version of the Wisdom of Ben Sira Compared to the Greek and Hebrew Materials* (SBLDS 107; Atlanta: Scholars Press, 1988), 113–14.

[118] Cf. Nelson, *Syriac Version,* 69–80. On Sir 13:17, see further the text-critical note in ch. 4 below.

"And so is a rich person toward a withdrawn [= poor] man." In his edition of G, Ziegler prints the many expansions of the later Greek recension (GII) in small print, whereas the earlier text (GI, found mostly in G^{BSA}) appears in print of a normal size.[119]

In view of the complexities of the textual situation for Ben Sira, no simple rules can solve all the problems; as Skehan and Di Lella assert, "the careful critic must take into account all these bewildering features and then make a judgment that seems the most reasonable for the particular text under consideration." In the next section I will explain my textual method, including the rationale for my Hebrew retroversions of Sir 19:13–17; 22:19–26; 27:16–21.

9. Method of Study

a. General Procedure

I shall offer a detailed discussion of Ben Sira's seven major pericopes on friendship (6:5–17; 9:10–16; 13:15–23; 19:13–17; 22:19–26; 27:16–21; 37:1–6).[120] Since (according to G^{B}) these seven passages account for thirty of the sage's forty-eight uses of φίλος ("friend"), this discussion will treat the majority of the sage's thoughts on friendship. My concluding chapter summarizes the findings from the exegesis of the seven pericopes. An appendix then provides a brief survey of the eighteen other uses of φίλος scattered throughout Ben Sira's book; a table of these eighteen occurrences lists the vocabulary of H (where extant) and S alongside each instance in G.

For each of the seven major pericopes, after an introduction, I begin by delimiting the pericope, using internal criteria (subject matter and style) and external factors (the context). Next I provide a Hebrew text, based on the Genizah MSS where extant (6:5–17; 9:10–16; 13:15–23; 37:1–6).[121] For those pericopes lacking a Hebrew text (19:13–

---

[119] Examples of expansion in GII include 13:14 (not in H^{A}, G^{BSA}, or S); 19:18–19 (not in G^{BSA} or S); 22:23ef (not in G^{BSA} or S). The text of GII appears mainly in G^{248}, G^{V}, and in the other Origenic and Lucianic witnesses. Sometimes, however, GII preserves an original bicolon omitted in GI, such as Sir 1:21; cf. Skehan and Di Lella, *Wisdom of Ben Sira*, 142. For the following quotation, see ibid., 60.

[120] Chapter 2 treats Sir 6:5–17 and 37:1–6 together because the two pericopes have many verbal and thematic resemblances. Similarly, ch. 5 considers 19:13–17 and 27:16–21 together because both these passages concern the effect of speech on friendship.

[121] Though the Qumran and Cairo Genizah MSS do not generally include vocalization, I have provided vowels to make my readings clear, following Segal, ספר בן־סירא השלם, in most cases.

17; 22:19–26; 27:16–21), I reconstruct one by means of retroversion. There follow text-critical notes and my English translation, which is rather literal to avoid obscuring the Hebrew idioms. Then I offer a poetic analysis, explaining the stanzaic structure of the pericope and examining its stylistic features (e.g., alliteration and assonance). Next I situate the pericope in its context within Ben Sira's book. The major part of the discussion of each pericope is the verse-by-verse exegesis, which comments on the words used and places the sage's thought against the background of other treatments of friendship in ancient literature (especially Greek and Egyptian). I finish the discussion of each pericope with a brief conclusion.

b. Text-Critical Method

The examination of the textual questions earlier in this chapter indicated the complexity of the textual criticism of Ben Sira's book. Here I outline my own method.[122]

Where extant, the text of H has initial priority. However, if the ancient versions or the context suggest that H is corrupt, I make corrections, usually on the basis of G or S. Frequently corruptions in H involve scribal error or orthographic confusion.[123] Another kind of corruption is an expansionary gloss, such as 13:17c H^A.

In the absence of H, I weigh both G and S. Where G agrees with S, I make a retroversion into Hebrew, often following Segal's retroverted text. Where G and S disagree, I seek the reason for the disagreement; for example, the translator of S has omitted the reference to the "law of the Most High" (19:17b G) because of his hostility to the law. An expanded text may indicate a corruption; thus, 22:22c G is overlong and probably inauthentic in its present form. Where no obvious cause exists for the difference between the readings in G and S, a text-critical decision is finally a matter of judgment; the reading of G is generally preferable, but sometimes that of S better fits a Semitic milieu.

---

[122] The following studies provided great assistance for my text-critical work: R. Smend, *Die Weisheit des Jesus Sirach, hebräisch und deutsch* (Berlin: Reimer, 1906) [henceforth: *Sirach, hebräisch und deutsch*]; idem, *Sirach, erklärt;* N. Peters, *Der jüngst wiederaufgefundene hebräische Text des Buches Ecclesiasticus* (Freiburg i.B.: Herder, 1902); idem, *Das Buch Jesus Sirach;* G. H. Box and W. O. E. Oesterley, "Sirach," *APOT* 1:268–517; Segal, ספר בן־סירא השלם; Skehan and Di Lella, *Wisdom of Ben Sira;* Di Lella, *Hebrew Text of Sirach;* Rüger, *Text und Textform;* Minissale, *La versione greca del Siracide.*

[123] See the text-critical notes on Sir 6:5–17 for examples of scribal error (6:14[e–e] and 6:16[g]) and orthographic confusion (6:5[a] and 6:7[b]).

c. Explanation for My Retroversions Where No Hebrew Text Is Extant

Discoveries from the Cairo Genizah and the Dead Sea area have failed to yield the Hebrew text of three of Ben Sira's friendship pericopes (19:13–17; 22:19–26; 27:16–21). Absence of a Hebrew original in these instances creates a problem of method: Which text should be chosen as the basis for study? Where the Hebrew is unavailable, most scholars select the Greek text as the primary basis for their translation and commentary. However, it seems to me that such a policy would be inadequate for the present study, because Ben Sira wrote in Hebrew (a Semitic language) rather than Greek (an Indo-European language). His thought-world and literary style are both fundamentally Semitic, and his work is full of subtle allusions to earlier books of the Hebrew Bible. Naturally, the grandson's Greek translation could generally not reproduce poetic devices such as assonance, alliteration, and rhyme, often found in Ben Sira's Hebrew. Moreover, in certain places the grandson misunderstood the Hebrew text. In other cases GI omitted parts of verses, while GII often added verses. The following discussion of three sample texts (24:1–34; 25:1–11; 25:13–26:27) will show some of the corruptions in GI and at the same time illustrate the benefits of an attempt at retroversion into Hebrew.[124]

i. 24:1–34.[125] In discussing his retroversion, Skehan notes the abundance of rhyming assonances, particularly with *-î* and *-â* suffixes.

24:13: Striking rhyme of לְבָנֹן ("Lebanon") and חֶרְמוֹן ("Hermon"); cf. עַרְמוֹן ("plane tree") in verse 14d.

24:26–27: Another remarkable rhyme of קָצִיר ("harvest," v. 26b) and בָּצִיר ("vintage," v. 27b).

---

[124] Where H is not extant, Segal has produced a retroversion based on G and (to a lesser extent) on S (ספר בן־סירא השלם, passim). In the case of Bar 3:9–5:9, D. G. Burke has made a similar attempt at retroversion from Greek (and sometimes Syriac); see *The Poetry of Baruch: A Reconstruction and Analysis of the Original Hebrew Text of Baruch 3:9–5:9* (SBLSCS 10; Chico, Calif.: Scholars Press, 1982). After providing his retroverted Hebrew text and textual notes, Burke presents a chapter entitled "An Analysis of the Baruch Poetry" (299–321), where he discusses such features as parallel word-pairs and Hebrew rhyme.

[125] In the case of ch. 24 (of which no Hebrew text is extant), P. W. Skehan has proposed a retroversion ("Structures in Poems on Wisdom: Proverbs 8 and Sirach 24," *CBQ* 41 [1979]: 374); he observes the frequency of rhyming assonances (377–79). See also his list of six earlier scholars who have made similar attempts at retroverting the passage (366 n. 3). In addition, note the comment of P. Faure ("Comme un fleuve qui irrigue: Ben Sira 24,30–34, I. Critique textuelle," *RB* 102 [1995]: 5–27): "La critique textuelle de Sir 24,30–34 nous porte à préférer le texte syriaque au texte grec" (27).

24:27: G has ὡς φῶς (= כְּאוֹר, "like light") for כַּיְאוֹר ("like the Nile," cf. S).

ii. 25:1–11. 25:1ab: G^{BSA} reads: "In three things I was beautified, and I arose in beauty before the Lord and human beings." This reading, out of context here, seems to be a Christian expansion referring to Jesus' three days in the tomb and his rising again. By contrast, S preserves the correct text; hence Ziegler emends G according to S.[126]

25:8b: Probably because of distaste for the Semitic animal imagery ("ox" and "ass"), G has omitted this colon, thereby losing one item from the decalogue of macarisms. By contrast, the colon appears in H^C and S.

25:9a: The reading of G, φρονήσιν ("sense"), is probably a sapiential interpretation, since L has "a true friend" and S may be revocalized to give "a friend."

iii. 25:13–26:27. 25:15: Missing the allusion to Deut 32:33, the grandson rendered ראשׁ ("poison") with its homonym, κεφαλή ("head"), and חֵמָה ("venom") with its homonym, θυμός ("wrath").[127]

25:21b: G reads אִשָּׁה (= γυναῖκα, "woman") instead of עַל יֵשׁ לָהּ ("what is hers") in H^C (cf. S).

26:22: G renders מְצוּדַת מָוֶת ("deadly snare") by its homonym πύργος θανάτου ("tower of death").

The above survey of several mistranslations and inadequacies of G in Sir 24:1–26:27 confirms the conclusion of Skehan and Di Lella: "Though GI remains the most reliable form of the book as a whole, it nevertheless contains many scribal errors and other corruptions as well as mistranslations due to the grandson's failure to understand the underlying Hebrew."[128] In this connection, our discussion of the above-mentioned sample passages has also illustrated the potential benefits of retroversion into Hebrew, especially in the recovery of Hebrew poetic features. Although the resultant text is obviously hypothetical, retroversion offers

---

[126] Cf. Ziegler, *Sapientia Iesu Filii Sirach,* 76–78. On Sir 25:1–11, see Reiterer, "Gelungene Freundschaft als tragende Säule einer Gesellschaft," as well as my discussion of 25:1, 9 in the appendix.

[127] On 25:15, see Skehan and Di Lella, *Wisdom of Ben Sira,* 346. On 26:22, see P. W. Skehan, "Tower of Death or Deadly Snare? (Sir 26:22)," in *Studies in Israelite Poetry and Wisdom* (CBQMS 1; Washington, D.C.: Catholic Biblical Association of America, 1971), 127.

[128] *Wisdom of Ben Sira,* 59. For an extensive tabular listing of differences between the Hebrew and Greek texts of Ben Sira, see Minissale, *La versione greca del Siracide,* 174–258.

the possibility of working in the Hebrew language and of deciding between G and S.[129] I do not wish to present my retroversions as the last word in reconstructing Ben Sira's Hebrew text, but rather as an attempt to get closer to the sage's original thought-world and to understand better the Semitic pattern of his poetry.

In my endeavor to reconstruct the Hebrew of Ben Sira, I aim to take into account the translation techniques of the ancient versions.[130] Although G tends toward lexical inconsistency, Wright concludes: "Many specific elements of the parent text may be reconstructed in spite of the grandson's general lack of consistency in some of these areas." Indeed, in exegetical discussions scholars often have recourse to Segal's retroverted text even if they do not usually favor such retroversions.[131] Hence, in this study I take the risk of producing retroversions for 19:13–17; 22:19–26; 27:16–21, in the hope that the benefits of this approach will outweigh the disadvantages.

---

[129] The alternative would be to present a composite text in several languages. Note that for his reconstructed Urtext of Sir 3:1–16 (15 bicola), R. Bohlen combines Hebrew, Greek, and Syriac texts (*Die Ehrung der Eltern bei Ben Sira* [TThSt 51; Trier: Paulinus, 1991], 39).

[130] See esp. B. G. Wright, *No Small Difference: Sirach's Relationship to Its Hebrew Parent Text* (SBLSCS 26; Atlanta: Scholars Press, 1989); Nelson, *Syriac Version;* Winter, "The Origins of Ben Sira in Syriac." For instance, Wright (*No Small Difference,* 115) notes G's flexibility in lexical representation; but see the following quotation from p. 235.

[131] Thus, Kieweler's exegesis of Sir 19:6–19 ("Freundschaft und böse Nachrede," 64–81), takes note of Segal's retroversion; see his comment (64): "Die Rückübersetzung vermag das mögliche Umfeld des fehlenden Textes aufzuzeigen, nicht aber den Text in seiner Originalität wiederherzustellen."

2

Sirach 6:5–17 and 37:1–6

1. Introduction

Sirach 6:5–17 is the first, and possibly the best-known, of Ben Sira's pericopes on friendship; hence I will treat it first here. In 1979 G. Krinetzki published a detailed study of the passage, focusing on Ben Sira's use of Hebrew Bible traditional material (especially from 1 Sam 25).[1] More recently, in 1996 P. C. Beentjes published a concise textual and literary examination of the poem.[2] Because the pericope as preserved by H^A mostly agrees with G and S, there are few textual problems.

In this chapter I will also discuss Sir 37:1–6. This shorter pericope evidences a number of serious textual problems, since the Hebrew manuscripts (H^B and H^D) and the versions all diverge considerably.

The chapter treats Sir 6:5–17 and 37:1–6 together because of their verbal and conceptual similarities. As well as textual and literary study, each pericope will receive verse-by-verse exegesis, with consideration of possible nonbiblical parallels. The chapter will conclude with a brief summary drawing together the exegesis of the two pericopes.

2. Sirach 6:5–17

a. Delimitation

The delimitation of 6:5–17 as a separate unit is evident from the subject matter.[3] The topic of friendship stands out in the context; whereas

---

[1] Krinetzki, "Die Freundschaftsperikope." Moreover, Irwin ("Fear of God") examines Ben Sira's analogy between human friendship (6:5–17) and God's relationship with those who serve him (2:1–18).

[2] Beentjes, "Ein Mensch ohne Freund." See also J. Corley, "Caution, Fidelity, and the Fear of God: Ben Sira's Teaching on Friendship in Sir 6:5–17," *EstBib* 54 (1996): 313–26. My study of the pericope has benefited from J. von Herrmann's unpublished paper, "A Stylistic and Poetic Study of Sirach 6:5–17."

[3] On the delimitation of 6:5–17, see Beentjes, "Ein Mensch ohne Freund," 3–4.

φίλος ("friend") occurs only once in 1:1–6:4 (at 6:1), the word occurs nine times in 6:5–17 and thereafter not until 7:12.[4]

The limits of the poem are indicated, not only by its distinctiveness of content, but also by the structure. The first colon of 6:5 and the first colon of 6:17 both contain internal rhyme; this device forms a stylistic *inclusio* for the pericope. Moreover, both the preceding poem (5:1–6:4) and the following wisdom poem (6:18–37) are twenty-two-line nonalphabetic acrostics[5] and hence distinct from 6:5–17.

b. Text[6]

I

5 חֵיךְ עָרֵב יַרְבֶּה אוֹהֵב   וְשִׂפְתֵי חֵן שׁוֹאֲלֵי[a] שָׁלוֹם׃
6 אַנְשֵׁי שְׁלוֹמְךָ יִהְיוּ רַבִּים   וּבַעַל סוֹדְךָ אֶחָד מֵאֶלֶף׃
7 קָנִיתָ אוֹהֵב בְּנִיסָּיוֹן[b] קְנֵהוּ   וְאַל תְּמַהֵר לִבְטֹחַ עָלָיו׃

II

8 כִּי יֵשׁ אוֹהֵב כְּפִי עֵת   וְאַל יַעֲמוֹד בְּיוֹם צָרָה׃
9 יֵשׁ אוֹהֵב נֶהְפָּךְ לְשׂנֵא   וְאֶת רִיב חֶרְפָּתְךָ יַחְשׂוֹף׃
10 יֵשׁ אוֹהֵב חֲבֵר שֻׁלְחָן   וְלֹא יִמָּצֵא בְּיוֹם רָעָה׃

III

11 בְּטוֹבָתְךָ הֻא כָמוֹךָ   [c]וּבְרָעָתְךָ יִתְנַדֶּה מִמְּךָ[c]׃
12 בְּשִׁפְלְךָ[d] יַהְפֹּךְ בְּךָ   וּמִפָּנֶיךָ יִסָּתֵר׃
13 מִשֹּׂנְאֶיךָ הִבָּדֵל   וּמֵאֹהֲבֶיךָ הִשָּׁמֵר׃

IV

14 אוֹהֵב אֱמוּנָה [e]אוֹהֶל תְּקוֹף[e]   וּמוֹצְאוֹ מָצָא הוֹן׃
15 לְאוֹהֵב אֱמוּנָה אֵין מְחִיר   וְאֵין מִשְׁקָל לְטוֹבָתוֹ׃
16 [f]צְרוֹר חַיִּים[f] אוֹהֵב אֱמוּנָה   יְרֵא אֵל יַשִּׂיגֶנּוּ[g]׃
17 [h]כִּי כָמוֹהוּ כֵּן רֵעֵהוּ[h]   [i]וְכִשְׁמוֹ כֵּן מַעֲשָׂיו[i]׃

---

[4] H[A] has two verbal uses of אוֹהֵב in 3:6–6:4. In 3:26 אוֹהֵב means "one who loves" (cf. G), while in 4:12 אֹהֲבֶיהָ signifies "those who love her" (cf. singular participle in G); cf. table 3 in the appendix.

[5] Skehan and Di Lella, *Wisdom of Ben Sira*, 74.

[6] For the *editio princeps* of 6:5–17 H[A], see Schechter and Taylor, *Wisdom of Ben Sira*, 5.

c. Text-Critical Notes

The above text follows H[A] throughout, except as noted below; S and G[S*] omit 6:9–10 by homoioteleuton.[7]

5[a]. For שׁוֹאֲלוֹ (H[A]) I read שׁוֹאֲלֵי.[8] The Cairo Genizah MSS often interchange *wāw* and *yōd;* for example, in Sir 5:4a H[A] correctly has לִי, whereas H[C] reads לוֹ.[9]

7[b]. Instead of ניסון (H[A]), I read ניסין vocalized as נִיסָּין (another case of *wāw/yōd* confusion).

11[c–c]. So H[A] (cf. S). G reads καὶ ἐπὶ τοὺς οἰκέτας σου παρρησιάσεται ("and toward your household servants he will speak freely"), which Smend retroverts as וּבַעֲבוֹדָתְךָ יִתְנַדֵּב.[10]

12[d]. Cf. G, ἐὰν ταπεινωθῇς ("if you are humbled"); S: *ʾen tēpēl* ("if you fall").[11] H[A] has the phrase: אִם תַּשִּׂיגְךָ רָעָה ("if adversity shall overtake you").[12]

14[e–e]. Where H[A] (cf. S) reads אוֹהֵב תְּקוֹף ("a strong friend"), G has σκέπη κραταιά ("a strong shelter"), which may be retroverted to give אוֹהֶל תְּקוֹף (lit., "a strong tent").[13]

---

[7] Two Qumran fragments from the first century B.C.E (2Q18) have been identified as broken portions of Sir 6:14–15, 20–31. From 6:14–15 the only complete word is אֵין ("there is no ...") in v. 15a. See M. Baillet, J. T. Milik, and R. de Vaux, *Les "petites grottes" de Qumrân* (DJD 3; Oxford: Clarendon, 1962), 76; Beentjes, *Book of Ben Sira in Hebrew,* 123. However, C. Martone identifies the smaller fragment not with Sir 6:14–15 but with 1:19–20; see his "Ben Sira Manuscripts from Qumran and Masada," in Beentjes, ed., *Book of Ben Sira in Modern Research,* 81–94, esp. 82; as well as the rejoinder by E. Puech, "Le livre de Ben Sira et les manuscrits de la Mer Morte," in Calduch-Benages and Vermeylen, eds., *Treasures of Wisdom,* 411–26, esp. 413–14.

[8] Smend, *Sirach, hebräisch und deutsch,* 54; cf. Beentjes, "Ein Mensch ohne Freund," 6.

[9] This interchange derives from the *Vorlage,* in which the two letters were often written almost identically, as in a number of Qumran texts; cf. F. M. Cross, "The Development of the Jewish Scripts," in *The Bible and the Ancient Near East: Essays in Honor of William Foxwell Albright* (ed. G. E. Wright; Garden City, N.Y.: Doubleday, 1961), 133–202, esp. 168–70. Di Lella (*Hebrew Text of Sirach,* 97–101) offers other examples of this orthographic interchange from the Cairo Genizah MSS.

[10] Smend, *Sirach, hebräisch und deutsch,* 55.

[11] Cf. von Herrmann, "Stylistic and Poetic Study," 9.

[12] The phrase of H[A] (perhaps a corruption based on Sir 22:26) unduly lengthens the bicolon and disrupts the rhyme pattern of 6:11–12a.

[13] So Smend, *Sirach, hebräisch und deutsch,* 55; it is also possible that the phrase's second word is the adjective תַּקִּיף ("strong"), with orthographic confusion of *wāw* and *yōd.* The reading of H[A], preferred by Beentjes ("Ein Mensch ohne Freund," 6–7), is somewhat tautological.

16^f–f^. So H^A (cf. 1 Sam 25:29: "bundle of the living" or "bundle of life"). G has φάρμακον ζωῆς ("a life-giving medicine") from צְרִי חַיִּים ("a life-giving balsam"; cf. S, L).

16^g^. Reading יַשִּׂיגֶנּוּ (cf. G, L) for יַשִּׂיגֵם ("will find them") in H^A.[14]

17^h–h^. So H^A. G reads ὁ φοβούμενος κύριον εὐθυνεῖ φιλίαν αὐτοῦ ("the one who fears the Lord will rightly direct his friendship"; cf. S, L). Here G appears to have a doublet of 6:16b: יְרֵא אֵל יְיַשֵּׁר אַהֲבָתוֹ ("the one who fears God will make straight his friendship").[15]

17^i–i^. So H^A, S^A (cf. Sir 2:18cd; 1 Sam 25:25). G (cf. S^{LMW}, L) replaces this colon with 6:17a.

d. Translation

I

5 Pleasant speech makes many a friend,
    and gracious lips multiply well-wishers.
6 Let those at peace with you be many,
    but the possessor of your confidence one in a thousand.
7 You have acquired a friend—with testing acquire him,
    and do not hasten to rely on him.

II

8 For there is a friend for a season,
    but he will not remain on a day of distress.
9 There is a friend, turned into an enemy,
    and he will expose a dispute to your disgrace.
10 There is a friend, a table associate,
    but he will not be found on a day of adversity.

III

11 In your prosperity he is like you,
    but in your adversity he will banish himself from you.
12 When you are humbled he will turn against you,
    and from your presence he will hide himself.

---

[14] Smend, *Sirach, hebräisch und deutsch*, 56.

[15] Cf. Segal, ספר בן־סירא השלם, 36. The reading of 6:17a G, preferred by Beentjes ("Ein Mensch ohne Freund," 8), may be an expansionary gloss by Ben Sira's grandson; the text of H^A makes good sense in its literary and historical context.

13 Separate yourself from your enemies,
and be wary of your friends.

IV

14 A faithful friend is a strong shelter,
and the one who finds him has found wealth.
15 For a faithful friend there is no price,
and there is no weighing of the benefit of him.
16 A faithful friend is a "bundle of the living";
the one who fears God will find him.
17 For as he is, so is his companion,
and as is his name, so are his deeds.

e. Poetic Analysis[16]

i. Stanzaic Structure. Sirach 6:5–17 consists of four stanzas: 3 + 3 + 3 + 4 bicola.[17] The distinctive literary feature of the pericope is the use of threefold repetition.[18] The second stanza is distinguished by the phrase "there is a friend" (יֵשׁ אוֹהֵב, vv. 8a, 9a, 10a), while the fourth stanza is characterized by the phrase "a faithful friend" (אוֹהֵב אֱמוּנָה, vv. 14a, 15a, 16a). The threefold stress on the danger of an unfaithful friend (vv. 8–10) corresponds to the threefold emphasis on the value of a faithful friend (vv. 14–16). Thus, the poem comprises three stanzas of three bicola on the perils of false friendship, and a final stanza of four bicola on the benefit of true friendship.

ii. Stanza 1. Caution in Making Friends (6:5–7). The first stanza contains three equal bicola of 4 + 4 words. The two opening verses are linked by an a:b::b:a chiasm: יַרְבֶּה : שׁוֹאֲלֵי שָׁלוֹם :: אַנְשֵׁי שְׁלוֹמְךָ : רַבִּים ("makes many: well-wishers [= those asking peace] :: those at peace with you : many"). Verse 7a also has its own a:b::b':a chiasm: קָנִיתָ : אוֹהֵב :: בְּנִיסָּיֹן : קְנֵהוּ ("you have acquired : a friend :: with testing : acquire him"); note the verb-noun-noun-verb pattern.

Verses 5–6a exhibit alliteration with *r* and *b* (עָרֵב יַרְבֶּה ... רַבִּים) and with *š* and *l* (שׁוֹאֲלֵי שָׁלוֹם ... אַנְשֵׁי שְׁלוֹמְךָ). Moreover, every word in verse

[16] Cf. Skehan and Di Lella, *Wisdom of Ben Sira,* 64 (assonance), 68 (chiasm); Beentjes, "Ein Mensch ohne Freund," 11–12.

[17] Segal, ספר בן־סירא השלם, 35–38; von Herrmann, "Stylistic and Poetic Study," 4.

[18] Cf. Beentjes, "Ein Mensch ohne Freund," 9.

5 except the final שָׁלוֹם ends with an *ē/e* vowel, and there is rhyme between עָרֵב and אוֹהֵב in verse 5a. In addition, assonance appears in verse 6 between שְׁלוֹמְךָ (v. 6a) and סוֹדְךָ (v. 6b). Ben Sira also utilizes antithesis in verse 6 in his contrast between רַבִּים ("many") and אֶחָד ("one").

This first stanza is parallel to the third stanza: it begins with two bicola (vv. 5–6; cf. vv. 11–12) containing third-person statements about friends and ends with a bicolon (v. 7; cf. v. 13) giving a second-person warning.

iii. Stanza 2. The Threefold Danger of an Unfaithful Friend (6:8–10). Like the first stanza, the second consists of three equal bicola of 4 + 4 words, except that verse 8a has an extra word (כִּי, "for"). In each bicolon there is a contrast between the opening words, "There is a friend," and the disappointing reality revealed in the course of time. This negative reality is expressed in different ways: verse 8 has the negation אַל ("not," here employed unusually with a third-person indicative verb);[19] verse 9 uses the word "enemy" (שׂנֵא, an intentional contrast with the previous אוֹהֵב, "friend"); verse 10 employs the normal negation לֹא ("not") in the second colon.

The stanza exhibits other instances of assonance and repetition. Verse 8a displays alliteration and assonance: כִּי יֵשׁ ... כְּפִי עֵת. There is also assonance in verse 9 between נֶהְפָּךְ ("turned") and חֶרְפָּתְךָ ("your disgrace"). In addition, verse 8b ("but he will not remain on a day of distress") is parallel to verse 10b ("but he will not be found on a day of adversity"), thus forming an *inclusio* for the second stanza.

This stanza is parallel to the fourth in its use of threefold repetition; that is, "there is a friend" (יֵשׁ אוֹהֵב, vv. 8–10) matches "a faithful friend" (אוֹהֵב אֱמוּנָה, vv. 14–16). Ben Sira frequently employs this pattern of threefold repetition,[20] which recurs in 2:1–18 (vv. 7–9, 10, 12–14, 15–17).

iv. Stanza 3. The Reality of an Unfaithful Friend (6:11–13). In this stanza of three bicola, the first three cola (vv. 11–12a) each contain three words, while the remaining three cola (vv. 12b–13) each have two. As in the first stanza, the two initial bicola consist of third-person statements (vv. 11–12), whereas the final bicolon contains two second-person commands

[19] This is a rare emphatic usage "to express the conviction that something cannot happen" (GKC §107p); cf. Pss 50:3; 121:3; Jer 46:6; 2 Chr 14:10; Sir 7:1 H^A; 16:13 H^A.

[20] A similar threefold pattern appears in Ps 136:1–3, as well as three times in Ps 118 (vv. 2–4, 10–12, 15–16).

(v 13). The third stanza also features an *inclusio,* formed by the use of contrast in both verse 11 ("in your prosperity"/"in your adversity") and verse 13 ("your enemies"/"your friends").

Verses 11–12a are bound together by the use of second-person singular suffixes: בְּטוֹבָתְךָ ... כָמוֹךָ׃ וּבְרָעָתְךָ ... מִמְּךָ׃ בְּשִׁפְלְךָ ... בְּךָ. These six suffixes appear two per colon.

Besides the rhymed ending *-kā,* verses 11–12a exhibit alliteration of *b, m,* and *t.* Verse 11 also presents a contrast between "good" (טוֹבָה) and "evil" (רָעָה): "in your prosperity" (בְּטוֹבָתְךָ, v. 11a), "in your adversity" (בְּרָעָתְךָ, v. 11b). In addition, the Hebrew word בְּרָעָתְךָ ("in your adversity," v. 11b) forms a *mot crochet* with בְּיוֹם רָעָה ("on a day of adversity," v. 10b) from the previous stanza.

The second three cola are linked by the fact that each phrase begins with the preposition מִן ("from"): "from your presence" (v. 12b), "from your enemies" (v. 13a), and "of [= from] your friends" (v. 13b); in each case a *nipʿal* verb follows the prepositional phrase. Indeed, verses 12b–13 have a forceful alliteration of *m* and *k,* as well as vowel rhyme and assonance: מִפָּנֶיךָ יִסָּתֵר׃ מִשֹּׂנְאֶיךָ הִבָּדֵל׃ מֵאֹהֲבֶיךָ הִשָּׁמֵר.

v. Stanza 4. The Threefold Benefit of a Faithful Friend (6:14–17). The final stanza consists of four equal bicola of 4 + 3 words. It is significant that in the stanza describing the faithful (= "perfect") friend each bicolon has seven words, since seven is the number denoting perfection or completeness in biblical usage.[21] In each of the first three bicola the same phrase occurs: אוֹהֵב אֱמוּנָה ("a faithful friend," vv. 14–16); this phrase balances the second stanza's threefold use of the words יֵשׁ אוֹהֵב ("there is a friend," vv. 8–10).

Chiastic patterns are found in the first two bicola. Verse 14 has an a:b::b:a' chiasm: אוֹהֵב אֱמוּנָה ... : מוֹצְאוֹ :: מָצָא : הוֹן ("a faithful friend . . . : the one who finds him :: has found : wealth"). In addition, verse 15 exhibits an a:b::b:a' chiasm: לְאוֹהֵב אֱמוּנָה : אֵין מְחִיר :: אֵין מִשְׁקָל : לְטוֹבָתוֹ ("for a faithful friend : there is no price :: there is no weighing : of the benefit of him"). Further alliteration and assonance appear in verses 14–15, especially assonance of *ô* (9x) and *ē/ê* (4x), and alliteration of *h* (4x), *m* (6x), *n* (5x), and *l* (4x).

The three favorable statements about a faithful friend (vv. 14–16) form a contrast with the three unfavorable statements about an unreliable friend (vv. 8–10). Indeed, one may discern a closer resemblance between

[21] Cf. the seven days of creation (Gen 1:1–2:3); seven priests with seven ram's horns march seven times around Jericho on the seventh day (Josh 6:4); Elisha tells Naaman to wash seven times in the Jordan River (2 Kgs 5:10).

the second and fourth stanzas by contrasting their respective grammatical and syntactic patterns. Verses 8–10 display one pattern: negative (אַל, "not," v. 8b); positive (but expressing a negative change from friend to enemy, v. 9); negative (לֹא, "not," v. 10b). By contrast, verses 14–16 evidence the opposite pattern: positive (v. 14); negative (אֵין, "there is no," but expressing the positive value of a faithful friend; bis, v. 15); positive (v. 16). In this way the grammatical and syntactic contrasts between the second and fourth stanzas emphasize the semantic opposition between the unfaithful and the faithful friends.

The fourth stanza concludes with a coda or tailpiece (v. 17) comprising one bicolon (continuing the pattern of 4 + 3 words of the previous three bicola). This bicolon is unified by the alliteration of *k* (5x)[22] and *m* (3x), as well as by the rhyme of כָּמוֹהוּ with רֵעֵהוּ (v. 17a). Moreover, both cola contain similar forms of comparison, in which כְּ ("as") is followed by כֵּן ("so"). The word כָּמוֹהוּ in verse 17a forms an *inclusio* with כָּמוֹךָ in verse 11a, binding the third and fourth stanzas together. Moreover, a rhyming pattern between verses 17 and 7 creates a stylistic *inclusio* for the poem, since the last bicolon in stanza 4 (רֵעֵהוּ ... מַעֲשָׂיו) rhymes with the final bicolon in stanza 1 (קֹנֵהוּ ... עָלָיו). In 7:36 (as in 6:17) Ben Sira ends a pericope (7:18–36) with one summarizing bicolon, while chapter 2 concludes with a couplet (2:18) containing a comparison similar to 6:17.[23]

f. Context

i. Place of Sir 6:5–17 within 4:11–6:17. The poem of 6:5–17 occurs within the second major unit (4:11–6:17) of Ben Sira's book. This major unit, which deals with "Applying Wisdom Personally,"[24] consists of four pericopes.

---

[22] On the frequent use of *kāp* to indicate the end of a Hebrew poem or section, see M. L. Barré, "'Terminative' Terms in Hebrew Acrostics," in *Wisdom, You Are My Sister: Studies in Honor of Roland E. Murphy, O. Carm., on the Occasion of His Eightieth Birthday* (ed. M. L. Barré; CBQMS 29; Washington, D.C.: Catholic Biblical Association of America, 1997), 207–15.

[23] Although Smend (*Sirach, erklärt,* 56) regards 6:17b H^A (cf. S^A) as displaced from 2:18d S, it seems more likely that Ben Sira intentionally concludes both 2:1–18 and 6:5–17 with a similar phrase (2:18d S = 6:17b H^A, S^A), in order to compare human friendship with God's relation to his servants. On the connection between the two pericopes, see Irwin, "Fear of God," 556–58.

[24] Cf. Harvey, "Toward a Degree of Order," 55. See also J. Marböck, "Structure and Redaction History of the Book of Ben Sira: Review and Prospects," in Beentjes, ed., *Book of Ben Sira in Modern Research,* 61–79, esp. 72–74. The ensuing division into four pericopes follows Skehan and Di Lella, *Wisdom of Ben Sira,* xiv.

4:11–19: Personal Challenge and Benefit of Wisdom[25]
4:20–31: Against Cowardice
5:1–6:4: Against Presumptuousness, Deceptive Speech, and Passionate Behavior (a twenty-two-line nonalphabetic acrostic)
6:5–17: Personal Challenge and Benefit of Friendship

Sirach 4:11–19 and 5:9–6:4 exhibit particular thematic links with the poem on friendship, as outlined below.

ii. Relation of 6:5–17 with 4:11–19. There are a number of connections between the wisdom poem in 4:11–19 and the friendship pericope in 6:5–17. According to 4:11–19 wisdom gives her rewards (4:12–16) only after imposing "tests" (נִסְיוֹנוֹת, 4:17) on "those who love her" (or "her friends": אֹהֲבֶיהָ, 4:12). A similar pattern emerges in 6:5–17: friendship yields its rewards (6:14–16), but only after the "friend" (אוֹהֵב, 6:7) has undergone "testing" (נִיסָּיוֹן, 6:7) by experience. Moreover, just as the seeker for wisdom will find "life" (חַיִּים, 4:12), so too the person acquiring a faithful friend has gained "a bundle of the living" (or "a bundle of life": צְרוֹר חַיִּים, 6:16). Just as those who rely on wisdom "will find" (יִמְצְאוּ, 4:13) glory, so the one who gains a faithful friend "has found" (מָצָא, 6:14) wealth. There is also a common emphasis on fidelity; in 4:16 (lacking in H^A^) wisdom is promised "if one remains faithful" (ἐὰν ἐμπιστεύσῃ), while 6:14–16 speaks of the great value of a "faithful friend" (φίλος πιστὸς). By means of these verbal connections the author suggests that, just as wisdom tests people before granting her friendship, so too the wise person should test any would-be friends.[26]

A chiastic pattern exists between 4:11–19 and 6:5–17.

A: אֹהֲבֶיהָ אָהֲבוּ חַיִּים ("those who love her love life," 4:12)
B: יִמְצְאוּ ("they will find," 4:13)
C: ἐὰν ἐμπιστεύσῃ ("if one remains faithful," 4:16)
D: בְּנִסְיוֹנוֹת ("with tests," 4:17)
D: בְּנִיסָּיוֹן ("with testing," 6:7)
C: πιστὸς ("faithful," 6:14, 15, 16)
B: מוֹצְאוֹ מָצָא ("the one who finds him has found," 6:14)
A: צְרוֹר חַיִּים אוֹהֵב ("a friend is a 'bundle of the living,'" 6:16)

[25] On this poem, see N. Calduch-Benages, "La sabiduría y la prueba en Sir 4,11–19," *EstBib* 49 (1991): 25–48; F. Saracino, "La sapienza e la vita: Sir 4,11–19," *RivB* 29 (1981): 257–72; L. Schrader, *Leiden und Gerechtigkeit*, 147–63.

[26] Cf. Harvey, "Toward a Degree of Order," 55; Irwin, "Fear of God," 558.

These connections between 4:11–19 and 6:5–17 serve a structural purpose: they form an envelope around part 2 of Ben Sira's book (4:11–6:17). Thus, such links not only relate the sage's teaching on friendship (6:5–17) to the search for wisdom (4:11–19) but also unify part 2 of his book.

iii. Relation of 6:5–17 with 5:9–6:4. Several connections exist between 6:5–17 and the preceding poem in 5:9–6:4 concerning control of one's speech (5:9–6:1) and of one's passions (6:2–4).[27] Whereas in 5:14 Ben Sira declares that "disgrace" (חֶרְפָּה) comes to the "two-faced person," 6:9 warns that such a person can cause "your disgrace" (חֶרְפָּתְךָ) by revealing a dispute. Furthermore, in 6:1 Ben Sira counsels his student: "Instead of a friend [אוֹהֵב], do not be an enemy [שׂוֹנֵא]" (through harmful speech), just as in 6:5–6a he advises the student to have many at peace with him. Moreover, using the same antithesis as in 6:1, he warns in 6:9 against "a friend [אוֹהֵב] turned into an enemy [שֹׂנֵא]," and in 6:13 he urges: "Separate yourself from your enemies [שֹׂנְאֶיךָ], and be wary of your friends [אֹהֲבֶיךָ]." Whereas a person with an evil character gains "a bad name" (שֵׁם רַע, 6:1) for his harmful speech, a person of good character can be a faithful friend whose actions are "as is his name" (כִּשְׁמוֹ, 6:17). Finally, 6:4 contains the saying: "Strong desire will destroy its possessors [בְּעָלֶיהָ], and the joy of an enemy [שׂוֹנֵא] will overtake them"; the occurrence of בַּעַל here creates a connection with 6:6, while the use of שׂוֹנֵא makes a link with 6:9 and 13.[28]

iv. Relation of 6:5–17 with 6:18–37. After considering the links between 6:5–17 and the preceding unit, I now discuss the connections between 6:5–17 and 6:18–37, a wisdom poem in the form of a nonalphabetic acrostic. Ben Sira's optimism that wisdom is attainable (6:18–19, 27–33, 37) matches his belief that a faithful friend is attainable (6:16), provided one seeks sincerely and devoutly. Indeed, in the poem's opening verse Ben Sira tells his student that by receiving instruction, "you will attain [תַּשִּׂיג] wisdom" (6:18 H^C), just as the God-fearing person seeking a faithful

---

[27] Elsewhere the sage juxtaposes control of the tongue and of the passions: tongue (19:4–12; 22:27–23:1; 23:7–15); passions (18:30–19:3; 23:2–6, 16–27). On 5:9–6:1, see Okoye, *Speech in Ben Sira;* and Di Lella, "Use and Abuse of the Tongue"; on 5:14–6:1, see Krammer, "Scham im Zusammenhang mit Freundschaft," 184–87.

[28] The sage occasionally makes use of a refrain to end pericopes. Here 6:4a H^A marks the close of 5:9–6:4, while the same colon in 19:3b H^C indicates the end of 18:15–19:3. In similar fashion, 20:30–31 G closes 19:20–20:31, while the same refrain in 41:14–15 G brings 41:5–15 to a close.

friend "will find him" (יַשִּׂיגֶנּוּ, 6:16).[29] Similarly, speaking of wisdom, 6:28 H^C promises: "Afterward you will find [תִּמְצָא] her refreshments," just as the one finding a friend "has found [מָצָא] wealth" (6:14).

According to 6:22, "Discipline—as is its name [כִּשְׁמָהּ], so it [= wisdom] is [כֵּן הִיא],[30] and not to many [רַבִּים] is it straightforward"; the assertion of verse 22a resembles the earlier statement on the nature of a faithful friend in 6:17b: "as is his name [כִּשְׁמוֹ], so [כֵּן] are his deeds." Moreover, the mention of "many" (רַבִּים, 6:22b) recalls the use of the same word in 6:6: "Let those at peace with you be many" (רַבִּים). In addition, 6:28 H^C says that despite initially causing suffering, wisdom later "will be changed [תֵּהָפֵךְ] for you into a delight." Here wisdom's encouraging "change" (הפך, *nipʿal*) contrasts with the discouraging "change" in a seeming friend "turned [נֶהְפָּךְ, 6:9] into an enemy." Furthermore, 6:29 H^A declares that wisdom's restrictive net will become "a strong foundation" (מְכוֹן עֹז); the phrase in G, σκέπη ἰσχύος (lit., "a shelter of strength"), recalls 6:14 G, which describes a faithful friend as a "strong shelter" (σκέπη κραταιά). Finally, both pericopes conclude by mentioning God (as do also 9:16; 19:17; 23:27; 25:11; 37:15). Ultimately wisdom is to be attained through meditation on "the commands of the Lord" (6:37a G; H^A reads "the fear of the Most High"), just as "the one who fears God" (יְרֵא אֵל) attains a faithful friend (6:16).[31]

g. Exegesis

i. Stanza 1. Caution in Making Friends (6:5–7). The first stanza of the poem urges a combination of politeness (6:5–6a) and reserve (6:6b–7). Such teaching, as we shall see, has parallels in Jewish tradition, in ancient Near Eastern wisdom texts, and in the Greek cultural world.

Sirach 6:5 urges pleasant speaking; the student is to avoid objectionable language (cf. Sir 20:13). Indeed, in 6:5–6a Ben Sira practices what he

---

[29] See the textual note above (16[g]). On Sir 6:18–37, see Argall, *1 Enoch and Sirach*, 60–63; Minissale, *La versione greca del Siracide*, 46–55; J. L. Crenshaw, "The Primacy of Listening in Ben Sira's Pedagogy," in Barré, ed., *Wisdom, You Are My Sister*, 172–87, esp. 185–87.

[30] Reading the feminine form הִיא (agreeing with חָכְמָה in 6:18b; cf. נְכוֹחָה in 6:22b H^A). Sirach 6:22a H^A reads הוּא, through confusion of *wāw* and *yōd* (as in 6:5b and 6:7a). Cf. Skehan and Di Lella, *Wisdom of Ben Sira*, 191.

[31] Sirach 6:5–17 also has links with 2:1–18 in its mention of "testing" (πειρασμός, 6:7; cf. 2:1), affliction (6:8, 10; cf. 2:11), faithfulness (πιστός, 6:14–16; cf. πιστεύω, 2:6, 8, 13), money (wealth in 6:14; cf. gold in 2:5), shelter (noun in 6:16; cf. verb in 2:13), and fear of Yahweh (6:16; cf. 2:7–9, 15–17); see further Irwin, "Fear of God," 556–58.

preaches by using euphonic alliteration of *r* (3x), *b* (4x), *š* (4x), *l* (3x), and *m* (3x). For "pleasant speech" H^A says literally "a sweet palate" (חֵיךְ עָרֵב); in the Song of Songs the bride praises her beloved by saying, "His speech [חִכּוֹ] is very sweet" (Cant 5:16). The phrase "gracious lips" (שִׂפְתֵי חֵן)[32] echoes the description of the bridegroom in the royal wedding song: "Graciousness has been poured out upon your lips" (הוּצַק חֵן בְּשִׂפְתוֹתֶיךָ, Ps 45:3). Moreover, similar phraseology occurs in the compact aphorism of Prov 22:11, אֹהֵב טְהָר־לֵב חֵן שְׂפָתָיו רֵעֵהוּ מֶלֶךְ, which the NRSV renders: "Those who love a pure heart and are gracious in speech will have the king as their friend."

Politeness and restraint of speech are common themes in wisdom literature. Proverbs 15:1 is well-known: "A gentle answer turns back wrath." Ben Sira himself devotes considerable space to the good or harm that the tongue can do (e.g., 5:9–6:1; 22:27–23:1; 23:7–15; 28:12–26).

The term שׁוֹאֲלֵי שָׁלוֹם (6:5b), rendered "well-wishers," refers to "those who give a greeting of peace." The idiom "to greet" (lit., "to ask peace," שָׁאַל לְשָׁלוֹם or שָׁאַל שָׁלוֹם) occurs elsewhere in the MT (e.g., 1 Sam 10:4; 17:22; 25:5; 30:21), as well as in Sir 41:20 H^BmgM. In fact, the idiom is one of several expressions common to 1 Sam 25 (the Nabal episode) and Sir 6:5–17.[33] In 1 Sam 25:5 David commands his servants to go to Nabal, saying: "and you shall greet him in my name" (וּשְׁאֶלְתֶּם־לוֹ בִשְׁמִי לְשָׁלוֹם).[34]

The fourth-century Greek orator Isocrates offers Demonicus teaching similar to Sir 6:5: "Be courteous in your manner, and cordial in your address. It is the part of courtesy to greet those whom you meet" (*Demon.* 20).[35] In a more cynical vein, Theognis advises Cyrnus: "Let thy tongue

---

[32] For the parallelism of "palate [= speech]" and "lips," see Prov 5:3; 8:7; cf. Beentjes, "Ein Mensch ohne Freund," 12.

[33] Krinetzki ("Die Freundschaftsperikope," 216–18) notes connections between Sir 6:9b and 1 Sam 25:39; Sir 6:16a and 1 Sam 25:29; and Sir 6:17b and 1 Sam 25:25. Adding the connection between Sir 6:5b and 1 Sam 25:5, Beentjes tabulates the parallels ("Ein Mensch ohne Freund," 15). My discussion of these four instances will suggest that 1 Sam 25 served as an exemplary narrative underlying Sir 6:5–17. Elsewhere Beentjes comments: "In Sir 6:5–17 we have the first occurrence of structural use of Scripture in the Book of Ben Sira"; see his "Canon and Scripture in the Book of Ben Sira (Jesus Sirach/Ecclesiasticus)," in *Hebrew Bible, Old Testament: The History of Its Interpretation* 1/2 (ed. M. Saebø et al.; Göttingen: Vandenhoeck & Ruprecht, 2000), 591–605; quotation from p. 600.

[34] Note that the word שָׁלוֹם is found three times in 1 Sam 25:6. Abigail's polite plea to David (1 Sam 25:24–31), later in the same episode, is an example of "pleasant speech."

[35] Norlin and van Hook, trans., *Isocrates,* 1:15. For the following quotation, see J. M. Edmonds, trans., *Elegy and Iambus* (2 vols.; LCL; New York: Putnam, 1931), 1:237.

give all men to think thou art their friend [φίλος], while in act thou mingle with no man any sober business whatsoever" (Theognis 63–65). However, whereas Theognis's advice may contain an element of deception, Ben Sira agrees with Isocrates in sincerely counseling his students to be polite.

Sirach 6:6 contrasts being at peace with "many" (רַבִּים; perhaps meaning "all") and trusting few, indeed only "one in a thousand."[36] The same phrase, "those at peace with you" (אַנְשֵׁי שְׁלוֹמְךָ, 6:6), occurs in Jer 38:22 in the context of betrayal. Psalm 41:10 employs an equivalent singular form, "one at peace with me" (אִישׁ שְׁלוֹמִי), in a similar context of the betrayal of friendship. In 6:6 Ben Sira echoes such expressions, with the result that while on the surface he is urging his students to be polite to all, at another level he is warning them not to trust everyone.

The contrast between "the many" and "the one" is a feature of the Greek philosophical search for a unifying principle of experience. However, in 6:6 Ben Sira simply uses a standard antithetical word-pair from biblical writing ("many"/"one": Ezek 33:24; cf. Luke 10:41–42; 1 Cor 10:17; 12:12), so as to add emphasis.

The phrase in 6:6b, "one in a thousand" (אֶחָד מֵאֶלֶף),[37] also occurs in Qoh 7:28 in reference to the rarity of a wise man. Elsewhere Ben Sira insists that his students should associate only with the wise (e.g., 6:34; 9:14). The sage's advice to restrict severely the number of one's confidants recurs in 8:17 H^{A}: "Do not share confidences with a simple person, for he will not be able to conceal your confidence" (סוֹדְךָ; cf. 37:10).

Like Sir 6:6, Theognis 73–75 teaches a cautious attitude toward making friends: "Share not thy device wholly with all thy friends; few among many, for sure, have a mind that may be trusted [παῦροί τοι πολλῶν πιστὸν ἔχουσι νοόν]. Make but few privy to it when thou takest in hand great matters."[38] Together with his worldly wise caution, Theognis displays a social preference for the upper classes (οἱ ἀγαθοί) and an aristocratic disdain for the lower classes (οἱ κακοί).[39] Xenophon

---

[36] While Aristotle recognizes that it is possible to befriend many people for political purposes, he asserts (*Eth. nic.* 9.10.6 §1171a) that "it is not possible to have many friends whom we love for their virtue and for themselves" (Rackham, trans., *Nicomachean Ethics,* 569). Elsewhere (*Eth. nic.* 9.5.3 §1167a) he states that "well-wishers are not necessarily friends" (ibid., 541).

[37] Ben Sira also contrasts "one" (אֶחָד) and "a thousand" (אֶלֶף) in 16:3. Moreover, in 39:11 G he asserts that the God-fearing scribe "will leave behind a name greater than a thousand."

[38] Edmonds, trans., *Elegy and Iambus,* 1:237.

[39] Cf. Theognis 43–47; 101–114; 183–192; 305–308. Donlan ("*Pistos Philos Hetairos,*" 234) explains Theognis's aristocratic view of friendship: "By shunning contact

expresses a similarly elitist outlook: "It is a far sounder plan to show kindness to the best [τοὺς βελτίστους], who are fewer in number, than to the worst [τοὺς χείρονας], who are the greater company" (*Mem.* 2.6.-27).[40] However, although Ben Sira may well have belonged to the upper class in the Jerusalem of his day (cf. Sir 31:12; 32:9; 38:24; 39:4), he does not disdain the poor (11:2–4) and warns of the danger in making friends with the rich (13:4–7).

Elsewhere in his book Ben Sira urges caution toward would-be friends. In 19:4 G, for instance, he declares: "One who quickly trusts is light-headed," and in 37:8 H^{BD} he urges: "Guard yourself from an advisor." Likewise, in 8:19 H^{A} he advises: "Do not reveal your heart to anyone."[41] Instead of trusting someone hastily, one should get to know the person by talking with him: "Before a conversation do not praise a man, for this is the test of human beings" (27:7 G).

In emphasizing the need to test a potential friend before relying on him, Sir 6:7 voices a common concern of many ancient writers. For example, the demotic wisdom text found in Papyrus Insinger (copied by the Egyptian scribe Phebhor or Phibis) urges a cautious attitude toward making friends. Sirach 6:7a resembles P. Insinger 12.15: "One does not discover the heart of a wise man if one has not tested him in a matter," while Sir 6:7b is similar to P. Insinger 11.23: "Do not trust one whom you do not know in your heart, lest he cheat you with cunning."[42] In fact, there are Egyptian parallels to Sir 6:7 from a wide time span, from the third millennium B.C.E. (Ptahhotep) to the late Ptolemaic era (Ankhsheshonq, P. Insinger).[43]

---

with the *kakoi/deiloi* (social and moral inferiors) who are, by nature, incapable of the refined ethical behavior of *agathoi*, the aristocrat is at least able to escape the most obvious source of bad effects from perverted friendships."

[40] E. C. Marchant, trans., *Xenophon: Memorabilia and Oeconomicus* (LCL; New York: Putnam, 1923), 139–41. Isocrates (*Demon.* 20) gives comparable advice: "Be pleasant to all, but cultivate the best" (Norlin and van Hook, trans., *Isocrates,* 1:15).

[41] Cf. Sanders, "Ben Sira's Ethics of Caution," 76–77. Ben Sira's emphasis on caution toward friends contrasts with the expectation of self-disclosure and frankness within Greek friendship; see further Konstan, *Friendship in the Classical World,* 93 (Isocrates), 112–13 (Philodemus).

[42] *AEL* 3:194–95. In the Hebrew Bible, Mic 7:5 issues a warning not to trust friends.

[43] Ptahhotep 33 advises: "If you probe the character of a friend, don't inquire, but approach him, deal with him alone, so as not to suffer from his manner. Dispute with him after a time, test his heart in conversation" (*AEL* 1:72). Ankhsheshonq 14.8 also counsels: "If you become the companion of a wise man whose heart you do not know, do not open your heart to him" (ibid., 3:170).

Greek parallels also exist from authors such as Theognis (sixth century B.C.E.), Xenophon and Isocrates (both fourth century B.C.E.), and Menander (third century B.C.E.).[44] For instance, Theognis declares: "Mind of man nor yet of woman shalt thou know till thou hast made trial [πειρηθείης] of it like a beast of burden" (Theognis 125–126).[45] Caution toward potential friends is also implied in Aristotle's dictum, "The wish to be friends is a quick growth, but friendship is not" (*Eth. nic.* 8.3.9 §1156b).

The need for testing friends arises from the ambiguity of the experience of friendship. Gerhard von Rad has pointed out that "the way in which Sirach often sharply confronts things in all their ambivalence reveals something of a consciously applied, didactic method" (cf. Sir 20:9–14).[46] Von Rad further explains:

> Where the judgment of a thing is unequivocal, such as the case of children or friends, Sirach can actually even confine himself to dwelling more on those aspects which are often thought about less. Many a friend turns into an enemy.

The element of testing occurs also in God's friendship with humanity.[47] In particular, divine testing appears prominently in the traditions about the ancient patriarchs. In Jdt 8:25–26 (NRSV) Judith says:

---

[44] In *Mem.* 2.6.1, Xenophon states that Socrates "gave instruction for testing the qualities that make a man's friendship worth winning" (Marchant, trans., *Xenophon,* 127). Similarly, in his oration *Ad. Nic.* 27 Isocrates advises: "Subject your associates to the most searching tests" (Norlin and van Hook, trans., *Isocrates,* 1:55). So too, one of Menander's *Fragments* (691K) states: "Gold knows how to be tested by fire, and loyalty among friends is tested when a crisis comes" (see F. G. Allinson, trans., *Menander: The Principal Fragments* [LCL; New York: Putnam, 1930], 523).

[45] Edmonds, trans., *Elegy and Iambus,* 1:243; cf. also Theognis 571–572 (= 1104A–B). The following quotation comes from Rackham, trans., *Nicomachean Ethics,* 465.

[46] G. von Rad, *Wisdom in Israel* (London: SCM, 1972), 247; the next quotation is from p. 248.

[47] Thus, Ben Sira's second chapter warns the student of divine testing: "My child, if you draw near to serve the Lord, prepare yourself for testing" (2:1). On 2:1–18, see Schrader, *Leiden und Gerechtigkeit,* 180–204; A. A. Di Lella, "Fear of the Lord and Belief and Hope in the Lord amid Trials: Sirach 2:1–18," in Barré, ed., *Wisdom, You Are My Sister,* 188–204; N. Calduch-Benages, "Trial Motif in the Book of Ben Sira with Special Reference to Sir 2,1–6," in Beentjes, ed., *Book of Ben Sira in Modern Research,* 135–51.

> In spite of everything let us give thanks to the Lord our God, who is putting us to the test as he did our ancestors. Remember what he did with Abraham, and how he tested Isaac, and what happened to Jacob.

Abraham, whom Israel's tradition calls the "friend of God" (Isa 41:8; 2 Chr 20:7; cf. Jas 2:23), was tested by God's command to sacrifice his son Isaac (Gen 22:1). Sirach 44:20 H^B affirms regarding Abraham: "In testing [נִיסּוּי] he was found faithful [נֶאֱמָן]" (cf. 1 Macc 2:52).[48]

The use of the verb קנה ("acquire, purchase, get") for gaining a friend (Sir 6:7) reflects an idiom found elsewhere in Hebrew; for instance, *m. ʾAbot* 1:6 advises: קְנֵה לְךָ חָבֵר ("Acquire for yourself an associate").[49] However, in 6:7 Ben Sira seems intentionally to utilize the same verb (קנה) that he employs elsewhere for "acquiring" wisdom (cf. Sir 51:25; Prov 4:7; 18:15; 19:8), since he views the quest for suitable friends in the context of the search for wisdom (cf. 9:14–15).[50]

ii. Stanza 2. The Threefold Danger of an Unfaithful Friend (6:8–10). The second stanza explains why the wise person must test any prospective friend (6:7): someone who first appears to be a friend can later turn into an enemy (6:9). The stanza is unified by the threefold phrase: "There is a friend" (יֵשׁ אוֹהֵב, 6:8, 9, 10). Although some translations (e.g. NAB and NJB) understand the threefold repetition to refer to three sorts of friends, it is more likely that Ben Sira is speaking of three aspects of the same unfaithful friend, just as the threefold repetition of "a faithful friend" in 6:14–16 refers to a single person.

Ben Sira's observations in this context appear to be based on Prov 18:24 (אִישׁ רֵעִים לְהִתְרֹעֵעַ וְיֵשׁ אֹהֵב דָּבֵק מֵאָח), which says literally: "A man of companions [is] to be broken in pieces, but there is a friend sticking [closer] than a brother."[51] Sirach 6:5–17 may be the sage's expansion of the thought of Prov 18:24.[52] Ben Sira explains the dangers of friendship in

---

[48] In 4:17 Ben Sira also describes how the person seeking the divine wisdom will experience her "tests" (נִסְיוֹנוֹת).

[49] For the Hebrew text, see B. T. Viviano, *Study As Worship: Aboth and the New Testament* (SJLA 26; Leiden: Brill, 1978), 12; the translation is mine. Sirach 20:23 H^C employs the same Hebrew verb to denote acquiring an enemy. Greek also uses the equivalent verb κτάομαι ("acquire, get") for gaining a friend; cf. Xenophon, *Mem.* 2.6.1; Sophocles, *Aj.* 1360; Euripides, *Orest.* 804.

[50] Cf. Harvey, "Toward a Degree of Order," 55.

[51] The sense of the verb לְהִתְרֹעֵעַ is not clear; perhaps we should emend it to לְהִתְרָעוֹת and translate 18:24a: "A man of companions will be companionable." For a Greek parallel to Prov 18:24b, see Euripides, *Orest.* 804–806.

[52] Cf. Sanders, *Ben Sira and Demotic Wisdom*, 7, 15.

6:8–13 (cf. Prov 18:24a) and its benefits in 6:14–17 (cf. Prov 18:24b). Just as Ben Sira uses a key phrase for 6:14–16 (אוֹהֵב אֱמוּנָה = "a faithful friend"), so too in 6:8–10 he borrows an expression (יֵשׁ אוֹהֵב = "there is a friend") from Prov 18:24b to introduce the actions of the unfaithful friend.

Sirach 6:8 speaks of the fair-weather friend; the first colon means literally: "For there is a friend according to a time." The usual human expectation is expressed in Prov 17:17: "At all times a companion loves, and a brother is born for adversity." However, with a fair-weather friend the "season" or "time" (עֵת) of his friendship ends as soon as a "day of distress" (יוֹם צָרָה, 6:8b) arrives. Ben Sira's hymn of praise (51:1–12) may reflect a similar personal experience of betrayal, since he thanks God for delivering him on the "day of distress" (51:10, 12). The distress, brought about by slander and deceit (51:2, 5–6), left him friendless (51:7), just as 6:8 speaks of desertion by a fair-weather friend.[53]

Elsewhere Ben Sira notes the change that comes over false friends at a time of distress (12:8–9). Such a change is also mentioned in P. Insinger 12.18: "One does not discover the heart of a friend if one has not consulted him in anxiety."[54] Moreover, Isocrates teaches: "Prove your friends by means of the misfortunes of life and of their fellowship in your perils" (*Demon.* 25).

Sirach 6:9 develops the thought of verse 8 by observing how a former friend can become an enemy who goes around saying uncomplimentary things. Similarly, Sir 37:2 H^D asks: "Is it not a sorrow reaching to death: a companion like oneself, turned into an adversary?" Indeed, the phrase "turned into an adversary" (נֶהְפָּךְ לְצַר, 37:2b) echoes the phrase "turned into an enemy" (נֶהְפָּךְ לְשׂוֹנֵא) in 6:9a. Moreover, Sir 6:1 advises: "Instead of a friend, do not be an enemy"; in both 6:1 and 6:9 there is the same contrast between אוֹהֵב and שׂוֹנֵא. Although Ben Sira urges caution toward potential friends, he is not as suspicious as Menander, who believes that any friend confided in can later become an enemy.[55]

Sirach 6:9b describes the false friend betraying the secret of a serious disagreement from the past. The actual phrase used here is another

---

[53] On the poem, see A. A. Di Lella, "Sirach 51:1–12: Poetic Structure and Analysis of Ben Sira's Psalm," *CBQ* 48 (1986): 395–407. The biblical phrase יוֹם צָרָה ("day of distress") also occurs in Sir 3:15 H^A.

[54] *AEL* 3:195; Sanders (*Ben Sira and Demotic Wisdom,* 64) notes this parallel. Similarly, Theognis 79–80 warns Cyrnus: "Few comrades, son of Polypaüs, wilt thou find worthy thy trust in difficulties" (Edmonds, trans., *Elegy and Iambus,* 1:239). The following quotation comes from Norlin and van Hook, trans., *Isocrates,* 1:19.

[55] In *Fragments* 695K he advises: "Don't tell your secret to your friend and you'll not fear him when he turns into an enemy" (Allinson, trans., *Menander,* 523).

allusion to the story of Nabal and Abigail (1 Sam 25).[56] When Ben Sira says that the renegade friend will reveal "a dispute to your disgrace" (אֶת רִיב חֶרְפָּתְךָ, lit. "the dispute of your disgrace"), he alludes to David's grateful response to Abigail's timely intervention: "Blessed be Yahweh who argued the case of my disgrace [אֶת־רִיב חֶרְפָּתִי] at the hand of Nabal and restrained his servant from evil, but Nabal's evil Yahweh has requited on his head" (1 Sam 25:39). In general, 1 Sam 25 contrasts the boorish Nabal, whose name means "fool" (1 Sam 25:25), with his prudent wife Abigail, who is described as being "of good insight" (טוֹבַת־שֶׂכֶל, 25:3) and whom David praises, saying: "Blessed be your discretion" (בָּרוּךְ טַעְמֵךְ, 25:33).[57] The use of wisdom vocabulary in 1 Sam 25 (נָבָל, "fool"; שֶׂכֶל, "insight, prudence"; טַעַם, "discretion") suggests that the story might easily have attracted the attention of a wisdom teacher such as Ben Sira.

The fact that here and in 6:16–17 Ben Sira clearly alludes to 1 Sam 25 suggests that he understands the story of Nabal and Abigail as exemplifying his teaching on friendship. As a negative example, the foolish Nabal refuses to respond peacefully to David's greeting (1 Sam 25:6–11; cf. Sir 6:5) but rather engages in a dispute to disgrace David (1 Sam 25:39; cf. Sir 6:9). As a positive example, the prudent Abigail responds to David in a friendly manner, offering gifts of food to David's troops (1 Sam 25:18–19) and gracious words to David himself (1 Sam 25:24–31; cf. Sir 6:5), with the result that her friendliness eventually leads to marriage with David (1 Sam 25:42).

Just as in 6:9 the sage alludes to Abigail because of her prudence in avoiding a dispute with David, so too he states elsewhere that the wise person is someone who does not enter into public disputes (Sir 11:9; cf. Prov 20:3; 26:17). Although friends may need to reprove one another (Sir

---

[56] Cf. Krinetzki, "Die Freundschaftsperikope," 216–17. On the literary contrast between Abigail and Nabal in 1 Sam 25, see J. D. Levenson, "1 Samuel 25 As Literature and As History," *CBQ* 40 (1978): 11–28; on Josephus's retelling of the biblical narrative, see C. Begg, "The Abigail Story (1 Samuel 25) according to Josephus," *EstBib* 54 (1996): 5–34.

[57] Trenchard comments on Sir 26:13: "Ben Sira uses *śkl* here to describe a good wife's trait" (*Ben Sira's View of Women,* 15). In n. 70 (pp. 193–94) he observes that "the only OT use of *śkl* in relation to a woman is 1 Sam 25:3. There Abigail is said to be a woman of good sense (*ṭwbt śkl*) and good looks (*ypt tʾr*). She demonstrates her *śkl* by providing for David and his men (25:18–22)." Trenchard adds (194) that "it is possible that this incident has influenced Ben Sira" in 26:13. Although Ben Sira never mentions Abigail by name, it seems that the story of her encounter with David was important to the sage.

19:13–17) and may even have a private quarrel, there is no cause for shame unless the disagreement is made public.[58]

The sage regards the revealing of a confidence as a serious matter. In 42:1 H^{BM} (the only other instance of the verb חשׂף ["expose"] in the Hebrew MSS of Ben Sira),[59] the sage tells his students to be ashamed "of exposing any matter [so H^{M}; 'confidence' in H^{B}] of advice." Likewise, Sir 27:16 declares: "One who reveals a confidence destroys faithfulness and will not find a friend for himself." In these utterances Ben Sira echoes the teaching of Prov 25:9–10: "Argue your case [רִיבְךָ] with your companion, but do not reveal another's confidence, lest one who hears will disgrace you, and the malicious talk about you will not cease." In light of these sayings, a renegade friend who betrays private disagreements appears all the more reprehensible.[60]

In restating the thought of Sir 6:8, 6:10 accentuates the intimacy of the earlier friendship by calling the former friend a "table associate." The story of Abraham's welcome of the three travelers (Gen 18:1–8) exemplifies the importance of hospitality in Jewish tradition.[61] Against this background, a breach of table fellowship represents a serious betrayal, as we see in Ps 41:10: "Even one at peace with me, in whom I trusted, who ate my bread, has raised high his heel against me."[62] The thought of Sir 6:10 (echoed in 37:4) seems to mirror the observation in Theognis 643–644: "Many become comrades dear [φίλοι ... ἑταῖροι] beside the bowl, but few in a grave matter."

Sirach 6:10b uses the phrase "day of adversity" (יוֹם רָעָה) to parallel the phrase of 6:8b, "day of distress" (יוֹם צָרָה). In Ps 41, the "day of adversity" (v. 2) denotes the day when one is betrayed by a close friend (v. 10).

iii. Stanza 3. The Reality of an Unfaithful Friend (6:11–13). The third stanza develops the thought of the second by spelling out the behavior of an

---

[58] Possibly Ben Sira implies a wordplay here between the verb חשׂף ("expose," 6:9b) and the Aramaic word חִסְפָּא ("shame").

[59] In Sir 42:1 H^{B} the root is spelled חסף.

[60] Among the Essenes there was a rule: "The secrets of a friend must not be divulged in enmity" (Philo, *Hypoth.* 7.8); the quotation is from F. H. Colson and G. H. Whitaker, trans., *Philo* (LCL; 10 vols.; Cambridge, Mass.: Harvard University Press, 1929–1962), 9:429.

[61] Moreover, according to the ancient custom of desert peoples in the Middle East, there is an obligation to show hospitality to visitors, whom the host may not harm after feeding them.

[62] According to John 13:18, Jesus uses the same psalm verse to refer to his forthcoming betrayal by a former friend. For the following Theognis quotation, see Edmonds, trans., *Elegy and Iambus,* 1:307 (cf. Theognis 115–116).

unfaithful friend (6:11–12) and drawing a lesson (6:13b). Ben Sira constructs the stanza around the twin polarities of "prosperity"/"adversity" (6:11) and "enemies"/"friends" (6:13). Both these contrasts recur in Sir 12:8 H^{A}: "A friend [אוֹהֵב] will not be recognized in prosperity [בְּטוֹבָה], but an enemy [שׂוֹנֵא] will not be concealed in adversity [בְּרָעָה]." Sirach 12:9 H^{A} explains why: "In a person's prosperity [בְּטוֹבַת אִישׁ], even an enemy [שׂוֹנֵא] is a companion, but in his adversity [בְּרָעָתוֹ], even a companion will separate himself."[63]

Sirach 6:11a depicts the unfaithful friend as appearing sincere in times of prosperity: "He is like you." Greek culture prized having a friend like oneself. Aristotle expresses this view of ideal friendship by citing several proverbs: "'Friends have one soul between them,' 'Friends' goods are common property,' 'Amity [φιλότης] is equality'" (*Eth. nic.* 9.8.2 §1168b).[64] However, whereas Sir 6:17 affirms that a true friend is like oneself (cf. 13:15) in action as well as in name, in 6:11 the sage speaks merely of the seeming similarity of a fair-weather friend.

Israelite sapiential tradition prior to Ben Sira notes the human tendency to fickleness in friendship, especially if one's friend becomes poor and needy. Thus, Prov 14:20 observes: "Even by his companions an impoverished person is hated, but the friends of a rich person are many" (cf. Sir 13:21–23; Theognis 929–930). So too, Prov 19:4 declares: "Wealth will add many companions, but a pauper will be separated from his companions."[65] Leaving aside an ethic of caution, however, Sir 22:23 urges fidelity toward an impoverished friend.

In 6:11b, where G seems to have read יִתְנַדֵּב ("he will speak freely"), H^{A} uses the *hitpaʿel* form of a rare verb נדה ("banish").[66] Only the *piʿel* of נדה occurs in the MT (Isa 66:5; Amos 6:3). Sirach 6:11b may be making

---

[63] I have emended the final word in H^{A} (בּוֹדֵד, "isolated") to יִבָּדֵל ("will separate himself"); cf. G and S. An observation similar to Sir 12:8–9 occurs in Theognis 697–698: "When I am in good plight my friends are many; if aught ill befall, there's but few whose hearts are true" (Edmonds, trans., *Elegy and Iambus,* 1:315).

[64] Rackham, trans., *Nicomachean Ethics,* 549–51. For a study of such terminology in Luke's picture of the early Christian church, see A. C. Mitchell, "The Social Function of Friendship in Acts 2:44–47 and 4:32–37," *JBL* 111 (1992): 255–72.

[65] For רֵעֵהוּ as a plural form ("his companions") in Prov 14:20; 19:4 (as in 1 Sam 30:26; Job 42:10), see GKC §91k. For similar sentiments, compare also Theognis 299: "Nobody's lief to be a man's friend when evil befalls him" (Edmonds, trans., *Elegy and Iambus,* 1:265); cf. Theognis 857–860; 645–646.

[66] The *hitpaʿel* of נדה occurs in *m. ʿEd.* 5:6, where הַמִּתְנַדֶּה refers to "the one under excommunication," someone banished from the community.

an allusion to Amos 6:3,[67] where the prophet proclaims doom to "those who banish the evil day" (הַמְנַדִּים לְיוֹם רָע), since Sir 6:10 has just mentioned "a day of adversity" (יוֹם רָעָה).

Sirach 6:12 elaborates how the false friend behaves in one's humiliation. Here Ben Sira may be alluding to the way Job's former friends turn against him in his adversity: "All the persons of my circle [סוֹדִי; cf. Sir 6:6] have abhorred me, and those whom I loved have turned against me" (נֶהְפְּכוּ־בִי, Job 19:19). Indeed, Sir 6:12 employs a similar phrase: "he will turn against you" (יֵהָפֵךְ בָּךְ). In contrast to such infidelity, Ben Sira teaches his students to be faithful to their friends: "If your friend becomes impoverished, do not put him to shame, and do not hide yourself from his presence" (Sir 22:25).[68]

Sirach 6:13 draws the lesson from 6:8–12: it is advisable not only to keep away from one's enemies, but also to beware of one's friends. The danger posed by foes is obvious (cf. 12:10),[69] but Ben Sira warns that friends can also be dangerous (cf. Theognis 575–576). According to his outlook, friendship is an ambiguous phenomenon that demands discernment (cf. 37:1).

Sirach 6:13 uses priestly language in its first verb (הִבָּדֵל) and Deuteronomic vocabulary in its second (הִשָּׁמֵר). In contrast with the sacral usage of the MT (e.g., Num 16:21; 1 Chr 23:13), Ben Sira here employs the cultic root בדל in a sapiential context. Whereas Ezra commands the Judeans: "Separate yourselves [הִבָּדְלוּ] from the peoples of the land and from the foreign wives" (Ezra 10:11), Ben Sira does not insist on separation from the Gentiles.[70] B. L. Mack avers that "Ben Sira did not share in the exclusivist notion of Jewish identity and ethic reflected in Ezra-Nehemiah."[71] Thus, even though Ben Sira is the first extant wisdom

---

[67] The context speaks of those enjoying sumptuous meals (Amos 6:4–6; cf. Sir 6:10).

[68] On the text of Sir 22:25, see ch. 6 below. Note also the contrasting insights of 6:12 and 12:8. Whereas 6:12 speaks of the supposed friend staying hidden at a time of adversity, 12:8 describes the identity of the enemy as not remaining hidden at such a time. Adversity makes the true situation clear: paradoxically, at a time of need the hiddenness of the supposed friend cannot hide his true identity as an enemy (rather than a real friend).

[69] In a vein similar to Sir 12:10, P. Insinger 12.8 warns: "Do not trust your enemy, lest his heart bring forth cursing" (*AEL* 3:195).

[70] On Ben Sira's relative "openness to foreigners," see J. G. Gammie, "The Sage in Sirach" in Gammie and Perdue, eds., *The Sage in Israel*, 355–72, esp. 363.

[71] B. L. Mack, *Wisdom and the Hebrew Epic* (CSHJ; Chicago: University of Chicago Press, 1985), 119; cf. Smend, *Sirach, erklärt*, 474. In fact, the sage does not even

writer to use the root בדל, he does so in the noncultic setting of 6:13. Elsewhere, the Hebrew MSS of Ben Sira employ בדל only in connection with his "doctrine of opposites" (33:11 H^E^).[72]

Using the *nipʿal* of שמר (as in Sir 6:13b), various biblical traditions mention the need to be heedful and wary. For instance, the usage is characteristic of Deuteronomy, where it occurs in Moses' warnings to the Israelites: "Take care" (e.g., Deut 4:9; 6:12; 8:11). In Job 36:21, too, Elihu warns: "Take heed [הִשָּׁמֶר]; do not turn to wickedness." Like Ben Sira, Jeremiah applies the idiom to the necessity for caution toward one's companions: "Be wary, each person of his companion" (אִישׁ מֵרֵעֵהוּ הִשָּׁמֵרוּ; Jer 9:3).[73]

A similar usage occurs in the story of David's rise, which presents Saul as an example of an unfaithful friend. Accordingly, Jonathan warns David to "be wary" (הִשָּׁמֶר, 1 Sam 19:2) of Saul, even though 1 Sam 16:21 notes that when David came to Saul "he loved him very much" (וַיֶּאֱהָבֵהוּ מְאֹד). Although David was invited to share the king's "table" (שֻׁלְחָן, 1 Sam 20:29; cf. Sir 6:10), Saul in fact "turned into an enemy" (cf. Sir 6:9, נֶהְפָּךְ לְשֹׂנֵא), as 1 Sam 18:29 records: "And Saul was the enemy [אֹיֵב] of David continually."

Elsewhere Ben Sira also advises caution toward the words of friends: "Guard yourself from an advisor" (Sir 37:8 H^BD^ ; cf. 13:13). Such an attitude of caution is likewise characteristic of Theognis; see, for instance, Theognis 575–576: "My friends [οἵ με φίλοι] it is that betray me; for mine enemy [τόν γ' ἐχθρόν] can I shun as the steersman the rock upstanding from the sea."[74]

iv. Stanza 4. The Threefold Benefit of a Faithful Friend (6:14–17). After the rather negative tone of Sir 6:5–13, the final stanza speaks positively of the benefit of having a "faithful friend" (H^A^ אוֹהֵב אֱמוּנָה, G φίλος πιστός).[75] In

mention Ezra, while he refers to Nehemiah only for his building activities (49:13); cf. C. Begg, "Ben Sirach's Non-mention of Ezra," *BN* 42 (1988): 14–18.

[72] However, by emendation I read the verb also in 12:9b; see my brief discussion in the appendix. On 33:11 see Prato, *Il problema della teodicea*, 36–38.

[73] The following colon of Jer 9:3, "and do not rely [אַל־תִּבְטָחוּ] on any relative," parallels Sir 6:7b, "and do not hasten to rely [בטח] on him." Jeremiah 9:2 also mentions "faithfulness" (אֱמוּנָה), an important virtue in Sir 6:14–16.

[74] Edmonds, trans., *Elegy and Iambus*, 1:297. Likewise, Theognis 1219–1220 observes: "'Tis hard in sooth for an enemy to deceive his foe, Cyrnus, but easy for a friend to deceive his friend" (ibid., 1:379).

[75] On the "faithful friend" in Greek literature, see briefly P. Hummel, "*Philos/pistos:* étude d'un cas de complémentarité métrique," *Informations*

emphasizing the need for fidelity in friendship, Ben Sira once again echoes a major concern of Greek authors such as Xenophon and Theognis. For example, in *Cyr.* 8.7.13 Xenophon states: "Faithful friends [οἱ πιστοὶ φίλοι] are a monarch's truest and surest sceptre."[76] Conversely, Theognis 209 laments the lack of fidelity in supposed friends: "Surely no man is friend [φίλος] and faithful comrade [πιστὸς ἑταῖρος] unto one that is in exile."[77]

The noun אֱמוּנָה ("faithfulness"), which Ben Sira employs to describe a loyal friend (6:14–16), recurs elsewhere in his work.[78] Often he uses the word to denote faithfulness to God; for instance, in 45:4 H^B he applies the term to Moses: "For his faithfulness and humility he [God] chose him from all [humanity]."[79] Likewise, in 44:20 H^B Ben Sira refers to Abraham's fidelity toward God: "In testing he was found faithful" (נֶאֱמָן; cf. 1 Macc 2:52; *Jub.* 17:18).

As one rooted in the Deuteronomic tradition, Ben Sira regards faithful human beings (whether famous figures of ancient Israel or living personal friends) as reflecting the faithfulness of God. Deuteronomy

---

Grammaticales 36 (1988): 17–19. For a survey of the concept of faithfulness in Ben Sira, see D. R. Lindsay, *Josephus and Faith:* ΠΙΣΤΙΣ *and* ΠΙΣΤΕΥΕΙΝ *As Faith Terminology in the Writings of Flavius Josephus and in the New Testament* (AGJU 19; Leiden: Brill, 1993), 39–51.

[76] W. Miller, trans., *Xenophon: Cyropaedia* (LCL; 2 vols.; New York: Macmillan, 1914), 2:429; Xenophon's statement applies in the first instance to "the friends of the king" (οἱ φίλοι τοῦ βασιλέως), i.e., court advisors. Compare also Euripides' declaration (*Orest.* 727–728): "A loyal friend in trouble's hour shows welcomer than calm to mariners"; see A. S. Way, trans., *Euripides* (LCL; 4 vols.; New York: Macmillan, 1912), 2:185. In addition, note Aristotle's assertion that a true friendship is permanent (*Eth. nic.* 8.3.7 §1156b).

[77] Edmonds, trans., *Elegy and Iambus,* 1:253 (cf. Theognis 332A). In Theognis 415–416 (= 1164E–F) we also read: "Seek as I will, I can find no man like myself that is a true comrade [πιστὸν ἑταῖρον] free of guile" (ibid., 1:279).

[78] Whereas in Greek literature (e.g., Theognis and Xenophon) the word "faithful" (πιστός) applies to friendship on a social ("horizontal") level, in the Hebrew Bible the term "fidelity" (אֱמוּנָה) often refers to one's ("vertical") attitude to God (Jer 7:28; Hab 2:4; cf. Sir 45:4). Thus, a "faithful friend" in the Hebrew sense may mean a "friend who is faithful [to God]" (cf. Sir 9:14–16) as much as a "friend who is faithful [to other human beings]"; cf. Lindsay, *Josephus and Faith,* 44. Likewise, in Israel's wisdom literature (e.g., Prov 11:13; 20:6; 28:20) the idea of faithfulness may encompass both the "horizontal" and the "vertical" aspects of fidelity.

[79] Where H^B has a lacuna, the final word of 45:4 is to be read as בָּשָׂר ("flesh, humanity"). Note that in its description of Moses, Num 12:7 G uses the adjective πιστός ("faithful") to render נֶאֱמָן ("trusted, faithful").

calls Yahweh both "the faithful God" (הָאֵל הַנֶּאֱמָן, Deut 7:9) and "a God of faithfulness" (אֵל אֱמוּנָה, Deut 32:4).[80] Since human beings are made in the image and likeness of God (Gen 1:27), who is faithful (Deut 7:9; 32:4), they are called to mirror God's faithfulness in their own lives (including their friendships); indeed, Prov 12:22 affirms God's pleasure in human faithfulness.

Faithfulness toward other human beings is a quality that Israel's sages prize. Proverbs 28:20 asserts that the "faithful person" will be blessed, while Prov 11:13 contrasts someone "trustworthy in spirit" (נֶאֱמַן־רוּחַ) with a "revealer of secrets." Moreover, Prov 27:6 acknowledges that a friend's loyalty may cause him to offer criticism: "Faithful [נֶאֱמָנִים] are the wounds of a friend [אוֹהֵב]." However, Prov 20:6 admits the rarity of human fidelity: "Many a human being will declare his loyalty, but a faithful person who can find?" (אִישׁ אֱמוּנִים מִי יִמְצָא). In an apparent allusion to Prov 20:6b, Ben Sira says of a faithful friend: "The one who finds him [מוֹצְאוֹ] has found [מָצָא] wealth" (6:14).[81]

Sirach 6:14 G portrays a faithful friend as a "strong shelter" (σκέπη κραταιά).[82] In LXX Exod 26:7 σκέπην renders the MT's אֹהֶל ("tent"), referring to the tent protecting the sanctuary. In 6:14 Ben Sira speaks of a faithful friend as fulfilling a similar protective role. Sirach 6:29 uses related language in describing wisdom: "Her net will become for you a strong foundation" (H^{A} מְכוֹן עֹז; G σκέπην ἰσχύος).[83] Moreover, in speaking of the strength provided by a faithful friend (6:14), the sage utters a thought comparable to Qoh 4:9, 12: "Two are better than one.... Even if one were to prevail against another, two would stand against him."

In its use of the idea of "wealth" to express the benefit of a faithful friend, Sir 6:14b echoes a motif found in such Greek authors as Hesiod, Euripides, and Xenophon.[84] Likewise, Theognis 77–78 speaks

---

[80] In both Deut 7:9 and 32:4, G adopts the rendering θεὸς πιστός ("a faithful God").

[81] The beneficial presence of the faithful friend forms an implied contrast with the unfaithful friend's absence: "he will not be found on a day of adversity" (6:10b).

[82] In *Fragments* 543K.1–3 Menander makes a comparable observation: "For ill words or ill-treatment suffered by any one of us, for us all there is a refuge, namely, in good friends" (Allinson, trans., *Menander*, 523).

[83] Krinetzki ("Die Freundschaftsperikope," 218) points out this connection. Note also that Sir 34:19 G calls God a "shelter" (σκέπη, cf. Ps 121:5 G).

[84] In *Op.* 347 Hesiod asserts: "He who enjoys a good neighbor has a precious possession"; see H. G. Evelyn-White, trans., *Hesiod, the Homeric Hymns and Homerica* (LCL; New York: Macmillan, 1914), 29. In *Orest.* 1155–1156a Euripides

of friendship using financial imagery: "In a sore dissension, Cyrnus, a trusty man [πιστὸς ἀνήρ] is to be reckoned against gold and silver."

The word Ben Sira uses for "wealth," הוֹן (6:14b; cf. 8:2 [bis]; 10:27; 31:3; 38:11), occurs in the MT mainly in wisdom literature. According to Prov 8:18, הוֹן exists where there is wisdom. Wisdom 7:14 calls wisdom "unfailing wealth" (ἀνεκλιπὴς ... θησαυρός), whose acquisition leads to "friendship toward God" (πρὸς θεὸν ... φιλίαν).[85] In Sir 6:14, however, wisdom is not the wealth that brings friendship with God; rather, true friendship is wealth in itself.

In referring to "price" and "weighing," Sir 6:15 develops the thought of verse 14b, which spoke of the "wealth" one acquires in having a faithful friend. The statement made in verse 15a, "For a faithful friend there is no price" (מְחִיר),[86] suggests a practical consequence that finds expression in 7:18a: "Do not exchange a friend for a price" (מְחִיר).

To emphasize the value of a faithful friend, the sage reiterates the thought of 6:15a in verse 15b: "There is no weighing [אֵין מִשְׁקָל] of the benefit of him." In 26:15 H^C Ben Sira employs a similar phrase about a modest wife: "There is no weighing [אֵין מִשְׁקָל] of a woman who is restrained in speech." Moreover, the grandson's Greek translation of Sir 26:14–15 offers a still closer parallel to his rendering of 6:15 in its use of both of the latter's terms: ἀντάλλαγμα ("exchange")[87] and σταθμός ("weight"). A comparison of Sir 26:13–18 with 6:14–16 suggests that Ben Sira advises his students to be just as selective in choosing a wife as they are in acquiring friends,[88] although someone (a potential wife or friend) who proves worthy after testing deserves eloquent praise.

declares: "Ha! nought is better than a loyal friend—nor wealth, nor lordship!" (Way, trans., *Euripides*, 2:227). In *Mem.* 2.4.1, 2, 5 Xenophon states: "Of all possessions the most precious is a good and sincere friend.... A friend is the greatest blessing.... Surely there is no other possession that can compare with a good friend" (Marchant, trans., *Xenophon*, 123). The following Theognis quotation is from Edmonds, trans., *Elegy and Iambus*, 1:239.

[85] Cf. von Herrmann, "A Stylistic and Poetic Study," 11.

[86] An identical phrase ("there is no price") occurs in a different context in 4QInstruction (4Q416 2 ii 7). Like Sir 6:15–16, Ptahhotep 35 also regards friends as more valuable than money: "Don't be mean toward your friends; they are one's watered field, and greater than one's riches, for what belongs to one belongs to another" (*AEL* 1:72).

[87] This noun is also used by Euripides (*Orest.* 1156b–1157) in speaking of a true friend: "Sure, of none account the crowd is, weighed against one noble friend" (ἀντάλλαγμα γενναίου φίλου; Way, trans., *Euripides*, 2:227).

[88] In Sir 40:23, however, the sage declares that a prudent wife is better than a friend.

In our consideration of Sir 6:7, we saw how the one sought as a friend must undergo rigorous testing comparable to that required of the person who seeks wisdom (cf. Sir 2:5; 4:17). Sirach 6:15 draws another sapiential parallel when it speaks of there being no price (מְחִיר) for a faithful friend and no weighing (מִשְׁקָל) of the benefit of such a person, since Job 28:15 employs related vocabulary in order to describe the search for wisdom: "Silver cannot be weighed as its price" (לֹא יִשָּׁקֵל כֶּסֶף מְחִירָהּ).

Sirach 6:16 contains the pericope's clearest reference to 1 Sam 25, since in the whole MT the phrase צְרוֹר חַיִּים ("bundle of the living, bundle of life") occurs only in 1 Sam 25:29.[89] It seems, however, that Ben Sira employs the phrase in a different sense from 1 Sam 25.[90] In 1 Sam 25:29 Abigail expresses her confidence in God's protection of David: "If anyone should rise up to pursue you and to seek your life, the life of my lord shall be bound in the bundle of the living [צְרוּרָה בִּצְרוֹר הַחַיִּים] under the care of the LORD your God" (NRSV). However, whereas 1 Samuel speaks of divine protection, Sir 6:16 alludes to the protective and supportive quality of human friendship. Ben Sira's point is that a faithful friend holds one safely among the living, just as God holds all the living in his "bundle" or "purse."[91]

The term צְרוֹר in 6:16 fits in with other poetic images of the pericope's final stanza. The predominant imagery of Sir 6:14–15 is financial: "wealth" (הוֹן), "price" (מְחִיר), and "weighing" (as of precious metals: מִשְׁקָל). Since the MT often uses the term צְרוֹר to refer to a "purse" or "moneybag" (Gen 42:35; Prov 7:20; Hag 1:6), Ben Sira is here employing another word with financial overtones.[92] At the same time, alluding to 1 Sam 25:29, Ben Sira modifies the term to speak of the "purse/bundle of the living." Thus, this phrase also suggests the idea of protectiveness, similar to the expression "strong shelter" in 6:14a.

Sirach 6:16b contains the first explicit mention of God in the pericope and asserts that a God-fearing person will not search in vain for a true friend. The poem in Sir 1:11–30 presents the fear of God as the path to blessing in life: "The fear of the Lord will delight the heart and will give

---

[89] The phrase also occurs in 1QH 10.20 (formerly 2.20); *b. Šabb.* 152b; *b. Ḥag.* 12b. See the discussion of the phrase in Krinetzki, "Freundschaftsperikope," 217.

[90] Beentjes ("Ein Mensch ohne Freund," 15) emphasizes the difference of context between 1 Sam 25 and Sir 6:5–17.

[91] The exact meaning of צְרוֹר is uncertain. Most scholars connect the noun with the verb צרר ("bind up"), hence "something tied up," "bundle" (cf. BDB, 865); see further O. Eißfeldt, *Der Beutel der Lebendigen* (Berlin: Akademie, 1960). In ancient times cloth was often bundled up around coins to create a "purse."

[92] Cf. Beentjes, "Ein Mensch ohne Freund," 7.

gladness and joy and length of days" (1:12). For Ben Sira, part of the joy resulting from the fear of God is the joy of friendship, which consists in having a few faithful friends (6:14–16). Moreover, 6:16b (like 6:7a) draws a parallel between friendship and wisdom, which are both gifts from God. Just as the God-fearing person will find a friend (reading יַשִּׂיגֶנּוּ for יַשִּׂיגֵם in H^A),[93] so too the one who chooses discipline will find wisdom (תַּשִּׂיג חָכְמָה, 6:18b H^C).

Verse 17 provides the final stanza with an asymmetric conclusion, adding a fourth bicolon but omitting the phrase "a faithful friend" (אוֹהֵב אֱמוּנָה, vv. 14–16). Such lack of symmetry highlights the conclusion of the pericope.

Sirach 6:17a speaks of the faithful friend resembling "his companion" (רֵעֵהוּ). Elsewhere Ben Sira states: "All flesh will love its own kind, and every human being one resembling him" (Sir 13:15). We may compare the French aphorism: "Qui se ressemblent s'assemblent." For the ancient Greeks, being like one's friend was an important component of friendship. For instance, after quoting a definition of a person's friend as one who "desires the same things as he does" (*Eth. nic.* 9.4.1 §1166a), Aristotle asserts that in the case of the good person, "A friend is another self" (9.4.5 §1166a).[94] Accordingly, the philosopher defines friendship: "Amity [φιλότης] consists in equality and similarity, especially the similarity of those who are alike in virtue" (8.8.5 §1159b; cf. Sir 13:15–16). This similarity can even lead a person to love his friend as himself, as Aristotle points out: "Very intense friendship resembles self-regard" (9.4.6 §1166b).

The biblical tradition is also aware of the inclination of friends to love one another as they love themselves. The clearest example in the MT is the story of the friendship between David and Jonathan. The affection between them is spoken of in 1 Sam 18:3: "Jonathan made a covenant with David, because he loved him as his own self" (בְּאַהֲבָתוֹ אֹתוֹ כְּנַפְשׁוֹ; cf. 1 Sam 18:1; 20:17). For both parties the covenant involved an attitude of "steadfast love" (חֶסֶד, 1 Sam 20:15), a disposition similar to the "faithfulness" (אֱמוּנָה) spoken of in Sir 6:14–16. Like the friendship of David and Abigail, the friendship of David and Jonathan seems to have been paradigmatic for Ben Sira.[95]

---

[93] See the text-critical note 16^g above.

[94] Rackham, trans., *Nicomachean Ethics*, 533, 535; the following two Aristotle quotations are from pp. 483 and 537.

[95] Cf. my exegesis of Sir 37:6a below. A connection between Sir 6:5–17 and the story of David and Jonathan is their shared contrast between good and evil (Sir 6:11; 1 Sam 20:12–13). This contrast also appears in Abigail's speech to David (1 Sam 25:24–31; cf. 25:21).

The Hebrew Bible not only celebrates friendship but also commands a friendly attitude to all in one's society. The classic expression of this appears in Lev 19:17–18: "You shall not hate your brother in your heart.... And you shall love your neighbor as yourself" (וְאָהַבְתָּ לְרֵעֲךָ כָּמוֹךָ; cf. Sir 6:17: כָּמוֹהוּ, "as he is"). Developing the teaching of Leviticus, Ben Sira urges: "Understand [the feelings] of your neighbor from yourself, and reflect over every action" (31:15 G).[96] Hence, a person should wish peace to all, even if one does not rely on everyone (Sir 6:6).

Sirach 6:17b completes the pericope by observing that in the case of a faithful friend, "as is his name, so are his deeds" (כִּשְׁמוֹ כֵּן מַעֲשָׂיו). This means that unlike false friends (6:8–12), a true friend lives up to the designation of "friend."[97] By contrast, Sir 37:1 speaks of "a 'friend' who is a friend in name only" (אוֹהֵב שֵׁם אוֹהֵב).

Sirach 6:17b also alludes to 1 Sam 25, where Abigail explains Nabal's unfriendly behavior: "My lord, do not pay attention to this worthless man, Nabal, for as is his name, so is he [כִּי כִשְׁמוֹ כֶּן־הוּא]; Nabal is his name, and folly [נְבָלָה] is with him" (1 Sam 25:25).[98] Whereas 1 Samuel depicts Nabal as being as foolish as his name suggests, Sir 6:17b speaks of a faithful friend who truly lives up to his name of friend. In addition, Ben Sira uses a similar phrase in 6:22a to assert that discipline lives up to its name: "For discipline—as is its name, so it is" (כִּי הַמּוּסָר כִּשְׁמָהּ כֶּן־הִיא).[99]

h. Summary

In Sir 6:5–17 Ben Sira expands the thought of Prov 18:24 and 20:6 into a poem on the dangers and benefits of friendship. He shares a number of counsels with Theognis and P. Insinger but has situated these within the context of Israelite tradition. For Ben Sira, it is "the one who fears God" (6:16) who finds true friendship.

Moreover, the placing of 6:5–17 as Ben Sira's first friendship poem is significant. It completes a section begun by the wisdom poem in 4:11–19 and is followed by another sapiential poem in 6:18–37. Both

---

[96] Likewise, Sir 31:15a H^B reads: "Know that your companion is like yourself [דְּעָה רֵעֲךָ כְּנַפְשֶׁךָ], and reflect on everything that you hate." While the exact wording of the original text is uncertain, the allusion to Lev 19:18 is clear in both H and G.

[97] Compare the Instruction of Any 5.7–8: "Befriend one who is straight and true, one whose actions you have seen. If your rightness matches his, the friendship will be balanced" (*AEL* 2:138).

[98] Citing the allusion to Prov 11:4 in Sir 5:8, Beentjes notes: "Many times Ben Sira uses a biblical quotation to conclude a paragraph" ("Canon and Scripture," 597).

[99] As mentioned in the section on context, instead of הִיא 6:22 H^A reads הוּא through confusion of *wāw* and *yōd*.

wisdom poems emphasize the joy given by wisdom (4:18; 6:28) after a process of testing and discipline (4:17; 6:20–21). Likewise, though attaining true friendship involves testing one's prospective friends (6:7), ultimately a faithful friend is of unlimited value (6:15). Thus, we could say that the quest for wisdom includes within it the search for faithful friends, and the same rules apply for both kinds of searching. Indeed, the fear of the Lord is the way to friendship (6:16), just as discipline is the path to wisdom (6:18).

Ben Sira's use of language in 6:5–17 shows that he is steeped in the biblical tradition. His treatment of friendship (especially 6:14–17) contains echoes of the story of the friendship between David and Jonathan. What is perhaps surprising, however, in view of Ben Sira's reputation as a misogynist,[100] is the number of allusions to the narrative of David's friendship with Abigail (1 Sam 25). There the male character, Nabal, appears as a fool, someone not to be imitated, whereas the female character, Abigail, is a model of prudence and friendliness. Ben Sira's verbal echoes of 1 Sam 25 imply that by contrast to the boorish Nabal, Abigail is the one whose friendly behavior is to be copied.

Ben Sira's ethic of caution makes him wary of instant friendships. However, this fact should not obscure his great appreciation of the value of good friends: "For a faithful friend there is no price" (6:15).

3. Sirach 37:1–6[101]

The second part of this chapter will discuss Sir 37:1–6. The following chart indicates its many similarities to 6:5–17.

A. 37:1 H$^{D/Bmg}$	יֵשׁ אוֹהֵב
6:8, 9, 10 H^{A}	יֵשׁ אוֹהֵב
B. 37:2 H^{D}	רֵיעַ כְּנֶפֶשׁ
6:17 H^{A}	כָּמוֹהוּ כֵּן רֵעֵהוּ
C. 37:2 H^{D}	נֶהְפָּךְ לְצַר
6:9 H^{A}	נֶהְפָּךְ לְשׂנֵא
D. 37:4 H^{B}	מַבִּיט אֶל שֻׁלְחָן
6:10 H^{A}	חֲבֵר שֻׁלְחָן
E. 37:4 H^{B}	בְּעֵת צוּקָה מִנֶּגֶד יַעֲמֹד

[100] Cf. Trenchard, *Ben Sira's View of Women*, 172–73.

[101] This study has benefited from Sauer's essay, "Freundschaft nach Ben Sira 37,1–6," 123–31.

	6:8 H[A]	כְּפִי עֵת וְאַל יַעֲמוֹד בְּיוֹם צָרָה
F.	37:5 H[D]	אוֹהֵב טוֹב
	6:14, 15, 16 H[A]	אוֹהֵב אֱמוּנָה

a. Delimitation

The poem in 37:1–6 is part of a larger unit, 36:23–37:15.[102] This larger unit is distinguished from its context by its subject, that is, discernment in the choice of associates (wife, friend, and advisor). Structural features also delimit 36:23–37:15. It is preceded by a prayer for the deliverance of Zion (36:1–22), a prayer marked off as a unit by an *inclusio*.[103] Following 37:15 stands a poem (37:16–31) on wise living, whose key word, חַיִּים ("life"), occurs six times. Furthermore, the unified internal structure of 36:23–37:15 (outlined below) confirms its status as a distinct unit.

The immediate context of 37:1–6 as a subunit within 36:23–37:15 deserves notice.

a. 36:23–25: Introduction: Discernment of the Right Foods
b. 36:26–31: Discernment of the Right Wife
c. 37:1–6: Discernment of the Right Friend
d. 37:7–11: Discernment of the Right Advisor
e. 37:12–15: Conclusion: Discernment, a Gift from God[104]

A clear pattern unites 36:23–37:15. Each subsection urging discernment in the choice of food (36:23–25), wife (36:26–31), friend (37:1–6), or advisor (37:7–11) starts with a similar verse (36:23, 26; 37:1, 7), opening with the word כָּל ("every") and beginning the second colon with the phrase אַךְ יֵשׁ ("yet there is").[105] Such structural features, therefore, indicate that 37:1–6 is a distinct subsection within 36:23–37:15.[106]

---

[102] Cf. Skehan and Di Lella, *Wisdom of Ben Sira,* xv.

[103] While 36:1a invokes the Deity as אֱלֹהֵי הַכֹּל ("God of all"), 36:22cd contains the words כָּל ("all") and אֵל ("God"); cf. Skehan and Di Lella, ibid., 74.

[104] The three subunits making up 36:26–37:11 form a twenty-three-line poem, which may be regarded as a nonalphabetic acrostic; note the *inclusio* of πάντα (36:26a) and πάσης (37:11j). A similar twenty-two-line nonalphabetic acrostic (24:3–22), marked off by *inclusio* with ἐγώ (24:3a, 17a), highlights wisdom's speech within the sapiential poem of ch. 24; see Skehan and Di Lella, *Wisdom of Ben Sira,* 332.

[105] Trenchard explains, "the general idea conveyed by this pattern is that, while there are many kinds of food, wives, friends, and counselors, not all are equally desirable" (*Ben Sira's View of Women,* 19). Cf. Harvey, "Toward a Degree of Order," 59.

[106] The fact that the word אוֹהֵב ("friend") occurs five times in 37:1–6 (but nowhere else in 36:23–37:15) confirms the delimitation.

b. Text

I

1 כָּל אוֹהֵב אוֹמֵר אָהַבְתִּי　　אַךְ יֵשׁ אוֹהֵב שֵׁם אוֹהֵב׃
2 הֲלֹא דָוֹן[a] מַגִּיעַ[b] עַד מָוֶת　　רֵיעַ כְּנֶפֶשׁ נֶהְפָּךְ לְצָר׃
3 הוֹי [c]יֵצֶר רַע[c] מַדּוּעַ נוֹצַרְתָּ[d]　　לְמַלֵּא פְּנֵי תֵבֵל תַּרְמִית׃

II

4 מֵרַע[e] אוֹהֵב מַבִּיט אֶל שֻׁלְחָן[f]　　וּבְעֵת[g] צוּקָה מִנֶּגֶד יַעֲמֹד׃
5 [h]אוֹהֵב טוֹב נִלְחָם עִם זָר[h]　　וְנֶגֶד עָרִים[i] יַחֲזִיק צִנָּה׃
6 אַל תִּשְׁכַּח חָבֵר בַּקְּרָב[j]　　וְאַל תַּעַזְבֵהוּ בִּשְׁלָלְךָ[k]׃

c. Text-Critical Notes

This pericope presents serious textual problems. The two Hebrew MSS, H^D and H^B, often differ both from each other and from the ancient versions. In a detailed textual study of 37:1, 2, 6, Di Lella has demonstrated that, despite its corruptions, the Hebrew text here is essentially authentic.[107] The present reconstruction takes as its base the text of H^D, except in 37:4 where H^B offers a better text.[108]

2[a]. For דִּין (H^BD) I read דָּוֹן ("sorrow, sickness"), corresponding to G λύπη ("grief"; cf. L).[109]

2[b]. For the verb G^B*, G^S*, G^A have ἔνι ("exists"), an inner-Greek corruption from ἐγγιεῖ ("will approach").[110]

3[c–c]. Both G (πονηρὸν ἐνθύμημα, "wicked thought") and L (*praesumptio nequissima,* "most wicked presumption") presuppose יֵצֶר רַע.[111] The

---

[107] Di Lella, *Hebrew Text of Sirach,* 70–77.

[108] So also Skehan and Di Lella, *Wisdom of Ben Sira,* 427; and Sauer, "Freundschaft nach Ben Sira 37,1–6," 126. In v. 3a, however, the reading of G is useful for recovering the original text.

[109] Di Lella (*Hebrew Text of Sirach,* 73) notes that "this same error is found in 14:1; 30:21, 23; and 38:18"; in each case G renders the word as λύπη ("grief"). In regard to the Hebrew MSS of Ben Sira, Di Lella also observes that "the misreading of *yod* for *waw* or vice versa is not uncommon in the Geniza fragments" (ibid.).

[110] P. Walters, *The Text of the Septuagint* (ed. D. W. Gooding; Cambridge: Cambridge University Press, 1973), 111–12; Ziegler, *Sapientia Iesu Filii Sirach,* 76. G uses ἐγγιεῖ in Sir 37:30 to render יַגִּיעַ ("will approach," H^B).

[111] So, for example, R. E. Murphy, "*Yēṣer* in the Qumran Literature," *Bib* 39 (1958): 334–44, esp. 338; Smend, *Sirach, erklärt,* 327. In the Hebrew MSS of Ben Sira the noun יֵצֶר occurs only twice; in 27:6 G renders it with ἐνθύμημα ("thought"), while in 15:14 G translates it as διαβούλιον ("counsel").

phrase occurs in 11QPs[a] 19.15–16 and in rabbinic literature (e.g., *Qoh. Rab.* 3.11) with the meaning "evil inclination."[112] Since such a signification does not fit the context here,[113] the phrase in Sir 37:3 is better understood as "evil creature."[114] Scribal error corrupted this original reading (יֵצֶר רַע) into רַע יֹאמַר (H^{D}) and into צַר וְרַע (S).

3[d]. The reading of L, *creata es,* presupposes an original verb נוֹצַרְתָּ ("you were formed"). G has the unusual expression ἐνεκυλίσθης ("you were rolled"), which Segal explains as a comparison with the action of the "potter" (יוֹצֵר, cf. Sir 33:13 H^{E}) who rolls clay to make a pot.[115] Both MSS of H have corrupted the original נוֹצַרְתָּ into נוֹצַרְתִּי ("I was formed").

4[e]. The opening word, written מרע in H^{BD}, is ambiguous. Whereas it was misunderstood as מֵרֵעַ ("associate") by G (ἑταῖρος) and L (*sodalis*), Segal (following S) correctly takes it as מֵרַע ("evildoer");[116] the latter meaning fits the sense of verse 4b.[117]

4[f]. While H^{B} has שֻׁלְחָן ("table," so S; cf. Sir 6:10), G misreads the word as שִׂמְחָה ("joy"). The reading of H^{BmgD} (שַׁחַת: "the pit") does not fit the context and is a corruption.

4[g]. So H^{D} (cf. G, S); H^{B} lacks the *wāw* ("and," "but").

5[h–h]. So H^{BD}. G presupposes a corrupt form of text, wherein the mention of the "stomach" (γαστήρ) may be influenced by the word קֶרֶב ("midst," "belly") as vocalized in 37:6a H^{D}.

5[i]. So H^{BD}. Ben Sira uses the Aramaizing form עָרִים (also found in Sir 47:7 H^{B}) in the sense of "foes" (cf. G^{V}, G^{248}: πολεμίου; L: *hostem*).[118]

---

[112] Cf. Prato, *Il problema della teodicea,* 241. This possible meaning has misled translators of Sir 37:3, from G onward.

[113] Murphy ("*Yēṣer* in the Qumran Literature," 338) notes that the Greek reading is "an abrupt intrusion into a context which deals with friendship."

[114] Genesis 2:7 uses the verb יצר to describe God "forming" the first man, like a potter (יוֹצֵר) shaping a pot out of clay (cf. Sir 33:10). The phrase יֵצֶר חֹמֶר ("creature of clay") occurs in the Qumran *Hodayot;* cf. Murphy, "*Yēṣer* in the Qumran Literature," 339–41.

[115] Segal, ספר בן־סירא השלם, 235. There is no MS support for Smend's suggestion (*Sirach, erklärt,* 327) that the Greek reading was originally ἐκτίσθης ("you were created").

[116] Segal, ספר בן־סירא השלם, 235; cf. Smend, *Sirach, erklärt,* 327; Skehan and Di Lella, *Wisdom of Ben Sira,* 428. S begins the colon: "Evil is the friend."

[117] Another possible meaning is "how evil!" (reading מָרַע for מָה־רַע); cf. Sauer, "Freundschaft nach Ben Sira 37,1–6," 125. For a similar elision, see Exod 4:2; Isa 3:15; Ezek 8:6 Kethib; cf. GKC §37c.

[118] Skehan and Di Lella (*Wisdom of Ben Sira,* 428) prefer to read צָרִים ("foes") because of sibilant alliteration; but the form עָר may be an intentional allusion to the story of David and Saul (1 Sam 28:16).

6[j]. H[D] vocalizes the word בְּקֶרֶב ("in the midst"); hence the reading of G and L: "in your soul." However, the military references of verses 5–6 demand instead the pointing בַּקְרָב ("in battle"; vocalized thus in 2 Sam 17:11).[119]

6[k]. So H[BD]. Instead of בִּשְׁלָלְךָ (lit., "in your spoil"), G presupposes the reading בְּשֶׁלְּךָ ("in what is yours");[120] but the reading of H fits the military context better.

d. Translation

I

1 Every friend says, "I am a friend,"
  yet there is a "friend," who is a friend in name only.
2 Is it not a sorrow reaching to death:
  a companion like oneself, turned into an adversary?
3 Alas, evil creature! Why were you formed,
  to fill the surface of the world with deceit?

II

4 An evildoer is a "friend" who gazes at the table,
  but at a time of stress he will stand aloof!
5 A good friend fights with a foreigner,
  and against foes he will take hold of a buckler.
6 Do not forget an associate in the battle,
  and do not abandon him among your spoil.

e. Poetic Analysis

i. Stanzaic Structure. Sirach 37:1–6 consists of two stanzas (each with three bicola) linked by the use of "evil" (רַע, v. 3a) and "evildoer" (מֵרֵעַ, v. 4a).

Antithesis is fundamental to both stanzas.[121] In the first stanza the antithesis is between the claim of the supposed friend ("I am a friend," v. 1) and his real identity ("adversary," v. 2; "evil creature," v. 3). Likewise, the second stanza revolves around the antithesis between the supposed "friend" (who is an "evildoer," v. 4) and the "good friend" (v. 5).

---

119 Cf. Smend, *Sirach, erklärt,* 328; Di Lella, *Hebrew Text of Sirach,* 75. Here we have another allusion to the story of David.

120 Peters, *Das Buch Jesus Sirach,* 301. The reading of S owes much to Sir 33:20–21.

121 Cf. Sauer, "Freundschaft nach Ben Sira 37,1–6," 129.

Besides employing antitheses, Ben Sira also provides balance between the two stanzas. For example, both stanzas contain "friend" (אוֹהֵב) as their second word (v. 1a, v. 4a), and in both the second bicolon speaks of enemies ("adversary," v. 2b; "foes," v. 5b). Moreover, the imperative negation in the second stanza (v. 6) balances the interrogative negation of the first stanza (v. 2a).

ii. Stanza 1. Warning about a Deceitful Friend (37:1–3). The first stanza makes abundant use of assonance and alliteration. Verse 1 exhibits rhyme and assonance (אוֹהֵב 3x; אוֹמֵר 1x). Verse 2 has two cases of alliteration: מַגִּיעַ עַד מָוֶת and כְּנֶפֶשׁ נֶהְפָּךְ. Verses 2b–3a also utilize alliteration of צ and ר: לְצַר ... יֵצֶר ... נוֹצַרְתָּ. The last two words of verse 3 have alliteration (תֵּבֵל תַּרְמִית), and in addition there is assonance of ē in the sequence לְמַלֵּא פְּנֵי תֵבֵל. Wordplay exists between רֵיעַ (v. 2b) and רַע (v. 3a), and antithesis between אוֹהֵב (v. 1) and צַר (v. 2b).

iii. Stanza 2. Contrast between a Bad and a Good Friend (37:4–6). The second stanza also makes plentiful use of assonance and alliteration. Verse 4 utilizes alliteration: מֵרַע ... מַבִּיט ... מִנֶּגֶד. There is also antithesis between מֵרַע ("evildoer," v. 4a) and טוֹב ("good," v. 5a). Indeed, the contrast between verses 4 and 5 is an extended one; whereas verse 4 declares מֵרַע אוֹהֵב ... מִנֶּגֶד, verse 5 states אוֹהֵב טוֹב ... נֶגֶד. In addition, assonance exists between verses 4a (אוֹהֵב מַבִּיט ... שֻׁלְחָן) and 5a (אוֹהֵב טוֹב נִלְחָם). A further sound pattern is evident between צוּקָה מִנֶּגֶד (v. 4b) and וְנֶגֶד ... צִנָּה (v. 5b). Assonance is also present between נִלְחָם עִם זָר (v. 5b) and נֶהְפָּךְ לְצַר (v. 2b). Moreover, in verse 6a the word קְרָב ("battle") reverses the last two letters of the previous word, חָבֵר ("associate").[122] The final two bicola exhibit end-rhyme (צִנָּה, v. 5b; בִּשְׁלָלְךָ, v. 6b), bringing the unit to a euphonious conclusion.

f. Context

i. Context of 37:1–6 within 36:23–37:15. The introductory section (36:23–25) uses food imagery in a metaphorical reference to discernment between types of persons.[123] Trenchard explains: "The statement—the stomach

[122] Skehan and Di Lella, *Wisdom of Ben Sira*, 432. For other examples of such alliterative rootplay in Hebrew, see Watson, *Classical Hebrew Poetry*, 240.

[123] On the difficult Hebrew text of 36:23–25, see Skehan and Di Lella, *Wisdom of Ben Sira*, 426–27. On 36:26–31, concerning choice of a wife (from a male viewpoint), see Trenchard, *Ben Sira's View of Women*, 19–26 (where he calls these verses 36:21–26). The following quotation of Trenchard is from p. 20.

receives all food alike, but the mouth distinguishes between tastes— ... is a symbolic introduction to the necessity of careful decisions in human relations." Thereafter, Ben Sira considers (in descending order of importance) three significant choices of associates (wife, friends, advisors).[124] The conclusion presents discernment as a gift from God, obtained through association with a devout person (37:12), through listening to one's conscience (37:13–14), and through prayer (37:15).

The complete poem, Sir 36:23–37:15, contains thirty-one bicola (3; 3 + 4; 3 + 3; 4 + 3 + 3; 5). We have already noted that 36:26–37:11 may be regarded as a nonalphabetic acrostic of twenty-three bicola. The opening line of each subunit (except the last)[125] is set out here to illustrate their similarity in structure.

23 כָּל מַאֲכָל אוֹכֵל גַּרְגֶּרֶת   אַךְ יֵשׁ אוֹכֶל מֵאוֹכֶל נָעִים׃
26 כָּל זָכָר תְּקַבֵּל אִשָּׁה   אַךְ יֵשׁ אִשָּׁה מֵאִשָּׁה יָפָה׃
1 כָּל אוֹהֵב אוֹמֵר אָהַבְתִּי   אַךְ יֵשׁ אוֹהֵב שֵׁם אוֹהֵב׃
7 כָּל יוֹעֵץ אוֹמֵר חֲזֵה   אַךְ יֵשׁ יוֹעֵץ דֶּרֶךְ עָלָיו׃

36:23 H[B]: Every food the throat eats,
    yet there is a food more pleasant than [another] food.[126]
36:26 H[B/Bmg]: Any male a woman will accept,
    yet there is a woman more beautiful than [another] woman.[127]
37:1 H[D/Bmg]: Every friend says, "I am a friend,"
    yet there is a "friend," [who is] a friend in name [only].
37:7 H[D]: Every advisor says, "Look!"
    yet there is an "advisor" [whose] way is for himself.

---

[124] Sirach 40:23 states that a wife is more important than a friend, while the advisor does not receive the high praise given to the faithful friend in 6:14–16. On the advisor, see G. Sauer, "Der Ratgeber (Sir 37,7–15): Textgeschichte als Auslegungsgeschichte und Bedeutungswandel," in Egger-Wenzel and Krammer, eds., *Der Einzelne und seine Gemeinschaft bei Ben Sira*, 73–85.

[125] The final subunit (37:12–15) is marked by a reversal of the key words. Thus, v. 12 begins with אַךְ ("yet"), while the first colon of v. 15 includes the word כָּל ("all").

[126] The Hebrew text of 36:23 is uncertain; where the second colon has a lacuna in H[B], I have followed the reconstruction of Segal (ספר בן־סירא השלם, 229). In the first colon H[B] has a feminine subject "throat" preceded by a masculine verb "eats"; such a lack of grammatical agreement sometimes occurs in poetry (cf. GKC §145o). However, Skehan and Di Lella (*Wisdom of Ben Sira*, 426) emend to the masculine synonym גָּרוֹן.

[127] Where H[B] has lacunae, I have followed Segal's reconstruction of the text (ספר בן־סירא השלם, 229).

It is noteworthy that 36:23 and 36:26 have a similar structure, just as do 37:1 and 37:7. In 36:23 and 36:26 the first two words ("every food"/"any male") denote the object of the verb, whereas in 37:1 and 37:7 the first two words ("every friend"/"every advisor") designate the subject. In both 36:23 and 36:26, the second colon implies the need for the student to make a discerning choice, since one kind of food or woman is better than another. In both 37:1 and 37:7, the first colon ends with a person's misleading words ("I am a friend"/"Look!"), while the second colon implies the need for discernment because the reality is not what it seems.

In particular, 37:1–6 shows a strong literary connection with 37:7–11. Just as both poems begin with a similar opening line (v. 1 and v. 7), so too both poems end with a prohibition (v. 6 and v. 11j G). There are also verbal links between verse 9b H^D: וְקָם מִנֶּגֶד לְהַבִּיט רֵאשְׁךָ ("but he will stand aloof to see your poverty"), and verse 4 H^B: מַבִּיט ... מִנֶּגֶד יַעֲמֹד ("who gazes ... he will stand aloof").

ii. Context of 36:23–37:15 within 32:14–38:23. The whole unit (36:23–37:15) occurs within the sixth portion (32:14–38:23)[128] of Ben Sira's book. This sixth portion consists of seven pericopes.

32:14–33:18: Wisdom Poem on God's Providence
33:19–33: Property and Servants
34:1–20: God As Trustworthy Rather than Dreams
34:21–36:22: True Worship of God
36:23–37:15: Discernment in the Choice of Associates
37:16–31: Wise Living
38:1–23: Sickness and Death

The whole section concerns the need to make wise decisions regarding whom or what to trust in life.[129] Ben Sira urges caution toward members of one's own household (33:20–21). One should trust in God (34:16) rather than in dreams (34:1). It is not right to trust in sacrifices made from the fruits of extortion (35:15); instead, one may rely on humble

---

[128] Where this sixth portion begins is disputed; e.g., Skehan and Di Lella (*Wisdom of Ben Sira*, 402) regard 33:19 as its opening verse. However, since all the previous portions begin with a wisdom poem, the sapiential composition in 32:14–33:18 seems better suited to introduce the sixth portion of the book; cf. Harvey, "Toward a Degree of Order," 53–54. The division into pericopes follows the outline given by Skehan and Di Lella, *Wisdom of Ben Sira*, xv.

[129] Cf. Harvey, "Toward a Degree of Order," 58–59.

prayer (35:21). When seeking advice, one is to trust in a God-fearing person (37:12) but also have confidence in one's own conscience (37:13–14) and seek divine help through prayer (37:15). In time of sickness one may rely on a physician (38:1), but above all one is to trust in God (38:9).

iii. Relation of 36:23–37:15 to 32:14–33:18. The sixth portion of the book (32:14–38:23) opens with a wisdom poem in 32:14–33:18[130] that introduces the idea of making the right choices. In its initial verse Ben Sira declares confidently: "One who seeks God will receive instruction" (32:14c H^B). The poem also insists on the importance of an advisor: "Without advice do not do anything" (32:19a H^B), just as chapter 37 gives attention to the right choice of an advisor (37:7–11). In 33:6 Ben Sira speaks of a friend who refuses to accept guidance: "Like a bridled horse is a hostile friend; under every rider he will neigh."[131]

The subunit of 33:7–15 focuses on the opposites in creation. Just as God's wise providence has made some days more distinguished than others (33:7–9), so God has also made distinctions between people: "Yahweh's wisdom will distinguish them, ... and he will differentiate their ways. Some of them he has blessed, and he has exalted them.... Some of them he has cursed, and he has humbled them" (33:11–12 H^E/G). Hence, in view of the God-given differences between human beings, it is necessary to be discerning in one's choice of wife, friends, and advisors (36:23–37:15).

W. Roth draws attention to Ben Sira's criteria for discernment, namely, "good and evil, and life and death" (37:18 H^B), and refers to his maxim: "Good is the opposite of evil, and life the opposite of death" (33:14 G; cf. Deut 30:15).[132] Roth paraphrases the sage's didactic principle thus: "Does the contemplated action result in good and affirm life or does it accomplish the opposite?" Applying this principle to friendship in 37:1–6, Ben Sira contrasts the "evildoer" (37:4) with the "good friend" (37:5) and observes that betrayal by a false friend is a "sorrow reaching to death" (37:2).

---

130 Skehan and Di Lella (*Wisdom of Ben Sira,* 397) note that the *inclusio* of παιδείαν (representing מוּסָר) in 32:14a and 33:18b delimits 32:14–33:18 as a unit. On the text of 32:14–33:6, see Minissale, *La versione greca del Siracide,* 78–89; on 33:7–15, see Prato, *Il problema della teodicea,* 13–61.

131 So H^F, except that I have substituted "rider" (רוֹכֵב, cf. G) for "friend" (אוֹהֵב) in the second colon; cf. the brief discussion in the appendix below.

132 W. Roth, "On the Gnomic-Discursive Wisdom of Jesus Ben Sirach," *Semeia* 17 (1980): 59–79, esp. 69 (whence the following quotation is taken).

g. Exegesis

i. Stanza 1. Warning about a Deceitful Friend (37:1–3). In 37:1 Ben Sira introduces his call for discernment in the choice of friends by observing that not every self-proclaimed friend is a real friend. This observation is a commonplace of ancient Greek writing. In Euripides' tragedy *Orestes* (454–455), the eponymous hero declares to Menelaus: "The name [ὄνομα] of friendship have they, not the truth, the friends that in misfortune are not friends."[133] Similarly, Theognis 979 declares: "I would have no man my friend with lips only, but also in deed." Indeed, many couplets of Theognis's poetry consist of laments over the insincerity of his friends or warnings based on this experience (e.g., Theognis 73–76, 79–82, 101–104, 575–576, 697–698).[134]

Proverbs 20:6 expresses a comparable insight into the insincerity of many self-proclaimed friends: "Many a human being will declare his loyalty, but a faithful person who can find?" Furthermore, the experience of both the historical Jeremiah and the fictional Job corroborates this observation. In Jer 9:4, for instance, the prophet declares, "Every companion goes about as a slanderer," while in Jer 20:10 he cites the accusations made by "everyone who was at peace with me." Likewise, Job recounts an experience of desertion by his friends (Job 19:19). Ben Sira's prayer (51:1–12) indicates that at a time of distressing accusations, he too was betrayed by his friends: "I turned around, and there was no helper for me" (Sir 51:7).

The wording of Sir 37:1b shows significant links with Sir 6:5–17. Whereas in Prov 18:24, the phrase יֵשׁ אוֹהֵב ("there is a friend") refers to "a true friend" (so NRSV), Ben Sira uses the same phrase to refer to someone who is not a real friend (37:1; cf. 6:8, 9, 10). Moreover, in 37:1 the pejorative use of the phrase שֵׁם אוֹהֵב ("a friend in name [only]"), contrasts with the positive use of the noun שֵׁם ("name") in the sage's description of the faithful friend: "As is his name, so are his deeds" (Sir 6:17b H^A).

---

133 Way, trans., *Euripides,* 2:165; cf. Middendorp, *Die Stellung Jesu ben Siras,* 23. The following Theognis quotation comes from Edmonds, trans., *Elegy and Iambus,* 1:345.

134 In Theognis 87–90 (= 1082C–F) the author pleads with Cyrnus for sincere friendship: "If thou lovest me and the heart within thee is loyal, be not my friend but in word, with heart and mind turned contrary; either love me with a whole heart, or disown me and hate me in open quarrel" (Edmonds, trans., *Elegy and Iambus,* 1:239). It is possible that Theognis 87–90 influenced Sir 37:1–2, just as Theognis 851–860 and 115–124 may have influenced Sir 37:3–4.

The term דְּוֹן, translated "sorrow"[135] in 37:2a, perhaps refers to "depression" or "morbid grief"; hence Ben Sira cautions his students against anything that might cause it. In Sir 30:21a H^B the sage counsels: "Do not give yourself to sorrow," while in Sir 30:23c H^B he warns: "Sorrow has killed many." In these sayings Ben Sira articulates the common sapiential counsel against grief and worry, found in wisdom texts from Israel (Qoh 11:9–10; Prov 17:22; cf. Sir 14:14–16), Greece (Theognis 765–768), and Egypt (P. Insinger 19.6–8).[136] Even in the case of bereavement Ben Sira advises against excessive grieving (38:20–23), because "from sorrow [דְּוֹן] comes forth harm [אָסוֹן]" (38:18a H^B).[137]

Sirach 37:2 regards the turning of a friend into an enemy as a source of sorrow and depression, so severe as to cause possible death (cf. Sir 30:23c H^B; 38:18a H^B). Psalm 107 (a thanksgiving hymn) offers praise to God for delivering those whose sins caused their sickness: "Their appetite loathed all food, and they reached to the gates of death" (Ps 107:18).[138] According to Ben Sira, a comparable grief reaching to death can be caused by the changed attitude of a former friend. Indeed, the sage uses some of the same language in his declarative psalm of praise: "And my soul reached to death" (Sir 51:6b H^B). It is possible that betrayal by a friend was the cause of the deep distress from which God delivered him (Sir 51:1–12).

Readers of the New Testament may detect an echo of Sir 37:2 in Jesus' doleful words in Mark 14:34 and Matt 26:38: περίλυπός ἐστιν ἡ ψυχή μου ἕως θανάτου ("my soul is very sorrowful, to the point of death"). Although the term περίλυπος is found with ψυχή in Pss 42:6, 12; 43:5 G, and although the petulant prophet says in Jonah 4:9 G: "I am deeply

---

[135] The noun דְּוֹן does not occur in the MT. Whereas in the MT the Hebrew root דוה means "be sick/faint" (cf. מַדְוֶה, "sickness," in Deut 28:60), the cognate Aramaic root דוא means "be sorrowful." G always uses λύπη ("sorrow") to render the term דְּוֹן (spelled דין in the Genizah MSS of Sir 14:1; 30:21, 23; 37:2; 38:18), and a similar meaning is evident in the parallel root עצב (verb "grieve" in Sir 14:1a). In 4Q385 3 i 1 the form דְּוֹנִי appears, meaning "my grief" (F. García Martínez, *The Dead Sea Scrolls Translated* [Leiden: Brill, 1994], 286).

[136] For example, P. Insinger 19.6 advises: "Do not let worry flourish lest you become distraught" (*AEL* 3:200). See also the Greek parallels to Qoh 11:7–10 cited by R. Braun, *Kohelet und die frühhellenistische Popularphilosophie* (BZAW 130; Berlin: de Gruyter, 1973), 140–42.

[137] Note the use of rhyme in H^B here (cf. Prov 11:2a). For the sentiment of Sir 38:20–23, compare Theognis 1069–1070B.

[138] The language of Ps 107:18b (וַיַּגִּיעוּ עַד־שַׁעֲרֵי מָוֶת) may have influenced the phraseology of Sir 37:2a (הֲלֹא דָוֹן מַגִּיעַ עַד מָוֶת) as well as of Sir 51:6b H^B (וַתִּגַּע לַמָּוֶת נַפְשִׁי).

grieved, to the point of death" (σφόδρα λελύπημαι ἐγὼ ἕως θανάτου), the context of Mark 14:34 more closely corresponds to that of Sir 37:2. Just as Ben Sira speaks of the sorrow (λύπη) that comes when a friend turns into an enemy, so Judas's departure to betray Jesus causes deep sorrow in Jesus' heart (Mark 14:17–21; Matt 26:20–25).[139]

To express the former closeness of the traitorous friend, Sir 37:2 describes him as רֵיעַ כְּנֶפֶשׁ, "a companion like oneself." Although Ben Sira's expression seems to mirror the Greek understanding of friendship as being μία ψυχή ("one soul"),[140] he reflects several biblical phrases as well. Most familiar, perhaps, is Lev 19:18: וְאָהַבְתָּ לְרֵעֲךָ כָּמוֹךָ ("And you shall love your neighbor[141] as yourself"). He may also be alluding to Jonathan's friendship with David: וַיֶּאֱהָבֵהוּ יְהוֹנָתָן כְּנַפְשׁוֹ ("And Jonathan loved him as his own soul," 1 Sam 18:1 Qere). A more exact parallel occurs in Deut 13:7, which urges each Israelite not to be swayed "if anyone secretly entices you—even if it is ... your most intimate friend [רֵעֲךָ אֲשֶׁר כְּנַפְשְׁךָ]—saying, 'Let us go worship other gods'" (NRSV). While Deut 13:7 speaks literally of a "companion like yourself" who turns away from Israel's God, Sir 37:2 describes a "companion like oneself" who turns into an enemy.

The phrase ending Sir 37:2, נֶהְפָּךְ לְצָר ("turned into an adversary"), echoes the lament of Job: וְזֶה־אָהַבְתִּי נֶהְפְּכוּ־בִי ("and those whom I loved have turned against me," Job 19:19). Sirach 6:9 has a similar expression: נֶהְפָּךְ לְשׂנֵא ("turned into an enemy"). A comparable lament, expressed in different words, occurs in Ps 55:13–14.

The language of Sir 37:3, on the other hand, echoes the Genesis creation stories. In particular, the use of the *nipʿal* of יצר ("form, create") and the cognate noun יֵצֶר ("creature") seems to allude to Gen 2:7: וַיִּיצֶר יְהוָה אֱלֹהִים אֶת־הָאָדָם עָפָר מִן־הָאֲדָמָה ("And Yahweh God formed the human being, dirt from the ground"). In 33:13a H[E] Ben Sira applies to

[139] In connection with Mark 14:34, R. E. Brown refers to Sir 37:2; see *The Death of the Messiah* (2 vols.; New York: Doubleday, 1994), 1:155. In the Johannine account of the Last Supper (13:18), the Evangelist presents Jesus as applying Ps 41:10 to his forthcoming betrayal by Judas. John further highlights the seriousness of Judas's betrayal by portraying Jesus' Last Supper and Farewell Discourse (chs. 13–17) using elements of the Hellenistic *symposium* (συμπόσιον) of friends (cf. John 15:13–15).

[140] Cf. Aristotle, *Eth. nic.* 9.8.2 §1168b; Aristotle, *Eth. eud.* 7.6.6 §1240b. However, Sir 37:2b G renders רֵיעַ כְּנֶפֶשׁ ("a companion like oneself") with the idiomatic phrase ἑταῖρος καὶ φίλος (lit., "a companion and friend"; cf. Isocrates, *Antid.* 96 and *De pace* 112).

[141] Or: "befriend your companion." In a similar vein Sir 31:15a H[B] advises: דְּעֵה רֵעֲךָ כְּנַפְשְׁךָ ("Know that your companion is like yourself").

God the biblical title יוֹצֵר ("fashioner, potter, creator").[142] Already in 33:10a H^E the sage calls the human being כְּלִי חֹמֶר ("a vessel of clay"), while in 33:10b H^E he clearly refers to Gen 2:7 when he declares: מִן עָפָר נוֹצַר אָדָם ("from dirt humankind was formed").[143] According to the text of H^E reconstructed by Prato, the first three cola of Sir 33:13 read:

כַּחוֹמֶר בְּיַד הַיּוֹצֵר   לֶאֱחוֹז כִּרְצוֹן
כֵּן אָדָם בְּיַד עוֹשֵׂהוּ

Like the clay in the hand of the potter,
to grasp according to his will,
so is humanity in the hand of its Maker.[144]

In Sir 37:3 Ben Sira uses the noun יֵצֶר in the sense of "creature" (= "something formed").[145] Similar terminology occurs in the Thanksgiving Hymns of the Qumran community. For example, in 1QH 9.21 (= 1.21) the person praying acknowledges: אֲנִי יֵצֶר הַחֹמֶר ("I am a creature of clay"), while in 1QH 21.16 (= 18.31) the petitioner declares: אֲנִי יֵצֶר הֶעָפָר ("I am a creature of dust").[146]

---

[142] Examples of biblical usage of יוֹצֵר for the Creator include Isa 45:18; 64:7; Jer 10:16; 51:19. Although Sir 51:12iv calls God יוֹצֵר הַכֹּל ("the Creator of all"; cf. Jer 10:16; 51:19), the attribution of the litany to Ben Sira is uncertain, since it is absent from G and S; cf. Di Lella, *Hebrew Text of Sirach,* 101–5.

[143] See further J. R. Levison, *Portraits of Adam in Early Judaism from Sirach to 2 Baruch* (JSPSup 1; Sheffield: Sheffield Academic Press, 1988), 48.

[144] See Prato, *Il problema della teodicea,* 15 (cf. 20). Because the text of 33:13 H^E is fragmentary, the exact meaning is unclear, and v. 13d is especially difficult; cf. Skehan and Di Lella, *Wisdom of Ben Sira,* 396. The image of the deity as a craftsman working in clay also occurs in the Egyptian Instruction of Amenemope 24.13–15: "Man is clay and straw, the god is his builder. He tears down, he builds up daily" (*AEL* 2:160).

[145] It is true that 11QPs^a 19.15–16 employs the same phrase יֵצֶר רָע in the sense of "evil inclination," and G understands it thus in Sir 37:3. But such a meaning (although possible in light of Sir 15:14; 27:6) does not fit the context in 37:3, in spite of the lengthy argumentation of Hadot, *Penchant mauvais et volonté libre,* 127–30; and Prato, *Il problema della teodicea,* 239–41. Noting the difficulty, Murphy asserts that the Greek reading is "extremely dubious" (" *Yēṣer* in the Qumran Literature," 338). The solution to the difficulty (not recognized by Murphy) is his distinction between (1) יֵצֶר חֹמֶר = creature of clay, and (2) יֵצֶר = nature, disposition, tendency (339–43). See further my textual note on Sir 37:3 above.

[146] García Martínez, *Dead Sea Scrolls Translated,* 327, 357. The supplicant uses the phrase יֵצֶר חֹמֶר ("a creature of clay") also in 1QH 11.23 (= 3.23); 12.29 (= 4.29); 19.3

Elsewhere in his work Ben Sira explicitly or implicitly alludes to Adam (see 15:14, 17; 17:1–4; 24:28; 33:10–14; 40:1; 49:16), while in 25:24 he probably refers to Eve.[147] In Sir 37:3 the sage seems to echo the story of the creation and sin of the first human beings in Gen 1–3. According to the Priestly tradition, God created humankind "good" (Gen 1:31) and gave them his blessing (Gen 1:28); but according to the Yahwist, they became evil through their sin, and God's curse came upon the ground (Gen 3:17; cf. Sir 37:3). Whereas God gave them the command: פְּרוּ וּרְבוּ וּמִלְאוּ אֶת־הָאָרֶץ ("Be fruitful and multiply and fill the earth," Gen 1:28, P), the man and the woman in Gen 3 (J) introduced treachery into the world by their sin.[148] Thus, by "filling the surface of the world[149] with deceit" (Sir 37:3), the false friend copies the first human beings, who broke faith with God.

For "deceit" Ben Sira employs the noun תַּרְמִית, which Jeremiah uses for the deceptive message of the false prophets (Jer 14:14); Jer 23:26 calls them נְבִיאֵי תַּרְמִת לִבָּם ("prophets of the deceit of their hearts"). Whereas honesty builds up a human relationship, deceit destroys it. Thus, Theognis testifies how painful it is to be the victim of a friend's deceit: "If the mind of a friend be false within him unbeknown, and the heart in his breast [be] deceitful, this hath God made most counterfeit for mankind, this is most grievous hard of all things to discover" (Theognis 121–124).[150] Similarly, in *Eth. nic.* 9.3.2 §1165b Aristotle asserts:

(= 11.3); 20.26, 32 (= 12.26, 32); 23.12 (= 18.12); see K. G. Kuhn, *Konkordanz zu den Qumrantexten* (Göttingen: Vandenhoeck & Ruprecht, 1960), 92–93. The phrase seems to derive from Isa 29:16; 45:9; 64:7; Jer 18:6; cf. Ps 103:14. On the imagery of the divine potter, see further Prato, *Il problema della teodicea,* 43–49.

[147] For a survey of Ben Sira's texts referring to Adam, see Levison, *Portraits of Adam in Early Judaism,* 33–48. Trenchard (*Ben Sira's View of Women,* 81) regards Sir 25:24 as a reference to Eve; contrast J. R. Levison, "Is Eve to Blame? A Contextual Analysis of Sirach 25:24," *CBQ* 47 (1985): 617–23.

[148] Commenting on the behavior of their descendants, Gen 6:13 (P) uses similar language: מָלְאָה הָאָרֶץ חָמָס ("the earth was filled with lawlessness"); cf. Sauer, "Freundschaft nach Ben Sira 37,1–6," 128.

[149] A similar phrase, וּמָלְאוּ פְנֵי־תֵבֵל ("and they shall fill the surface of the world"), occurs in Isa 14:21; 27:6.

[150] Edmonds, trans., *Elegy and Iambus,* 1:243. While Theognis 122 describes the friend's disloyal heart as "deceitful" (δόλιον), Ben Sira's grandson uses the cognate noun δολιότης ("deceit") to render תַּרְמִית in Sir 37:3. Moreover, whereas Theognis 123 states explicitly that "God made" (θεὸς ... ποίησε) the deceitful heart, Sir 37:3 implies the divine creation of the deceitful friend by using the *nipʿal* form נוֹצַרְתָּ ("you were formed"). Theognis 851–852 also invokes the deity in the

> When he has been deceived by his friend's pretence, there is ground for complaint against the deceiver: in fact he is a worse malefactor than those who counterfeit the coinage, inasmuch as his offence touches something more precious than money.[151]

ii. Stanza 2. Contrast between a Bad and a Good Friend (37:4–6). In its statement concerning the evil friend, 37:4 both continues the thought of verse 3 and sets up a contrast with verse 5. The opening word of the stanza, the noun מֵרַע ("an evildoer," v. 4), provides the transition by echoing the adjective רַע ("evil," v. 3) and preparing for the antithesis, אוֹהֵב טוֹב ("a good friend," v. 5).

The phrase in H[B], מַבִּיט אֶל שֻׁלְחָן ("who gazes at the table"), describes someone who is ready to enjoy meals at a friend's table but not to share his troubles. Here Ben Sira seems to allude to the Greek custom of holding banquets (cf. 31:12–32:13). The *symposium* was a favored custom among the Hellenistic upper classes, and in 31:12–32:13 the sage advises his students on proper behavior while eating and drinking. O. Murray explains the importance of the *symposium* in Greek culture:

> The *symposium* or male drinking group ... embodies essentially an aristocratic form of culture still practised in the classical age, but no longer dominant. Earlier much of Greek poetry, Greek music, and Greek pottery had been created for such groups.[152]

Mention of the table in 37:4 recalls Ben Sira's similar statement in 6:10: "There is a friend, a table associate, but he will not be found on a day of adversity." The thought of both 6:10 and 37:4 echoes the assertion of Theognis: "Many, for sure, are cup-and-trencher friends [ἑταῖροι], but few a man's comrades in a grave matter" (Theognis 115–116; cf. 643–644).[153]

---

context of a friend's deceitfulness: "Olympian Zeus destroy the man that is willing to deceive his comrade with the babbling of soft words" (ibid., 1:331).

[151] Rackham, trans., *Nicomachean Ethics,* 529. Note that counterfeiters of money were subject to the death penalty in Aristotle's time (528).

[152] O. Murray, "Life and Society in Classical Greece," in *The Oxford History of the Classical World* (ed. J. Boardman, J. Griffin, and O. Murray; Oxford: Oxford University Press, 1986), 204–33; the quotation is from p. 224. Both Plato and Xenophon wrote works describing discussions at such *symposia.*

[153] Edmonds, trans., *Elegy and Iambus,* 1:243. The duty to help a friend in need is presumed in ancient Greek culture (cf. Euripides, *Orest.* 665–667, 802–803). On the "table" as a symbol of friendship in 1 and 2 Samuel, see Sauer, "Freundschaft nach Ben Sira 37,1–6," 129–30. In particular, in 1 Sam 20:34 the table is the place

Sirach 37:4b notes the unreliability of the evil friend: "But at a time of stress[154] he will stand aloof." In the comparable case of the self-centered advisor Ben Sira warns of his aloofness when he is most needed: "He will say to you, 'How good your way is!', but he will stand aloof to see your poverty" (Sir 37:9, $H^{B/D}$).[155] As an illustration of Ben Sira's teaching one might think of Ahithophel, "David's advisor" (יוֹעֵץ דָּוִד, 2 Sam 15:12), who caused the king much sorrow by his disloyalty (2 Sam 15:30–31).

Sirach 37:4b also echoes the psalmist's lament in Ps 38:12: "My friends and companions stand aloof from my affliction, and my neighbors stand far off."[156] Theognis 857–858 makes a similar complaint: "If any friend of mine see me in evil plight, he turneth away his head and will not so much as look at me."

According to Sir 37:5, the "good friend" is a person who will join in fighting one's battles. Although the grandson's translation of verse 5 does not use the term, there seems to be a reference here to the Greek idea of the σύμμαχος ("ally," "comrade-in-arms," "helper"). For instance, Demosthenes 9.12 speaks of Philip of Macedon entering Thessaly (treacherously) as a "friend and ally" (φίλος καὶ σύμμαχος),[157] while Xenophon speaks of the need to reward "those who are willing to fight at your side" (συμμαχεῖν; *Mem.* 2.6.27).

---

where Jonathan's friendship for David becomes apparent, even as it becomes evident that Saul has changed from a friend to an adversary.

[154] The term צוּקָה ("stress") occurs in Isa 30:6 and Prov 1:27 as a synonym for צָרָה ("distress"). Whereas Sir 6:8 has בְּיוֹם צָרָה ("on a day of distress") in a similar context, Sir 37:4 uses the parallel expression בְּעֵת צוּקָה ("at a time of stress").

[155] Reading: וְיֹאמַר לְךָ מַטּוֹב דַּרְכְּךָ וְקָם מִנֶּגֶד לְהַבִּיט רֵאשְׁךָ.

[156] MT: אֹהֲבַי וְרֵעַי מִנֶּגֶד נִגְעִי יַעֲמֹדוּ וּקְרוֹבַי מֵרָחֹק עָמָדוּ. Sirach 37:4b also contains an indirect allusion to Edom's failure to help his brother Jacob: בְּיוֹם עֲמָדְךָ מִנֶּגֶד ("on the day that you stood aloof," Obad 11) during an attack by "foreigners" (Obad 11). In contrast, Sir 37:5a praises the good friend who fights against a "foreigner." Note that the following Theognis quotation is from Edmonds, trans., *Elegy and Iambus,* 1:331.

[157] J. H. Vince, trans., *Demosthenes* (LCL; New York: Putnam, 1930), 231. Demosthenes explains that Philip "understood that they were suffering from acute internal trouble, and it was the duty of true friends and allies to be at their side on such occasions" (ibid.). Similar terminology occurs in 1 Macc 10:16, which recounts King Alexander Balas's wish to make the Maccabean leader Jonathan his "friend and ally" (φίλον καὶ σύμμαχον); see 1 Macc 8:20, 31; 12:14; 14:40; 15:17 for further examples. The following Xenophon quotation comes from Marchant, trans., *Xenophon,* 139; for other instances of similar terminology in Xenophon, see Konstan, *Friendship in the Classical World,* 83–86.

Although the exact referent of the term זָר ("a foreigner")[158] is unclear, the most common meaning is a non-Israelite (as in Ezek 28:7, 10; 30:12; 31:12).[159] Accordingly, Ben Sira may be referring to Israel's nationalistic hopes as expressed in the preceding prayer for his people (Sir 36:1–22): "Raise your hand against an alien nation [עַם נֵכָר], that they may see your powerful deeds" (36:2 H^B).[160] However, Ben Sira does not show the fiercely militaristic opposition to Israel's Hellenistic overlords that Antiochus IV Epiphanes (175–164 B.C.E) provoked among the Maccabees in the subsequent generation.[161] It is more probable, therefore, that in 37:5a the sage makes symbolic use of military terminology to refer to friendly support against adversaries.

Parallel to זָר ("a foreigner," collective) is the term עָרִים ("foes," an Aramaism). The use of עָרִים here (H^BD) matches the phrase in Ben Sira's eulogy of David: "And he encamped against hostile Philistines" (47:7b H^B).[162] In the MT the only occurrence of the Hebrew term עָר ("foe")[163] is in the context of David's rise and Saul's downfall; in the episode of Saul and the necromancer at Endor, Samuel says: "Yahweh has turned from you and become your foe" (1 Sam 28:16).

The mention of צִנָּה (a "buckler" or "shield") provides another echo of the story of David's rise, since the account of David's conflict with Goliath twice mentions the giant's "shield-bearer" (נֹשֵׂא הַצִּנָּה, 1 Sam 17:7, 41). In light of 1 Sam 17, the "foreigner" whom the good friend fights (Sir 37:5a) may possibly be an allusion to Goliath, whom David calls "this uncircumcised Philistine" (1 Sam 17:36); indeed, Sir 37:5a uses the same

---

[158] זָר has this sense in both 37:5a and 10:22a; in both cases the grandson's Greek translation eliminates the word. Elsewhere Ben Sira uses this term for a "stranger" (8:18), "another person" (14:4; 40:29), or an "outsider" (45:13; plural 45:18). In 9:3 the sage employs the feminine form זָרָה for a "loose woman," as in Proverbs (e.g., Prov 2:16; 7:5).

[159] However, in a Hellenistic context זָר may possibly denote "barbarian," if the word is equivalent to ξένος or βάρβαρος.

[160] Likewise, in 36:9 H^B Ben Sira prays: "Subjugate the adversary and push down the enemy," possibly referring to the battles for control over Palestine between the Ptolemies and the Seleucids around 200 B.C.E.

[161] Alternatively, Sir 37:5a could refer to the activity of Jewish soldiers fighting in the armies of the Ptolemies or the Seleucids. Hengel (*Judaism and Hellenism*, 1:15–17) gives examples of such mercenaries; for instance, in Elephantine there were colonies of Jewish soldiers serving the Ptolemaic Empire. Hengel further notes that "Ptolemy I took a large number of Jewish prisoners into his army" (2:11 n. 85).

[162] Reading וַיִּחַן בִּפְלִשְׁתִּים עָרִים; so Skehan and Di Lella, *Wisdom of Ben Sira*, 524.

[163] Here I leave aside the dubious case of עָרֶיךָ in Ps 139:20.

nipʿal verb as in David's plea to Saul: "Let your servant go and fight [יֵלֵךְ וְנִלְחַם] with this Philistine" (1 Sam 17:32). In addition, the whole of Sir 37:5 reflects the opening of Ps 35 (a prayer attributed to David), where the psalmist asks for Yahweh's help in distress: "Contend, Yahweh, with those who contend with me; fight with those who fight me [לְחַם אֶת־לֹחֲמָי]! Take hold of shield and buckler [הַחֲזֵק מָגֵן וְצִנָּה], and arise to help me!" (Ps 35:1–2).

After the Davidic allusions in 37:5, the expression בַּקְרָב ("in the battle") in verse 6 may be a further echo of the story of David, since this exact form occurs only once in the MT. In 2 Sam 17:11 Hushai[164] (opposing the advice given earlier by Ahithophel) counsels Absalom that he gather all Israel and that "your presence go into the battle" (פָּנֶיךָ הֹלְכִים בַּקְרָב).[165] The verbal root (קרב) also appears in the sense "draw near for battle" in the Goliath narrative.[166]

Ben Sira's advice in 37:6a, "Do not forget an associate in the battle,"[167] resonates with David's regard for Jonathan after the Philistine attack at Mount Gilboa (1 Sam 31:1–13). Although David was absent from the battle, he did not forget his friend, and the news of Jonathan's death caused him to lament deeply (2 Sam 1:19–27).

Sirach 37:6b uses the root עזב ("abandon") in parallel with שׁכח ("forget").[168] The injunction to remain loyal to one's friend echoes Prov 27:10 (Qere): רֵעֲךָ וְרֵעַ אָבִיךָ אַל־תַּעֲזֹב ("Do not abandon your companion or your father's companion"). Trusting in the bond of friendship with God, the psalmist offers the prayer: אַל־תַּעַזְבֵנִי יְהוָה ("Do not abandon me, Yahweh," Ps 38:22).

The pericope's military imagery concludes with mention of שְׁלָלְךָ ("your spoil"). Ben Sira urges the listener not only to help a friend in time of conflict (37:6a) but also to share the fruits of victory with him (37:6b).

---

[164] Note that 2 Sam 15:37; 16:16 refer to Hushai as רֵעֶה דָוִד ("the companion of David").

[165] So MT, although the phrase is difficult. In 2 Sam 17:11, G read בַּקְרָב as בְּקֶרֶב ("in the midst") and hence rendered it by ἐν μέσῳ αὐτῶν. In Sir 37:6 the grandson fell into a similar misunderstanding, translating בקרב with ἐν τῇ ψυχῇ σου ("in your soul"); cf. Di Lella, *Hebrew Text of Sirach*, 75–76.

[166] In 1 Sam 17:41 the Philistine is described as "walking and drawing near" (הֹלֵךְ וְקָרֵב) to David; cf. also 1 Sam 17:48.

[167] Sirach 37:6a provides a deliberate contrast with v. 4b. Whereas v. 4 refers to the evil friend who lets one down "at a time of stress," v. 6a speaks of remembering a comrade in his greatest hour of need, namely, "in the battle" (v. 6a).

[168] This parallel word-pair also occurs in Isa 49:14; 65:11; Job 9:27; Prov 2:17; Lam 5:20; 4Q525 2 ii 5.

The joy of those dividing the spoil (שָׁלָל) after a military triumph was proverbial (cf. Isa 9:2). It is noteworthy that the Davidic tradition recalls his generosity in sharing the spoils of war; according to David's instructions, not only the actual combatants were to benefit from a victory, but also those who remained behind with the baggage and the local elders (1 Sam 30:22–26; cf. 2 Sam 3:22). Thus, 1 Sam 30:26 declares that on David's arrival at Ziklag, "he sent some of the spoil [שָׁלָל] to his comrades, the elders of Judah." David's mindfulness and generosity accords with Sir 37:6, which expresses positively what Theognis asserts negatively: "A bad man ... would neither save thee from sore trouble and ruin, nor wish to share with thee any good thing he had" (Theognis 103–104).[169]

h. Summary

In 37:1–6 Ben Sira applies to the topic of friendship his call for wise decision making. Sirach 37:1–6 forms an integral part of a larger pericope (36:23–37:15), linked thematically and stylistically, on the subject of discernment in the choice of associates. The unit makes use of alliteration, assonance, and antithesis. The basic contrast is between the "evil friend" (37:1–4) and the "good friend" (37:5–6). Ben Sira points out that it is not words (37:1) but actions (37:4–5) that indicate the difference between a good friend and a bad one. The basic idea for the passage may show the influence of Theognis (especially 87–90; 121–124; 857–860), but Ben Sira develops the thought using allusions to biblical characters, particularly Adam (37:3) and David (37:2, 4–6). As in 6:5–17, the sage is not afraid to echo the ideas of pagan authors when he believes they have valid insights into human nature. However, by also including a number of biblical allusions, he has brought the material into the context of Israelite thinking. Ben Sira thereby expands the traditional caution of Prov 20:6 into an appropriate warning for his students about the need to discern between true and false friends.

4. Conclusion

In 6:5–17 and 37:1–6 Ben Sira contrasts the disloyalty of the false friend with the loyalty of the faithful friend. In both pericopes a longer

---

[169] Edmonds, trans., *Elegy and Iambus,* 1:241. Compare Socrates' advice in Xenophon, *Mem.* 2.6.27: "Those who are willing to fight at your side must be well treated, that they may be willing to exert themselves" (Marchant, trans., *Xenophon,* 139).

passage warning of the false friend's disloyalty (6:8–12; 37:1–4) precedes a shorter sequence praising the loyalty of the good friend (6:14–17; 37:5–6). Ben Sira's thought has points of resemblance to Greek and Egyptian works. His caution regarding would-be friends is reminiscent of an attitude found in the writings of the Greek poet Theognis, as well as in the late Egyptian wisdom tradition represented by P. Insinger. When Ben Sira praises the good friend, he echoes sentiments voiced by Xenophon and Euripides (although such sayings may have entered the general Hellenistic culture, or perhaps he may have known a few sayings of these writers through chrestomathies). The whole development of his thought, however, is permeated with biblical allusions, especially to the story of David in 1 and 2 Samuel. Confronting a society in the process of hellenization, when the special Greek esteem for friendship was becoming influential in Judea, he attempts to show his students that the wisest Greek teachings on friendship harmonize with the insights from Israel's Bible, because "all wisdom is from the Lord" (Sir 1:1).

3

Sirach 9:10–16

1. Introduction

The third major unit of the Wisdom of Ben Sira, namely, 6:18–14:19, offers the longest treatment of friendship in the book, since both 9:10–16 and 13:15–23 (as well as 7:12, 18; 12:8–9; 14:13) deal with the theme. This chapter will consider 9:10–16. The pericope speaks positively of the old friend (9:10), one who is wise and just (9:14–16), while warning against friendship with the wicked and the proud (9:11–13). In 9:10–16 the primary text is H^A, supplemented in its few lacunae by G and S.[1]

2. Delimitation

This section will first examine the indicators that 9:1–16 is a pericope separate from 8:1–19 and 9:17–10:18, and then will delimit 9:10–16 as the second half of 9:1–16, distinct from 9:1–9.

a. Delimitation of 9:1–16 from 8:1–19

Sirach 8:1–19, a poem on prudence in social relationships,[2] is a series of prohibitions; every bicolon contains either אַל ("do not") or an explanatory כִּי ("because"). The pericope does not mention women, who form the whole subject of 9:1–9.

b. Delimitation of 9:1–16 from 9:17–10:18

The content of 9:17–10:18, which Prato considers to be a tract on government, distinguishes it as a separate pericope from 9:1–16. The first

---

[1] For the text of 9:10–16 H^A, see Adler, "Some Missing Chapters of Ben Sira," 469. On Sir 9:1–18, see Botha, "Through the Figure of a Woman," with discussion of delimitation on p. 23.

[2] Skehan and Di Lella, *Wisdom of Ben Sira*, 209. Note that the final bicolon (8:19) contains end-rhyme, which emphasizes the conclusion of 8:1–19.

subsection on rulers (9:17–10:5) is marked off as a distinct unit by a double *inclusio:* יָדַיִם ("hands," 9:17a) matches יַד־ ("hand," 10:4a, 5a), and איש ("man") occurs in both 9:18a and 10:4b.[3]

c. Delimitation of 9:1–16 As a Pericope

As regards the subject matter, 9:1–16 is a pericope concerning two kinds of relationships: with women (vv. 1–9) and with male friends (vv. 10–16). Although 9:1–16 has some verbal links with the preceding and following pericopes, its sharp focus on women (vv. 1–9) and on desirable and undesirable male friends (vv. 10–16) marks it as a discrete pericope.

Stylistic features also indicate that 9:1–16 is a separate pericope. If the text of H^A is accepted, the passage is a nonalphabetic acrostic of twenty-two bicola, although the pericope has twenty-one bicola in G (and twenty-three in S). The passage displays rhyme in its opening bicola (vv. 1–3) and its last bicolon (v. 16).

d. Delimitation of 9:10–16 within 9:1–16

Sirach 9:10–16 forms the second half of a unit dealing with relationships. Whereas in the first half (9:1–9) concerning relationships with women, the noun אִשָּׁה ("woman") occurs five times (H^A, vv. 1a, 2a, 3a, 8a, 8c),[4] it never appears in 9:10–16. Similarly, whereas 9:10–16 thrice employs איש ("man, person"),[5] twice in the singular (vv. 11a, 13a) and once in the plural (v. 16a), the term never appears in 9:1–9. Moreover, while 9:10–16 twice employs אוֹהֵב ("friend," vv. 10a, 10c), the root אהב occurs only once (v. 8d) in 9:1–9.[6] The same sequence of women (9:1–9) followed by friends (9:10–16) also occurs in 36:26–37:6, where 36:26–31 discusses women and 37:1–6 deals with friends.

Stylistic features also indicate that 9:1–16 is a pericope in two parts. Both units begin with prohibitions; אַל ("do not," vv. 1a, 2a, 3a) opens the first three bicola of 9:1–9 (according to H^A), while three of the first four bicola of 9:10–16 also begin with אַל (H^A, vv. 10a, 11a, 12a). Furthermore, just as 9:1–9 opens with rhyme in the first three bicola (H^A, vv. 1ab, 2ab, 3ab), so 9:10–16 begins with rhyme between the first two bicola (vv. 10b, 10d). Likewise, just as 9:1–9 includes a rhymed wordplay within the last bicolon (תַּטֶּה, "you will incline," v. 9c; תִּטֶּה, "you

[3] See further the discussion of 9:17–10:18 in Prato, *Il problema della teodicea,* 369–72; cf. Haspecker, *Gottesfurcht bei Jesus Sirach,* 138–39.

[4] As well as these five instances, G uses γυνή ("woman") also in 9:9a.

[5] G once utilizes ἄνθρωπος ("human being, man," 9:13a) and once ἀνήρ ("man," 9:16a [plural]).

[6] On the textual question in 9:8d H^A, see table 2 in the appendix.

will decline," v. 9d), so 9:10–16 closes with rhyme (vv. 16a, 16b) in the final bicolon.[7]

Moreover, each half of the pericope ends with a concluding theme typical of Ben Sira. The last word of 9:1–9 is שַׁחַת ("the pit/grave," v. 9d),[8] just as other pericopes close with mention of "worms" (7:17b, concluding 7:1–17), "the end" (7:36a, concluding 7:18–36), "death" (11:28a, concluding 11:7–28; 28:6b, concluding 27:22–28:7), and "Sheol" (41:4d, concluding 41:1–4). In like manner, 9:10–16 finishes with the mention of the "fear of God" (9:16b),[9] a theme that often concludes Ben Sira's pericopes elsewhere (1:30e; 6:16b; 23:27c; 25:10–11; 38:34c S; 40:26–27; 50:29).[10]

3. Text of 9:10–16

I

10 אַל תִּטֹּשׁ אוֹהֵב יָשָׁן   כִּי חָדָשׁ [a]לֹא יִשְׁוֶנּוּ[a]:
יַיִן חָדָשׁ אוֹהֵב חָדָשׁ   וְיָשָׁן אַחַר תִּשְׁתֶּינּוּ[b]:

II

11 אַל תְּקַנֵּא [c]בְּאִישׁ רָשָׁע[c]   כִּי לֹא תֵדַע מַה יּוֹמוֹ:
12 אַל תְּקַנֵּא[d] [e]בְּזֵדוֹן מַצְלִיחַ[e]   זְכֹר כִּי עֵת[f] מָוֶת לֹא יִנָּקֶה:

III

13 רְחַק מֵאִישׁ [g]שַׁלִּיט לַהֲרוֹג[g]   וְאַל תִּפְחַד פַּחֲדֵי מָוֶת:
וְאִם קָרַבְתָּ לֹא תֶאְשַׁם   פֶּן יִקַּח אֶת נִשְׁמָתְךָ:
דַּע כִּי בֵין פַּחִים תִּצְעַד   וְעַל מְצוּדוֹת[h] תִּתְהַלָּךְ:

IV

14 כְּכֹחֲךָ עֲנֵה רֵעֲךָ   וְעִם חֲכָמִים הִסְתַּיֵּיד:

---

[7] Skehan and Di Lella, *Wisdom of Ben Sira,* 219, 220.

[8] This word also concludes 3:25–4:10 in H^A (4:10d), but the reading of G seems preferable there.

[9] Cf. Haspecker, *Gottesfurcht bei Jesus Sirach,* 136 n. 30. For further discussion, see my exegesis of 9:16b below.

[10] The versions of Ben Sira often confuse the "fear" (יִרְאָה) and the "law" (תּוֹרָה) of God, given their interconnection for the sage; compare 6:37 G with H^A and S; also 9:15 G with S^W.

15 עִם נָבוֹן יְהִי חֶשְׁבּוֹנְךָ   וְכָל סוֹדְךָ [i]בְּתוֹרַת עֶלְיוֹן[i]:
16 אַנְשֵׁי צֶדֶק בַּעֲלֵי לַחְמְךָ   וּבְיִרְאַת אֱלֹהִים תִּפְאַרְתְּךָ:

4. Text-Critical Notes

The text follows H[A] throughout, except where noted below. Although generally reliable, H[A] has suffered damage in the case of a few letters in verses 10–13, but the restoration from G and S is probable.

10[a–a]. The phrase לֹא יְשַׁוֶנּוּ ("will not equal him")[11] represents G[BSCV] οὐκ ἔστιν ἔφισος αὐτῷ ("is not equal to him") and the reading of S ("does not equal him"). Although the final Hebrew letter is uncertain, the damaged phrase in H[A] seems to read לֹא יד__ך, possibly לֹא יִדְמֶה לְךָ ("will not resemble you") or לֹא יְדָעֲךָ ("has not known you"). Peters suggests the possible reading לֹא יִדְמֶה לוֹ ("will not resemble him").[12] However, besides the evidence of G and S, poetic considerations also favor יְשַׁוֶנּוּ, which rhymes with תִּשְׁתֶּינּוּ (v. 10d) and exhibits assonance with יָשָׁן (v. 10a).[13]

10[b]. In the word תִּשְׁתֶּינּוּ the שׁ has to be supplied in a MS lacuna, while the י is an example of plene spelling sometimes found in H[A] (compare the unusual plene verbs in 7:17a and 10:6a). G adds the explanatory phrase μετ᾽ εὐφροσύνης ("with joy"), absent in H[A] and S.

11[c–c]. Whereas H[A] (followed by S) has בְּאִישׁ רָשָׁע ("a wicked person"), G reads δόξαν ἁμαρτωλοῦ ("the glory of a sinner").

12[d]. Where H[A] has a lacuna, I supply the verb תְּקַנֵּא ("envy") from S.[14] G has εὐδοκήσῃς ("be pleased"), possibly from תִּרְצֶה ("delight"). However, the verb תְּקַנֵּא provides a wordplay with the final verb in verse 12b, יִנָּקֶה, and similar anaphoric repetitions of an opening phrase occur elsewhere in the book (e.g. 4:29–31; 5:3–4; 16:8–9).

12[e–e]. The form זדון is best vocalized זֵדוֹן ("arrogant"). Psalm 124:5 uses the word symbolically (spelled plene); here Ben Sira employs it as a noun, "an arrogant person" (cf. *Der. Er. Rab.* 2).[15] Where H[A] (followed by

[11] Cf. I. Lévi, "Notes sur les ch. VII.29–XII.1 de Ben Sira," *JQR* 13 (1900–1901): 1–17; Lévi makes his suggestion on p. 9.

[12] Peters, *Der jüngst wiederaufgefundene hebräische Text*, 12.

[13] Also in connection with wine, G[SC] uses the word ἔφισος in Sir 31:27a: ἔφισον ζωῆς οἶνος ἀνθρώποις ("for human beings wine is something equal to life"). See briefly C. Wagner, *Die Septuaginta-Hapaxlegomena im Buch Jesus Sirach* (BZAW 282; Berlin: de Gruyter, 1999), 216.

[14] So Lévi, "Notes sur les ch. VII.29–XII.1 de Ben Sira," 10.

[15] Comparison with G suggests that the adjectival noun זֵדוֹן ("arrogant person") also be read in Sir 12:14 (G: ἁμαρτωλῷ); 13:24 (G: ἀσεβοῦς); 35:23 (G: ὑβριστῶν).

S) has בְּזֵדוֹן מַצְלִיחַ ("a prosperous arrogant person"), G^{BA} reads ἐν εὐδοκίᾳ ἀσεβῶν ("in the pleasure of impious persons," = בִּרְצוֹן זֵדִים).

12[f]. For עֵת ("time," H^A), G (ἕως) and S presuppose עַד ("even till"); but עֵת מָוֶת ("[at] the time of death")[16] in verse 12b provides a better parallel to יוֹמוֹ ("his day") in verse 11b.

13[g–g]. Damage to H^A has obscured some letters in the phrase שַׁלִּיט לַהֲרוֹג ("empowered to kill"), but the above restoration on the basis of G and S is highly probable.

13[h]. For the noun רֶשֶׁת ("net"; cf. plural noun in S) in H^A, G reads ἐπάλξεων πόλεως ("the battlements of a city"). Thus, the original reading may be מְצוֹדוֹת (or perhaps מְצוּדוֹת), meaning either "nets" (S; cf. H^A) or "fortifications" (G);[17] the word provides assonance with תִּצְעַד (v. 13e), and also occurs in 9:3b ("nets," "snares"). Probably a scribe substituted רֶשֶׁת by analogy with Job 18:8.[18]

15[i–i]. Where H^A has בֵּינוֹתָם ("among them," or with initial *î* vowel "their discernments";[19] in either case the plural suffix is difficult), G has ἐν νόμῳ ὑψίστου ("in the law of the Most High"), equivalent to בְּתוֹרַת עֶלְיוֹן (cf. L: *in praeceptis Altissimi*); the Hebrew phrase occurs in 41:4 H^B; 41:8 H^M; 42:2 H^{BM}; 49:4 H^B. However, S^W reads "in the fear of the Lord" (equivalent to בְּיִרְאַת יְהוָה).[20]

5. Translation

I

10 Do not abandon an old friend,
 for a new one will not equal him.

[16] For the lack of an initial preposition such as בְּ ("at"), compare the phrase עת נוחו ("[at] the time of his resting," Sir 40:5 and 46:19); see also Ps 69:14: עֵת רָצוֹן ("[at] a time of favor").

[17] For a similar ambiguity underlying Sir 26:22, see Skehan, "Tower of Death or Deadly Snare?" 127.

[18] For a similar scribal alteration, see how H^B alters the second word of Sir 43:8a H^M on the basis of Num 28:14.

[19] Botha ("Through the Figure of a Woman," 23) translates "their understanding" (presumably an intensive plural, as in Isa 27:11). For the emendation according to G, see Smend, *Sirach, erklärt*, 88.

[20] Elsewhere S shows a tendency to avoid mentioning "the law of the Most High" (e.g., 19:17b; 41:8b); cf. Winter, "The Origins of Ben Sira in Syriac," 498. Note that S^L reads "in the ways of the Lord" in 9:15b.

A new friend is new wine,
    and when it has grown old, afterward you may drink it.

II

11 Do not envy a wicked person,
    for you cannot know when his day will be.
12 Do not envy a prosperous arrogant person;
    remember that at the time of death he will not be held guiltless.

III

13 Keep far from anyone empowered to kill,
    and you will not be terrified of the terrors of death.
But if you have approached, commit no offense,
    else he may take away your life-breath.
Know that you will be stepping among traps,
    and upon nets you will be walking about.

IV

14 In accordance with your ability, respond to your companion,
    and confide in wise persons.
15 Let your planning be with someone discerning,
    and let all your confidence be in the law of the Most High.
16 Let righteous persons be your meal-partners,
    and let your glory be in the fear of God.

6. Poetic Analysis

The poem consists of four stanzas (2 + 2 + 3 + 3 bicola).[21] The first stanza (9:10) compares old and new friends, using the adjectives חָדָשׁ ("new," 3x) and יָשָׁן ("old," 1x), as well as the verb יָשַׁן ("grow old," 1x). The second stanza (9:11–12) warns the student not to be envious of the wicked, who are doomed to death; both bicola begin with the prohibition אַל תְּקַנֵּא ("do not envy"). The third stanza (9:13), urging extreme care in dealing with the ruling power, is bound together by the assonance between פַּחֲדֵי מָוֶת ("the terrors of death," v. 13b) and פַּחִים ("traps," v. 13e). Finally, the fourth stanza (9:14–16) returns to an appreciation of wise friends and is

[21] Cf. Botha, "Through the Figure of a Woman," 22–23.

held together by the related terms חֲכָמִים ("wise persons," v. 14b), נָבוֹן ("someone discerning," v. 15a), and אַנְשֵׁי צֶדֶק ("righteous persons," v. 16a).

The two middle stanzas are linked by the explicit mention of death (מָוֶת, 9:12b, 13b).[22] Its antithesis, life, is implied in the first stanza by the mention of "wine" (cf. Sir 31:27). In the fourth stanza life is also suggested by the reference to its characteristic virtues of "righteousness" (9:16a; cf. Deut 16:20; Ps 119:144) and "the fear of God" (9:16b; cf. Deut 4:10; 6:24; 31:13). Indeed, this antithesis between life and death gives the pericope an a:b::b:a chiastic pattern.

Stanza 1: The Life-Giving Value of an Old Friend
  Stanza 2: Avoiding Company Leading to Death
  Stanza 3: Avoiding Company with One Empowered to Kill
Stanza 4: The Life-Giving Value of Wise Friends

The poem also exhibits *inclusiones* of meaning and sound. A word-pair (found in Prov 4:17 and 9:5, for instance) frames the whole pericope, which begins with יַיִן ("wine," 9:10c) and ends with לַחְמְךָ (lit., "your bread," 9:16a). The whole passage is also bracketed by a rhyming *inclusio,* since one rhyme occurs between verses 10b and 10d, and another between verses 16a and 16b. In addition, below I will note a phonetic *inclusio* for each stanza.[23]

a. Stanza 1. The Life-Giving Value of an Old Friend (9:10)

The first stanza exhibits a pattern of repetition, chiasm, and antithesis. The couplet repeats אוֹהֵב ("friend," 2x), חָדָשׁ ("new," 3x), and the root ישׁן ("old," v. 10a; "grow old," v. 10d). Indeed, repetition of "new" and "old" forms an a:b::b:a chiastic pattern: יָשָׁן : חָדָשׁ :: חָדָשׁ (2x) : וְיָשַׁן ("old : new :: new [2x] : and when it has grown old").[24] In this way, Ben Sira utilizes the antithesis between old and new to generate a chiastic structure for the couplet. Moreover, there is an explicit contrast between אוֹהֵב יָשָׁן ("an old friend," v. 10a) and אוֹהֵב חָדָשׁ ("a new friend," v. 10c).

Sound patterns also contribute to the poetic effect of the stanza. If יְשַׁוֶנּוּ ("will equal him") is the correct retroversion for the verb in verse

[22] The middle stanzas also have an *inclusio:* לֹא תֵדַע ("you cannot know," 9:11b) in the first bicolon of the second stanza matches דַּע ("know," 9:13e) in the last bicolon of the third stanza.

[23] Another device serves to bracket the poem: its first word begins with *ʾālep* (9:10a), while its last word begins with *tāw* (9:16b). The same device occurs in Ps 1, as well as Sir 5:1–6:4 H[A] and 7:18–36 H[A].

[24] Skehan and Di Lella, *Wisdom of Ben Sira,* 69.

10b (cf. G), it offers a striking rhyme with תִּשְׁתֶּינּוּ ("you may drink it") in verse 10d.[25] Ben Sira also creates a phonetic *inclusio* for the stanza, since assonance exists between אַל תִּטֹּשׁ (v. 10a) and אַחַר תִּשְׁתֶּינּוּ (v. 10d). Indeed, the letter *š* occurs twice in each of the four cola. There is further alliteration with initial *y* (once in each colon). Finally, there is a clever wordplay between יָשָׁן ("old") and יִשְׁוֶנּוּ ("will equal him").

b. Stanza 2. Avoiding Company Leading to Death (9:11–12)

The second stanza makes use of repetition, synonymy, and alliteration. Both bicola have the words: אַל תְּקַנֵּא בְּ ... כִּי ... לֹא ("do not envy ... for/that ... not").[26] In addition, the term זֵדוֹן ("arrogant person," v. 12a) serves as a synonym for אִישׁ רָשָׁע ("wicked person," v. 11a), while the phrase עֵת מָוֶת ("the time of death," v. 12b) parallels יוֹמוֹ ("his day," v. 11b). Sirach 9:12 exhibits an a:b::b:a' chiasm in its pattern of alliteration: *l-q-n* : *z-m* :: *z-m* : *l-n-q*[27] (אַל תְּקַנֵּא ... : זֵדוֹן מַצְלִיחַ :: זְכֹר ... מָוֶת : לֹא יִנָּקֶה).

In addition, the series אַל ... כִּי ... לֹא ("do not ... for/that ... not," 9:11–12) repeats the pattern of verse 10ab. Finally, as in stanza 1, a phonetic *inclusio* unites stanza 2, which begins with אַל תְּקַנֵּא ("do not envy," v. 11a) and ends with לֹא יִנָּקֶה ("he will not be held guiltless," v. 12b).

c. Stanza 3. Avoiding Company with One Empowered to Kill (9:13)

The third stanza employs antithesis and assonance. Antitheses exist between רְחַק ("keep far," v. 13a) and קָרַבְתָּ ("you have approached," v. 13c), as well as between מָוֶת ("death," v. 13b) and נִשְׁמָתְךָ ("your life-breath," v. 13d). The second bicolon exhibits alliteration of *q*, *t*, *š*, and *m*, with קָרַבְתָּ ... תֶּאְשַׁם (v. 13c) followed by יִקַּח ... נִשְׁמָתְךָ (v. 13d). Like the other stanzas, the third stanza contains a phonetic *inclusio*, with תִּפְחַד פַּחֲדֵי (v. 13b) matching פַּחִים תִּצְעַד (v. 13e). Assonance is also apparent in the phrase תִּפְחַד פַּחֲדֵי (v. 13b), as well as between תִּצְעַד (v. 13e) and מְצוֹדוֹת (v. 13f).

Moreover, the third stanza plays on the syntactic pattern of the previous two. Whereas the first two stanzas contain the sequence אַל ... כִּי ... לֹא ("do not ... for/that ... not"), Ben Sira distributes this sequence throughout

[25] Ben Sira often begins a pericope with rhyming bicola; see, for instance, 6:18b, 19b, 19d; 9:1b, 2b, 3b; 51:1b, 2a, 2c. Cf. my discussion of rhyme under "Ben Sira's Poetry" in ch. 1 above.

[26] Here we assume the reconstruction (cf. S) of תְּקַנֵּא in the lacuna of H^{A} (9:12a); see textual note 12[d] above. For stylistic reasons G tends to avoid repeating the same verb in consecutive bicola and prefers synonyms instead; e.g., אַל תְּהִי (4:29a, 30a) corresponds to μὴ γίνου in 4:29a but to μὴ ἴσθι in 4:30a.

[27] Note the reversal of *q* and *n* in the final verb.

the third stanza: אַל (v. 13b), לֹא (v. 13c), and כִּי (v. 13e). In addition, the sage has linked the second and third stanzas by the common use of אִישׁ ("person, anyone," vv. 11a, 13a), מָוֶת ("death," vv. 12b, 13a), and the root ידע ("know," vv. 11b, 13e).

d. Stanza 4. The Life-Giving Value of Wise Friends (9:14–16)

The fourth stanza uses alliteration and assonance. Verse 14a has *k* four times (כְּכֹחֲךָ עֲנֵה רֵעֲךָ), while verse 14b employs *m* three times (עִם חֲכָמִים). In verse 15 Ben Sira continues the assonance between נָבוֹן ("someone discerning") and חֶשְׁבּוֹנְךָ ("your planning") as far as עֶלְיוֹן ("the Most High") at the conclusion of the verse.[28] All of the last four cola contain *-kā* once, always at the end of the colon except in verse 15b. Indeed, the final stanza has a phonetic *inclusio* formed by the suffixed and plural endings: the threefold series כְּכֹחֲךָ/רֵעֲךָ/חֲכָמִים (v. 14) matches the subsequent threefold sequence לַחְמְךָ/אֱלֹהִים/תִּפְאַרְתְּךָ (v. 16). Furthermore, the stanza ends with rhyme between לַחְמְךָ ("your meal," v. 16a) and תִּפְאַרְתְּךָ ("your glory," v. 16b).[29]

Stanza 4 also utilizes synonyms. The adjectives חָכָם ("wise"; plural in 9:14b) and נָבוֹן ("discerning," v. 15a) occur together in the MT.[30] Likewise, the MT often connects the concepts of "righteousness" (צֶדֶק, v. 16a) and "the fear of God" (יִרְאַת אֱלֹהִים, v. 16b).[31] Moreover, the noun רֵעֲךָ ("your companion," v. 14a) and the phrase בַּעֲלֵי לַחְמְךָ ("your meal-partners," v. 16a) are also virtually synonyms. Finally, the use of the noun סוֹדְךָ ("your confidence," v. 15b) and the cognate verb הִסְתַּיֵּיד ("confide," v. 14a) contributes to the unity of the stanza.

7. Context

a. Context of 9:1–16 within 6:18–14:19

Harvey sees the third part of Ben Sira's book (6:18–14:19) as concerned with "Applying Wisdom Socially."[32] He explains:

---

[28] Sirach 9:15 has an a:b::b:a chiastic rhyme: נָבוֹן : חֶשְׁבּוֹנְךָ :: סוֹדְךָ : עֶלְיוֹן.

[29] Skehan and Di Lella, *Wisdom of Ben Sira,* 220.

[30] E.g., Gen 41:33, 39; Deut 4:6; 1 Kgs 3:12. According to Prov 4:4–5, the way to gain life is by acquiring חָכְמָה ("wisdom") and בִּינָה ("discernment").

[31] For instance, Deut 6:24–25 equates "to fear [לְיִרְאָה] Yahweh our God" with "righteousness" (צְדָקָה); cf. also Pss 15:2, 4; 112:1–3; 119:74–75; Prov 8:13, 18.

[32] Harvey, "Toward a Degree of Order," 55, whence comes the following quotation.

> The wisdom poem of 6:18–37 exhorts the student to submit to wisdom's discipline because of the many benefits she bestows. The teaching of the body of the section applies that discipline to social and relational issues raised when the wise person associates with others.

More specifically, Roth suggests that the key word of this section is גַּאֲוָה ("pride" or "arrogance": 7:17; 10:6–8; 13:20),[33] a sin that spoils all relationships.

In keeping with the emphasis on social relations in 6:18–14:19, several of its pericopes discuss friendship. According to the outline given by Skehan and Di Lella, this section comprises eleven pericopes.[34]

6:18–37: Encouragement to Strive for Wisdom
7:1–17: Conduct toward God and Neighbor
7:18–36: Maxims for Family Life, Religion, and Charity
8:1–19: Prudence in Dealing with Others
9:1–16: Advice concerning Women and the Choice of Friends
9:17–10:18: About Rulers and the Sin of Pride
10:19–11:6: True Glory
11:7–28: Providence and Trust in God
11:29–12:18: Care in Choosing Friends
13:1–14:2: The Rich and the Poor[35]
14:3–19: The Use of Wealth

Within this section of eleven pericopes, there are at least three nonalphabetic acrostics: 6:18–37, the opening wisdom poem (twenty-two

---

[33] Roth, "On the Gnomic-Discursive Wisdom," 74. Although the terms גַּאֲוָה ("pride") and גֵּאֶה ("proud") do not occur in 9:10–16, a synonym of the latter term, זֵדוֹן ("arrogant"), appears in 9:12.

[34] Skehan and Di Lella, *Wisdom of Ben Sira,* xiv. On 6:18–31, see Schrader, *Leiden und Gerechtigkeit,* 164–77; on 10:19–11:6, see A. A. Di Lella, "Sirach 10:19–11:6: Textual Criticism, Poetic Analysis, and Exegesis," in *The Word of the Lord Shall Go Forth: Essays in Honor of David Noel Freedman in Celebration of His Sixtieth Birthday* (ed. C. L. Meyers and M. O'Connor; Winona Lake, Ind.: Eisenbrauns, 1982), 157–64; on 12:8–12, see L. Schrader, "Unzuverlässige Freundschaft und verläßliche Feindschaft: Überlegungen zu Sir 12,8–12," in Reiterer, ed., *Freundschaft bei Ben Sira,* 19–59.

[35] Although Skehan and Di Lella (*Wisdom of Ben Sira,* xiv) regard the pericope on "The Rich and the Poor" as comprising 13:1–14:2, it is better to limit the unit to 13:1–23, since 13:24–14:19 is a twenty-three-line nonalphabetic acrostic (ibid., 258–59). For lists of *inclusiones* and nonalphabetic acrostics, see pp. 73–74.

bicola); 12:1–18 (also twenty-two bicola); and 13:24–14:19, the section's closing poem (twenty-three bicola). According to H^A 9:1–16 is also a twenty-two-line poem, although the text of G has only twenty-one bicola. Two other pericopes in 6:18–14:19 are marked off by *inclusiones:* 10:19–11:6 with the adjectives נִכְבָּד ("honored": 10:19ab; 11:6b) and נִקְלֶה ("dishonored": 10:19cd; 11:6c); and 13:1–23 by the root נגע ("touch, reach": 13:1a, 23b).

b. Links between 9:10–16 and the Wisdom Poem in 6:18–37

Ben Sira's advice to associate with wise and understanding persons who fear God (9:14–16) echoes his earlier exhortation to search for wisdom (6:18–37). The table below illustrates some connections between the two pericopes.

9:13c H^A: אִם קָרַבְתָּ "if you have approached"	6:19a H^AC: קְרַב אֵלֶיהָ "approach her"
9:14b G: μετὰ σοφῶν "with wise persons"	6:34b G: τίς σοφός "who is wise?"
9:15a H^A: נָבוֹן "someone discerning"	6:35b H^AC: בִּינָה "discernment"
9:15b G: νόμῳ ὑψίστου "the law of the Most High"	6:37a G: τοῖς προστάγμασιν κυρίου "the commands of the Lord"[36]
9:16b H^A: תִּפְאַרְתֶּךָ "your glory"	6:31b H^A2Q: תִּפְאֶרֶת "glory"

These connections imply that for Ben Sira, one's choice of friends should contribute to one's quest for wisdom.

c. Links between 9:10–16 and 8:1–19

Sirach 8:1–19, urging prudence in various social relationships, also exhibits several links with 9:10–16. In both 8:18 and 9:11 Ben Sira emphasizes the limits of human knowledge, while the injunction to זְכֹר ("remember") the fact of death occurs in both 8:7b and 9:12b. The advice of 8:8a, אַל תִּטֹּשׁ שִׂיחַת חֲכָמִים ("Do not abandon the conversation of wise persons"), is, moreover, distributed in 9:10–16 between the opening bicolon of stanza 1, אַל תִּטֹּשׁ אוֹהֵב יָשָׁן ("Do not abandon an old friend," 9:10a), and the opening bicolon of stanza 4, עִם חֲכָמִים הִסְתַּיֵּיד ("Confide in wise persons," 9:14b).

---

[36] However, Sir 6:37a H^A reads יִרְאַת עֶלְיוֹן ("the fear of the Most High"), which parallels יִרְאַת אֱלֹהִים ("the fear of God") in 9:16b H^A.

d. Links between 9:10–16 and 9:1–9

In addition, there are connections in H^{A} between 9:10–16 and 9:1–9,[37] as the following table illustrates.

9:11a: אַל תְּקַנֵּא "Do not envy"	9:1a: אַל תְּקַנֵּא "Do not be jealous"
9:13c: אִם קָרַבְתָּ "if you have approached"	9:3a: אַל תִּקְרַב[38] "Do not approach"
9:13f: עַל מְצוֹדוֹת[39] "upon nets"	9:3b: בִּמְצוֹדֹתֶיהָ "into her nets"
9:14b: הִסְתַּיֵּיד "confide"	9:3c: אַל תִּסְתַּיֵּיד "do not confide"

This series of similarities (in the same order) may indicate that 9:1–9 and 9:10–16 form two parallel panels of a diptych, although the textual confusion in 9:1–9 makes it difficult to gain precision in the matter.[40]

Several motifs in 9:8–9 foreshadow themes in 9:10–16. The mention of "strong drink, beer" (שֵׁכָר)[41] in 9:9b anticipates the imagery of "wine" (יַיִן) in 9:10c. Likewise, the root אהב ("love") in 9:8d H^{A} anticipates the occurrence of אוֹהֵב ("friend") in 9:10a, 10c. Finally, the reference to שַׁחַת ("the pit/grave") in 9:9d foreshadows the allusion to מָוֶת ("death") in 9:12b, 13b. Such shared ideas knit 9:1–16 together as a pericope.

e. Links between 9:10–16 and 9:17–10:18

Just as 9:10–16 contrasts the "arrogant person" (זֵדוֹן, 9:12a) with "someone discerning" (נָבוֹן, 9:15a), so too 9:17–10:18 contrasts the "arrogance" (זָדוֹן, 10:13a, 18a) of the proud with the well-ordered modesty of

---

[37] Cf. Botha, "Through the Figure of a Woman," 30. The text of 9:1–9 is confused in places; cf. Skehan and Di Lella, *Wisdom of Ben Sira,* 216–18; Trenchard, *Ben Sira's View of Women*, 29–30, 87–88, 108–15, 118–21, 162–63.

[38] G presupposes אַל תִּקָּרֶה ("do not encounter").

[39] H^{A} reads עַל רֶשֶׁת ("upon a net").

[40] Botha ("Through the Figure of a Woman," 30–31) summarizes the links between 9:1–9 and 9:10–16: "Both sets [of directives] dwell on relations which can be described as intimate (the wife; the close friend). Both sets warn against being jealous. Both sets warn against people with questionable morality (prostitutes; evil and arrogant men). Both sets compare certain relationships with stepping between snares (a prostitute; a man with authority to kill).... Both sets contain instructions on whom one should dine with (never with a married woman; always with just and God-fearing men)."

[41] Cf. G; H^{A} mistakenly has שִׁכּוֹר ("drunkard").

"the government of a discerning person" (מֶמְשֶׁלֶת מֵבִין, 10:1b). Moreover, in both pericopes Ben Sira warns against pride in view of the certain fact of death. Just as 9:11–12 declares that the arrogant cannot escape "death" (מָוֶת, 9:12b), so 10:9–11 notes that "at the death of a human being [בְּמוֹת אָדָם] he will inherit worms" (10:11a), even if he has been a king (10:10b).

8. Exegesis

a. Stanza 1: The Life-Giving Value of an Old Friend (9:10)

The first stanza is a rhymed couplet that urges the student not to abandon an old friend. A comparable sentiment occurs in Prov 27:10a: רֵעֲךָ וְרֵעַ אָבִיךָ אַל־תַּעֲזֹב ("Do not abandon your companion or your father's companion"). Within the biblical tradition the classic illustration of enduring loyalty in friendship is the story of David's friendship with Jonathan, which was sealed by a covenant (1 Sam 18:1–3). After Jonathan's death in battle (1 Sam 31:2), David showed covenant loyalty to his friend's crippled son Mephibosheth (2 Sam 9:1–13), acting "for the sake of Jonathan" (2 Sam 9:1).

Theognis also offers advice similar to Sir 9:10a: "Never be thou persuaded by the words of men of the baser sort to leave the friend thou hast and seek another" (Theognis 1151–1152 = 1238A–B).[42] Similarly, Sophocles knows the value of an old friend, for his tragic hero Philoctetes describes Nestor as "my good old friend" (παλαιὸς κἀγαθὸς φίλος τ᾽ἐμός, *Phil.* 421). Likewise, Aristotle asserts that one should honor an old friend even after a rupture in the friendship.[43]

Sirach 9:10 shows the sage's esteem for an "old friend,"[44] which accords with the general "conservatism" of his outlook.[45] Di Lella has

[42] Edmonds, trans., *Elegy and Iambus,* 1:367; cf. Middendorp, *Die Stellung Jesu ben Siras,* 16. The following Sophocles quotation comes from F. Storr, trans., *Sophocles* (LCL; 2 vols.; New York: Macmillan, 1913), 2:399.

[43] See *Eth. nic.* 9.3.5 §1165b: "Are we then to behave toward a former friend in exactly the same way as if he had never been our friend at all? ... Some attention should be paid, for the sake of old times, to those who were our friends in the past" (Rackham, trans., *Nicomachean Ethics,* 531–33).

[44] As distinct from an "aged friend" (= אוֹהֵב זָקֵן), the term אוֹהֵב יָשָׁן denotes principally a "long-standing friend," one whose friendship has matured like old wine. However, Ben Sira would also tend to favor an older person (cf. 8:9; 25:4–6); indeed, perhaps he was already advanced in years when he composed the pericope.

[45] For example, he urges: "Endure in your covenant and be engaged in it, and in your work grow old" (11:20 G; H^{A} has lacunae). Sirach 11:20b H^{A} may be

contrasted Ben Sira's "conservative" theology with the more "progressive" theology of the Wisdom of Solomon, in relation to Hellenism, anthropology, and retribution.[46] With reference to Sir 2:10, Di Lella remarks that "as a genuine conservative in the best sense of the word, Sirach urges his readers to look to the past for answers to the present crisis."[47] Hence it is not surprising to find the sage asserting the value of an old friendship.

Ben Sira plays on the contrast between יָשָׁן ("old," 9:10a) and חָדָשׁ ("new," 9:10bc), using an antithesis that also occurs in the MT (Lev 26:10; Cant 7:14). Luke 5:38–39 draws an explicit contrast between new and old wine: "New wine [οἶνον νέον] is to be put into new skins. And no one drinking the old [παλαιὸν] desires the new [νέον], for he says, 'The old [ὁ παλαιὸς] is pleasant.'"[48] However, whereas Sir 9:10 refers approvingly to the pleasantness of vintage wine[49] (symbolizing an old friendship), Luke 5:39 uses the same imagery to point out the comfortable inertia that can prevent acceptance of anything new.

Greco-Roman literature often praises old wine. For example, from the fifth century B.C.E. one of Pindar's *Olympian Odes* (9.48–49) contrasts the delight of old wine with the beauty of new songs: "While thou praisest the wine that is old [παλαιὸν οἶνον], thou shalt also praise the flowers of songs that are new [νεωτέρων]."[50]

About a century and a quarter after Ben Sira compared an old friend to old wine, Cicero made a similar comparison (*Amic.* 19 §§67–68):

> Are new friends who are worthy of friendship, at any time to be preferred to old friends? ... The doubt is unworthy of a human being, for

---

completed to read וּבִמְלַאכְתְּךָ הִתְיַשָּׁן ("and in your work grow old"), using the same root (ישן) as in 9:10.

[46] Di Lella, "Conservative and Progressive Theology," 139–54.

[47] Ibid., 141. Di Lella also observes (142) that "in the section entitled 'Praise of the Fathers' (44:1–50:24), Sirach pulls out all the stops to celebrate the glories of Israel's past."

[48] The latter saying (Luke 5:39), absent from Mark and Matthew but paralleled in the Gospel of Thomas §47, is doubtless an ancient proverb; cf. J. A. Fitzmyer, *The Gospel According to Luke* (2 vols.; AB 28, 28A; New York: Doubleday, 1981–1985), 1:601.

[49] Ancient Israelites prized such vintage wine. More than a dozen of the eighth-century B.C.E. Samaritan ostraca mention נבל.ין.ישן ("a jar [or skin] of old wine"); cf. G. I. Davies, *Ancient Hebrew Inscriptions* (Cambridge: Cambridge University Press, 1991), 39–42.

[50] J. E. Sandys, trans., *The Odes of Pindar* (2d ed.; LCL; New York: Putnam, 1930), 101. The Latin dramatist Plautus (a contemporary of Ben Sira) also writes appreciatively of old wine (*Cas.* Prologue 5–6).

> there should be no surfeit of friendships as there is of other things; and as in the case of wines that improve with age, the oldest friendships ought to be the most delightful.[51]

A comparison of aged persons to old wine occurs in *m. ʾAbot* 4:20:

> R. José b. Judah of Kefar ha-Babli said: He that learns from the young, to what is he like? To one that eats unripe grapes and drinks wine from his winepress. And he that learns from the aged, to what is he like? To one that eats ripe grapes and drinks old wine [יַיִן יָשָׁן].[52]

R. José b. Judah expects that the aged will be able to teach mature wisdom, which is as pleasant as old wine, just as Ben Sira believes that an old friend's company is as agreeable as old wine.

Proverbs 9 employs the poetic imagery of wisdom's banquet, where wine is served. Proverbs 9:5 presents wisdom's invitation to the simple: לְכוּ לַחֲמוּ בְלַחֲמִי וּשְׁתוּ בְּיַיִן מָסָכְתִּי ("Come, eat of my bread, and drink of the wine I have mixed"). This imagery may underlie Sir 9:10–16, which also mentions the "wise" and the "righteous" (cf. Prov 9:9). Not only does Sir 9:10 speak of an old friend as "old wine," but verse 14 also advises, "Confide in wise persons" (חֲכָמִים), while verse 16 counsels, "Let righteous persons be your meal-partners" (בַּעֲלֵי לַחְמְךָ).[53]

In the world of both Israelite and Greco-Roman literature, wine was an integral part of festal meals. The Hebrew Bible mentions wine in connection with various celebrations of friends, such as parties (Isa 5:12; cf.

---

[51] W. A. Falconer, trans., *Cicero: De Senectute, De Amicitia, De Divinatione* (LCL; New York: Putnam, 1923), 177–79. On Cicero's view of friendship, see Konstan, *Friendship in the Classical World,* 122–36; Steinberger, *Begriff und Wesen der Freundschaft,* esp. 62–79; B. Fiore, "The Theory and Practice of Friendship in Cicero," in Fitzgerald, ed., *Greco-Roman Perspectives on Friendship,* 59–76.

[52] Viviano, *Study As Worship,* 101. A contrasting saying (ibid.) concludes *m. ʾAbot* 4:20: "Rabbi [= R. Judah the Patriarch] said: Look not on the jar but on what is in it; there may be a new jar that is full of old wine and an old one in which is not even new wine." The aphorism of R. Judah the Patriarch may be an allusion to Elihu's speech in Job 32. In Job 32:9b Elihu declares, "[It is not] the old who understand judgment," while in 32:19 he says, "Behold, my belly is like wine which has no vent; like wineskins it will burst open." The utterances of Elihu and R. Judah the Patriarch in favor of youth contrast with the statements of Ben Sira and R. José b. Judah on behalf of maturity.

[53] Sirach 9:10 begins with the phrase אַל תִּטֹּשׁ ("Do not abandon"), which occurs in Prov 1:8 and 6:20 in a sapiential context: "Do not abandon your mother's instruction." Ben Sira uses the phrase in an explicitly sapiential statement in 8:8a H[A]: "Do not abandon the conversation of wise persons" (אַל תִּטֹּשׁ שִׂיחַת חֲכָמִים).

Wis 2:7) and royal banquets (Esth 5:6; 7:2, 7, 8; Neh 2:1). In Greek culture the drinking of wine was the centerpiece of a *symposium* (Plato, *Leg.* 665b–666c). Since in the Hellenistic world friends from the wealthy classes (such as Ben Sira's students) would gather to drink wine at *symposia,*[54] the sage's comparison of an "old friend" with "old wine" was appropriate.

Sirach 9:10 indicates the sage's positive appreciation of wine, which we see most clearly in 31:27cd H^B: "What is life for one lacking wine, which from the beginning was formed for joy?" Similarly, 32:5 G states: "A seal of carnelian on an adornment of gold is a band of musicians at a *symposium* of wine."[55] In 40:20a H^B the sage also praises wine for its cheering effects: "Wine and beer make the heart rejoice."[56]

Being also aware of the negative results of drinking alcohol (19:2; 31:25), Ben Sira understands the ambiguity of wine, which brings delight when consumed moderately but pain when imbibed excessively (31:28–29). Hence he sums up his view of wine in 31:27ab H^{BF}: לְמִי הַיַּיִן חַיִּים לֶאֱנוֹשׁ אִם יִשְׁתֶּנּוּ בְּמַתְכֻּנְתּוֹ ("Wine is life for whom? For a human being, if he drinks it in its measure").[57] Just as an appropriate measure of wine is life-giving, so too mature and God-fearing friends safeguard one's life (Sir 6:16a) and enhance it (9:10).

b. Stanza 2: Avoiding Company Leading to Death (9:11–12)

Having spoken positively of an old friend in the first stanza, Ben Sira now speaks negatively of the wicked and the arrogant, who constitute unsuitable friends. The reason for the sage's warning is that God may at any time bring death upon such persons, and hence joining them in friendship may be harmful. The whole sentiment seems to allude to Prov 24:19–20:

---

[54] Cf. Sir 31:25–31. For Ben Sira's teaching on meals and *symposia,* see Wischmeyer, *Die Kultur des Buches Jesus Sirach,* 106–13. On wine drinking at Greek *symposia,* see Murray, "Life and Society in Classical Greece," 224.

[55] H^B has two versions of this verse. The actual phrase "banquet of wine" (מִשְׁתֵּה הַיַּיִן) occurs in H^B here (bis) as well as in 31:31; 32:6; 49:1.

[56] For שֵׁכָר ("beer") G reads שִׁיר ("song").

[57] Cf. Minissale, *La versione greca del Siracide,* 67–68. Note the contrast with Prov 23:29; see A. A. Wieder, "Ben Sira and the Praises of Wine," *JQR* 61 (1970): 155–66. Here I vocalize לֶאֱנוֹשׁ ("for a human being"; cf. G ἀνθρώποις, "for human beings"), where Wieder reads לָאָנוּשׁ ("for the sick," 162). Di Lella prefers to read לְמִי as לְמוֹ (through orthographic confusion); cf. A. A. Di Lella, "The Newly Discovered Sixth Manuscript of Ben Sira from the Cairo Geniza," *Bib* 69 (1988): 226–38, esp. 231.

אַל־תִּתְחַר בַּמְּרֵעִים אַל־תְּקַנֵּא בָּרְשָׁעִים׃
כִּי לֹא־תִהְיֶה אַחֲרִית לָרָע נֵר רְשָׁעִים יִדְעָךְ׃

Do not be vexed at the evildoers;
do not envy the wicked;
for there will be no future for the evil person;
the lamp of wicked persons will be extinguished.

Sirach 9:11 also echoes Prov 24:1:

אַל־תְּקַנֵּא בְּאַנְשֵׁי רָעָה וְאַל־תִּתְאָו לִהְיוֹת אִתָּם׃

Do not envy persons of evil,
and do not desire to be with them.

Likewise, Prov 3:31a (also alluded to in Sir 10:23b H^B) warns readers: "Do not envy a person of lawlessness" (אַל־תְּקַנֵּא בְּאִישׁ חָמָס); this is the first of several points of contact between Sir 9:10–16 and Prov 3:21–35. Similarly, just as Ben Sira urges his students not to envy the wicked (Sir 9:11a), so 4QInstruction suggests keeping a distance from evil and hostile persons: "Do not count a man of iniquity as a helper. And moreover let there be no enemy [among thy acquaintances]" (4Q417 2 i 7).[58]

Next, Ben Sira explains the motivation for the admonition of 9:11a: לֹא תֵדַע מַה יוֹמוֹ ("you cannot know when his day will be," v. 11b). The term "his day" (יוֹמוֹ) denotes "the day of his death," as it also does in 1 Sam 26:10: "His day will come and he will die" (יוֹמוֹ יָבוֹא וָמֵת).[59] Moreover, Ps 37, which begins with the counsel אַל־תְּקַנֵּא בְּעֹשֵׂי עַוְלָה ("Do not envy those who do wrong," cf. Sir 9:11a), says of the "wicked person" (רָשָׁע; cf. Sir 9:11a):

אֲדֹנָי יִשְׂחַק־לוֹ כִּי־רָאָה כִּי־יָבֹא יוֹמוֹ׃

The Lord will laugh at him,
for he sees that his day will come (Ps 37:13).

---

[58] J. Strugnell et al., *Sapiential Texts, Part 2: Qumran Cave 4.24* (DJD 34; Oxford: Clarendon, 1999), 176; cf. Harrington, *Wisdom Texts from Qumran*, 49. The exact reading of this text is uncertain.

[59] Likewise, speaking of the "wicked" (רְשָׁעִים, Job 18:5; cf. רָשָׁע, Sir 9:11a), Job 18:20a says: "Westerners are appalled at his day" (יוֹמוֹ), that is, the day of his death.

According to Ben Sira, a terrible death may serve as punishment for an evildoer (11:25–28). God knows the day when he will judge the wicked by causing their death, even if human beings are ignorant of when that day will be (9:11).

Human ignorance about the future is a common theme in the wisdom literature of Israel and Egypt. Thus, Prov 27:1 advises, "Do not boast about tomorrow, for you cannot know what the day will bring forth" (כִּי לֹא־תֵדַע מַה־יֵּלֶד יוֹם). Similarly, Qoh 11:2 counsels giving a portion to seven or eight different persons: "For you cannot know what evil there will be on the earth" (כִּי לֹא תֵדַע מַה־יִּהְיֶה רָעָה עַל־הָאָרֶץ). In addition, Qoh 11:5 affirms: "You cannot know the activity of God" (לֹא תֵדַע אֶת־מַעֲשֵׂה הָאֱלֹהִים).

Such human ignorance is also a theme in ancient Egyptian sapiential texts; for example, Amenemope 19.13 declares: "Man ignores how tomorrow will be," while Amenemope 22.5 asserts: "Indeed you do not know the plans of god."[60] Closer to Sir 9:11 is the Instruction of Any 5.2: "You do not know your death." Similarly, P. Insinger 4.8 offers the counsel: "Do not be greedy for wealth in a lifetime which you cannot know," while P. Insinger 17.6 notes: "Death and the life of tomorrow, we do not know their [nature]." A Greek parallel occurs in Theognis 159–160: "No man living knoweth what a night and a day have to accomplish for us."

Elsewhere in his book (e.g., 3:21–22; 11:4; 43:32), Ben Sira points out the limits of human knowledge. Sirach 8:18 H^A advises: "Before a stranger do not do anything secret, for you cannot know what its end will bring forth" (כִּי לֹא תֵדַע מַה יֵּלֵד סֹפוֹ). In addition, Sir 11:18–19 warns against becoming like a selfish miser, who "cannot know what will be his portion [לֹא יֵדַע מה יִּהְיֶה חֶלְקוֹ],[61] and he will leave it to another and die" (11:19cd H^A). Sirach 9:11 implies that since the rich miser cannot be sure of enjoying his possessions, there is no need to envy the wicked, whose appointed day has been decreed by God.

Sirach 9:12 emphatically reiterates the advice of verse 11, introducing the term מָוֶת ("death," v. 12b). The first colon presents one way to avoid death: אַל תְּקַנֵּא בְּזֵדוֹן מַצְלִיחַ ("Do not envy a prosperous arrogant person"). In the Deuteronomic law code the root זיד ("be arrogant") refers to a presumptuous sin deserving death; Deut 17:12 speaks of the זָדוֹן ("arrogance") of someone who rejects the decision of the priest or judge,

[60] *AEL* 2:157, 159. The following quotations of Egyptian texts come from 2:138 (Instruction of Any) and 3:188, 198 (P. Insinger), while the Theognis quotation is from Edmonds, trans., *Elegy and Iambus*, 1:247.

[61] I complete the lacuna of H^A in light of Qoh 11:2.

while Deut 18:20 uses the cognate verb הֵזִיד ("act arrogantly," "be presumptuous") to denote the action of a false prophet. However, whereas in Deuteronomy the root זיד tends to denote a specific arrogant action, in Ben Sira the presumptuousness that deserves death seems to refer more to a general attitude.

The root זיד ("be arrogant") belongs largely to Israel's sapiential writings.[62] Proverbs 11:2 contrasts arrogance (זָדוֹן) with wisdom (חָכְמָה; cf. Prov 13:10), just as Sir 9:10–16 contrasts the arrogant person (זֵדוֹן, v. 12a) with wise persons (חֲכָמִים, v. 14b). Similarly, Sir 32:18d H[BmgE] asserts: "An arrogant person [זֵד] and a scoffer will not accept the commandment," while 15:7b H[A] declares of wisdom: "Arrogant persons [אַנְשֵׁי זָדוֹן] will not behold her." In sapiential texts the noun זֵד ("arrogant person") occurs in parallel with לֵץ ("scoffer": Prov 21:24; Sir 32:18) and רַע ("evil person": Sir 12:4).

Where Sir 9:11–12 warns against associating with those whose power derives from arrogance, 12:8–18 spells out the harmful effects of such associations. Thus, 12:14a warns that no one pities "one who associates with an arrogant person,"[63] and hence the sage cautions his students not to envy a "prosperous arrogant person" (זֵדוֹן מַצְלִיחַ; 9:12a). Since such a person is dangerous for "all who approach" (כָּל הַקָּרֵב, 12:13b), in 9:13c Ben Sira advises how to behave "if you have approached" (אִם קָרַבְתָּ) someone powerful.

In two particular passages Ben Sira speaks strongly against the arrogance of proud sinners. Sirach 10:12–18 addresses the topic of pride and concludes: "Arrogance [זָדוֹן] is not fitting for a human being, nor fierceness of anger for one born of woman" (10:18 H[A]). Sirach 16:1–4 insists that one God-fearing child is of greater value than a thousand sinners and maintains: "Better is ... dying childless ... than a posterity of arrogance" (אַחֲרִית זָדוֹן; 16:3d H[A]).[64] For Ben Sira, any worldly advantages of the "arrogant person" are completely offset by the certainty that God will punish him, whether in the course of his life or at the actual moment of his death.

Sirach 9:12a warns against envying an arrogant person who is "prosperous" (or "successful," מַצְלִיחַ). Ben Sira here echoes Ps 37:7bc:

---

[62] Just as Sir 9:11–12 uses the terms רָשָׁע ("wicked") and זֵדוֹן ("arrogant") almost as synonyms in successive bicola, so Ps 154:15 (11QPs[a] 18.15) employs רְשָׁעִים ("the wicked") and זֵדִים ("the arrogant") as a parallel word-pair.

[63] Read חוֹבֵר אֶל אִישׁ זֵדוֹן (cf. G), where H[A] has חוֹבֵר אֶל אֵשֶׁת זָדוֹן (lit., "one who associates with a woman of arrogance").

[64] Cf. 16:3d G; the text of H[A] here contains doublets and expansions.

אַל־תִּתְחַר בְּמַצְלִיחַ דַּרְכּוֹ בְּאִישׁ עֹשֶׂה מְזִמּוֹת

Do not be vexed at someone who makes his way prosperous,
at a person who makes scheming plans.

The certainty of death (Sir 9:12b; cf. Ps 37:20) marks the sage's answer to the problem of the prosperity of the wicked, a perennial problem that caused Israel's prophets and sages so much trouble.[65] Ben Sira elaborates his answer in Sir 41:1–2, where he presents the ambiguity of death.[66] Whereas death is bitter for "a person at peace and prosperous [מַצְלִיחַ] in everything" (41:1c H^{BM}), it is welcome for "a person stumbling and tripping at everything" (41:2c H^{Bmg}). Thus, death will be a much more serious blow for the arrogant person who prospers in his earthly life than for a devout pauper.

The phrase "the time of death" (עֵת מָוֶת) corresponds to the phrase ἡμέρα τελευτῆς ("the day of death") occurring elsewhere in Ben Sira (1:13; 11:26; 18:24; 40:2). Also found in H^E is the expression בְּיוֹם הַמָּוֶת ("on the day of death," 33:24b), which G renders ἐν καιρῷ τελευτῆς ("at the time of death").

The phrase "remember that" (זְכֹר כִּי, 9:12b) also occurs in 7:11 H^A with reference to God's judgment.

אַל תְּבֶז לֶאֱנוֹשׁ בְּמַר רוּחַ זְכֹר כִּי יֵשׁ מֵרִים וּמַשְׁפִּיל

Do not despise a human being in the bitterness of his spirit;
remember that there is one who exalts and humbles.

In 8:7 H^A Ben Sira uses the same imperative verb "remember" (זְכֹר) to remind his students of the certainty of death:

אַל תִּתְהַלֵּל עַל גֹּוֵעַ זְכֹר כֻּלָּנוּ נֶאֱסָפִים

Do not glorify yourself above a dying person;
remember, we are all being gathered in.

---

[65] Cf., e.g., Jer 12:1; Job 21:7; Ps 73:3. On Ben Sira's theodicy, see Prato, *Il problema della teodicea;* and J. L. Crenshaw, "The Problem of Theodicy in Sirach: On Human Bondage," *JBL* 94 (1975): 47–64.

[66] On Sir 41:1–4, see Reiterer, "Deutung und Wertung des Todes"; Schrader, *Leiden und Gerechtigkeit,* 233–52. To compare the treatment of the topic in the Wisdom of Solomon (where there is belief in the afterlife), see M. Kolarcik, *The Ambiguity of Death in the Book of Wisdom 1–6* (AnBib 127; Rome: Pontifical Biblical Institute, 1991).

Thus, although the sage does not promise rewards in the afterlife for the God-fearing pauper, he does insist that death will bring low the arrogance of the prosperous who turn away from God, and hence one should not envy such persons.

Death plays a significant role in Ben Sira's theology.[67] For the sage a happy death is extremely desirable, and according to 1:13 G the God-fearing person "will be blessed on the day of his death." Conversely, the worst form of divine punishment is a painful death in disgrace; hence the sage warns against delaying to fulfill one's vows: "Remember [the Lord's] wrath in the days of death, and the time of [his] punishment at the turning away of [his] face" (18:24 G[BA]). Similarly, among the sufferings of life is the "thought of expectation" which is "the day of death" (ἡμέρα τελευτῆς; 40:2 G). But the most forceful of Ben Sira's death-inspired admonitions occurs in 11:25–28. In particular, 11:26–27a G warns: "In the sight of the Lord it is easy on the day of death to repay a human being according to his ways. The evil of an hour causes forgetfulness of enjoyment."[68] Hence, since God can punish one's misdeeds by causing a painful and shameful death, one should take timely preventive action. Thus, Ben Sira advises keeping away from the arrogant, who will receive God's punishment.[69]

Death also plays an important part in both 9:10–16 and 13:24–14:19. Just as in 13:24–14:19 human mortality affects one's outlook on wealth, so in 9:10–16 death serves as a reason for behaving cautiously toward the wicked. In 9:12 Ben Sira seeks to turn his students' attention away from the wealth currently enjoyed by the proud: "Do not envy a prosperous arrogant person; remember that at the time of death he will not be held guiltless" (זְכֹר כִּי עֵת מָוֶת לֹא יִנָּקֶה). In 14:12b, 13a the sage urges his pupil to practice generosity and avoid avarice:

---

[67] In the extant Hebrew MSS of Ben Sira מָוֶת ("death") occurs twenty-two times, while in G θάνατος ("death") is found twenty-eight times, and τελευτή ("end, death") occurs nine times.

[68] Cf. Di Lella, "Conservative and Progressive Wisdom," 143–46; and Crenshaw, "The Problem of Theodicy in Sirach," 126.

[69] Possibly in Sir 9:11–12 the sage alludes to the story of Eli's family, punished for the sins of the priest's two wicked sons, Hophni and Phinehas (1 Sam 2:12). The punishment prophesied against them was that "on one day both of them will die" (1 Sam 2:34; cf. "his day" in Sir 9:11b). On the very day of their death together in battle (1 Sam 4:11–12), their father Eli died of shock (1 Sam 4:17–18) and "the time for her death" (עֵת מוֹתָהּ; cf. עֵת מָוֶת, "the time of death," Sir 9:12b) came upon Phinehas's wife as she gave birth (1 Sam 4:20). On the pride of Hophni and Phinehas, see Josephus, *Ant.* 5.10.1 §339.

זְכוֹר כִּי ... לֹא מָוֶת יִתְמַהְמֵהַּ
בְּטֶרֶם תָּמוּת הֵיטֵב לְאוֹהֵב

Remember that ... death will not linger.
Before you die, be good to a friend.

The phrase לֹא יִנָּקֶה ("will not be held guiltless") is characteristic of ancient Israel's wisdom literature; the exact phrase occurs seven times in Proverbs. In speaking of the punishment of the proud, Sir 9:12 follows Prov 16:5: "An abomination to Yahweh is everyone whose heart is haughty; assuredly he will not be held guiltless" (לֹא יִנָּקֶה). Elsewhere Ben Sira speaks of God's punishment of those involved in the unbridled pursuit of wealth. Echoing Prov 28:20, Sir 11:10b H[AB] declares: אָץ לְהַרְבּוֹת לֹא יִנָּקֶה ("One hasty to gain increase will not be held guiltless"). Moreover, Sir 31:5 H[B] asserts (cf. 26:29 G): רוֹדֵף חָרוּץ לֹא יִנָּקֶה ("One who pursues gold will not be held guiltless"). Ben Sira recognizes that the "prosperous arrogant person" (9:12) is often someone whose relentless pursuit of wealth has blinded him to moral values and made him liable to divine judgment (11:10; 31:5).[70]

By making multiple allusions to Israel's earlier wisdom literature, Sir 9:12 reinforces the sage's point that prosperity gained by ungodly means is bound to end in punishment, even if such punishment occurs only at the person's death. Hence one should avoid befriending such people who are on the road to disaster.

c. Stanza 3: Avoiding Company with One Empowered to Kill (9:13)

Ben Sira begins the third stanza by urging his students to keep their distance from the authorities who hold the power of the sword. Doubtless the sage is referring to the Hellenistic rulers of Palestine, either the Ptolemies until the Battle of Panium (ca. 200 B.C.E.), or the Seleucid authorities in the years thereafter. From the Hephzibah inscription (ca. 195 B.C.E.) we know of a provincial governor (στρατήγος) named Ptolemaios son of Thraseas; having served the Ptolemies as a general, he changed his allegiance and became Seleucid governor of Syria and Phoenicia.[71] Answerable to the provincial governor were the high priest (ἀρχιερεύς) and the senate (or council of elders,

[70] Possibly the sage may be thinking of the Tobiads who administered the heavy tax burden imposed on Jerusalem by the Ptolemies in the latter part of the third century B.C.E. (cf. Hengel, *Judaism and Hellenism,* 1:47–55).

[71] Josephus, *Ant.* 12.3.3 §138; cf. R. S. Bagnall, "Palestine, Administration of (Ptolemaic)," *ABD* 5:90–92.

γερουσία).[72] Although the Hellenistic governor (στρατήγος) and his staff held the "power of the sword," it is unclear whether the Jewish senate (γερουσία) in Jerusalem was also "empowered to kill."[73] Accordingly, Ben Sira doubtless urges his students to keep away from the circle of the provincial governor.[74] Instead of an attitude of familiarity with the authorities, in 4:7b H[A] he urges submissiveness: לְשִׁלְטוֹן עִיר הַכְאֵף רֹאשׁ ("To the ruler of a city[75] bow the head").

Ben Sira's advice in 9:13a accords with his ethics of caution,[76] which matches the teaching of Egyptian wisdom literature. For example, P. Insinger 3.14 warns, "Do not tie yourself to one who is [greater] than you, for then your life will be ruined," while P. Insinger 27.8 advises, "Do not approach the strong man even when you have protection behind you."[77]

---

[72] In *Ant.* 12.3.3 §142 Josephus mentions "the senate, the priests, the scribes of the temple and the temple-singers" (Thackeray et al., trans., *Josephus,* 7:73).

[73] Possibly the "power of the sword" was reserved to the Hellenistic governor and not exercised by the Jerusalem senate, but historical evidence for the period 220–180 B.C.E. is scarce. On the same topic during the Roman occupation in the first century C.E., see Brown, *Death of the Messiah,* 1:363–72.

[74] Similar advice is given in *m. ʾAbot* 1:10: "Seek not acquaintance with the ruling power" (Viviano, *Study As Worship,* 18). On Ben Sira's attitude to the Hellenistic authorities, see N. Calduch-Benages, "Fear for the Powerful or Respect for Authority?" in Egger-Wenzel and Krammer, eds., *Der Einzelne und seine Gemeinschaft bei Ben Sira,* 87–102. If Ben Sira belonged to the "scribes of the temple" (Josephus, *Ant.* 12.3.3 §142), as Hengel has tentatively suggested (*Judaism and Hellenism,* 1:133), he might be urging his students to resist economic pressure to work for the provincial governor. This interpretation appears to contradict 39:4: "In the midst of magnates he [the scribe] will serve, and before rulers he will appear; he will pass through the land of alien nations." However, in light of 9:13a, 39:4 presumably has in view an official of the high priest and *gerousia* (rather than an official of the Hellenistic rulers). Thus, 2 Macc 4:11 speaks of John, father of Eupolemus, being sent to Antiochus III on behalf of the high priest (= Simeon II, ca. 198 B.C.E.), while a generation later Judas Maccabeus sent Eupolemus to Rome on a diplomatic mission (1 Macc 8:17, probably in 161 B.C.E.; cf. Josephus, *Ant.* 12.10.6 §415).

[75] For עוֹד ("still," H[A]), read עִיר ("city") with S; so Skehan and Di Lella, *Wisdom of Ben Sira,* 163.

[76] See Sanders, "Ben Sira's Ethics of Caution." In 33:20–21 H[E] the sage commends preserving control of oneself even from family members: "While you are still living and there is breath [נְשָׁמָה] in you, do not let anyone human have power [תַּשְׁלֵט] over you" (33:21). As in 9:13, the sage advises saving one's life-breath by keeping power over oneself.

[77] *AEL* 3:188, 206; see also the Instruction of Any 5.7: "Keep away from a hostile man; do not let him be your comrade" (ibid., 2:138). Cf. Fuß, "Tradition und Komposition," 80.

By his warning in 9:13a Ben Sira draws out the practical consequences of biblical sayings like Prov 20:2: "The dread of a king is like the growling of a young lion; one who makes him angry sins against his life." Whereas Qoh 7:19 declares that wisdom is stronger than ten "rulers" (שַׁלִּיטִים) in a city, Sir 9:13a indicates that wisdom entails keeping far from a ruler who is "empowered to kill" (שַׁלִּיט לַהֲרוֹג).

By repeating in 9:13b the word "death" (מָוֶת, already used in v. 12b), Ben Sira emphasizes the need to keep away from someone holding the power of the sword. Here the sage develops the observation of Prov 16:14: "A king's wrath means messengers of death, and a wise person will pacify it."

For Ben Sira wariness toward the ruling power is an example of wise behavior that will eliminate a source of fear from one's life. Here again (as in 9:11a) the sage is probably alluding to the wisdom poem, Prov 3:21–35. Just as Sir 9:11a echoed Prov 3:31a, so Sir 9:13b contains echoes of Prov 3:24–25.

> If you lie down you will not be terrified [לֹא־תִפְחָד],
> and you will lie down and your sleep will be pleasant;
> you will not fear a sudden terror [פַּחַד פִּתְאֹם],
> or the devastation of the wicked when it comes.

Biblical phraseology (cf. Deut 28:67; Pss 14:5; 53:6; Job 3:25) is also apparent in the sage's cognate accusative, פָּחַד פַּחַד ("be terrified of a terror"). Instead of suffering a terrible untimely death brought about by ambitious friendships, Ben Sira wishes his students to live on until their natural death, which is not to be feared.[78]

Both 9:13 and 13:9–10 use the antithesis between "near" (קָרֹב) and "far" (רָחֹק) to warn against too close an association with those bearing political authority. Just as 9:13a advises, "Keep far [רְחַק] from anyone empowered to kill," so 13:9a counsels, "When a prince is near, keep far away" (קָרֵב נָדִיב הֱיֵה רָחוֹק, H^{A}). In 13:10 Ben Sira continues the contrast:

אַל תִּתְקָרֵב פֶּן תִּתְרַחֵק   וְאַל תִּתְרַחֵק פֶּן תִּשָּׂנֵא

> Do not come near, lest you be kept far away,
> and do not keep far away, lest you be hated.

Similarly in 9:13, after urging the reader to "keep far" (רְחַק) from such a powerful person (9:13a), the sage gives advice on how to behave if one

[78] In 41:3a H^{M} the sage teaches: "Do not be terrified of death, the decree for you" (אַל תִּפְחַד מִמָּוֶת חֻקֶּךָ).

has indeed come close to someone in authority: "If you have approached [אִם קָרַבְתָּ], commit no offense" (9:13c).

To underscore the seriousness of his admonition to avoid committing an offense, Ben Sira warns that the ruler "may take away your life-breath." The verb אשם ("commit an offense, become guilty") occurs most often in a priestly or cultic context (e.g., Lev 5:19; Num 5:7), although in Prov 30:10 it appears in a wisdom setting. Whereas Gen 2:7 employs the phrase נִשְׁמַת חַיִּים ("breath of life"), here Ben Sira contrasts נִשְׁמָתְךָ ("your life-breath," Sir 9:13d) with "death" (מָוֶת, v. 13b).

In the MT the formulation that opens Sir 9:13e, דַּע כִּי ("know that"), often introduces serious admonitions. In Gen 20:7, for instance, King Abimelech of Gerar receives a warning to return Sarah to Abraham: "If you do not return her, know that you shall surely die" (דַּע כִּי־מוֹת תָּמוּת). Similarly, David warns Jonathan about Saul: "If he is indeed angry, know that [דַּע כִּי] evil has been determined by him" (1 Sam 20:7).

The warning of Sir 9:13ef alludes to Job 18:7–9, part of Bildad's speech concerning God's punishment of the wicked.[79]

יֵצְרוּ צַעֲדֵי אוֹנוֹ וְתַשְׁלִיכֵהוּ עֲצָתוֹ׃
כִּי־שֻׁלַּח בְּרֶשֶׁת בְּרַגְלָיו וְעַל־שְׂבָכָה יִתְהַלָּךְ׃
יֹאחֵז בְּעָקֵב פָּח יַחֲזֵק עָלָיו צַמִּים׃

His vigorous steps will be narrowed,
    and his advice will cast him away,
for he has been dispatched into the net by his feet,
    and upon netting he will be walking about.
A trap will seize his heel;
    it will cause snares to prevail over him.

Sirach 9:13ef H^A has four words in common with Job 18:7–9: פַּח ("trap"), צַעַד ("step"), רֶשֶׁת ("net"), and הִתְהַלֵּךְ ("walk about"). However, in view of G's misunderstanding,[80] I discount רֶשֶׁת ("net") as a scribal alteration (to harmonize with Job 18:8a). Nevertheless, the other three words in common suggest that Ben Sira here alludes to Job 18:7–9. Just as Bildad insists that the wicked person will be caught in his own traps, so Ben Sira counsels that keeping away from the powerful will enable one to avoid falling into their fatal snares.

---

[79] We have already seen that Sir 9:11ab alludes twice to Job 18 (v. 5: "wicked"; v. 20: "his day").

[80] The word מְצוֹדוֹת (taken as original here) means either "nets" (cf. H^A) or "battlements" (cf. G); see textual note 13^h above.

The imagery of "traps" and "nets" (9:13ef), taken from the world of hunting, occurs frequently in the MT.[81] Indeed, just as Ps 124:5–7 combines imagery of "the arrogant waters" (הַמַּיִם הַזֵּידוֹנִים) and the hunter's "trap" (פַּח), so Sir 9:12–13 speaks of the "arrogant person" (זֵדוֹן) and the ruler's "traps" (פַּחִים). Moreover, Qoh 9:12 offers a parallel to Ben Sira at this point: "For a human being cannot even know his time [cf. Sir 9:11b], like the fish that are caught in an evil net [מְצוֹדָה, cf. Sir 9:13f], and like birds caught in a trap [פָּח, cf. Sir 9:13e]." Whereas Qoheleth speaks of death as the fate that comes unbidden upon human beings, Ben Sira warns against inducing death by rash association with the powerful.[82]

d. Stanza 4. The Life-Giving Value of Wise Friends (9:14–16)

After the warnings of stanzas 2 and 3, Ben Sira again dispenses positive advice, as in the first stanza. As countless teachers before and after him have urged, he advises his students to choose wise and God-fearing friends.

Since communication is such an important part of friendship, Ben Sira begins the last stanza by appealing to his hearers to give generous and wise answers to their companions. Sirach 9:14a has affinities to 5:12 H^A:

אִם יֵשׁ אִתְּךָ עֲנֵה רֵעֲךָ   וְאִם אַיִן יָדְךָ עַל פִּיךָ

If you have something [to say] answer your companion,
and if not, [place][83] your hand over your mouth.

In 9:14a the sage counsels his students to respond to their companions to the best of their ability, in other words, by sharing the wisdom they have acquired.

Sirach 9:14b then recommends associating with wise people. This age-old advice appears in Israelite sapiential tradition; for instance, Prov 13:20a (Qere) asserts: הֹלֵךְ אֶת־חֲכָמִים יֶחְכָּם ("One who walks with wise persons will become wise").[84] Similarly, Ben Sira often advises learning

---

[81] Ben Sira too has a fondness for hunting imagery (cf. 27:19–20); compare his use of מוֹקֵשׁ ("snare") in 31:30; 32:2; 51:3 (all H^B). Note that the wordplay between פַּחַד ("terror," 9:13b) and פַּח ("trap," 9:13e) also occurs in the MT (Isa 24:17; Jer 48:43).

[82] In 9:3b H^A Ben Sira uses the noun מְצוֹדָה ("net") to describe the entrapping enchantment of foreign (or "loose") women: "Do not approach a strange woman, lest you fall into her nets." The sage's warning is comparable to Qoh 7:26, which speaks of a woman's heart as "nets" (מְצוֹדִים).

[83] H^C adds the imperative verb שִׂים ("place") here.

[84] Compare the admonition of Tob 4:18 and the observations in Prov 13:14; 15:31. Similar advice occurs in *m. ʾAbot* 1:4: "Let thy house be a meeting-house for the sages" (חֲכָמִים; Viviano, *Study As Worship*, 9).

from the "wise" (חֲכָמִים), as in 8:8 H^A. Moreover, in 27:12 G the sage counsels: "In the midst of the senseless keep track of time, but in the midst of the discerning stay continually."[85]

Ben Sira's advice to associate with the wise accords with the counsel of many sages from the ancient world.[86] For example, Ankhsheshonq 13.6 declares, "The friend of a fool is a fool; the friend of a wise man is a wise man," while P. Insinger 13.19 asserts that "he who walks with a wise man shares his praise." In addition, since Greek culture held wisdom in high esteem (cf. Aristotle, *Eth. nic.* 6.7.2 §1141a; Plato, *Apol.* 20d), it is not surprising that its literature encourages association with the wise. Thus, one of the fragments of Menander (694K) states: "If you go in for wisdom, do not make intimates of those who lack wisdom."

The *hitpaʿel* verb הִסְתַּיֵּיד ("confide [in]" or "associate [with]")[87] occurs thrice elsewhere in Ben Sira (8:17a H^A; 9:3c H^A; 42:12b H^B). In 42:12b the sage gives advice concerning a daughter, "Let her not associate among women,"[88] and in 9:3c he says, "Do not associate with a prostitute."[89] The message of 9:14b is the converse of 8:17, which declares:

עִם פּוֹתֶה אַל תִּסְתַּיֵּיד כִּי לֹא יוּכַל לְכַסּוֹת סוֹדְךָ׃

Do not confide in a simple person,
for he will not be able to conceal your confidence.

---

[85] Sirach 6:34 G^{BAC} also makes this appeal (using the question idiom borrowed from Hos 14:10; Ps 107:43): "Stand in the multitude of elders. And who is wise? Attach yourself to him."

[86] For a brief discussion, see M. Lichtheim, *Late Egyptian Wisdom Literature in the International Context* (OBO 52; Göttingen: Vandenhoeck & Ruprecht, 1983), 46–47. For the following two quotations, see *AEL* 3:169, 196. For Menander's aphorism, see Allinson, trans., *Menander*, 523.

[87] No verbal form of the root סוד occurs in the MT, although the *paʿel* and *etpaʿal* forms occur in Syriac. Commenting textually on 9:3c, Skehan and Di Lella (*Wisdom of Ben Sira*, 217) assert: "There is the strongest of evidence that *hstyd* as a verb stem based on the noun *sôd*, and meaning 'make oneself the familiar companion/associate of (another)' was a real part of Ben Sira's personal vocabulary."

[88] I read וּבֵין נָשִׁים אַל תִּסְתַּיֵּד (with Smend, *Sirach, hebräisch und deutsch*, 44; cf. G).

[89] I read עִם זוֹנָה אַל תִּסְתַּיֵּיד (H^A); on 9:3, see the text-critical note in Skehan and Di Lella, *Wisdom of Ben Sira*, 216–17.

As in 8:17, 9:14b–15b plays on the root סוד (verb in 8:17a and 9:14b; noun in 8:17b and 9:15b); while the noun סוֹד means "confidence, secret," the *hitpaʿel* verb denotes either "to confide [in]" or "to associate [with]."[90]

Sirach 9:15a reiterates the thought of verse 14b. In the MT (e.g., Prov 1:5; 17:28; 18:15; Qoh 9:11) the adjective נָבוֹן ("discerning") occurs frequently as a synonym of חָכָם ("wise"); for instance, Prov 16:21a declares: "Someone wise of heart [חֲכַם־לֵב] will be called discerning [נָבוֹן]." In the Hebrew text of Ben Sira as well, the roots בין ("be discerning") and חכם ("be wise") occur together.[91] For example, 4:11 H[A] opens a sapiential poem with the words: "Wisdom [חָכְמוֹת] teaches her children, and testifies to all who discern [מְבִינִים] her."[92]

Ben Sira employs the adjective נָבוֹן ("discerning") to describe the ideal wise and God-fearing person.[93] Similar to 9:15 is the thought of 33:3a H[B]: "A discerning person [אִישׁ נָבוֹן] will understand the Word [= the Torah, cf. 33:3b],"[94] since in 9:15 the "discerning" person worth befriending is one who is occupied in the "law of the Most High."

The term חֶשְׁבּוֹן (here rendered "planning"), from the root חשב ("think," "reckon," "plan"), may refer to either financial or cognitional reckoning. In Qoh 7:25, 27 the noun חֶשְׁבּוֹן means "reckoning," "account," "sum total," and Sir 42:3a H[M] presumes a similar sense: "[Do not be ashamed] of keeping accounts [חֶשְׁבּוֹן] with a partner or a traveler." In Qoh 9:10 and Sir 27:5–6 (as in Sir 9:15b), the same word may simply mean "plan, thought."[95]

---

[90] Seemingly, the *piʿel* of the verb סוד occurs in 7:14a H[A]: אַל תְּסַוֵּד בַּעֲדַת שָׂרִים ("Do not give counsel in the assembly of elders"), but the versions diverge here.

[91] The noun בִּינָה ("discernment") does not occur in the extant MSS of Ben Sira, unless the word בינותם at the end of 9:15 H[A] represents בִּינוֹתָם ("their discernments"), which is awkward syntactically. However, the form תְּבוּנָה ("discernment") occurs in parallel with חָכְמָה ("wisdom") in Sir 4:24; 14:20 (both H[A]).

[92] The two roots also occur together in 3:29 H[A]; 6:37 H[A]; 11:15 H[A] (probably an expansionary gloss); 32:16cd H[BEF] (probably a doublet); 42:21 H[M].

[93] Sirach 7:25b H[C] suggests that if you have a daughter, "bestow her upon a discerning man" (גֶּבֶר נָבוֹן), while 31:19a H[B], urging moderation in eating, asks: "Is not a little sufficient for a discerning human being?" (אֱנוֹשׁ נָבוֹן).

[94] Compare G's reading of 33:3a: "A discerning person will believe in the law."

[95] Sir 27:5–6 H[A] is difficult. I would paraphrase the couplet: "Just as the potter's plan of the pot he makes is tested when it is fired in the kiln, so a person's planning is tested in the heat of experience. On the basis of a tree's cultivation there will be fruit; equally on the basis of a person's imagination there will be planning."

The term סוֹד ("confidence," "secret," "council") is important in Ben Sira's thinking on friendship (cf. 6:6 H[A]; 8:17 H[A]; 37:10 H[D]; 42:1 H[B]). Whereas elsewhere he warns against revealing confidences (cf. 27:16–21), in Sir 9:15b he urges his students to spend their time positively, not in secret intrigues with courtiers, but in meditation on the "law of the Most High."[96]

The phrase תּוֹרַת עֶלְיוֹן ("the law of the Most High," absent here in H[A] but supplied from G)[97] occurs in 41:4 H[B]; 41:8 H[M]; 42:2 H[BM]; 49:4 H[B].[98] In 42:2a H[BM] Ben Sira places it at the head of his list of things that are no cause for shame. By contrast, in 41:8 H[M] the sage condemns the wicked who abandon it, and in 49:4 H[B] he laments over Judah's rulers who "abandoned the law of the Most High" (תּוֹרַת עֶלְיוֹן).[99]

The theme of the Torah is significant for Ben Sira, who often connects it with wisdom and the fear of the Lord.[100] Sirach 9:14–16 makes these connections with successive mention of "wise persons" (חֲכָמִים, v. 14b), "the law of the Most High" (νόμῳ ὑψίστου, v. 15b), and "the fear of God" (יִרְאַת אֱלֹהִים, v. 16b).[101] Sirach 19:20 states the connections more directly:

---

[96] In Ben Sira's time the Torah may have served not only as religious legislation but also as civil law for the Jewish community centered around Jerusalem; cf. the decree of Antiochus III confirming the right of the Jews to live according to their ancestral laws (Josephus, *Ant.* 12.3.3 §142).

[97] The phrase νόμος ὑψίστου ("law of the Most High") is present eight times in the Greek text (9:15; 19:17; 23:23; 38:34; 41:8; 42:2; 44:20; 49:4); see further my exegesis of 19:17.

[98] In 41:4b Ben Sira calls death תּוֹרַת עֶלְיוֹן ("the law of the Most High"), which is equivalent to חוֹק כָּל בָּשָׂר ("the decree for all flesh," 41:4a). In 41:4a I read חוֹק ("decree," cf. G) for H[B]'s חֵלֶק ("portion"); instead of חוֹק H[M] has קֵץ ("end," cf. S).

[99] In addition, for 6:37a Smend suggests תּוֹרַת עֶלְיוֹן ("the law of the Most High"; cf. G) where H[A] reads יִרְאַת עֶלְיוֹן ("the fear of the Most High"); see *Sirach, hebräisch und deutsch,* 6. The phrase תּוֹרַת עֶלְיוֹן ("the law of the Most High") occurs also in 11QPs[a] 18.14 (= Ps 154:14); 4Q525 2 ii 4.

[100] Cf. Jolley, "The Function of Torah in Sirach," 86–150; Schnabel, *Law and Wisdom from Ben Sira to Paul,* 8–92; J. Marböck, "Gesetz und Weisheit: Zum Verständnis des Gesetzes bei Jesus Ben Sira," *Gottes Weisheit Unter Uns,* 52–72. In 37:12 H[BD] the sage urges his students: "[Take advice] with a person always reverent, who you know keeps the commandment."

[101] A similar series, with parallels to Sir 9:14–16, occurs in Ps 154:10–14 (11QPs[a] 18.9–14): "The man who gives glory to the Most High is accepted.... Her [= wisdom's] voice is heard in the gates of just men [צַדִּיקִים] ... ; they speak about it when they eat to bursting ... ; their meditation is on the Law of the Most High [שִׂיחָתָם בְּתוֹרַת עֶלְיוֹן]" (García Martínez, *Dead Sea Scrolls Translated,* 305).

πᾶσα σοφία φόβος κυρίου, καὶ ἐν πάσῃ σοφίᾳ ποίησις νόμου.

The fear of the Lord is all wisdom,
and the doing of the law is in all wisdom.[102]

Similarly, 1:26–27a G links wisdom, commandments, and the fear of the Lord: "If you desire wisdom, keep the commandments, and the Lord will lavish her on you; for the fear of the Lord is wisdom and instruction." Moreover, the central sapiential poem in Ben Sira's book equates the wisdom dwelling in Israel (24:8) with "the law that Moses commanded us" (24:23).[103]

In Sir 9:16a the sage advises his students to share meals with righteous persons, because their conversation and example will be beneficial. This advice is the corollary of the saying of Menander (*Thaïs,* fragment 218) quoted in 1 Cor 15:33: "Bad company corrupts good habits." Hence the psalmist prays to be saved from the ill effects of bad company: "Do not turn my heart to anything evil, to do wanton deeds in wickedness, with those who are doers of iniquity, and let me not eat of their delicacies" (Ps 141:4).

Ben Sira employs the noun לֶחֶם ("bread," "meal") in both a literal and a metaphorical sense. Using the term in the physical sense (Sir 31:12, 23, 24), 31:12–32:13 offers instructions on proper conduct at banquets. Understood in a metaphorical sense, "bread" represents "insight" (Sir 15:3; cf. Prov 9:5). The connection between "bread" (Sir 9:16a) and "wine" (Sir 9:10c) that frames this pericope recurs often in the MT.[104]

Ben Sira uses the noun צֶדֶק ("righteousness")[105] to describe both divine and human activity; thus, in 35:22 H^{B} he affirms of God that "as judge of righteousness [= righteous judge] he will perform judgment," while in 49:9 H^{B} the sage praises Job as "the one upholding all [the ways of] righteousness." In 9:16 Ben Sira's concern is that his

[102] Likewise, Sir 21:11 declares: "One who keeps the law controls his thoughts, and complete fear of the Lord is wisdom." Note that P. Insinger 23.23 also connects wisdom and reverence: "It is the god who gives the heart to the wise man for the sake of having respect" (*AEL* 3:204).

[103] Cf. 23:27. Note, however, that 25:10 G declares: "How great is the one who has found wisdom, but he is not superior to the one who fears the Lord."

[104] E.g., Gen 14:18; Deut 29:5; 1 Sam 10:3; 16:20; 25:18; Prov 4:17; 9:5; Qoh 9:7; 10:19; cf. C. Begg, "'Bread, Wine and Strong Drink' in Deut 29:5a," *Bijdr* 41 (1980): 266–75, esp. 269–70.

[105] Note that in Ben Sira צְדָקָה (e.g., 3:14, 30; 40:17) generally means "almsgiving" rather than "righteousness."

students will take their meals with upright persons, so as to learn their righteousness.

Just as Ben Sira urges his hearers to associate and eat with righteous persons, so too ancient Egyptian and Greek writers offer similar advice. Thus, the Instruction of Any (5.7) teaches: "Befriend one who is straight and true."[106] Similarly, Theognis 31–34 advises: "This then I would have thee to know, nor [*sic*] to consort with the bad but ever to cleave unto the good, and at their tables to eat and to drink, and with them to sit" (cf. Theognis 563–566). Likewise, Xenophon (*Mem.* 1.2.20) asserts: "The society of honest men is a training in virtue, but the society of the bad is virtue's undoing."[107]

To conclude this pericope, Ben Sira brings the whole subject of friendship into the context of the fear of God, just as he did in 6:16b (at the end of 6:5–17). According to Haspecker, fear of God is the overall theme of Ben Sira's book.[108] In fact, if we discount the sage's foreword (1:1–10) and appendix (ch. 51), the whole book is united by an *inclusio:* φόβος κυρίου ("fear of the Lord," 1:11a) and יִרְאַת ייי ("fear of Yahweh," 50:29 H^B).

Ben Sira likes to conclude his pericopes by mentioning the fear of God.[109] Indeed, this theme concludes the opening nonalphabetic acrostic on the fear of God (1:11–30; cf. v. 30e); the first friendship pericope (6:5–17; cf. v. 16b);[110] the present poem on friendship (9:10–16; cf. v. 16b); the double nonalphabetic acrostic on self-control (22:27–23:27; cf. 23:27b G); the decalogue of macarisms (25:7–11; cf. vv. 10b–11); the nonalphabetic acrostic on the trades (38:24–34; cf. v. 34c S); the decalogue of good things (40:18–27; cf. vv. 26b–27); and the postscript (50:27–29; cf. v. 29).[111]

---

[106] *AEL* 2:138. The following quotation comes from Edmonds, trans., *Elegy and Iambus,* 1:233.

[107] Marchant, trans., *Xenophon,* 21. Note also Aristotle's dictum (*Eth. nic.* 9.9.5 §1170a) that "good men find pleasure in the actions of other good men who are their friends" (Rackham, trans, *Nicomachean Ethics,* 561).

[108] Haspecker, *Gottesfurcht bei Jesus Sirach,* 87–105. The term "fear of God" occurs more than fifty-five times in Ben Sira (p. 82); see the chart comparing G, S, and H (pp. 48–50).

[109] The sage probably borrows this feature from Prov 31:10–31 (the acrostic on the "capable woman"), whose penultimate bicolon (31:30b) mentions "the fear of Yahweh" (יִרְאַת יְהוָה). Note also that in P. Insinger the didactic units close with a religious refrain, as in 13.7: "The fate and the fortune that come, it is the god who determines them" (*AEL* 3:195); cf. Sanders, *Ben Sira and Demotic Wisdom,* 90.

[110] Moreover, in H^A "the fear of the Most High" occurs at the end of 6:18–37 (in v. 37a); but it is better to read "the law of the Most High" (cf. G).

[111] Fuß comments: "Sirach likes to top what was previously said in a unit by a final religious declaration, which may point to the fear of God, the law, or prayer

The expression of 9:16b resembles that of 10:22b. Whereas 9:16b H^{A} urges: בְּיִרְאַת אֱלֹהִים תִּפְאַרְתֶּךָ ("Let your glory be in the fear of God"), 10:22 H^{B} asserts:

גֵּר זָר נָכְרִי וָרָשׁ   תִּפְאַרְתָּם יִרְאַת ייי׃

Immigrant, foreigner, alien and pauper,
their glory is the fear of Yahweh.

Ben Sira teaches that just as those who are helpless or inglorious by human standards can find glory in fearing God, so too a person seeking friendship should glory not in the wealth or rank of his friends but in their fear of God.[112]

A related phrase also occurs in 25:6 G: "The crown of the aged is great experience, and their glory (καύχημα, as in 9:16b; 10:22b) is the fear of the Lord." Just as the aged, who possess wisdom (25:5 G), can rightly glory in the fear of God, so too Ben Sira's students will be able to glory in fearing God if they choose wise and upright friends. Similarly, the opening nonalphabetic acrostic of the book (1:11a G) asserts: φόβος κυρίου δόξα καὶ καύχημα ("The fear of the Lord is glory and exultation"). Thus, at the end of his second poem on friendship, Ben Sira has returned to the theme of fear of God with which he began his book.

9. Conclusion

After discussing the dangers of liaisons with women in 9:1–9, Ben Sira treats relations with male friends in 9:10–16. His basic advice is to find God-fearing friends and stick with them, instead of being attracted by the unscrupulous persons who wield power. In the context of its sociopolitical setting, the sage's message has a "conservative" tone, implying that one should remain faithful to those who obey the Torah in Jerusalem, instead of advancing one's career by forging connections with Hellenistic rulers. Ben Sira restates the traditional wisdom instruction to

---

(e.g., 7:36; 28:6–7; 35:10; 37:15)" ("Tradition und Komposition," 278–79; translation mine); cf. Haspecker, *Gottesfurcht bei Jesus Sirach*, 136 n. 30.

[112] Compare the prayer in Ps 119:63: "I am a comrade to all who fear you—to those who keep your precepts." Like Sir 9:16, Prov 31:30b links glory with the fear of God: "A woman whose fear is Yahweh—she will be praised"; cf. T. P. McCreesh, "Wisdom As Wife: Proverbs 31:10–31," *RB* 92 (1985): 25–46, esp. 28–29 n. 11.

shun the arrogant and the wicked (doubtless the proud rulers of 9:17–10:18). He also follows earlier sapiential tradition in his advice to associate with wise, discerning, and righteous persons. Although this pericope offers no new teaching, it spells out clearly and succinctly the way to be avoided in one's friendships (arrogance) and the way to be taken (the fear of God).

4

Sirach 13:15–23

1. Introduction

This chapter concerns the final unit (Sir 13:15–23) of a long segment (11:29–13:23) devoted to social relationships. Much of the advice in this segment is negative, reflecting an ethic of caution: warnings about friendship (e.g., 12:8–9; 13:1–2) introduce descriptions of mistreatment at the hands of false friends (e.g., 12:10–18; 13:3–7). Similarly, in 13:15–23 the general statement that people associate with their own kind (13:15–16) leads Ben Sira to explain why he considers friendship between rich and poor to be impossible (13:17–23). In 13:15–23 the text of H^A is mostly authentic, and the sage's literary skill is evident in his use of imagery (from the world of animals) and poetic devices (such as alliteration and repetition).[1]

2. Delimitation

As a didactic poem on friendship, Sir 13:15–23 is marked off as a unit by both its content and its form.[2] Its unifying theme is the impossibility of friendship between rich and poor, while an *inclusio* delimits the unit poetically: כָּל ("all," 13:15a) opens the pericope, while the concluding verse contains הַכֹּל ("everyone," 13:23a).[3] In regard to content, the unit consists of two parts: an axiom with illustrations from animal life (13:15–20);[4] and an application to rich and poor (13:21–23).[5]

---

[1] For the text of Sir 13:15–23 H^A, see Schechter and Taylor, *Wisdom of Ben Sira*, 8.

[2] Skehan and Di Lella (*Wisdom of Ben Sira*, 254) consider 13:15–23 as a separate subunit within 13:1–14:2.

[3] There is a second *inclusio*, with the accusative particle אֶת occurring in 13:15b, 23b.

[4] In the axiom (13:15–16) מִין ("kind") occurs three times, while the illustrations (13:17–19) mention three pairs of animals.

[5] In 13:21–23 both עָשִׁיר ("rich") and דַּל ("poor") occur three times.

The preceding unit (13:9–13), offering advice on approaching a nobleman, is delimited by an *inclusio:* חֱיֵה ("be") occurs in 13:9a, 13a. The following unit (13:24–14:2), concerning one's attitude to wealth, is also marked off by an *inclusio:* פִּי ("mouth," "speech") appears in 13:24b, while פִּיהוּ ("his mouth," "his speech") occurs in 14:1a.[6]

3. Text

I

15 כָּל הַבָּשָׂר יֶאֱהַב מִינוֹ   וְכָל אָדָם [a]אֶת הַדּוֹמֶה לוֹ[a]׃

16 מִין[b] כָּל בָּשָׂר אֶצְלוֹ[c]   וְאֶל מִינוֹ יְחוּבַּר[d] אָדָם׃

17 מַה יְּחוּבַּר זְאֵב אֶל כֶּבֶשׂ   כֵּן[e] רָשָׁע לְצַדִּיק[f]׃

18 [g]מַה יֵּשׁ[g] שְׁלוֹם צָבוּעַ אֶל כֶּלֶב   מֵאַיִן[h] שְׁלוֹם עָשִׁיר אֶל רָשׁ׃

19 מַאֲכַל אֲרִי פִּרְאֵי מִדְבָּר   כֵּן מַרְעִית עָשִׁיר דַּלִּים׃

20 תּוֹעֲבַת גַּאֲוָה[i] עֲנָוָה   וְתוֹעֲבַת עָשִׁיר אֶבְיוֹן׃

II

21 עָשִׁיר מוֹט[j] [k]נִסְמָךְ מֵרֵעַ[k]   וְדַל נָמוֹט[l] נִדְחֶה [m]מֵרֵעַ אֶל רֵעַ[m]׃

22 עָשִׁיר מְדַבֵּר[n] וְעֹזְרָיו רַבִּים   וּדְבָרָיו [o]מְכוֹעָרִין מוֹפִין[o]׃

דַּל מְדַבֵּר[p] [q]גַּע גַּע יִשְׂאוּ[q]   וְדִבֶּר מַשְׂכִּיל וְאֵין לוֹ מָקוֹם׃

23 עָשִׁיר דּוֹבֵר הַכֹּל נִסְכָּתוּ   וְאֶת שִׂכְלוֹ[r] עַד עָב יַגִּיעוּ׃

דַּל דּוֹבֵר מִי זֶה יֹאמְרוּ   וְאִם נִתְקַל גַּם הֵם יֶהְדְּפוּהוּ[s]׃

4. Textual Notes

The text given above follows H^A, except where indicated otherwise below. H^A mostly preserves a good text, although it contains some Aramaisms.[7]

---

[6] A careful study by P. C. Beentjes concludes, by contrast, that 13:24 (which he calls 13:23) forms the last verse of the preceding pericope rather than the first verse of what follows ("'How Can a Jug Be Friends with a Kettle?' A Note on the Structure of Ben Sira Chapter 13," *BZ* 36 [1992]: 87–93). In the section on context below I explain in greater detail why I nevertheless consider that 13:24 opens a new pericope (13:24–14:19).

[7] H^A reads מא ("what") in v. 18a, and the two participles מכוערין ("loathsome") and מופין ("they call beautiful") or מהופין ("[are] called beautiful") in v. 22b have Aramaizing endings.

15[a–a]: So H^A and S. G and L paraphrase: "his neighbor."

16[b]: So H^A. S presupposes מִן ("from,""some of"), while G paraphrases κατὰ γένος ("according to kind").

16[c]: So H^A (cf. S). G and L presuppose נֶאֱצָל ("is joined").

16[d]: So H^A and L. G and S presuppose יְדַבֵּק ("will stick").

17[e]: I replace the Mishnaic form כָּךְ ("so") in verse 17b (H^A) with its biblical synonym כֵּן ("so") from verse 17c (H^A).[8]

17[f]: After verse 17b H^A has a gloss that is lacking in G, S, and L: וְכֵן עָשִׁיר אֶל אִישׁ נֶאֱצָל ("and so is a rich person joined to a man;"[9] or "and so is a rich person toward a withdrawn [= poor] man").

18[g–g]: H^A reads מאיש (= מַא־יֵשׁ, "what is there?"), written as one word under the influence of מֵאַיִן ("whence?"; "how?") in verse 18b. Instead of the Aramaizing spelling מא (cf. Ezra 6:8) I read מה.[10]

18[h]: So H^A.[11] G repeats τίς ("what?") from verse 18a (cf. S).

20[i]: So H^A; this abstract noun corresponds to the following abstract noun, עֲנָוָה ("humility"). G presupposes גֵּאֶה ("a proud person"). S omits verse 20, seemingly because the translator considered it uncomplimentary toward the poor.[12]

21[j]: So H^A; מוֹט is a *qal* infinitive absolute (cf. GKC §113gg) serving for the participle מָט ("tottering"; cf. S: "falling"); cf. Qoh 4:2; Isa 59:4 for a similar use of the infinitive. However, G presupposes נָמוֹט ("made to totter," "shaken").

21[k–k]: Cf. G ("is supported by friends"). H^A reads בִּסְמָךְ מֵרֵעַ ("with the support of a companion"), while S has "and is thrust away to evil."

21[l]: So H^A. Both G and S, rendering "falling," presuppose מָט ("tottering").

21[m–m]: So H^A. S presumes מֵרַע אֶל רַע ("from bad to worse"; cf. Jer 9:2), while G repeats ὑπὸ φίλων ("by friends") from verse 21a.

22[n]: So H^A and S. G reads σφαλέντος ("made to totter" = נָמוֹט).

22[o–o]: So H^A (cf. S); the Aramaizing endings, found elsewhere in biblical Hebrew poetry (GKC §87e), may here be due to dissimulation, so as to avoid a succession of *m* sounds (as in Job 4:2b). Above the first two letters of מוֹפִין ("they call beautiful") in H^A a scribe has added ה, perhaps to

---

[8] So Smend, *Sirach, erklärt,* 126.

[9] Possibly emend אִישׁ ("man") to רָשׁ ("pauper"); cf. Skehan and Di Lella, *Wisdom of Ben Sira,* 251.

[10] So Smend, *Sirach, erklärt,* 127.

[11] For מֵאַיִן (lit., "from where?") meaning "how?" see 2 Kgs 6:27. Note that this interrogative particle occurs in parallel with מָה ("what?") in 2 Kgs 20:14; Isa 39:3; Jonah 1:8.

[12] Cf. Winter, "The Origins of Ben Sira in Syriac," 245–46.

indicate an unusual *hopʿal* form מְהוּפִּין ("called beautiful").[13] G paraphrases verse 22b: "He spoke unutterable things, and they justified him."

22p: So S.[14] G presupposes the reading of HA, נָמוֹט ("made to totter"), borrowed from verse 21b.

22q–q: HA has the ambiguous phrase נַּע נַּע וְשָׂא, which might mean "Strike [him], strike [him], and take [him] away"[15] or "Come, come, and speak up";[16] but these meanings do not fit the context well. For נַּע נַּע S has a similar onomatopoeic form *gûʿ* ("Pooh!") expressing contempt.[17] Moreover, instead of ושׂא (HA), it is better to read יִשְׂאוּ ("they will utter");[18] cf. S ("they say to him"). For the whole phrase G reads, "and they further rebuked him," either a paraphrase or perhaps reflecting וּגְעָרָה יִשְׂאוּ ("and they will utter a rebuke").

23r: So HA. G presupposes שִׂיחוֹ ("his talk"), while S ("his benefactors") presumes מַשְׂכִּילָיו ("those who cause him to prosper").

23s: So HA and S. GBS presupposes יַהַפְכוּהוּ ("they will overturn him"); cf. Sir 12:12b G for the same confusion.

5. Translation

I

15 All flesh will love its own kind,
    and every human being one resembling him.
16 All flesh has its kind close to it,
    and with his own kind a human being will be associated.
17 How can a wolf be associated with a lamb?
    So is a wicked person toward a righteous person.
18 What peace can a hyena have toward a dog?
    How can a rich person have peace toward an impoverished person?

---

[13] Segal, ספר בן־סירא השלם, 86. However, Peters (*Das Buch Jesus Sirach*, 118) suggests that the word may also be *hipʿil* (מְהוֹפִּין, "they call beautiful").

[14] Cf. Smend, *Sirach, erklärt*, 127–28.

[15] Peters, *Das Buch Jesus Sirach*, 118; a common meaning of נגע is "strike" (Isa 53:4; Job 1:19; 19:21).

[16] Cf. Skehan and Di Lella, *Wisdom of Ben Sira*, 250. For נגע with the meaning "come," see Job 4:5; Jonah 3:6.

[17] So Smend, *Sirach, erklärt*, 128.

[18] Cf. Schechter and Taylor, *Wisdom of Ben Sira*, 47; for the verb נשׂא in the sense "lift up [one's voice], utter" see Isa 3:7; 42:2, 11. Probably the initial י of יִשְׂאוּ was confused with a ו, while the final ו was lost by haplography with the following word.

19 The wild asses of the desert are a lion's food;
so paupers are the feeding-ground of the rich person.
20 Humility is an abomination to pride,
and a needy person is an abomination to a rich person.

II

21 A rich person tottering is supported by a companion,
but a pauper made to totter is thrust away from companion to companion.
22 A rich person speaks and his helpers are many,
and they call his loathsome words beautiful.
A pauper speaks; "Pooh-pooh!" they will utter;
and he will speak giving insight but there is no place for him.
23 A rich person speaks; all have been silenced,
and they make his insight reach to the clouds.
A pauper speaks; "Who is this?" they will say,
and if he has stumbled they too will push him down.

6. Poetic Analysis

The whole poem (Sir 13:15–23) is united by *inclusio* and rhyme. There is a double *inclusio* between the first and last couplets (vv. 15–16 and v. 23). Whereas verses 15–16 thrice employ כָּל ("all," "every"), verse 23a uses הַכֹּל ("all"). Additionally, both verses 15b and 23b contain the accusative particle אֶת.[19] There is also opening and closing rhyme. The first three cola (vv. 15–16a) exhibit end-rhyme (מִינוֹ, לוֹ, and אֶצְלוֹ), as do the last four cola in verse 23 (נִסְכְּתוּ, יַגִּיעוּ, יֹאמְרוּ, and יֶהְדְּפוּהוּ).[20] Thus, *inclusio* and rhyme serve to indicate the boundaries of the poetic unit.

---

[19] Because the previous occurrence of the particle אֶת is in 9:6 H^{A}, while the next appearance is in 15:11 H^{AB}, the sage's double use of the particle in 13:15–23 is stylistically significant. Note that the particle often occurs in the opening line of a pericope (9:1 H^{A}; 15:11 H^{AB}; 44:1 H^{M}) or in the closing line (39:35 H^{B}; 43:33 H^{B}; 51:12 H^{B}). On the sage's use of אֶת see F. V. Reiterer, "Markierte und nicht markierte direkte Objekte bei Ben Sira: Präliminaria zur Untersuchung der Hebraizität Siras anhand der Verben mit את-Verwendung," in *Text, Methode und Grammatik: Wolfgang Richter zum 65. Geburtstag* (ed. W. Gross et al.; St. Ottilien: EOS, 1991), 359–78.

[20] This fourfold rhyme in v. 23 also signals the end of the longer unit 13:1–23, which began with a rhyming bicolon (13:1).

The division into two stanzas (vv. 15–20 and vv. 21–23) is also indicated stylistically, namely, by means of further rhyme and patterns of three. The last bicolon of stanza 1 is marked by internal rhyme (נַאֲוָה עֲנָוָה, v. 20a), and the opening bicolon of stanza 2 also exhibits rhyme (מֵרֵעַ, v. 21a; רֵעַ, v. 21b). In addition, stanza 1 employs three words three times: כָּל ("all," "every": vv. 15ab, 16a); מִין ("kind": vv. 15a, 16ab); and עָשִׁיר ("rich": vv. 18b, 19b, 20b). Stanza 2 also employs three words three times: עָשִׁיר ("rich": vv. 21a, 22a, 23a); דַּל ("pauper": vv. 21b, 22c, 23c); and רֵעַ ("companion": v. 21ab). The root דבר ("speak" or "word": vv. 22abcd, 23ac) is present six times (= twice 3x).

a. Stanza 1: Creatures Associate with Their Own Kind (13:15–20)

We have already observed that the first stanza is united by a pattern of threes (3x "all/every," "kind," and "rich"), as well as by opening end-rhyme (vv. 15–16a) and closing internal rhyme (v. 20a). Other patterns also indicate the unity of stanza 1. Both cola of the opening line begin with כָּל ("all," "every," v. 15ab), while both cola of the closing line begin with תּוֹעֲבַת־ ("abomination," v. 20ab).

The stanza may be subdivided into three couplets. The first couplet (vv. 15–16) features the parallelism between בָּשָׂר ("flesh": vv. 15a, 16a) and אָדָם ("human being": vv. 15b, 16b). Both lines of the central couplet (vv. 17–18) begin with מַה־ ("what," "how?"). The second bicolon of the second couplet repeats שְׁלוֹם־ ("peace": v. 18ab), just as the second bicolon of the third couplet repeats תּוֹעֲבַת־ ("abomination": v. 20ab).

The stanza makes use of three rhetorical questions (vv. 17a, 18a, 18b). It also employs three animal comparisons (vv. 17a, 18a, 19a), which develop the phrase "all flesh" in vv. 15a and 16a. In addition, the term רָשָׁע ("wicked," v. 17b) not only exhibits assonance with רָשׁ ("impoverished," v. 18b), but also reverses the root consonants of עָשִׁיר ("rich"), which appears six times in verses 18–23.

A complex pattern of alliteration is apparent in the stanza, whereby the consonants of מִין כָּל בָּשָׂר (lit., "the kind of all flesh") generate most of the sound patterns in the stanza. In the opening couplet, for instance, ל occurs six times, and both ב and מ occur four times. Each colon in verses 17–19 begins with either מ or כ. More striking are the two animal names, כֶּבֶשׂ ("lamb," v. 17a) and כֶּלֶב ("dog," v. 18a), whose consonants use the letters of כָּל בָּשָׂר ("all flesh," v. 16a) in the same order. Moreover, the interrogative particle מֵאַיִן ("how?": v. 18b) is reminiscent of מִין ("kind," v. 16a), while מַאֲכַל ("food," v. 19a) ends with the two consonants of כָּל ("all," v. 16a). There is further assonance between בָּשָׂר ("flesh," v. 16a), יְחוּבַּר ("will be associated," vv. 16b, 17a) and מִדְבָּר ("desert," v. 19a).

Other instances of alliteration and assonance also abound. Verse 15b has אָדָם and הַדּוֹמֶה, while לוֹ in verse 15b is echoed in אֶצְלוֹ in verse 16a. Verse

18b has sibilant and liquid alliteration with its series שְׁלוֹם עָשִׁיר אֶל רָשׁ. In verse 19, too, there is alliteration in אֲרִי פִּרְאֵי, plus the series מִדְבָּר, מַאֲכַל, and מַרְעִית.[21] Alliteration is also evident in verse 20 between עֲנָוָה ("humility") and עָשִׁיר ("rich"), despite their contrasting meanings.

Finally, verses 17a, 18a, and 18b exhibit a similar structure with alliteration and assonance:

17a:	אֶל כֶּבֶשׂ	זְאֵב	מַה יְחוּבַּר
18a:	אֶל כֶּלֶב	צָבוּעַ	מַה יֵּשׁ שְׁלוֹם
18b:	אֶל רָשׁ	עָשִׁיר	מֵאַיִן שְׁלוֹם

b. Stanza 2: Rich and Poor Receive Unequal Treatment (13:21–23)

We have already noted that the second stanza is united by the frequent use of the pattern of three (3x "rich," "pauper," and "companion"; 6x דבר, "speak" or "word"). We also observed the presence of opening rhyme (v. 21ab) and the extensive use of closing rhyme (v. 23abcd). The unity of the stanza is further evident from the threefold contrast between the "rich person" and the "pauper" (vv. 21, 22, 23), a pattern that provides the basic structure for verses 21–23.

In the second stanza, each of the three contrasting statements exhibits an elaborate parallel structure, enhanced by repetition and assonance. Thus, verse 21 repeats the word רֵעַ ("companion," 3x) and the root מוט ("totter," 2x):

עָשִׁיר מוֹט נִסְמָךְ מֵרֵעַ
וְדַל נָמוֹט נִדְחֶה מֵרֵעַ אֶל רֵעַ

Two antithetical word-pairs are present: עָשִׁיר ("rich person") and דַּל ("pauper"); סמך ("support") and דחה ("thrust away"). In an additional contrast, מֵרֵעַ in verse 21a has a positive meaning ("by a companion"),[22] whereas in verse 21b it has a negative connotation ("from a companion"). In verse 21 three words begin with מ and three with נ; both these letters belong to the key word מִין ("kind," v. 16a) of the first stanza.

Verse 22 also exhibits a complex parallel structure with alliteration and repetition:

מוּפִין	וּדְבָרָיו מְכוֹעָרִין	מְדַבֵּר וְעוֹזְרָיו רַבִּים	עָשִׁיר
וְאֵין לוֹ מָקוֹם	וְדִבֶּר מַשְׂכִּיל	מְדַבֵּר גַּע גַּע יִשְׂאוּ	דַּל

[21] Cf. Skehan and Di Lella, *Wisdom of Ben Sira*, 66.

[22] For מִן ("by") with the agent of a passive verb, see Ps 37:23; Job 24:1; Qoh 12:11; cf. GKC §121f.

The first colon of each line employs מְדַבֵּר ("speaks"), while each second colon uses another form of the root דבר ("his words" in v. 22b; "he will speak" in v. 22d). Antithesis is evident, not only between the two bicola ("rich person" in v. 22a; "pauper" in v. 22c), but also within each bicolon. The first bicolon of v. 22 implies the contrast between what is "loathsome" (מְכוֹעָר) and what is "beautiful" (יָפֶה), while the second bicolon describes the rejection of someone whose insight should be heeded. The first letter of עָשִׁיר ("rich person," v. 22a) recurs in the word עֹזְרָיו ("his helpers," v. 22a), while the opening letter of דַּל ("pauper," v. 22c) occurs four times in verse 22 in the root דבר ("speak" or "word"). Many letters from the key phrase מִין כָּל בָּשָׂר (lit., "the kind of all flesh," v. 16a) recur in a series in verse 22: וְדֶבֶר מַשְׂכִּיל, מְדַבֵּר, וּדְבָרָיו מְכוֹעָרִין מוֹפִין, רַבִּים, מְדַבֵּר. Moreover, in the first bicolon of verse 22 three words begin with מ (מְדַבֵּר, מְכוֹעָרִין, and מוֹפִין), as also in the second bicolon of verse 22 (מְדַבֵּר, מַשְׂכִּיל, and מָקוֹם). Internal rhyme occurs as well: וְעֹזְרָיו and וּדְבָרָיו; מְכוֹעָרִין מוֹפִין; and נַּע גַּע.

A further example of parallelism (with contrast, repetition, and alliteration) is present in the structure of the two bicola of verse 23:

עָשִׁיר דּוֹבֵר הַכֹּל נִסְכְּתוּ   וְאֶת שִׂכְלוֹ עַד עָב יַגִּיעוּ׃
דַּל דּוֹבֵר מִי זֶה יֹאמְרוּ   וְאִם נִתְקַל גַּם הֵם יֶהְדְּפוּהוּ׃

Verse 23 employs antithesis, not only between עָשִׁיר ("rich person") and דַּל ("pauper"), but also between נִסְכְּתוּ ("they have been silenced") and יֹאמְרוּ ("they will say"). The assonance of the phrase עַד עָב ("to the clouds") matches the alliteration of גַּם הֵם ("they too"). Three words in verse 23 begin with ע: עָשִׁיר, עַד, and עָב; similarly, three words begin with ד: דַּל and דּוֹבֵר (twice). Many letters from the key phrase מִין כָּל בָּשָׂר ("the kind of all flesh," v. 16a) occur in verse 23: דּוֹבֵר הַכֹּל, דּוֹבֵר מִי, יֹאמְרוּ וְאִם נִתְקַל. In addition, two Hebrew roots connect verses 23ab and 22cd: דבר ("speak") and שׂכל ("give insight"). Such poetic patterns contribute to the artistic effect of the sage's composition.

7. Context of Sirach 13:15–23

a. Context within Part 3 of Ben Sira's Book (6:18–14:19)

Sirach 13:15–23 belongs to part 3 of Ben Sira's book (6:18–14:19), concerned with "Applying Wisdom Socially."[23] Sirach 13:1–23 itself comes

[23] Harvey, "Toward a Degree of Order," 55. In my discussion in ch. 3 concerning the context of Sir 9:10–16, I present the structure of 6:18–14:19.

toward the end of a long segment concerning the right attitude to wealth and poverty (10:19–14:19).

10:19–11:6: True Glory
11:7–28: Providence and Trust in God
11:29–12:18: Care in Choosing Friends[24]
13:1–23: The Rich and the Poor[25]
13:24–14:19: The Use of Wealth[26]

Haspecker regards 11:9–14:19 as a unity because this segment deals with problems arising from economic and social differences.[27] He observes that all the pericopes in 11:9–14:19 (apart from 11:29–12:6) assume the viewpoint of the poor:

> Admittedly no destitute persons are to be understood among them, but rather a pious but economically weaker middle class that always stands in danger, either of falling victim to the allurements of a speedy but morally questionable economic rise (11:10–28), or else of allying itself to unscrupulous rich and aristocratic persons and of being exploited by these or morally contaminated (13:1–23; from the context doubtless also 12:8–18).

In addition, Haspecker notes that Ben Sira often employs sociological and moral terminology in tandem:

> Throughout these texts an antithesis occurs between poor and rich, small and mighty, good and evil, humble and proud, righteous and iniquitous (cf. especially 11:21–22; 13:17–20).

---

[24] On 12:1–6, see L. J. Prockter, "Alms and the Man: The Merits of Charity," *JNSL* 17 (1991): 69–80, esp. 75–77; on 12:8–12, see Schrader, "Unzuverlässige Freundschaft und verläßliche Feindschaft," in Reiterer, ed., *Freundschaft bei Ben Sira*, 19–59.

[25] On ch. 13 of Ben Sira, see Beentjes, "How Can a Jug Be Friends with a Kettle?" Because Beentjes rightly regards 13:14 G as a gloss, he (like the NAB) numbers as Sir 13:14–25 what I (following Ziegler and the NRSV) call 13:15–26. On 13:1–24, see also Baldauf, "Arme und Armut im Buch Ben Sira," 55–69.

[26] Sirach 13:24–14:19 is a twenty-three-line nonalphabetic acrostic; cf. Skehan and Di Lella, *Wisdom of Ben Sira*, 74. On 14:11–19, see Schrader, *Leiden und Gerechtigkeit*, 264–78.

[27] Haspecker, *Gottesfurcht bei Jesus Sirach*, 187; the following two quotations (my translation) come from pp. 187–88.

Sirach 13:15–23 shares certain characteristics with 10:19–11:6: the use of rhetorical questions (10:19, 29; 13:17–18), the antithesis between rich and poor (10:30; 13:19–23), and a sympathetic attitude toward the poor (10:23; 11:2, 4; 13:18–23). Sirach 13:15–23 also shares some features with 11:7–28, particularly the contrast between popular opinion and true judgment (11:11–13, 21; 13:22–23), the association of righteous and poor (11:17, 22; 13:17), and the antithesis between rich and poor (11:14, 21; 13:19–23).

b. Context of Sirach 13:15–23 within 11:29–13:23

Sirach 11:29–13:23 forms a poetic segment focused on the theme of social relationships. Since H^A leaves a space after 13:1 and begins a new indented line with 13:2,[28] some scholars assert that 13:1 concludes the material in chapter 12 and that a fresh section begins with 13:2.[29] However, several poetic factors indicate that it is 13:1 (not 13:2) that opens a new section. While 12:1–18 is a twenty-two-line nonalphabetic acrostic,[30] the unity of 13:1–23 is evident from an *inclusio* with the root נגע ("touch," "reach": 13:1a, 23b) and from the use of rhyme in its opening and closing verses (13:1ab and 13:23abcd). Ben Sira generally uses analogies from the natural world (such as "touching pitch" in 13:1a) to open rather than close pericopes.[31] Moreover, the word יָדוֹ ("his hand") in 13:1 forms a *mot crochet* with יָד ("hand") in 12:18, thereby linking 13:1–23 with 11:29–12:18.[32]

When 13:1 is recognized as opening a new poem, the segment 11:29–13:23 falls into two equal portions: 11:29–12:18 (28 bicola)[33] and

[28] Schechter and Taylor, *Wisdom of Ben Sira*, 7.

[29] So Smend (*Sirach, hebräisch und deutsch*, 15), Peters (*Der jüngst wiederaufgefundene hebräische Text*, 70; but see his revised opinion in *Das Buch Jesus Sirach*, 113), Baldauf ("Arme und Armut im Buch Ben Sira," 61–64), and Beentjes ("How Can a Jug be Friends with a Kettle?" 88).

[30] Skehan and Di Lella, *Wisdom of Ben Sira*, 74.

[31] There are many examples of analogies from nature at the start of the sage's poems: thus, Sir 3:25 opens 3:25–29; 3:30 begins 3:30–4:6; 5:9 opens 5:9–6:1; 9:10 begins 9:10–16; 13:15–19 opens 13:15–23; 22:19–20 begins 22:19–26.

[32] Among those who regard 13:1 as the opening verse of a new pericope are Segal (ספר בן־סירא השלם, 81), Peters (*Das Buch Jesus Sirach*, 113; a revision of his earlier opinion), Fuß ("Tradition und Komposition," 96), Haspecker (*Gottesfurcht bei Jesus Sirach*, 188), Prato (*Il problema della teodicea*, 375), and Skehan and Di Lella (*Wisdom of Ben Sira*, 252).

[33] The numeration follows G, omitting 12:6c (lacking in G^{BSA} and H^A) and 12:7 (lacking in H^A, a doublet of 12:4). H^A contains many corruptions and expansions, especially in 11:29–34; cf. Skehan and Di Lella, *Wisdom of Ben Sira*, 244.

13:1–23 (28 bicola).[34] The segment may be further divided into subunits, as indicated below.

A 11:29–34: Wariness in Offering Hospitality to Strangers (6 bicola)[35]
  B 12:1–6: Giving to the Good Person but Not to the Bad (7 bicola)
    C 12:8–9: In Prosperity Enemies Pretend to be Friends (2 bicola)
A' 12:10–12: Caution toward Enemies (6 bicola)
  B' 12:13–18: Mistreatment by the Arrogant (7 bicola)[36]

X 13:1–4: Friendship Impossible between Rich and Poor (5 bicola)
  Y 13:5–8: Mistreatment of the Poor by the Rich (6 bicola)
    Z 13:9–13: Caution before Princes (6 bicola)[37]
X' 13:15–20: Friendship Impossible between Rich and Poor (6 bicola)
  Y' 13:21–23: Mistreatment of the Poor by Society (5 bicola)

In 11:29–12:18 the aphoristic couplet on friendship (12:8–9) stands at the heart of the segment, being both preceded and followed by thirteen bicola (11:29–12:6; 12:10–18). Similarly, in 13:1–23 the admonition to maintain caution toward princes (13:9–13) stands at the center of a series of warnings about the impossibility of friendship between rich and poor, because of the mistreatment that the rich perpetrate (13:1–8 = 11 bicola; 13:15–23 = 11 bicola).

c. Relationship of 13:15–23 with 13:24–14:19

Sirach 13:24 begins a new pericope, concerned with the use and misuse of wealth.[38] Although a number of scholars regard 13:24 as a concluding verse (with v. 25 starting a new pericope),[39] several stylistic

[34] The numeration again follows G, but disregarding 13:14 (a gloss lacking in G^{BSA} and H^{A}). Note the *inclusio* between נוֹגֵעַ ("one who touches," 13:1a) and יַגִּיעוּ ("they make [his insight] reach," 13:23b).

[35] Note the *inclusio:* οἶκόν ("house," 11:29a); ἐνοίκισον ("lodge," 11:34a).

[36] Both 12:13–18 and 13:1–4 employ the word חוֹבֵר ("snake charmer," 12:13a; "one who associates," 13:1b) in the opening bicolon, while both 12:13–18 and 13:9–13 exhibit the word קָרֵב ("approaching": 12:13b; 13:9a) in the opening bicolon.

[37] Note the *inclusio* with הֱיֵה ("be") in 13:9a, 13a. Both 13:5–8 and 13:9–13 end with a warning introduced by הִשָּׁמֵר ("be on guard": 13:8a, 13a).

[38] Scholars who regard 13:24 as the opening verse of a new unit include Peters (*Das Buch Jesus Sirach,* 118) and Haspecker (*Gottesfurcht bei Jesus Sirach,* 188), as well as Skehan and Di Lella, who note the use of end-rhyme in the bicolon (*Wisdom of Ben Sira,* 255).

[39] Those regarding 13:25 as the opening verse of the subsequent pericope include Smend (*Sirach, erklärt,* 129); Segal (ספר בן־סירא השלם, 87); Fuß ("Tradition und

indications suggest rather that verse 24 opens the next pericope. Verse 24 says:

טוֹב הָעוֹשֶׁר אִם אֵין עָוֹן וְרַע הָעוֹנִי עַל פִּי זֵדוֹן

Riches are good if there is no iniquity,
but poverty is evil according to the speech of an arrogant person.

To indicate the opening of a new poem, the bicolon exhibits end-rhyme, following the fourfold rhyme in 13:23 that closed the previous pericope. Whereas 13:15–23 utilizes the word עָשִׁיר ("rich") six times as a key word (but not the noun עוֹשֶׁר, "riches"), the adjective is absent in 13:24–14:19, while the noun occurs twice (13:24a; 14:3).[40] Thus, whereas 13:15–23 is concerned with persons (the "rich"), 13:24–14:19 deals with material things ("riches"); while 13:15–23 concerns the disparity of treatment that the rich and the poor receive from society, 13:24–14:19 is about the use and misuse of riches.[41] In addition, whereas Sir 13:20 speaks of the reluctance of the rich to have dealings with the poor (possibly out of fear of having to share their wealth), 14:13a H^A offers the admonition that one should show generosity toward friends with one's possessions: בְּטֶרֶם תָּמוּת הֵיטֵב לְאוֹהֵב ("before you die be good to a friend").

8. Exegesis

a. Stanza 1: Creatures Associate with Their Own Kind (13:15–20)

Using analogies from the animal world, the first stanza teaches that both rich and poor associate with their own kind. The Priestly creation theology of Gen 1–11 underlies the sage's initial statement that "all flesh will love its own kind." Sirach 13:15 H^A parallels "all flesh" with "every human being." Although the anarthrous phrase כָּל בָּשָׂר ("all flesh") occurs frequently in the MT (12x in Gen 1–11 and 26x elsewhere), as well as in the Hebrew MSS of Ben Sira,[42] the arthrous phrase כָּל הַבָּשָׂר (lit., "all

Komposition," 100); Prato (*Il problema della teodicea*, 375); Baldauf ("Arme und Armut im Buch Ben Sira," 61–64); Beentjes ("How Can a Jug be Friends with a Kettle?" 90).

[40] In fact, the root עשר ("rich") in 13:23–24 serves as a *mot crochet* linking 13:1–23 with 13:24–14:19.

[41] Furthermore, the contrast between טוֹב ("good") and רַע ("evil"), which occurs nowhere in 13:1–23, appears repeatedly in 13:24–14:19 (13:24, 25; 14:5, 7).

[42] Twice in H^A (8:19; 13:16) and five times in H^B (39:19; 41:4; 44:18; 48:12; 50:17). The fragmentary form כל ב[שׂר] ("all f[lesh]") also occurs in 40:8 H^Bmg and 45:4 H^B.

the flesh") occurs only twice in the MT (Gen 7:15; Isa 40:6) and twice also in Ben Sira (13:15; 14:17). In Gen 7:15 the arthrous phrase denotes all the species of animals (of which a representative pair entered the ark), whereas in Isa 40:6 it refers primarily to all humanity (seen as mortal). Ben Sira's use of the arthrous term in 14:17 H^A depends on Deutero-Isaiah; the theme of mortality in 14:17 and the comparison to "a bud of a leaf" (פֶּרַח עָלֶה) in 14:18 reflect the thought of Isa 40:6, where כָּל־הַבָּשָׂר ("all flesh") is called חָצִיר ("grass"). By contrast, in Sir 13:15 H^A the phrase reflects the usage in Gen 7:15, where it refers to all the kinds of animals. The links to Gen 7:14–16 are evident; while Sir 13:15a employs כָּל הַבָּשָׂר ("all flesh") and מִין ("kind"), Gen 7:14 uses מִין four times, Gen 7:15 has כָּל־הַבָּשָׂר, and Gen 7:16 utilizes the anarthrous equivalent כָּל־בָּשָׂר.[43]

The occurrence of מִין ("kind") in Sir 13:15a reinforces the sage's allusion to Gen 7:13–16, which tells of the entry of the animals into Noah's ark:

> On that same day Noah, and Shem and Ham and Japheth, Noah's sons, and Noah's wife, and his sons' three wives with them, came into the ark, they and every living thing according to its kind [לְמִינָהּ] and every beast according to its kind [לְמִינָהּ] and every creeping thing that creeps on the earth according to its kind [לְמִינֵהוּ] and every bird according to its kind [לְמִינֵהוּ], every fowl, every winged thing. And they came to Noah at the ark, two by two from every creature [מִכָּל־הַבָּשָׂר] in which there was the breath of life. And those that came, male and female from every creature [מִכָּל־בָּשָׂר], came as God had commanded him.[44]

The text of Gen 7:13–16 itself refers back to Gen 1:24:

> And God said, "Let the earth bring forth living beings according to their kinds, beasts and creeping things and living things of the earth according to their kinds," and it was so.

The close linguistic parallel between Sir 13:15a and Gen 7:14–16 (cf. Gen 1:24) suggests that in the former מִין refers to a "kind" or "species" of

[43] Ben Sira's allusion here to the Priestly section of the Genesis flood narrative supports Burton's finding: "The formative influence of the primeval history in Genesis 1–11 upon Sirach's doctrine of creation cannot be outweighed by any other OT document" ("Sirach and the Judaic Doctrine of Creation," 8).

[44] Burton (ibid., 22) notes that the sage's characteristic teaching on paired opposites (33:15 H^E; cf. 42:24 G) also derives from the Genesis flood story. The expression שְׁנַיִם שְׁנַיִם ("two by two," "in pairs") in Sir 33:15 H^E echoes the same phrase in Gen 7:9, 15.

creature and that כָּל הַבָּשָׂר denotes every creature (such as beast or reptile or bird, as in Gen 7:14).[45] An analogous use of מִין ("kind") occurs in the reference to sea creatures in Sir 43:25 H^B, where the sage describes מִין כָּל חַי ("every living thing's own kind") as marvels of God's making.[46]

In Ben Sira's book the context determines whether the phrase "all flesh" refers to every creature or to all humanity (or to both). In certain other passages besides 13:15–16, the term כָּל בָּשָׂר (= πᾶσα σάρξ = "all flesh") can denote every creature. In Sir 17:4, for example, the sage declares that God placed the fear of human beings ἐπὶ πάσης σαρκὸς ("upon all flesh" = "upon every creature"), an allusion to Gen 9:2. In Sir 17:4 and perhaps in 13:15–16, "all flesh" refers to animals as distinct from human beings.[47] In other of the sage's poems, however, "all flesh" has the inclusive sense of "every creature, whether human or animal" (as in Num 18:15). For instance, in Sir 40:8 the sage speaks of various kinds of trouble that remain μετὰ πάσης σαρκὸς ἀπὸ ἀνθρώπου ἕως κτήνους ("with all flesh, from human being to beast"). Similarly, in a further reference to the story of the Genesis flood, Sir 44:18 H^B declares of Noah: "With an eternal sign a covenant was made with him not to destroy all flesh" (כָּל בָּשָׂר), an allusion to God's promise in Gen 9:15.[48]

In observing that human beings love their own kind, Sir 13:15 may contain an echo of Lev 19:18–19. In particular, the verb יֶאֱהַב ("will love," Sir 13:15a) may be an allusion to the prescription in Lev 19:18: וְאָהַבְתָּ לְרֵעֲךָ כָּמוֹךָ ("and you shall love your neighbor [or 'companion'] as yourself"). Furthermore, in prohibiting mixtures Lev 19:19 stipulates that animals must breed only according to their kind: בְּהֶמְתְּךָ לֹא־תַרְבִּיעַ כִּלְאַיִם ("You shall not let your beasts lie with a different species").[49] Ben Sira

---

[45] A. Caquot observes that the MT reserves the term מִין ("kind") for plants (Gen 1:11, 12 [bis]) and animals (Gen 1:21 [bis], 24 [bis], 25 [3x]; 6:20 [3x]; 7:14 [4x]; 9x Leviticus; 4x Deuteronomy; 1x Ezekiel); hence, the term does not refer to "humankind, the human species" ("Le Siracide a-t-il parlé d'une 'espèce' humaine?" *RHPR* 62 [1982]: 225–30, esp. 225–26).

[46] Prato (*Il problema della teodicea,* 196) notes that the phrase alludes to an expression in Gen 7:14, כָּל־הַחַיָּה לְמִינָהּ ("every living thing according to its kind"). In fact, Sir 43:25b is an example of the "inverted quotation" (of Gen 7:14), just as Sir 46:19 quotes 1 Sam 12:3 in reverse order; cf. P. C. Beentjes, "Inverted Quotations in the Bible: A Neglected Stylistic Pattern," *Bib* 63 (1982): 506–23. On מִין ("kind"), see P. Beauchamp, *Création et séparation* (Paris: Aubier Montaigne, 1969), 240–47.

[47] Cf. Caquot, "Le Siracide," 227.

[48] Elsewhere, to be sure, the phrase "all flesh" can denote "all humanity" or "every person," as in Sir 18:13 G; 45:4 H^B; 50:17 H^B.

[49] Beauchamp (*Création et séparation,* 245 n. 24) observes the implicit connection between Lev 19:19 and Gen 1.

connects these laws (juxtaposed in Lev 19) by recognizing that just as one should not mix kinds of animals, so too one should befriend only one's own kind of human being.[50]

The phrase כָּל אָדָם ("every human being," Sir 13:15b)[51] here serves to balance כָּל הַבָּשָׂר ("all flesh," v. 15a). Indeed, Sir 13:15 exhibits staircase parallelism: if every animal associates with its own kind, how much more should human beings do so. Here Ben Sira modifies a traditional contrasting word-pair (Ps 36:7; Qoh 3:19, 21), namely אָדָם ("humanity") and בְּהֵמָה ("beasts"). In place of בְּהֵמָה, which usually refers to domesticated livestock such as cattle, he employs בָּשָׂר ("flesh"), so as to echo the Priestly tradition in the primeval history of Genesis (cf. Gen 7:15).[52]

In speaking of every human being's love for "one resembling him" (אֶת הַדּוֹמֶה לוֹ), Sir 13:15b contains a further echo of the Priestly primeval history. Whereas Gen 1:26 recounts God's creative words, נַעֲשֶׂה אָדָם בְּצַלְמֵנוּ כִּדְמוּתֵנוּ ("let us make humanity in our own image, according to our likeness"), Sir 13:15b speaks of a "human being" (אָדָם) "resembling" (דּוֹמֶה) another human being. A rather more pessimistic view of humanity appears in Ps 144:4: אָדָם לַהֶבֶל דָּמָה ("humanity resembles a mere breath"), a view echoed in Sir 41:11a.

In its teaching that "every creature will love its own kind, and every human being one resembling him," Sir 13:15 mirrors a commonplace of Greek thought. An ancient example occurs in Homer's *Odyssey* (17.217–218), where Melantheus mocks Odysseus (who is disguised as a swineherd): "Lo, now, in very truth the vile leads the vile. As ever, the god is bringing like and like together" (ὡς αἰεὶ τὸν ὁμοῖον ἄγει θεὸς ὡς τὸν ὁμοῖον).[53] Plato quotes comparable aphorisms in the *Symposium* and in *Gorgias*. Thus, in *Symp.* 195b Agathon declares that similar persons have a tendency to come together: "Like and like together strike" (ὡς ὅμοιον ὁμοίῳ ἀεὶ πελάζει; lit., "one always approaches together to a similar person"). Socrates expresses the same thought more amply when he comments in *Gorg.* 510b: "The closest possible friendship between man

[50] Cf. P. Beauchamp, "מִין *mîn*," *TDOT* 8:288–91, esp. 290; Söding, "Nächstenliebe bei Jesus Sirach," 245.

[51] The phrase is also present in Sir 16:14 H[A]; 31:31 H[F]; 33:30 H[E]; 46:19 H[B]. In the MT כָּל־הָאָדָם ("all humanity, every human being") occurs in Qoh 3:13; 5:18; 7:2; 12:13.

[52] Note that Job 34:15 also employs אָדָם ("humanity") in parallel with כָּל־בָּשָׂר ("every creature").

[53] A. T. Murray, trans., *Homer: The Odyssey* (LCL; 2 vols.; New York: Putnam, 1919), 2:167; Middendorp notes this parallel (*Die Stellung Jesu ben Siras*, 18). For the following two quotations of Plato, see Lamb, trans., *Plato*, 153 and 477.

and man is that mentioned by the sages of old time as 'like to like'" (ὁ ὅμοιος τῷ ὁμοίῳ).

Some of the clearest formulations of this Greek proverbial tradition occur in the works of Aristotle, especially in books 8–9 of *Nicomachean Ethics,* the parts that treat friendship. Discussing the nature of friendship in *Eth. nic.* 8.1.6 (§1155a), the philosopher says:

> Some define it as a matter of similarity; they say that we love those who are like ourselves [τοὺς ὁμοίους φίλους]: whence the proverbs "Like finds his like [τὸν ὅμοιόν ... ὡς τὸν ὅμοιον]," "Birds of a feather flock together," and so on.[54]

Later in the same paragraph (8.1.6 §1155b) the philosopher quotes the view of Empedocles: "Like seeks after like" (τὸ ... ὅμοιον τοῦ ὁμοίου ἐφίεσθαι), while in 9.3.3 (§1165b) Aristotle asserts that "like is the friend of like" (τὸ ὅμοιον τῷ ὁμοίῳ φίλον).

Just as Ben Sira states that "all flesh will love its own kind, and every human being one resembling him" (Sir 13:15), so Aristotle (*Eth. nic.* 8.1.3 §1155a) compares animal bonding and human friendship:

> The affection of parent for offspring and of offspring for parent seems to be a natural instinct, not only in man but also in birds and in most animals; as also is friendship between members of the same species; and this is especially strong in the human race.[55]

A further discussion of similarity in friendship, also using animal references, occurs in Aristotle's *'Art' of Rhetoric,* composed about a century and a half before Ben Sira's book. The philosopher states in *Rhet.* 1.11.25 (§1371b):

> All things akin and like are for the most part pleasant to each other, as man to man, horse to horse, youth to youth. This is the origin of the proverbs: the old have charms for the old, the young for the young; like to like [ὡς αἰεὶ τὸν ὁμοῖον]; beast knows beast; birds of a feather flock together; and all similar sayings.[56]

---

[54] Rackham, trans., *Nicomachean Ethics,* 453; the latter proverb is lit. "jackdaw to jackdaw" (cf. Sir 27:9). The following two quotations come from pp. 455, 531.

[55] Ibid., 451–53. Whereas Aristotle holds that a "natural affinity and friendship exist between man and man universally" (ibid., 453), Ben Sira in practice divides human beings into two broad groups, the righteous poor and the arrogant rich, and affirms that each group should stick to its own kind.

[56] J. H. Freese, trans., *Aristotle: The 'Art' of Rhetoric* (LCL; New York: Putnam, 1926), 127. Commenting on the pentateuchal prohibition of mixed crops (Lev

It is noteworthy that both Aristotle and Ben Sira employ animal analogies to illustrate their thoughts on human friendship.[57]

Whereas Ben Sira applies his general statements (13:15–16) to the relations between rich and poor (13:17–19), other wisdom writings apply the teaching on "like to like" to the case of the wise and the foolish. Thus, Prov 13:20 (Qere) declares: "One who walks with wise persons will become wise, but one who befriends fools will suffer harm" (cf. Sir 13:1). Similarly, Ankhsheshonq 13.6 says: "The friend of a fool is a fool; the friend of a wise man is a wise man."[58]

Sirach 13:16 largely restates the thought of 13:15 for emphasis, while the use of the root חבר ("associate") in 13:16b paves the way for its use in 13:17a. By means of the *puʿal* form יְחוּבַּר ("will be associated"), Ben Sira may be echoing Qoh 9:4: "Whoever is associated [Qere, יְחֻבַּר] with all the living has hope, for it is better for a living dog [כֶּלֶב] than a dead lion [אַרְיֵה]."[59] In subsequent verses Ben Sira will contrast the "dog" (כֶּלֶב, 13:18a) as a victim (of hyenas) with the "lion" (אֲרִי, 13:19a) as a predator (attacking wild asses).

Ben Sira employs the root חבר ("associate") elsewhere in 11:29–13:23 H^A. In 12:13–14 the sage plays on two meanings of חוֹבֵר: "Who will pity[60] a snake-charmer [חוֹבֵר] who is bitten, or anyone approaching a predatory animal? So is one who associates [חוֹבֵר] with an arrogant person."[61] Sirach 13:1 declares: "One who touches pitch—his hand will stick, and one who associates [חוֹבֵר] with a scoffer will learn his way." In both 12:14 and 13:1 the sage urges his students to avoid contact with those who despise God's law (the arrogant and the scoffers).

Sirach 13:2 employs the *hitpaʿel* of חבר to apply the thought of 13:1 to the relations between rich and poor. Thus, 13:2ab (cf. 13:18b) asks: "Why will you lift what is too heavy for you, and why will you associate yourself [תִּתְחַבֵּר] with someone richer than you?" Sirach 13:2cd continues:

19:19; Deut 22:9) in *Ant.* 4.8.20 §228, Josephus states: "Nature delighteth not in the conjunction of things dissimilar" (Thackeray et al., *Josephus*, 4:587).

[57] A parallel Talmudic saying (*b. B. Qam.* 92b), comparing birds and human friends, freely combines Sir 27:9a and 13:15b: כָּל עוֹף לְמִינוֹ יִשְׁכּוֹן וּבֶן אָדָם לַדּוֹמֶה לוֹ ("Every bird will dwell with its own kind, and a human being with one resembling him"). Cf. Segal, ספר בן־סירא השלם, 85.

[58] *AEL* 3:169; cf. Sir 9:14–16.

[59] We shall also see below that Sir 13:22–23 may echo Qoh 9:13–16.

[60] Reading מִי יָחוֹן with G and S, where the first hand of H^A reads מַה יּוּחַן ("how will be pitied?").

[61] Reading אִישׁ זָדוֹן with G and S. The reference to "a predatory animal" in 12:13b anticipates the mention of wolf, hyena, and lion in 13:17–19.

"How can an earthen pot associate itself [יִתְחַבֵּר] with a caldron, against which it knocks and is broken?"[62] This image of the caldron smashing the pot, like the descriptions of the activity of the predatory animals in 13:17–19, depicts how the rich crush the poor, and hence expresses the impossibility of friendship between rich and poor.[63]

Sirach 13:17–19 makes plain the meaning of מִינוֹ ("his own kind") in 13:16b. Verse 17b offers a contrast between the "righteous person" (צַדִּיק) and the "wicked person" (רָשָׁע), while verses 18b and 19b contrast the "impoverished person" (v. 18b: רָשׁ) or "paupers" (v. 19b: דַּלִּים) with the "rich person" (vv. 18b, 19b: עָשִׁיר). Hence, in verse 16b the sage refers to two "kinds" of person, the righteous pauper and the wicked rich person.[64]

Employing antitheses common in the book of Proverbs, Ben Sira separates human beings into two opposing categories: "righteous"//"wicked" (13:17b); "poor"//"rich" (13:18b, 19b); "good"//"evil" (12:2–5). In 33:14 he also uses antitheses to express his doctrine of opposites.[65]

Although Ben Sira alludes to the Genesis creation story in his use of מִין ("kind," 13:15–16), he makes subtle changes to the theology of the Priestly tradition. Whereas Gen 1 employs מִין ("kind") seven times of animals (Gen 1:21–25) and three times of plants (Gen 1:11–12), it never applies the term to human beings; there is thus an implied distinction between the multiplicity of animal species and the unity of humankind.[66] In Sir 13:15–16, however, the emphasis is on separating the human race into two different kinds, as specified in 13:17 (righteous and wicked) and 13:18–19 (poor and rich). While Gen 1 stresses the difference between human beings and animals, Sir 13:17–19 implies a similarity by using animal imagery to refer to types of human beings.

---

[62] I take Sir 13:2e H^{A} as a gloss, since it is absent in G.

[63] When Ben Sira suggests the impossibility of friendship between rich and poor, he sympathizes with the viewpoint of the victimized weaker party (13:2, 18–20). Aristotle also observes that such unequal friendship does not happen but implies that the reason is the weaker party's sense of inferiority (*Eth. nic.* 8.7.4 §1158b).

[64] Compare Caquot's interpretation of Sir 13:16b: "It is the just who seek the just, and the wicked who seek the wicked" ("Le Siracide," 230; translation mine). According to Xenophon (*Mem.* 2.6.20), "Neither can rogues ever join in friendship with honest men, for how can wrongdoers become friendly with those who hate their conduct?"; see Marchant, trans., *Xenophon*, 137.

[65] On Ben Sira's doctrine of opposites, see Prato, *Il problema della teodicea*, 49–55; Collins, *Jewish Wisdom in the Hellenistic Age*, 84–85.

[66] Cf. Beauchamp, "מִין *mîn*," 8:290.

After two bicola (13:15–16) consisting of general statements (based on observation of the animal world) that "like belongs with like," Sir 13:17a begins a series of three specific animal comparisons (vv. 17–19): a lamb is not attracted to a wolf, nor a dog to a hyena, nor a wild ass to a lion.

The imagery in 13:17a utilizes the proverbial contrast between the lamb (as prey) and the wolf (as predator). This antithesis is a widespread motif in ancient Near Eastern literature. For instance, the second-millennium B.C.E. Sumerian myth of Enki and Ninsikila (Ninhursaga) depicts the state of paradisal harmony by referring to the animal world: "The lion slew not, the wolf was not carrying off lambs."[67] Isaiah 11:6a employs similar imagery in prophesying a return to paradisal bliss: "And the wolf shall dwell with the lamb" (וְגָר זְאֵב עִם־כֶּבֶשׂ; cf. Isa 65:25a).

Various ancient proverbs note that such a state of paradisal harmony no longer exists, but rather that the wolf is the enemy of the lamb. Homer's *Iliad,* for instance, speaks of the impossibility of friendship between wolves and lambs.[68] Closer to Sir 13:17a is Trygaeus's question in Aristophanes' play *The Peace* (1076): καὶ πῶς, ὦ κατάρατε, λύκος ποτ' ἂν οἶν ὑμεναιοῖ; ("How, you scoundrel accurst, can the wolf and the lamb be united?").

Similarly, the opposition between wolf and sheep underlies several of Aesop's fables. For instance, Fable 217 (according to E. Chambry's numbering) concerns "wolves [λύκοι] wishing to surprise a flock of sheep [προβάτων]"; after persuading the sheep to part from their sheep-dogs, the wolves devoured the flock.[69] Similarly, Fable 218 begins: "Wolves

[67] T. Jacobsen, *The Harps That Once...: Sumerian Poetry in Translation* (New Haven, Conn.: Yale University Press, 1987), 186. Similarly, another second-millennium B.C.E. Sumerian myth, Enmerkar and the Lord of Aratta, portrays a primeval age without predators: "In those days..., there being no hyenas, there being no lions, there being no wild dogs or wolves..., mankind had no opponents" (ibid., 289). Sirach 13:17–19 also lists wolf, hyena, and lion as predators.

[68] Achilles says to Hector (*Il.* 22.261–265): "Hector, talk not to me, thou madman, of covenants. As between lions [λέουσι] and men [ἀνδράσιν] there are no oaths of faith, nor do wolves [λύκοι] and lambs [ἄρνες] have hearts of concord but are evil-minded continually one against the other, even so it is not possible for thee and me to be friends [φιλήμεναι]"; translation from A. T. Murray, *Homer: The Iliad* (LCL; 2 vols.; New York: Putnam, 1924–1925), 2:475. Middendorp (*Die Stellung Jesu ben Siras,* 18) notes this parallel; cf. also Homer, *Il.* 16.352. The following quotation comes from B. B. Rogers, trans., *Aristophanes* (LCL; 3 vols.; New York: Putnam, 1924), 2:99.

[69] E. Chambry, *Esope: Fables* (Paris: Les Belles Lettres, 1927), 96; the translations (here and below) are mine. The ensuing quotations come from p. 97 (Fable 218) and p. 98 (Fable 221).

[λύκοι] sent ambassadors to the sheep [προβάτοις] to make a perpetual peace [εἰρήνην] with them"; only the warning of a wise old ram prevented the foolish sheep from accepting this alleged offer of peace. Most similar, perhaps, is Fable 221, which begins: "A wolf [λύκος], having seen a lamb [ἄρνα] drinking from a certain river, wished with a certain fine-sounding excuse to devour it"; when these pretexts failed, the wolf said to the lamb: "If you are experienced in giving excuses, I will nonetheless devour you." The moral of the fable follows: "In the face of those whose intention is to do wrong, no just defense prevails." Thus, in referring to the opposition between wolf and lamb, both Aesop and Ben Sira highlight the defenselessness of the "lambs."[70]

Animal imagery also features prominently in *1 En.* 85–90 (the Animal Apocalypse), which was probably written within a generation after Ben Sira.[71] In its retelling of early biblical history *1 En.* 89 compares the Israelite exodus from Egypt to the escape of sheep from wolves.[72]

The prophetic dimension of the metaphors in Sir 13:17a becomes evident in light of Ezekiel's and Zephaniah's use of animal imagery in their social criticism. Thus, Ezek 22:27 depicts Judah's ruling class as wolves: "Its officials in its midst are like wolves [זְאֵבִים] tearing the prey, to shed blood, to destroy lives, for the sake of gaining dishonest gain." Speaking of Jerusalem, Zeph 3:3 employs a similar image: "Its judges are wolves of the evening" (זְאֵבֵי עֶרֶב).[73] The echoes of Ezek 22:27 and Zeph 3:3 in Sir

[70] Cf. Kieweler, *Ben Sira zwischen Judentum und Hellenismus*, 123–24. The New Testament, too, employs the contrast between wolves and sheep: Matt 7:15; 10:16; Luke 10:3; John 10:12; Acts 20:29. According to 1 Sam 17:34–35, David used to rescue defenseless lambs from a marauding lion or bear.

[71] According to P. A. Tiller, the Animal Apocalypse dates from between 165 and 160 B.C.E. (*A Commentary on the Animal Apocalypse of 1 Enoch* [SBLEJL 4; Atlanta: Scholars Press, 1993], 78–79).

[72] A fragmentary Qumran text of Aramaic Enoch (4Q206 4 ii 17–21; 4 iii 14–15) recounts the exodus events: "[The wolves] began to harass the flock.... [The flock groaned and shrieked horribly] until the Lo[rd of the flock] came down.... [All the] wolves who went on chasing that flock [died sinking and drowning, and] the water covered them" (García Martínez, *Dead Sea Scrolls Translated*, 257); the lacunae have been completed from Ethiopic Enoch. If the symbolism of *1 En.* 89 is already operative in Sir 13:17a, Ben Sira's implied message may be that Israel (the lamb) should not be allied to Ptolemaic Egypt (the wolf). Note that Hos 4:16 compares Israel ironically to a lamb, while Jer 5:6 speaks of Judah's enemies as a wolf.

[73] On the textual crux (עֶרֶב), see A. Berlin, *Zephaniah* (AB 25A; New York: Doubleday, 1994), 128. We shall further see that אֲרִי ("lion," Ezek 22:25; Zeph 3:3) also occurs in Sir 13:19a.

13:17a suggest that the sage may be engaged in a prophetic critique of the mistreatment of the poor by the rich. This interpretation matches his mention of how the rich disregard the poor (Sir 13:21–23), as well as his scathing attack on those who defraud the needy (Sir 34:21–27).[74]

Thus, the image of the wolf in Sir 13:17a operates on several levels. First, the antithesis between the predatory wolf and the preyed-upon lamb is a common feature of proverbial wisdom, found in Mesopotamian, Israelite, and Greek texts. Second, on the political level, in the Enoch tradition the wolf represents Egypt and the lamb Israel. Third, in the prophetic tradition and closest to Ben Sira's own thought, the wolf symbolizes the rich person who preys on the poor, represented by the lamb.

In Sir 13:17a, then, Ben Sira employs the metaphor of the "lamb" (כֶּבֶשׂ) for the righteous pauper who is the victim of the wicked rich person. In the MT the term כֶּבֶשׂ mostly denotes a sacrificial lamb.[75] Indeed, the Priestly laws of sacrifice frequently use phrases such as "an unblemished lamb, a year old" (כֶּבֶשׂ תָּמִים בֶּן־שְׁנָתוֹ; Lev 23:12). Since a righteous person (צַדִּיק, Sir 13:17b) could also be called תָּמִים, meaning morally "unblemished" or "blameless,"[76] the metaphor of the lamb alludes to the innocence of the righteous pauper.

The concept of sacrifice associated with the lamb also suggests the idea of the suffering (and even slaughter) of the righteous paupers at the hands of the rich and powerful. In Jeremiah's "Confessions" the prophet depicts his suffering in sacrificial language (even though he was not actually killed): "And I like a gentle lamb [כֶּבֶשׂ] was led for slaughter, and I did not know that against me they had devised plans: 'Let us destroy the tree with its fruit'" (Jer 11:19).[77] Thus, the term "lamb" may hint at the mistreatment (and even execution) of innocent members of the population at the hands of the Tobiads.[78]

---

[74] Cf. Marböck, "Macht und Mächtige im Buch Jesus Sirach," 188–91; Corley, "Social Responsibility in Proverbs and Ben Sira," 10.

[75] Cf. C. Dohmen, "כֶּבֶשׂ κτλ," *TDOT* 7:43–52, esp. 7:48.

[76] For instance, Gen 6:9 says of Noah: "He was a righteous [צַדִּיק] man, blameless [תָּמִים] in his generation." Likewise, Job laments that as a "blameless righteous person" (צַדִּיק תָּמִים), he must suffer mockery from his supposed friends (Job 12:4).

[77] Isaiah 53:7 applies a comparable image to the suffering Servant of Yahweh: "Like a sheep [שֶׂה] that was led to the slaughter, and like a ewe that was dumb before its shearers, he did not open his mouth." Moreover, the pauper's ewe lamb in Nathan's parable falls victim to the power of the rich man (2 Sam 12:1–4).

[78] Josephus records examples of the cruelty of Joseph son of Tobias in the late third century B.C.E.; for example, he executed civil leaders in Ashkelon and Scythopolis for the nonpayment of taxes (*Ant.* 12.4.5 §§181–183).

A further political resonance for the term "lamb" is present in Sir 13:17. Like other ancient Near Eastern and Mediterranean literature, the MT often calls members of Israel's ruling class "shepherds"[79] and regards their task as caring for the people, who are often depicted under the image of "sheep."[80] Prophets such as Jeremiah and Ezekiel criticize Judah's leaders for failing to look after the flock entrusted to them (cf. Jer 23:1–4; Ezek 34:2–10). Thus, the political nuance of כֶּבֶשׂ ("lamb"), deriving from the prophetic critique of Israel's government, may also underlie Sir 13:17a. Whereas Jerusalem's ruling class should care for the righteous poor, the supposed shepherds have turned into wild beasts, crushing the poor like wolves devouring the flock. In view of this situation, Ben Sira may perhaps be warning his students of the danger of associating with the Tobiads and their circle.

In contrasting the "righteous person" (צַדִּיק) and the "wicked person" (רָשָׁע), Sir 13:17b utilizes a common antithesis of Israel's sapiential tradition (cf. Prov 10:16, 28; 11:8, 10, 31; Qoh 7:15; 8:14; 9:2). Thus, Prov 29:7 asserts: "The righteous person [צַדִּיק] knows judgment for paupers [דַּלִּים]; a wicked person [רָשָׁע] will not understand knowledge." Similarly, in 12:2–3 H^A Ben Sira contrasts the giving of good treatment to the "righteous person" (צַדִּיק) with the avoidance of consoling the "wicked person" (רָשָׁע). Sometime in the second century B.C.E., the biblical antithesis between the righteous and the wicked (present in Ben Sira) became sharpened into the Qumran community's dualism; for instance, 1QS 3.20–21 contrasts the "sons of justice" (בְּנֵי צֶדֶק) with the "sons of deceit (בְּנֵי עָוֶל)."[81]

The word שָׁלוֹם ("peace," Sir 13:18ab) is closely connected with friendship. In its political sense שָׁלוֹם has in view an alliance that may be described in the language of friendship.[82] In its social sense the word

[79] For Israel see, e.g., 2 Sam 7:7; Jer 23:1–4; Ezek 34:2–10; Mic 5:4; Zech 11:16–17; 1 Chr 17:6. In Homer the ruler is named ποιμὴν λαῶν ("shepherd of subjects," *Il.* 2.243), while Plato calls the rulers ποιμένες πόλεως ("shepherds of the city," *Resp.* 4.15 §440d).

[80] The MT frequently uses צֹאן ("sheep," "flock") for Israel; see, e.g., 2 Sam 24:17; Jer 23:1–3; Ezek 34:2–6; Zech 11:17; Ps 74:1; 1 Chr 21:17. Jeremiah 50:17 calls Israel a "hunted sheep" (שֶׂה פְזוּרָה).

[81] García Martínez, *Dead Sea Scrolls Translated*, 6.

[82] Thus, 1 Kgs 5:15 employs friendship language in speaking of the alliance between David and King Hiram of Tyre: "Hiram was always a friend [אֹהֵב] to David." This alliance continued in the covenant of "peace" (שָׁלֹם) between Solomon and Hiram (1 Kgs 5:26). The phrase בְּרִית שָׁלוֹם ("covenant of peace") occurs in Num 25:12; Isa 54:10; Ezek 34:25; 37:26.

refers to peace between members of society; thus, Sir 6:6 H^A employs a phrase from Jer 38:22 and Obad 7, אַנְשֵׁי שְׁלוֹמְךָ ("those at peace with you"), as a periphrasis for "your friends." Presupposing the human tendency to mistreat the poor, Ben Sira asks: "How can a rich person have peace [שָׁלוֹם] toward an impoverished person [רָשׁ]?" (13:18b). By contrast, Sir 4:8 H^A insists that one should be attentive to the poor: "Turn your ear to the poor person [עָנִי], and return to him a greeting [שָׁלוֹם, lit. peace) with humility [עֲנָוָה]."

The saying in 13:18a reflects the hostility shown by the predatory hyena (צָבוּעַ) toward the less ferocious dog (כֶּלֶב). In the MT the noun צָבוּעַ ("hyena") occurs only in place names, such as גֵּי הַצְּבֹעִים ("Valley of the Hyenas," 1 Sam 13:18). Hyenas are mentioned in ancient Greek literature. In his *History of Animals* (7.5 [= 8.5] §594b), for instance, Aristotle explains that the hyena catches dogs by making a retching noise: "It hunts dogs by vomiting like men."[83]

In contrast to the hyena, Ben Sira cites the dog (כֶּלֶב) to symbolize someone of low status (as in 1 Sam 17:43; Prov 26:11; cf. Job 30:1; Qoh 9:4). In Israel, as elsewhere in the ancient Near East, the term "dog" frequently served as a term of self-abasement; in 2 Kgs 8:13, for instance, the future Syrian king says to Elisha: "What is your servant, the dog [מָה עַבְדְּךָ הַכֶּלֶב], that he will do this great thing?"[84] In Ben Sira's day also, the term would fittingly describe the humble status of the poor, who lived like "servants."

In Sir 13:18a the sage asserts that just as hyenas devour dogs, so the rich destroy the poor. With prophetic verve he subverts the traditional formula for humility: given society's view of the poor as humble "dogs," Ben Sira declares that the rich are no better than "hyenas."

With the use in 13:18b of the word-pair עָשִׁיר ("rich") and רָשׁ ("impoverished"; cf. דַּל, "poor," in vv. 19, 21–23), Ben Sira reaches the heart of his message, which he will elaborate in 13:19–23. His basic point

---

[83] A. L. Peck and D. M. Balme, trans., *Aristotle: History of Animals* (LCL; 3 vols.; Cambridge, Mass.: Harvard University Press, 1965–1991), 3:113. Similarly, in his *Cynegetica* (3.265) the later author Oppian (ca. 210 C.E.) describes the hyena as "the foe of dogs and mighty hounds" (cf. A. W. Mair, trans., *Oppian, Colluthus, Tryphiodorus* [LCL; New York: Putnam, 1928], 137). For two of Aesop's fables concerning hyenas, see Chambry, *Esope*, 147–48.

[84] Similar expressions appear in the Lachish letters (2.4; 5.4; 6.3); for instance, 2.4 asks: "Who is thy servant (but) a dog that my lord hath remembered his servant?" (*ANET* 322). The phrase "dead dog" also occurs as a term of self-abasement in 1 Sam 24:15; 2 Sam 9:8; 16:9. See further D. W. Thomas, "*Kelebh*, 'Dog': Its Origins and Some Usages of It in the Old Testament," *VT* 10 (1960): 410–27, esp. 414.

is that the poor are mistreated by the wealthy (vv. 18–20) and ignored by society (vv. 21–23).[85]

Sirach 13:15–20 may suggest a critique of the misuse of power by the Hellenistic overlords and Tobiad ruling class of the sage's time. After noting the rise of government officials, tax-collectors, and merchants in Jerusalem around 200 B.C.E., V. Tcherikover states: "No wonder class enmity between rich and poor became so acute in Jerusalem at the beginning of the Seleucid rule."[86] Similarly, Hengel cites Sir 13:15, 17–20 as an illustration of the "unbridgable opposition between poor and rich" in Ben Sira's age.[87]

Aware of the danger of pride arising from an attachment to wealth (e.g., 31:5), Ben Sira observes that "gold has made many reckless, and wealth can make the heart of princes go astray" (8:2 H^A; cf. 11:10). On the basis of such experience, therefore, he regards friendship between rich and poor as impossible.

Scholars have detected a prophetic tone to many of Ben Sira's utterances regarding the wealthy; indeed, Hengel describes the sage's outlook thus:

> He can value riches honestly gained.... Much stronger, however, is his warning against the dangers of riches and his admonition to a merciful social attitude which corresponds with the will of God.[88]

---

[85] On the poor in Ben Sira, see Baldauf, "Arme und Armut im Buch Ben Sira" (she provides word studies of the Hebrew and Greek terms for "poor," as well as exegesis of 4:1–10; 11:10–28; 13:1–24); Morla Asensio, "Poverty and Wealth." On wealth and poverty in biblical wisdom literature, see R. N. Whybray, *Wealth and Poverty in the Book of Proverbs* (JSOTSup 99; Sheffield: JSOT Press, 1990); J. D. Pleins, "Poverty in the Social World of the Wise," *JSOT* 37 (1987): 61–78; A. George, "Pauvre: Dans l'Ancien Testament," *DBSup* 7: 387–95.

[86] V. Tcherikover, "Social Conditions," in *The Hellenistic Age* (ed. A. Schalit; WHJP 6; New Brunswick, N.J.: Rutgers University Press, 1972), 87–114; citation from pp. 112–13. Tcherikover goes on to quote Sir 13:15–16, 18–19 as demonstrating class hostility between rich and poor. On the heavy taxation imposed on Palestine by the Ptolemies (and retained in mitigated form by the Seleucids after 200 B.C.E.), see Hengel, *Judaism and Hellenism,* 1:18–29.

[87] Hengel, *Judaism and Hellenism,* 1:137. Hengel comments: "Ben Sira gives an impressive description of the power of the rich aristocracy, which makes unscrupulous use of it" (1:136–37). Commenting elsewhere on the sage's attack on arrogance in 10:6–18, Hengel states: "One might feel that the Tobiads, who represented the most powerful group in Jerusalem after the high-priestly family of the Oniads, or the Ptolemaic or Seleucid rulers, were particular embodiments of this 'arrogance'" (1:151).

[88] Ibid., 1:136. On Sir 34:24–27 Hengel states that "in his polemic against the 'sacrifices of the lawless' his accusations have an almost prophetic ring" (1:137); cf. Skehan and Di Lella, *Wisdom of Ben Sira,* 87–88.

By juxtaposing 13:18 with 13:17, Ben Sira suggests a connection between his two antitheses of "wicked"//"righteous" and "rich"//"poor"; indeed, he implies a large overlap between the rich and the wicked, as also between the poor and the righteous.[89] The sage here takes over an idea from the psalms of lament; for instance, in Ps 140:13–14 the "righteous" and the "upright" parallel the "poor person" and the "needy."

V. Tcherikover analyzes the social gulf present in the sage's society:

> Ben Sira recognizes a threefold antagonism which existed in his time in the Jewish community: the social antagonism between rich and poor; the moral antagonism between sinners and righteous; and the religious antagonism between unbelievers and the pious. These three antagonisms naturally tended to combine into one all-inclusive antagonism; on one side the wealthy, morally transgressing in their oppression of the poor, their perversion of justice and their dishonesty, also rejecting the fundamentals of Judaism; opposed to them stands the great mass of the poor and humble, who are morally "righteous" and religiously "devout."[90]

In view of this chasm between the "haves" and the "have-nots," Ben Sira questions how there can be peace between the two social groups.

After referring to the wolf (13:17a) and the hyena (v. 18a), Ben Sira's series reaches a climax in the third predator mentioned, the "lion" (אֲרִי, v. 19a).[91] Proverbs 30:30 calls the lion (לַיִשׁ) "the mightiest of beasts" (גִּבּוֹר בַּבְּהֵמָה), analogous to a king among his people (Prov 30:31).[92] Similarly, 1 Macc 3:4 says of the leader of the Jewish revolt against Antiochus Epiphanes, Judas Maccabeus: "He was like a lion in his deeds." Proverbs 28:15, however, employs the image of a lion to stress the cruelty of a bad ruler:

---

[89] To be sure, "rich" does not automatically mean "wicked," as 13:24; 31:8–11 show. Likewise, "poor" is not entirely equivalent to "righteous," since 18:32–19:1 acknowledges that some kinds of poverty may be self-inflicted.

[90] V. Tcherikover, *Hellenistic Civilization and the Jews* (Philadelphia: Jewish Publication Society of America, 1959), 150–51. Note that *Jub.* 23:19 also contrasts "the poor with the rich, the lowly with the great"; see O. S. Wintermute, "Jubilees," *OTP* 2:35–142, esp. 2:101.

[91] The danger that lions presented for the ancient Israelites is clear from 1 Kgs 13:24; 20:36; 2 Kgs 17:25; Amos 3:4, 12; Prov 22:13; 26:13.

[92] Note also that Gen 49:9 calls Judah, the ancestor of King David and his descendants, גּוּר אַרְיֵה ("a lion's whelp"). Moreover, the "young lion" (כְּפִיר) has royal associations in Prov 19:12; 20:2.

אֲרִי־נֹהֵם וְדֹב שׁוֹקֵק מֹשֵׁל רָשָׁע עַל עַם־דָּל

A growling lion or a charging bear
is a wicked ruler over a poor people.[93]

In comparing Israel's leaders to lions, the prophets also tend to emphasize their cruelty. In particular, Zeph 3:3 says of Jerusalem, "Her officers in her midst are roaring lions" (אֲרָיוֹת), while Ezekiel condemns those in power in the land of Israel, saying: "A band of its leaders[94] is in its midst, like a roaring lion [אֲרִי] tearing the prey; they devour lives, they take treasure and valuables, they multiply its widows in its midst" (Ezek 22:25).[95] Moreover, Ezek 19:6 depicts the cruelty of one of Judah's last kings[96] using leonine imagery: "He walked about in the midst of lions [אֲרָיוֹת]; he was a young lion [כְּפִיר], and he learned to tear prey; he devoured human beings."

In the Aramaic Ahiqar tradition the lion's attitude to its prey symbolizes "man's inhumanity to man." Saying 9 (lines 88–89a) declares: "The lion [אריא] catches the scent of the stag in its hidden den, and he ... sheds its blood and eats its flesh. Just so [כן] is the meeting of [men]."[97] Saying 10 (lines 89b–90) asserts that because of the lion, "the ass [חמר] abandons his load and will not carry it," while Saying 28 (line 110) refers to an encounter between the lion (אריא) and the ass (חמרא).

Just as the mention of a "lion" (אֲרִי) in 13:19a may suggest an allusion to the Tobiad dynasty, so may its reference to the "desert" (מִדְבָּר). Reporting on the activities of the Tobiad leader Hyrcanus son of Joseph, Josephus says that he "settled in the country across the Jordan.... And he built a strong fortress ... and had beasts of gigantic size carved on it"

---

93 Using the image of a lion (אַרְיֵה), Sir 4:30a H^{C} depicts a householder who is domineering toward his servants; on the textual problem here, see Skehan and Di Lella, *Wisdom of Ben Sira*, 177.

94 Reading נְשִׂיאֶיהָ ("its leaders," cf. G) instead of נְבִיאֶיהָ ("its prophets," MT).

95 Jeremiah 5:6 also speaks figuratively of Judah's enemies as a "lion" (אַרְיֵה). P. D. Miller ("Animal Names As Designations in Ugaritic and Hebrew," *UF* 2 [1970]: 177–86) suggests that in some biblical Hebrew texts (e.g., Ezek 32:2; 38:13; Nah 2:14b) "young lion" (כְּפִיר) functions as "a kind of designation or title for soldiers, leaders, dignitaries, or functionaries of some sort" (183).

96 It is unclear whether Ezek 19:6 refers to Jehoiakim, Jehoiachin, or Zedekiah; for discussion, see M. Greenberg, *Ezekiel 1–20* (AB 22; Garden City, N.Y.: Doubleday, 1983), 355–56.

97 Lindenberger, *Aramaic Proverbs of Ahiqar*, 60. The ensuing quotations come from pp. 62, 96.

(*Ant.* 12.4.11 §§229–230).[98] The walls of the Tobiad fortress of ʿIraq el-Emir (ten miles west of Amman) still display friezes of lions (as well as panthers and eagles).[99] In this context, the "wild asses of the desert" (פִּרְאֵי מִדְבָּר) may refer to the victims of the heavy Tobiad taxation, especially those who lived in desert villages outside Jerusalem.[100]

One fable of Aesop (Chambry 207), linking "lion and wild ass" (λέων καὶ ὄναγρος), concludes with the statement that it is good "neither to join nor to associate [κοινωνεῖν] with those more powerful than oneself."[101] The fact that Ben Sira uses the same symbolic animals to make a similar point may suggest that he knew some form of this folktale.

Ben Sira skillfully combines this folk wisdom with imagery from the book of Job. Employing the metaphor of "wild asses in the desert," Job 24:4–5b graphically depicts the plight of the poor at the hands of the wicked:

> They turn away needy persons [אֶבְיוֹנִים] from the path,
> the poor of the land [עֲנִיֵּי־אָרֶץ] are all hidden.
> Behold, like wild asses in the desert [פְּרָאִים בַּמִּדְבָּר] they go out
> for their task seeking prey.[102]

Ben Sira takes up Job's description of the plight of the impoverished desert dwellers to portray the fate of the poor under Tobiad rule in Palestine. Moreover, just as Jer 14:6 depicts the desperate state of the wild asses in a time of drought, when there is no vegetation for them to eat, so Sir 13:19 uses the wild asses as symbols of the poor who have no assured means of support.

Jeremiah 25:36–38 pictures Israel as a pasture ground (מַרְעִית) threatened by a lion (symbolizing God). While Jer 25:36 declares, "There is the sound of the cry of the shepherds … for Yahweh despoils their pasture

---

[98] Thackeray et al., trans., *Josephus*, 7:117.

[99] Cf. E. Will, "ʿIraq el-Emir," *ABD* 3:454–56; the author suggests that "the eagles and the lions … could have a political significance: they are symbols of royal power" (3:456).

[100] Note that Josephus (*Ant.* 12.4.11 §229) reports an attack by the Tobiad leader Hyrcanus on some desert Arabs. See also Gen 16:12, which calls Ishmael "a wild ass of a man" (פֶּרֶא אָדָם) because he inhabited the desert (Gen 25:18).

[101] Chambry, *Esope*, 91–92 (translations mine). Cf. Middendorp, *Die Stellung Jesu ben Siras*, 9; Kieweler, *Ben Sira zwischen Judentum und Hellenismus*, 124.

[102] For the scansion of Job 24:5 as a tricolon, see M. H. Pope, *Job* (AB 15; Garden City, N.Y.: Doubleday, 1965), 174. Job 39:5–8 also pictures the free roaming of the wild asses in the desert.

ground" (מַרְעִיתָם)," Jer 25:38 announces that God "has left his lair like a young lion" (כְּפִיר). Whereas Ben Sira uses the image of lions to refer to the predatory ruling class of southern Palestine, Jeremiah boldly pictures God himself as a lion.

To conclude the first stanza, Ben Sira summarizes his thought on rich and poor with the assertion: "Humility is an abomination to pride, and a needy person is an abomination to a rich person."[103] Here the sage adapts Prov 29:27, which uses the antithesis "righteous"//"wicked" (cf. Sir 13:17b):

תּוֹעֲבַת צַדִּיקִים אִישׁ עָוֶל   וְתוֹעֲבַת רָשָׁע יְשַׁר־דָּרֶךְ

A wrongdoer is an abomination to the righteous,
and one whose way is upright is an abomination to a wicked person.[104]

Whereas the word תּוֹעֵבָה ("abomination") in the MT generally denotes actions abhorred on religious grounds,[105] Sir 13:20b draws on Prov 24:9b; 29:27 in applying the noun to persons instead. Given the widespread abhorrence shown by the wealthy toward the poor (Sir 13:20b), Sir 11:2b H^B exhorts: "Do not abominate [אַל תְּתַעֵב] a human being who is broken[106] in his appearance."

In 13:20a Ben Sira employs polar opposites, גַּאֲוָה ("pride") and עֲנָוָה ("humility"). Here he adapts the biblical antithesis (cf. Ps 10:2; Prov 16:19; Sir 10:14) between גֵּאֶה ("proud") and עָנִי ("poor," "afflicted").

[103] The pattern of Sir 13:20, in which abstract nouns in the first colon introduce persons in the second colon, copies Prov 24:9: "The devising of folly is sin, and a scoffer is an abomination to humanity."

[104] 1QS 4.17 preserves a saying based on Prov 29:27 and similar to Sir 13:20:
תּוֹעֲבַת אֱמֶת עֲלִילוֹת עַוְלָה   וְתוֹעֲבַת עַוְלָה כוֹל דַּרְכֵי אֱמֶת
Deeds of injustice are an abhorrence to truth,
and all the paths of truth are an abhorrence to injustice.
For the Hebrew text, see E. Lohse, *Die Texte aus Qumran: hebräisch und deutsch* (2d ed.; Munich: Kösel, 1971), 14; for the translation, see García Martínez, *Dead Sea Scrolls Translated*, 7.

[105] E.g., idolatrous practices (Deut 13:15; 17:4; Ezek 16:51; 18:12) or unchaste behavior (Lev 18:22; 20:13; Ezek 22:11; 33:26). Sirach 49:2 H^B praises King Josiah's successful campaign to root out idolatry in Judah: "He destroyed vain abominations" (תּוֹעֲבוֹת הֶבֶל), while Sir 15:13 H^A says emphatically: "Yahweh hates evil and abomination" (תֹּעֵבָה).

[106] For the reading מְשֻׁבָּר ("broken"), see A. A. Di Lella, "The Recently Identified Leaves of Sirach in Hebrew," *Bib* 45 (1964): 153–67, esp. 156.

Many biblical texts play on the ironic reversal of a person's situation (from exaltation to humiliation, or vice versa); thus, Prov 29:23a asserts: גַּאֲוַת אָדָם תַּשְׁפִּילֶנּוּ ("A human being's pride will bring him low").[107] Ben Sira refers to God as one who brings down human pride (e.g., 7:11; 10:14; 11:4–6). Elsewhere he employs the noun גַּאֲוָה ("pride") particularly in his tract on government in 9:17–10:18; for instance, Sir 10:6b–7a H^A teaches: "Do not walk in the way of pride [גַּאֲוָה]; hated by the Lord and human beings is pride."

In line with his attacks on human pride, Ben Sira commends humility. According to H^A Sir 3:17a advises: "My child, in your riches [בְּעָשְׁרְךָ][108] walk in humility [בַּעֲנָוָה]"; in other words, wealth should not lead to pride, as it did among the Tobiad ruling class in Palestine. Hence, Sir 3:18a H^C continues: "If you are wealthy, humble yourself all the more."[109]

The sage frequently speaks of the importance of humility. In his opening chapter (1:27 G) he asserts: "Fear of the Lord is wisdom and discipline, and his delight is faithfulness and humility" (πραΰτης).[110] Sirach 4:8 plays on the related terms עָנִי ("poor") and עֲנָוָה ("humility"): "Turn your ear to the poor person, and return to him a greeting [lit., peace] with humility." The sure fact of death motivates Ben Sira's call to a lowly attitude in the rhymed saying of 7:17 H^A: "Very much, very much humble pride [גַּאֲוָה], for a mortal's hope is worms [רִמָּה]." Nevertheless, the humility that the sage advocates is not a denial of God-given gifts (10:28–29) but rather an unpretentious modesty (10:26–27).

Just as Ben Sira links "humility" (13:20a) with the "righteous person" (v. 17b) and the "poor" (v. 19b), so Zeph 2:3 makes similar connections: "Seek Yahweh, all the afflicted of the land [כָּל־עַנְוֵי הָאָרֶץ], who perform his justice; seek righteousness [צֶדֶק], seek humility [עֲנָוָה]" (cf. Amos 2:6; 5:12). Furthermore, humility also characterizes the outlook of the Qumran community (1QS 2.24; 3.8; 4.3; 5.3). Whereas Lev 19:17 commands that one offer reproof to a neighbor (cf. Sir 19:13–17), the *Community Rule* stipulates how one is to do so: "Each should reproach his

---

[107] The humbling of human pride is a frequent theme of Isaiah (Isa 2:12–17; 13:11; 14:12–15). For other examples of this antithesis, see J. Krašovec, *Antithetic Structure in Biblical Hebrew Poetry* (VTSup 35; Leiden: Brill, 1984), 130.

[108] G presupposes בְּמַעֲשֶׂיךָ ("in your deeds").

[109] H^A reads a different text here; cf. Di Lella, "Recently Identified Leaves," 164–65.

[110] Moses embodies both the qualities in Sir 1:27b; thus, in 45:4 H^B Ben Sira praises him not just for "his faithfulness" (cf. Num 12:7) but also for "his humility" (עַנְוָתוֹ; cf. Num 12:3).

fellow in truth, in meekness [עֲנָוָה] and in compassionate love for the man" (1QS 5.24–25).[111]

b. Stanza 2: Rich and Poor Receive Unequal Treatment (13:21–23)

The structure of the second stanza (13:21–23) hinges upon a triple antithesis between the rich and the poor. Whereas the first comparison contrasts the reaction of others when a person totters (13:21), the second and third comparisons (13:22–23) contrast people's reactions to someone's speech. While the wealthy receive both support when they stumble and praise for their words (however repugnant), people abandon the needy when they totter and ignore what they say (however wise it may be).

In making his threefold antithesis between the rich person (עָשִׁיר) and the pauper (דַּל), Ben Sira uses a standard parallel word-pair of biblical Hebrew poetry (cf. Exod 30:15; Prov 22:16; 28:11; Ruth 3:10). Thus, Prov 10:15 teaches: "The wealth of the rich person [עָשִׁיר] is his strong city; the ruin of paupers [דַּלִּים] is their poverty." Sirach 10:30 employs a similar antithesis: "A pauper [דַּל] is honored on account of his insight, and a rich person [עָשִׁיר] is honored on account of his riches."[112] Sirach 13:3 H^A reworks Prov 18:23 to create a stark antithesis between society's respect for the rich and its mistreatment of the poor: "When a rich person [עָשִׁיר] afflicts, he will be the one to preen himself; but when wrong is done against a pauper [דַּל], he will be the one to supplicate." Having returned to the same thought in 13:19, Ben Sira develops this antithesis at greater length in 13:21–23.[113]

Although he believes in a just cosmic order (cf. Sir 18:1–15; 33:7–15; 39:16–35) in which God will punish human injustice to the poor (cf. 35:15–20), the sage (like the book of Proverbs) is also aware that the rich and the poor are not treated equally in society.[114] Thus, Prov 14:20 declares: "Even by his companions[115] an impoverished person is hated, but

[111] García Martínez, *Dead Sea Scrolls Translated,* 9.

[112] For textual criticism here, see Di Lella, "Sirach 10:19–11:6," 158 (text), 161 (notes).

[113] Note also that 30:14 H^B creates an antithesis between a poor person (מִסְכֵּן) and a rich person (עָשִׁיר), while 31:3–4 H^B contrasts the rich person (עָשִׁיר) with the poor person (עָנִי); cf. also 25:2 G; 26:4 G.

[114] Cf. Whybray, *Wealth and Poverty,* 32; Schrader, "Unzuverlässige Freundschaft und verläßliche Feindschaft," in Reiterer, ed., *Freundschaft bei Ben Sira,* 32–33. A similar awareness pervades Nathan's parable of the rich man (עָשִׁיר) and the poor man (רָאשׁ) in 2 Sam 12:1–4.

[115] For רֵעֵהוּ as plural (cf. "friends" in the second colon), see GKC §91k.

the friends of a rich person are many" (אֹהֲבֵי עָשִׁיר רַבִּים). Similarly, Prov 19:4 asserts: "Wealth will add many companions, but a pauper will be separated from his companions." Moreover, Prov 19:7ab teaches: "All the relatives of an impoverished person hate him; how much more do his companions keep far from him!" In Greek poetry a comparable contrast occurs in Theognis 621: "Every man honoureth a rich [πλούσιον] man and despiseth a poor [πενιχρόν]."[116]

In Sir 13:21a the verb סמך ("support") denotes the activity of a friend to help someone in difficulty. Just as 51:7 H^B^ employs the participle סוֹמֵךְ ("supporter") in parallel with עוֹזֵר ("helper"), so 13:21a places the verb סמך ("support") in parallel with עזר ("help," 13:22a); the same parallel word-pair also appears in Isa 63:5 and Ps 54:6. Sirach 12:17 H^A^ describes the false friendship of an enemy who pretends to be a "supporter" (סוֹמֵךְ) while at the same time placing obstacles before one. By contrast, Sir 22:23 advises: "Support [סְמֹךְ] your companion in his poverty [דַּלּוּתוֹ]."[117]

The verb מוט ("totter"), occurring in the *qal* in 13:21a and in the *nipʿal* in 13:21b H^A^, refers to the result of an attack on a person's welfare and stability. The underlying metaphor, common in biblical usage, is of someone "standing" (= having a secure status) or "walking" (= playing a role in society). Thus, Ps 38:17 speaks of those who boast at "the tottering of my foot" (מוֹט רַגְלִי), that is, my insecure position in society. Sirach 3:31 H^A^ says of the generous person, "At the time of his tottering [מוטו] he will find support," whereas 12:15 H^A^ says of the insolent person: "If you are made to totter [נָמוֹט], he will not restrain himself."

Despite the difficulties involved for his belief in the Deuteronomic scheme of retribution,[118] Sir 13:21b acknowledges that in reality the pauper may be made to totter (נָמוֹט) even if he is righteous (צַדִּיק, 13:17b), just as Prov 25:26 envisages (albeit unhappily) "a righteous person tottering before a wicked person" (צַדִּיק מָט לִפְנֵי־רָשָׁע). Ultimately the poor but righteous person who faces threats to his stability and welfare can only trust in God (Pss 37:3; 55:23; 94:17–18; 118:13; Sir 2:6–9). It is such a faith in God that leads Israel's aphoristic tradition to affirm: "The righteous person will not be made to totter [בַּל־יִמּוֹט] forever" (Prov 10:30; cf. Ps 112:6).

The fate of the tottering pauper is to be "thrust away" (נִדְחֶה) from one companion to another (Sir 13:21b). Whereas Prov 14:32 employs the

---

[116] Edmonds, trans., *Elegy and Iambus,* 1:303.

[117] See my retroversion of Sir 22:23 in ch. 6 below. According to Xenophon (*Mem.* 2.4.6), true friendship means being foremost in helping one's friend by "raising him up when he falls" (see Marchant, trans., *Xenophon,* 125).

[118] Ben Sira is, however, aware of probationary suffering (2:1–5); cf. Skehan and Di Lella, *Wisdom of Ben Sira,* 83–85.

same verb to describe the situation of the wicked ("For his evil a wicked person will be thrust away" [יִדָּחֶה]), Ben Sira has to admit that the innocent pauper often suffers such a fate in society.

Sirach 13:22ab asserts that when the wealthy person speaks, "his helpers are many" (עֹזְרָיו רַבִּים),[119] and they applaud his repugnant words. The sage's thought here echoes Prov 19:4a: "Wealth will add many companions" (רֵעִים רַבִּים; cf. Prov 14:20b; 19:6b). A comparable sentiment appears in Theognis 929–930: "If thou be rich, thy friends are many [πολλοὶ φίλοι], and if poor, they are few."[120]

Wishing to please the rich person, the hearers "call his loathsome words beautiful";[121] instead of speaking truly, they defer to the wealthy person out of fear or a desire to win favor.[122] The root כער ("abhor"), of which the *puʿal* participle ("abhorred," "loathsome") occurs in 13:22b, is not attested in the MT. However, the same *puʿal* participle also occurs in 11:2b H^{BmgA}: "Do not abominate a human being abhorrent [מְכוֹעָר] in his appearance."[123]

Whereas the wealthy person's talk receives public acclaim, society rejects the pauper's words, however sensible they may be. Ben Sira uses

---

[119] Here the root עזר has the nuance of "support" (as in Ezra 10:15).

[120] Edmonds, trans., *Elegy and Iambus*, 1:339; cf. Sanders, *Ben Sira and Demotic Wisdom*, 30–31.

[121] The word מוֹפִין ("they call [lit., make] beautiful") is a *hipʿil* participle of יפה with an Aramaizing plural ending; in the MT the *piʿel* ("beautify") occurs in Jer 10:4. Greco-Roman teachers (such as Aristotle and Isocrates) urged their students to be wary of flatterers; see Konstan, *Friendship in the Classical World*, 98–103.

[122] The sixth line of a medieval Hebrew poem from the Cairo Genizah reworks the thought of Sir 13:22:

עָשִׁיר מְקוּלְקָל וּבְפִי כֹל מְהוּלָּל
וְהַדַּל מְפַלֵּס צְעָדָיו וְהוּא נִקְרָא מְהוֹלָל׃

A rich person is corrupt but is praised by the mouths of all;
the pauper makes his steps level but he is called mad.

The whole poem includes seven bicola (lines 4–10) contrasting the rich person with the pauper; cf. S. Schechter, "A Further Fragment of Ben Sira," *JQR* 12 (1899–1900): 456–65 (text on 459–60).

[123] The MSS have lacunae: H^{Bmg} reads מכוע[ר], while H^{A} has מכ[וע]ר; however, H^{B} reads a different participle, מְשֻׁבָּר ("broken"), which Di Lella accepts as original ("Sirach 10:19–11:6," 162). Ziegler ("Zwei Beiträge zu Sirach," 282–83) suggests that in 13:22b מְכוֹעָר means "unclear" or "stupid" (rather than "loathsome"), but since ἀπόρρητος often denotes "unfit to be spoken" or "abominable" (cf. Plato, *Leg.* 854E), the reading of G in fact attests to the meaning "loathsome" for מְכוֹעָר. See further Wagner, *Die Septuaginta-Hapaxlegomena im Buch Jesus Sirach*, 161–62.

an onomatopoeic phrase, נַע נַע ("Pooh-pooh!"), to express the contemptuous response of the hearers.[124]

As a contrast with the rich person whose words are "loathsome," Ben Sira takes the case of a pauper who "will speak[125] giving insight" (דִּבֶּר מַשְׂכִּיל). The word מַשְׂכִּיל is the *hipʿil* masculine participle from the root שׂכל ("have insight," "be prosperous"); the cognate noun שֵׂכֶל ("insight") occurs in 13:23b. The exact syntactic function of מַשְׂכִּיל in 13:22d is uncertain. It could refer to what is spoken,[126] since the form occurs thirteen times in the MT as a title for various psalms, possibly in the sense of "didactic poem" or "skillful composition."[127] However, the uncertainty over the meaning of מַשְׂכִּיל as a psalm title makes this suggestion suspect, and so it seems better to understand the word as describing the action of a person "giving insight." In the book of Proverbs the participle מַשְׂכִּיל refers to "one giving insight" or "an insightful person"; for example, Prov 10:19 teaches: "One who restrains his words is an insightful person" (מַשְׂכִּיל; cf. Prov 15:24).

Ben Sira often utilizes phrases from Proverbs concerning persons with insight. For instance, Sir 47:12 calls Solomon "an insightful son" (בֵּן מַשְׂכִּיל, cf. Prov 10:5), Sir 7:21 and 10:25 refer to "an insightful servant" (עֶבֶד מַשְׂכִּיל, cf. Prov 14:35; 17:2), and three times (Sir 7:19; 25:8; 40:23) the sage employs the phrase "an insightful wife" (אִשָּׁה מַשְׂכֶּלֶת, cf. Prov 19:14). In the phrase "an insightful pauper" (דַּל מַשְׂכִּיל, Sir 10:23), however, the sage creates an expression not found in Proverbs. There he voices his opposition to the natural human tendency (noted also in 13:22) to attend to the mighty while ignoring the pauper's speech: "One should not despise an insightful pauper [דַּל מַשְׂכִּיל], and one should not honor any lawless person" (10:23 H[B]).

During the Maccabean revolt a generation after Ben Sira, the word מַשְׂכִּילִים became a technical term for "the Jewish leaders of the anti-Hellenistic resistance, who are later called in Greek *Hasidaioi*."[128]

[124] See the text-critical note 22[q–q] for alternative explanations of the phrase.

[125] I understand וְדִבֶּר ("and he will speak") as a converted perfect, following the imperfect verb יִשְׂאוּ ("they will utter"). Other examples of the converted perfect in Ben Sira include וְאָמַרְתָּ ("nor shall you say," 5:6a H[AC]) and וְהָיְתָה ("and it shall become," 6:29a H[A]).

[126] G reads σύνεσιν ("prudence"), while S paraphrases with "what is fine."

[127] Other interpretations include "successful song" and "antiphon"; for a survey, see K. Koenen, "שָׂכַל *śākal*," *ThWAT* 7:781–95, esp. 793–94. For a general study of the term מַשְׂכִּיל, see H. Kosmala, "*Maśkîl*," *JANESCU* 5 (1973): 235–41.

[128] So L. F. Hartman and A. A. Di Lella, *The Book of Daniel* (AB 23; Garden City, N.Y.: Doubleday, 1978), 299.

Daniel 11:33 describes how these leaders raised the people's awareness of what was at stake in the struggle against Antiochus IV Epiphanes: מַשְׂכִּילֵי עָם יָבִינוּ לָרַבִּים ("the insightful ones of the people gave understanding to the multitude").[129] In the Qumran community's writings the term מַשְׂכִּיל refers to "someone whose function it is to make others wise, that is, an 'Instructor' or 'Master.'"[130]

Sirach 13:22d ends with the sad statement about the wise pauper: "there is no place for him" (אֵין לוֹ מָקוֹם).[131] In a similar vein, Sir 4:4–5 depicts a pauper whose only "opportunity" (מָקוֹם) is to curse those who refuse to help him.[132]

The thought of Sir 13:22–23 parallels Qoheleth's exemplary story concerning a besieged city (Qoh 9:15–16):

> In it there was found a poor wise man, and he could have delivered the city by his wisdom, but nobody took notice of that poor man. And I said, "Although wisdom is better than strength, the poor man's wisdom is despised and his words [דְּבָרָיו] are not heeded."[133]

Sirach 13:23a declares that when the rich person speaks, "all have been silenced" (הַכֹּל נִסְכָּתוּ).[134] Here the sage uses a rare root סכת ("be silent"), occurring in MT as a *hapax legomenon;* in Deut 27:9 Moses and the Levitical priests preface their instructions to the people with a call to attention: הַסְכֵּת וּשְׁמַע יִשְׂרָאֵל ("Be silent and hear, O Israel"). In Sir 13:23, however, the people give their reverent attention, not to Moses' teaching but to the

---

[129] Further references to the מַשְׂכִּילִים occur in Dan 11:35; 12:3, 10.

[130] So C. A. Newsom, "The Sage in the Literature of Qumran: The Functions of the *Maśkîl,*" in Gammie and Perdue, eds., *The Sage in Israel,* 373–82; the quotation is from p. 374. She cites 1QS 3.13: "The *maśkîl* shall instruct all the sons of light and shall teach them" (ibid.). Whereas in Proverbs and Ben Sira the term has a general sense of "insightful" or "giving insight," in both Daniel and Qumran the term acquires a technical meaning of "Instructor," either of the people threatened by hellenization (Daniel) or of the sectarian community (Qumran).

[131] The word מָקוֹם may mean either "place" or "opportunity [for him to be heard]" (cf. 4:5; 38:12). Compare the use of τόπος in 19:17b G; see my exegesis of that verse in the next chapter.

[132] Sirach 4:3–5 H^{A} advises: "Do not withhold a gift from your pauper…, and you will not give him an opportunity [מָקוֹם] to curse you."

[133] For this interpretation of Qoh 9:15–16, cf. J. L. Crenshaw, *Ecclesiastes* (OTL; Philadelphia: Westminster, 1987), 166–67. The parallel with Sir 13:22–23 is noted by Skehan and Di Lella, *Wisdom of Ben Sira,* 255.

[134] Although הַכֹּל ("all, everyone") is grammatically singular, it here takes a plural verb because of its collective sense; cf. GKC §145b–e.

utterances of an arrogant rich person. Whereas in Job 29:9 the formerly wealthy patriarch had earned a respectful silence from people by his care of the poor (Job 29:12–17), Ben Sira speaks of the awe commanded by the rich person simply by virtue of his powerful economic position.

Next, Ben Sira avoids repetition of the *piʿel* participle מְדַבֵּר ("speaks," v. 22ac) by shifting to the *qal* participle דּוֹבֵר ("speaks," v. 23ac) for the sake of variety, and perhaps also for its echoing of prophetic denunciations of the rich and powerful. Micah 7:3, for instance, states: "The powerful person speaks [דֹּבֵר] what he himself desires"; that is, he names the amount of the bribe he will accept. Closer to Sir 13:17–23 is the condemnation of the wealthy class recorded in Amos 5:10: "They hate the reprover at the gate, and they abhor the one who speaks blamelessly" (דֹּבֵר תָּמִים יְתָעֵבוּ). Besides censuring their trampling on the "pauper" (דַּל, Amos 5:11) and affirming, "Your transgressions are many" (רַבִּים, Amos 5:12), the prophet declares that they "harass the righteous person [צַדִּיק], take a ransom, and turn aside the needy [אֶבְיוֹנִים] at the gate. Therefore the insightful person [הַמַּשְׂכִּיל] at that time will be silent" (Amos 5:12–13).[135] Just as the animal analogies in 13:17–19 use prophetic imagery, so too the comparison of rich and poor in 13:21–23 echoes the prophetic denunciations of the callous behavior of the wealthy.

In 13:23b the sage refers to the "insight" (שֵׂכֶל) popularly (but hypocritically) attributed to the wealthy person. Though Sir 10:30a H^B declares that "a pauper [דַּל] is honored on account of his insight [שִׂכְלוֹ],"[136] in 13:22–23 the pauper stands in the shadow of the rich person, who receives all the glory because of "his [supposed] insight" (שִׂכְלוֹ). Whereas in 10:19–11:6 the sage is outlining his ideal for the relation between rich and poor, in 13:17–23 he depicts the sad reality of the situation.

Using poetic hyperbole (tinged with irony) Ben Sira describes the popular admiration for the rich person: "They make his insight reach to the clouds" (אֶת שִׂכְלוֹ עַד עָב יַגִּיעוּ; 13:23b). Here the sage borrows a phrase from Job 20:6–7, where Zophar says of the impious person: "Even if his exaltation will mount to the skies, and his head will reach to the clouds [רֹאשׁוֹ לָעָב יַגִּיעַ], he will perish forever like his dung; those who have seen him will say, 'Where is he?'"[137] Moreover, Sir

[135] Thus, Sir 13:17–23 shares seven words with Amos 5:10–13: צַדִּיק (13:17), דַּל (13:19, 21, 22, 23), the root תעב (13:20), אֶבְיוֹן (13:20), רַבִּים (13:22), מַשְׂכִּיל (13:22), and דּוֹבֵר (13:23).

[136] Similarly, Prov 12:8 states: "According to his insight [שִׂכְלוֹ] a person will be praised."

[137] The implication of Ben Sira's allusion to Job 20:6–7 is that such high praise (Sir 13:23) will also be brought down to earth.

35:21 H^B employs a similar idiom in mentioning what truly deserves to reach the heavens.[138]

שַׁוְעַת דַּל עָבִים חָלְפָה   וְעַד תַּגִּיעַ לֹא תָנוּחַ

The cry of the pauper passes through the clouds,
and until it arrives it will not rest.

In Sir 13:23c the public reaction to the pauper's words is full of contempt: "Who is this?" A comparable contempt is evident in God's first address to Job: "Who is this [מִי זֶה] obscuring counsel by words without knowledge?" (Job 38:2).[139]

Sirach 13:23d depicts what will happen to the pauper "if he has stumbled" (אִם נִתְקַל). The verb תקל ("trip"), absent from the MT, occurs twice elsewhere (in a metaphorical sense) in the Hebrew MSS of Ben Sira. Sirach 32:20 H^B advises: "Do not walk on a road of snares, and do not stumble [אַל תִּתָּקֵל] on an obstacle twice," while Sir 15:12 H^A reports the sinner's accusation against God: "It was he who made me slip" (הוּא הִתְקִילַנִי).[140]

When the pauper stumbles, the public "will push him down" (יֶהְדְּפוּהוּ), according to 13:23d.[141] Here Ben Sira employs exactly the same word as in Job 18:18, in which Bildad describes the fate of the wicked person: "They will push him down [יֶהְדְּפֻהוּ] from light into darkness." The root הדף ("push down") occurs thrice elsewhere in the Hebrew MSS of Ben Sira (12:12; 36:9; 47:5). Sirach 12:12 H^A advises keeping a distance from an enemy: "Do not let him stand beside you, lest he push you down [יֶהְדָּפְךָ] and stand in your place." The nationalistic prayer of 36:9 H^B beseeches God: "Subjugate the adversary and push down the enemy" (הֲדוֹף אוֹיֵב). The sad irony of Sir 13:23d is that it is not the wicked person (Job 18:18), a personal enemy (Sir 12:12), or a national foe (Sir 36:9) that is pushed down, but the innocent pauper in trouble.

---

[138] I read עָבִים חָלְפָה with H^{Bmg}.

[139] A similar rebuke occurs in Job 42:3. Elsewhere in the MT, too, questions with מִי ("who?") may express scorn, as in Judg 9:36; 1 Sam 17:26; 25:10.

[140] Using a cognate noun, Sir 31:7 H^B calls love of gold a "stumbling block" (תַּקָּלָה). According to Xenophon (*Mem.* 2.4.6) a good person will help a friend who is stumbling.

[141] Ben Sira's use of גַּם הֵם ("they too [will push him down]") in 13:23d may be an echo of the same phrase in Ps 38:11, where it may perhaps refer elliptically to עֵינַי, "my eyes" (cf. GKC §32n for such lapses in gender agreement). Note the sentiment of Ps 38:12a: "My friends and companions stand aloof from my affliction" (cf. Sir 37:4b).

In Sir 13:21–23 the sage completes the lesson begun in 10:19–11:6. Whereas 11:1–2 outlines what should happen (the wise pauper receiving recognition), 13:21–23 portrays the grim reality that society often pushes aside the poor and ignores them. Although this observation does not make Ben Sira a radical revolutionary, it does indicate his sympathy for the poor and his distaste for the arrogance of the rich. The behavior of the rich shows that they are not following the social teachings of the Torah, and hence Ben Sira advises the righteous to avoid making friends with such persons. On the other hand, since the poor tend to be humble, the sage teaches that one should befriend them.

9. Conclusion

In providing guidance for Ben Sira's students regarding friendships, Sir 13:15–23 presupposes a social gulf between the wealthy but wicked members of the hellenized ruling class and the poor but righteous Jewish population. The pericope opens with the general axiom that like associates with like; although this principle is akin to the Greek philosophy of nature found in Aristotle, it is couched in vocabulary taken from the Priestly tradition in Gen 1–11. Three animal comparisons follow (Sir 13:17–19), combining international sapiential traditions (e.g., Aesop) with Israel's prophetic heritage; by means of these the sage asserts the impossibility of friendship between rich and poor, and perhaps obliquely criticizes the abuse of power by the Tobiad rulers. The first stanza ends with another axiomatic statement (13:20) noting the distaste felt by the wealthy toward the poor. The second stanza (13:21–23) focuses on the way society ignores the poor; this theme, mirroring the thought of Israel's wisdom tradition (Job and Qoheleth), may suggest further criticism of the Tobiad rulers. Thus, Ben Sira implies a warning to his students against making friends with members of the arrogant wealthy class.

5

Sirach 19:13–17 and 27:16–21

1. Introduction

Chapters 5 and 6 discuss three pericopes from the central portion of the book: Sir 19:13–17; 22:19–26; 27:16–21. Developing the sapiential theme of the right and wrong uses of speech, all three passages warn of dangers to friendship: failure to reprove a friend to his face (19:13–17); slandering a friend behind his back (22:19–26); and revealing a friend's secrets (27:16–21). This chapter will consider the two shorter pericopes, 19:13–17 and 27:16–21.

Unfortunately, discoveries from the Cairo Genizah and the Dead Sea area have failed to yield the Hebrew original for these three pericopes.[1] However, I provide a reconstructed Hebrew text for them on the basis of the ancient versions.[2]

2. Sirach 19:13–17

Sirach 19:13–17,[3] a didactic poem of five bicola, inculcates the need to reprove a friend for wrongdoing. This passage, therefore, concerns the right use of the tongue, by contrast with the previous passage on misuse of the tongue (19:4–12).

a. Delimitation

The clearest feature indicating the unity of Sir 19:13–17 is the fourfold repetition of the key word הוֹכַח (= ἔλεγξον, "reprove") at the start of

---

[1] In the case of Sir 22:19–26, however, a medieval Hebrew poem (MS Adler 3053), based on 22:22–23:9, exists among the Genizah texts; see further the introduction to ch. 6.

[2] For an explanation of my decision to employ retroversion, see the section on method of study at the end of ch. 1.

[3] On the pericope, see H. V. Kieweler, "Freundschaft und böse Nachrede," 61–85, especially 76–81.

verses 13, 14, 15, 17. In addition, there is an alternating pattern with אוֹהֵב (= φίλον, "friend") in verses 13a and 15a, and רֵעַ (= πλησίον, "companion," "neighbor") in verses 14a and 17a. Thus, the whole of 19:13–17 considers reproof of one's friends.

While the preceding passage (19:4–12)[4] concerns gossip (a misuse of speech), the present text (19:13–17) is about reproof (a right use of speech). Indeed, 19:4–12 uses the term "word" (λόγος) four times (vv. 7, 10, 11, 12), by contrast with only one occurrence (v. 15) in 19:13–17.

The following passage (19:20–24)[5] discusses the relationship among wisdom, the fear of God, and the law. The term "wisdom" (σοφία), which last appeared in 18:28, occurs four times (19:20 [bis], 22, 23). A double *inclusio* marks off the passage; just as 19:20 uses "fear" (φόβος) and "the law" (νόμου), so 19:24 employs "reverent" (ἔμφοβος) and "the law" (νόμον).

b. Retroverted Text of Sirach 19:13–17

I

13 הוֹכַח אוֹהֵב[a] [b]אֲשֶׁר לֹא יַעֲשֶׂה[b]   וְאִם עָשָׂה פֶּן יוֹסִיף׃
14 הוֹכַח רֵעַ[c] [d]אֲשֶׁר לֹא יֹאמַר[d]   וְאִם אָמַר פֶּן יִשְׁנֶה׃

II

15 הוֹכַח אוֹהֵב כִּי [e]פְּעָמִים דִּבָּה[e]   וּלְכָל דָּבָר [f]אַל תַּאֲמֵן[f]׃
16 [g]יֵשׁ נִתְקָל[g] וְלֹא מִלִּבּוֹ[h]   [i]וּמִי לֹא חָטָא בִלְשׁוֹנוֹ[i]׃
17 הוֹכַח רֵעַ[j] [k]בְּטֶרֶם תִּזְעֹם[k]   [l]וְתֵן מָקוֹם לְתוֹרַת עֶלְיוֹן[l]׃

c. Text-Critical Notes

This reconstruction is based mainly on G, while also taking into account S and L. Note that G[A] lacks 19:13b–14a (homoioarchton).

13[a]: So G and L; S has "your friend" here and in 19:15a.

13[b–b]: Compare S: "so that he may not do anything evil." G has "perhaps he did not do [it]."[6]

14[c]: So G[SC] and L; S has "your neighbor," while G[B] reads, "the friend."

---

[4] Cf. ibid., 64–76, on Sir 19:6–12. The context section (below) explains why I regard 19:4 as the beginning of the unit.

[5] Here I ignore 19:18–19 (a gloss found only in GII), on which see ibid., 81–83.

[6] See Segal, ספר בן־סירא השלם, 115; and J. L. Kugel, "On Hidden Hatred and Open Reproach: Early Exegesis of Leviticus 19:17," *HTR* 80 (1987): 43–61, esp. 48 n. 12.

14[d–d]: Following S; G has "perhaps he did not say [it]."

15[e–e]: So G; S has "how many times empty slander happens."

15[f–f]: So most MSS of G; S and G^{248} read, "Let not your heart believe."

16[g–g]: So most MSS of G; G^{248} adds "with a word," while L specifies "with his tongue." S, however, reads, "For there is one who sins."

16[h]: So S; G and L read, "from the soul," with a similar meaning (as 4:17 illustrates).

16[i–i]: So G; S^{ALW} reads, "and there is one who stumbles, but not with his tongue."

17[j]: So G^{SV} and L; G^{BAC} reads, "your neighbor." S, however, has "a wicked person," from רַע ("evil," "an evil person").

17[k–k]: So G; S^{LM} reads, "who has wronged many."[7]

17[l–l]: So G; S has "and do not believe every word," by analogy with 19:15b.[8]

After 19:17 GII has two further bicola:

18 Fear of the Lord is the origin of acceptability,
  and wisdom procures love from him.
19 Knowledge of the Lord's commands is an education in life,
  and those who do what is pleasing to him will harvest fruit from the tree of immortality.

Since these two bicola are absent from GI, S, and L, I regard them as a later gloss and hence do not discuss them here.

d. Translation

I

13 Reprove a friend so that he may not do it,
  and if he has done it, lest he do it again.

---

[7] For discussion of the Syriac translator's advocacy of the poor against the powerful, see Winter, "The Origins of Ben Sira in Syriac," 245–49. See also R. J. Owens, "The Early Syriac Text of Ben Sira in the Demonstrations of Aphrahat," *JSS* 34 (1989): 39–75; Owens disputes Winter's claim that the Syriac text of Ben Sira comes from Ebionite circles.

[8] Winter ("The Origins of Ben Sira in Syriac," 498) observes that in eight verses S removes or alters references to the "law" or "commandments" found in G (9:15b, 17b, 20b; 28:6b; 29:11a; 34:8a; 38:34d; 39:8b). These changes are probably due to a Christian translator or reviser.

14 Reprove a companion so that he may not say it,
and if he has said it, lest he repeat it.

II

15 Reprove a friend because often there is malicious talk,
but do not believe every word.
16 There is one who stumbles but not intentionally;
and who has not sinned with his tongue?
17 Reprove a companion before you become indignant,
and give place to the law of the Most High.

e. Poetic Analysis

The alternation between אוֹהֵב ("friend," 19:13a, 15a) and רֵעַ ("companion," 19:14a, 17a) indicates that the poem consists of two stanzas (19:13–14 and 19:15–17). Both stanzas open with the phrase: "Reprove a friend" (vv. 13a, 15a), while the closing bicolon of both stanzas begins with the phrase: "Reprove a companion" (vv. 14a, 17a).[9]

The clearest feature uniting the first stanza (19:13–14) is the parallel syntactic structure (הוֹכַח ... לֹא ... וְאִם ... פֶּן ...). The parallelism also involves two word-pairs, first אוֹהֵב ("friend") and רֵעַ ("companion"),[10] and second הוֹסִיף ("do again") and שָׁנָה ("repeat"). In addition, there is rhyme between the last word of the first colon, יַעֲשֶׂה ("he may do," v. 13a), and the last word of the final colon, יִשְׁנֶה ("he may repeat," v. 14b).

The sound patterns of the second stanza (19:15–17) add to the poetic effect. Verse 15 exhibits assonance between דִּבָּה ("malicious talk," v. 15a) and דָּבָר ("word," v. 15b). In verse 16 rhyme occurs between מִלִּבּוֹ ("from his heart" = "intentionally") at the end of verse 16a and בִּלְשׁוֹנוֹ ("with his tongue") at the end of verse 16b. Verse 16 contains alliteration of *l* (5x), while verse 17 exhibits alliteration of *t* (4x).

f. Context

i. Context of 19:13–17 within 14:20–23:27. Part 4 of the book, 14:20–23:27, consists of two major segments: a theological section (14:20–18:14)

---

[9] Note how the fourfold repetition of the imperative verb הוֹכַח (= ἔλεγξον, "reprove": 19:13a, 14a, 15a, 17a) unifies the poem. Moreover, "the law of the Most High" (19:17b) indicates the end of the pericope, just as the same phrase in 9:15b G draws attention to the approaching conclusion of 9:10–16, and mention of the "commandments" (6:37b G; 28:7a G) marks the ending of 6:18–37 and 27:22–28:7.

[10] This word-pair also occurs in Pss 38:12; 88:19; Prov 14:20; 18:24; Sir 31:2 H^B (a gloss); 33:20 H^E.

concerning topics such as theodicy and free will, and an ethical section (18:15–23:27) concerning speech and self-control. Whereas 14:20–18:14 deals mainly with theoretical wisdom, 18:15–23:27 has to do principally with practical wisdom.[11]

ii. Context of 19:13–17 within 18:15–23:27. The section 18:15–23:27 consists of several poems.

18:15–19:3: Prudential Warnings[12]
19:4–17: Misuse and Proper Use of Speech[13]
19:20–20:31: Wisdom and Folly in Word and Deed[14]
21:1–21: Sin Contrasted with Wisdom[15]
21:22–22:18: Sin and Folly of Various Kinds[16]

---

[11] On 14:20–15:10, see Rickenbacher, *Weisheitsperikopen bei Ben Sira,* 73–98; and Marböck, *Weisheit im Wandel,* 104–13. On 15:11–18:14, see Prato, *Il problema della teodicea,* 209–99.

[12] A twenty-two-line nonalphabetic acrostic in G; S adds two extra bicola in 18:21. The address τέκνον ("child") in 18:15 indicates the start of a new pericope, as often (e.g., 2:1; 3:17; 6:18) but not always (cf. 3:12; 4:1). The end of the pericope is apparent from the allusion to death ("rottenness and worms," 19:3a; compare "worms," 7:17b), as well as from the use of a concluding refrain in 19:3b that is the same as 6:4a.

[13] I regard 19:4–17 as a unit, along with Haspecker (*Gottesfurcht bei Jesus Sirach,* 159), Fuß ("Tradition und Komposition," 125), and Segal (ספר בן־סירא השלם, 115). The end of the pericope recapitulates its opening motifs; thus, "believe" (πίστευε, 19:15b) corresponds to "trusting" (ἐμπιστεύων, 19:4a), "from his heart" (מִלִּבּוֹ, 19:16a; cf. S) parallels "in heart" (καρδίᾳ, 19:4a), and "has ... sinned" (ἥμαρτεν, 19:16b) matches "sinning" (ἁμαρτάνων, 19:4b).

[14] Note the *inclusio* of σοφία ("wisdom," 19:20a) and σοφίαν ("wisdom," 20:31b). On the poem, see P. C. Beentjes, "'Full Wisdom Is Fear of the Lord': Ben Sira 19,20–20,31: Context, Composition and Concept," *EstBib* 47 (1989): 27–45. On Sir 19:20–30, see K. Weber, "Wisdom False and True (Sir 19,20–30)," *Bib* 77 (1996): 330–48; on Sir 20:1–3, 5–8, 13, 18–20, 27, see Krinetzki, "Die Sprüche über das Reden und Schweigen." On the structure of Sir 19:20–23:27, see Marböck, "Structure and Redaction History of the Book of Ben Sira," in Beentjes, ed., *Book of Ben Sira in Modern Research,* 61–79, esp. 74–75.

[15] A twenty-three-line nonalphabetic acrostic (Skehan and Di Lella, *Wisdom of Ben Sira,* 74); whereas vv. 1–10 concern sin, vv. 11–21 are about wisdom. On 21:11–21, see A. J. Desečar, *La sabiduría y la necedad en Sirac 21–22* (Rome: Edizioni Francescane, 1970), 21–44.

[16] On 21:22–22:18, see Desečar, *La sabiduría y la necedad,* 44–74. On 22:9–15, see A. A. Di Lella, "Sirach 22:9–15: 'The Life of a Fool Is Worse Than Death,'" in

22:19–26: Preserving Friendship
22:27–23:27: Control of the Tongue and of Bodily Desires[17]

Much of 18:15–23:27 concerns wise speaking, which is contrasted with the utterances of the fool (cf. 20:13).

iii. Relationship of 19:13–17 with 19:4–12. Sirach 19:4–12, concerning sins of the tongue, is the antithesis of 19:13–17, which discusses a right use for the tongue (reproving a friend).[18] Not only does 19:15–16 return to the motifs of 19:4 (belief/trust; heart; sin); 19:13–14 also develops the motifs of 19:7–8 ("repeat" and "friend").[19]

iv. Relationship of 19:13–17 with 19:20–24. Sirach 19:20–24 forms the opening unit of the segment 19:20–20:31.[20] Beentjes has observed a twofold *inclusio* for the unit: ἔμφοβος ("reverent," 19:24a) balances φόβος κυρίου ("fear of the Lord," 19:20a), while παραβαίνων νόμον ("transgressing the law," 19:24b) corresponds antithetically to ποίησις νόμου ("the doing of the law," 19:20b).[21] Mention of the "law" in 19:17b forms a link-word with 19:20–24,[22] while discussion of sinning with the tongue (19:16b) leads into a concern about sinners in general (19:22b).

Calduch-Benages and Vermeylen, eds., *Treasures of Wisdom*, 159–68. On 22:19–26, see the next chapter of this study.

[17] A nonalphabetic double acrostic of forty-four bicola. Ben Sira makes use of further nonalphabetic double acrostics in 25:13–26:27 (46 bicola) and 42:15–43:26 (45 bicola), following the example of Pss 105 (45 bicola) and 107 (43 bicola); note also the alphabetic double acrostics in Ps 37 (45 bicola) and Pss 9–10 (41 bicola, a damaged acrostic). On Sir 22:27–23:27, see P. C. Beentjes, "Sirach 22:27–23:6 in zijn context," *Bijdr* 39 (1978): 144–51; Desečar, "La necedad en Sirac 23,12–15," *SBFLA* 20 (1970): 264–72; I. Krammer, "Die Auswirkungen des Verhaltens zum Mitmenschen auf die Beziehung zu Gott im Buch Ben Sira" (Th.D. diss., University of Salzburg, 1997), 186–93 (on Sir 23:16–21).

[18] Cf. Kieweler, "Freundschaft und böse Nachrede," 62.

[19] In S the verb "repeat" also occurs in 19:6, while seemingly G has misread שׁוֹנֶה ("one who repeats") as שׂוֹנֵא ("one who hates"); see Skehan and Di Lella, *Wisdom of Ben Sira*, 289. Moreover, 19:6a in G[248] contains γλώσσῃ ("with the tongue"), which matches the mention of the tongue in 19:16b.

[20] Skehan and Di Lella, *Wisdom of Ben Sira*, 299; Beentjes, "Full Wisdom Is Fear of the Lord," 35–36; Rickenbacher, *Weisheitsperikopen bei Ben Sira*, 99–101.

[21] Beentjes, "Full Wisdom Is Fear of the Lord," 35. In addition, the use of the noun σοφία ("wisdom") in 19:23b matches its double use in 19:20.

[22] Haspecker, *Gottesfurcht bei Jesus Sirach*, 52 n. 7.

v. Relationship of 19:13–17 with 22:27–23:27. Ben Sira often juxtaposes word and deed (3:8a; 37:16a); thus, in 19:13–14 reproof for a friend's faulty action immediately precedes reproof for a companion's sinful speech. This juxtaposition occurs several times in Ben Sira.

Deed (sins of passion): 6:2–4; 18:30–19:3; 23:2–6; 23:16–27
Word (sins of the tongue): 5:9–6:1; 19:4–12; 22:27–23:1; 23:7–15[23]

Through such juxtapositions the sage wishes to stress that the wise person will be self-controlled in both action and speech.

g. Exegesis

i. Stanza 1: The Benefit of Reproof (19:13–14). The first stanza opens emphatically with the key word of the whole pericope, "reprove" (19:13a, 14a, 15a, 17a); the imperative verb ἔλεγξον[24] in G represents the Hebrew הוֹכַח[25] (cf. Sir 31:31a H^F). The fundamental text underlying Sir 19:13–17 is Lev 19:17, whence Ben Sira borrows the verb "reprove."[26]

Leviticus 19:17, one of the prescriptions of the Holiness Code, legislates for a matter that is hard to regulate by law:[27]

---

[23] On this juxtaposition in 22:27–23:27, see Beentjes, "Sirach 22:27–23:6 in zijn context," 149–50.

[24] I. de la Potterie (*La Vérité dans Saint Jean, I* [AnBib 73; Rome: Pontifical Biblical Institute, 1977], 399–404) distinguishes six meanings of the verb ἐλέγχειν: make an inquiry; cross-examine; expose; refute; reprove; punish. Here the meaning "reprove" fits best.

[25] In his article "יכח κτλ" (*TDOT* 6:64–71), G. Mayer distinguishes between two main senses of the Hebrew root, a forensic usage (65–68) and a pedagogical usage (68–70). Thus, the verb הוֹכִיחַ has two basic meanings in the MT: in an educational or social context it means "reprove," "correct" (e.g., Lev 19:17; Prov 3:12; 24:25), while in a judicial context it denotes "decide," "adjudicate," "judge," "convict" (e.g., Isa 2:4; 11:3, 4).

[26] In addition, the words אוֹהֵב("one who loves" = "friend," Sir 19:13a, 15a) and רֵעַ ("companion," 19:14a, 17a) may reflect the language of Lev 19:18, which reads: וְאָהַבְתָּ לְרֵעֲךָ כָּמוֹךָ ("and you shall love your neighbor as yourself"). On Lev 19:18, see Mathys, *Liebe deinen Nächsten wie dich selbst*, passim. On the importance of Lev 19 for the Hellenistic-Jewish author Pseudo-Phocylides, see P. W. van der Horst, *The Sentences of Pseudo-Phocylides* (SVTP 4; Leiden: Brill, 1978), 66–67.

[27] Cf. Kugel's comment on Lev 19:15–18: "All of the things enjoined are very difficult to enforce simply by legal fiat—they ultimately depend on the heart of each individual and a desire to comply even when, sometimes, non-compliance is undetectable" ("On Hidden Hatred," 44).

לֹא־תִשְׂנָא אֶת־אָחִיךָ בִּלְבָבֶךָ
הוֹכֵחַ תּוֹכִיחַ אֶת־עֲמִיתֶךָ
וְלֹא־תִשָּׂא עָלָיו חֵטְא׃

You shall not hate your brother in your heart;
you shall surely reprove your compatriot,
so that you will not incur guilt because of him.[28]

Leviticus 19:17 forms part of a section of apodictic laws concerning interpersonal behavior (Lev 19:11–18).[29]

The link between reproof and love, spelled out in Lev 19:17–18 ("you shall surely reprove.... you shall love"), is part of Israel's wisdom tradition. Proverbs 3:12 sees God's reproof as an expression of his parental love: "Yahweh reproves the one whom he loves" (אֶת אֲשֶׁר יֶאֱהַב יְהוָה יוֹכִיחַ ; cf. Prov 13:24; Sir 18:13). Closer to Sir 19:13 are the aphorisms of Prov 27:5–6:

טוֹבָה תּוֹכַחַת מְגֻלָּה מֵאַהֲבָה מְסֻתָּרֶת׃
נֶאֱמָנִים פִּצְעֵי אוֹהֵב וְנַעְתָּרוֹת נְשִׁיקוֹת שׂוֹנֵא׃

Better a revealed reproof
than a hidden love.
Faithful are the wounds of a friend,
but abundant are the kisses of an enemy.[30]

Furthermore, Prov 9:8 observes that "love" is the wise student's reaction to reproof (cf. Ps 141:5; Prov 15:12). Just as Israel's wisdom tradition often situates reproof in the context of "loving" (אהב), so too Ben Sira insists that love of a "friend" (אוֹהֵב) may entail reproving him. In Sir 19:13, therefore, the sage has skillfully combined the teaching of Lev 19:17 with Prov 27:5–6, thereby applying the Levitical prescription to the context of friendship.[31]

---

[28] This understanding of עָלָיו ("because of him") is supported by the rendering of Lev 19:17 G, δι' αὐτὸν.

[29] On Lev 19:17 in its context, see Mathys, *Liebe deinen Nächsten wie dich selbst*, 38–39, 63–67; and G. Barbiero, *L'Asino del Nemico* (AnBib 128; Rome: Pontifical Biblical Institute, 1991), 268–77.

[30] From Prov 27:5–6 Ben Sira derived two features of his teaching on friendship: "reproof" (תּוֹכַחַת; cf. Sir 19:13–17) and faithfulness (נֶאֱמָנִים = "faithful"; cf. Sir 6:14–16).

[31] Leviticus 19:17 is also applied to the context of friendship in 4 Macc 2:13, saying that, with the help of reason, the law (ὁ νόμος) "is master over the intimacy of friends, reproving [ἐξελέγχων] them because of wickedness."

Elsewhere Ben Sira speaks of the value and necessity of reproof. Sirach 20:2–3, for instance, declares: "How much finer to reprove [ἐλέγξαι] than to be angry, and the one confessing will be prevented from disgrace"[32] (because he has heeded the reproof). By way of contrast, using a phrase from Prov 12:1b (שֹׂנֵא תוֹכַחַת, "one who hates reproof"), Sir 21:6a warns: "One who hates reproof is in a sinner's path." Similarly, Sir 32:17 ($H^{B/Bmg}$) observes that "a lawless person will turn aside reproofs" (אִישׁ חָמָס יַטֶּה תוֹכָחוֹת), refusing to listen to criticism.

Although Sir 19:13–17 interprets Leviticus's idea of fraternal correction in a moral and educational sense, as befits wisdom literature,[33] Lev 19:17b also came to be interpreted in a judicial sense during the Second Temple period. Such a legal understanding clearly occurs in the *Damascus Document* found in the Cairo Genizah and paralleled among the Qumran finds.[34] L. H. Schiffman speaks of a "law of reproof" in CD 9.2–8, a law that the community derived from Lev 19:17–18.[35] Schiffman further explains how the community combined the prohibition of grudges (Lev 19:18) with the admonition to reprove (Lev 19:17):

> Lev 19:18 has been interpreted here to mean that a member who sees an offense must immediately perform the required "reproof." If he does not, but later makes an accusation, he violates Lev 19:18 by "bearing a grudge" and "taking vengeance."[36]

---

[32] 20:3 G has ἐλαττώσεως ("indigence"), presupposing חֶסֶר ("lack"), but חֶסֶר can also mean "disgrace"; see N. M. Bronznick, "An Unrecognized Denotation of the Verb *ḤSR* in Ben-Sira and Rabbinic Hebrew," *HAR* 9 (1985): 91–105, esp. 100.

[33] Kugel ("On Hidden Hatred," 45) notes how the stipulation of reproof in Lev 19:17 reflects the world of Israelite wisdom.

[34] For a translation of the Qumran fragments of the *Damascus Document,* see García Martínez, *Dead Sea Scrolls Translated,* 47–71. 4Q269 10.1–3 contains part of CD 9.5–8; 4Q270 10 iii 17–20 has part of CD 9.2–6, while 5Q12 1.2 provides CD 9:7–8 (ibid., 61, 65, 70). For the Hebrew text, see J. M. Baumgarten et al., *Qumran Cave 4.13: The Damascus Document (4Q266–4Q273)* (DJD 18; Oxford: Clarendon, 1996). On the use of Lev 19:17–18 in CD (and also in 1QS), see Mathys, *Liebe deinen Nächsten wie dich selbst,* 120–23.

[35] L. H. Schiffman, *Sectarian Law in the Dead Sea Scrolls* (BJS 33; Chico, Calif.: Scholars Press, 1983), 89; note that CD 7.2 also alludes to the Levitical "law of reproof."

[36] Ibid. The text of CD 9.2–4, 6–8, according to the translation of García Martínez (*Dead Sea Scrolls Translated,* 40) reads: "And what it says: [*Lev 19:18*]: 'Do not avenge yourself or bear resentment against the sons of your people': everyone of those who entered the covenant who brings an accusation against his fellow, unless it is with reproach [בְּהוֹכֵחַ] before witnesses, or who brings it when

A New Testament parallel to CD 9.2–8, Matt 18:15–17, also employs the verb "reprove" (ἔλεγξον [Matt 18:15], exactly as in Sir 19:13, 14, 15, 17 G), in conjunction with the legal requirement of two or three witnesses (cf. Deut 19:15).

The Qumran community took seriously the "law of reproof" in Lev 19:17. The *Rule of the Community* prescribes reproof as part of the way of life for members (1QS 5.24–6.1):

> Each should reproach [לְהוֹכִיחַ] his fellow in truth, in meekness and in compassionate love for the man. [*Blank*] No-one should speak to his brother in anger or muttering, ... and he should not detest him [וְאַל יִשְׂנָאֵהוּ] [in the stubbornness] of his heart, but instead reproach him [יוֹכִיחֶנּוּ] that day so as not to incur a sin for his fault. And in addition, no-one should raise a matter against his fellow in front of the Many unless it is with reproof [בְּתוֹכַחַת] in the presence of witnesses.[37]

Also parallel to Sir 19:13–17 and dependent on Lev 19:17 is chapter 6 of the *Testament of Gad*.[38] In particular, Gad's exhortatory words

---

he is angry, or he tells it to his elders so that they despise him, he is 'the one who avenges himself and bears resentment'.... If he kept silent about him from one day to the other, or accused him of a capital offence, he has witnessed against himself, for he did not fulfil the commandment of God which tells him: [*Lev 19:17*] 'You shall reproach your fellow so as not to incur sin because of him.'"

[37] Ibid., 9. One fragmentary Qumran text (4Q477) lists persons who had been reproved at the community meeting according to the sect's procedure for judicial discipline. Thus, 4Q477 1 ii 3–5 records: "[They reproached] Johanan, son of Mata[thias because he] ... was quick for anger, ... and has the evil eye, and also has a boastful spirit.... And they reproached [הוֹכִיחוּ] Hananiah Notos" (ibid., 90). In her article "4Q477: The Rebukes by the Overseer" (*JJS* 45 [1994]: 111–22), E. Eshel notes: "Apparently, this text preserves remnants of a legal record, compiled by the sect's Overseer (מבקר), of those members who were rebuked after committing a sin" (111). Note that some of Eshel's readings of the text differ from those of García Martínez. See further E. Eshel, "4QRebukes Reported by the Overseer," in *Qumran Cave 4.26: Cryptic Texts and Miscellanea, Part 1* (ed. S. J. Pfann et al.; DJD 36; Oxford, Clarendon, 2000), 474–83, esp. 481.

[38] Although the present form of the *Testaments of the Twelve Patriarchs* shows the influence of Christian redaction, its origins are Jewish, possibly from the second century B.C.E.; J. H. Ulrichsen dates the basic text of the work to 200–175 B.C.E. (*Die Grundschrift der Testamente der Zwölf Patriarchen* [Uppsala: Almqvist & Wiksell, 1995], 339). Nothing in ch. 6 of the *Testament of Gad* demands a Christian source; indeed, the similarities to Ben Sira (especially to Sir 19:8–9, 13–17; 20:2–3; 28:1–2) support Ulrichsen's suggested date for the original of this passage.

concerning loving reproof (*T. Gad* 6.3) are in harmony with Ben Sira's sentiments:

> Love one another from the heart, and if a man sins against you, speak to him in peace, after having cast away the poison of hatred; and do not hold guile in your soul. And if he confesses and repents, forgive him.[39]

In Greek culture also, candid reproof was viewed as a mark of true friendship. Thus, the Greeks referred to the παρρησία ("frankness" or "boldness") with which the genuine friend offered criticism, by contrast with the fine words uttered by the flatterer who spoke only to please (cf. Aristotle, *Eth. nic.* 10.3.11). Indeed, in his letter *To Antipater* 4, Isocrates offers a commendation of his pupil Diodotus for his "frankness ... which would rightly be regarded as the surest indication of devotion to his friends."[40]

According to my reconstructed text of Sir 19:13a, which echoes the wording of S ("so that he may not do anything evil"), the sage advocates reproving a friend before he actually sins. However, G understands the phrase differently, that is, as introducing an element of doubt whether the friend actually did the wrong deed. A similar divergence between S and G occurs in 19:14a (concerning speech).

In Sir 19:14a (and 19:17a) the sage urges: "Reprove your companion" (ἔλεγξον τὸν πλησίον). While for the sake of variety Ben Sira may have used the synonym רֵעַ ("companion") instead of אוֹהֵב ("friend"), this reading also corresponds more exactly with the form of Lev 19:17b found in other texts. Whereas the MT urges, "You shall surely reprove your compatriot" (עֲמִיתֶךָ), the quotation in CD 9.7–8 reads, "You shall surely reprove your companion" (רֵעֵיךָ).[41] Similarly, Lev 19:17b G states: "With a reproof[42] you shall reprove your companion" (τὸν πλησίον σου). Thus, it is evident that the reading רֵעֵיךָ ("your neighbor") for Lev 19:17b represents an early tradition.

---

[39] H. W. Hollander and M. de Jonge, *The Testaments of the Twelve Patriarchs: A Commentary* (SVTP 8; Leiden: Brill, 1985), 331.

[40] Norlin and van Hook, trans., *Isocrates*, 3:415. On the contrast between flattery and frankness, see the following essays in Fitzgerald, ed., *Friendship, Flattery, and Frankness of Speech:* D. Konstan, "Friendship, Frankness, and Flattery," 7–19; C. E. Glad, "Frank Speech, Flattery, and Friendship in Philodemus," 21–59; T. Engberg-Pedersen, "Plutarch to Prince Philopappus on How to Tell a Flatterer from a Friend," 61–79; see also Konstan, *Friendship in the Classical World*, 93–95, 98–105.

[41] Note the plene spelling of the singular noun, as in 2 Sam 12:11.

[42] G uses this circumlocution to render the Hebrew infinitive absolute.

Elsewhere, out of a concern for shame, Ben Sira moderates the demand of Lev 19:17b, by warning against choosing the wrong time to reprove a companion. Thus, in 20:1a he advises: "There is a rebuke [ἔλεγχος] that is untimely" (NRSV). In particular, the middle of a banquet is an inappropriate time (31:31–32a H^F^): "At a banquet of wine do not reprove a companion [אַל תּוֹכַח רֵעַ], and do not grieve him when he is joyful. Do not say to him a disgraceful word."

Human reproof of companions parallels God's reproving of humanity, an aspect of the divine mercy: "A human being's mercy is toward his neighbor, but the Lord's mercy is toward all humanity, reproving [ἐλέγχων] and disciplining and teaching" (18:13 G). Thus, Ben Sira teaches that mercy, whether human or divine, involves an element of discipline and reproof.[43]

The verb "say" (אמר) in 19:14a corresponds to the verb "do" (עשׂה) in 19:13a. The same linkage occurs in Sir 3:8: "In speech and in deed [בְּמַאֲמָר וּבְמַעֲשֶׂה] honor your father."[44] Middendorp observes that the connection between "word" and "deed" appears also in Xenophon's *Memorabilia*.[45] However, the biblical tradition already attests to this connection in the first chapter of Genesis.[46]

In Sir 19:14 the sage teaches that reproof will stop a companion from saying unhelpful things in the first place, or else from repeating them once they have been said. Already Prov 17:9 warned of the harm done by continually repeating such negative words: "One who seeks friendship [אַהֲבָה] covers over transgression, but one who repeats a matter [שֹׁנֶה בְדָבָר] alienates an associate." Similarly, Sir 19:6–7 S teaches: "One who repeats a matter is lacking in sense. Never repeat a matter, and no one will disgrace you." Moreover, 42:1 H^BM^ urges: "[Be ashamed] of repeating a matter [מִשְּׁנוֹת דָּבָר] that you may have heard."

---

43 On the analogy between human friendship and God's relationship to his servants, see Irwin, "Fear of God," 557–58.

44 Moreover, Sir 37:16a H^D^ states: "The origin of every work [or deed] is speech" (ראשׁ כָּל מַעֲשֶׂה מַאֲמָר), possibly an allusion to God's creation of the world in Gen 1.

45 Middendorp (*Die Stellung Jesu Ben Siras*, 13) refers to *Mem.* 2.3.8, 15, 17; 2.10.6; 3.11.10. *Memorabilia* 3.11.10 declares: "That your friends [φίλοι] give you satisfaction, you convince them, I know, not by words but by deeds [οὐ λόγῳ ἀλλ' ἔργῳ]" (Marchant, trans., *Xenophon*, 245). See also Sanders, *Ben Sira and Demotic Wisdom*, 43–44.

46 See, for example, Gen 1:6–7: "And God said [וַיֹּאמֶר], 'Let there be a dome in the midst of the waters. . . .' And God made [וַיַּעַשׂ] the dome." Note that the verbs in Gen 1:6–7 G (εἶπεν: "he said"; ἐποίησεν: "he made") are identical with those at the end of Sir 19:13a, 14a G.

ii. Stanza 2: The Need for Reproof (19:15–17). "Malicious talk" (דִּבָּה, representing διαβολή in 51:2)[47] is something against which wisdom teachers warn. For example, Prov 10:18b declares, "The one who brings forth malicious talk [דִּבָּה] is a fool," while Prov 25:10b, warning against revealing the confidence of another person, says, "The malicious talk about you (דִּבָּתְךָ) will not cease."

Living in a society with a strong culture of honor and shame, Ben Sira is concerned that his students avoid any actions that might give rise to such disgrace.[48] According to 26:5c G "the malicious talk of a city" (διαβολὴν πόλεως) is worse than death, while in 42:11c H^BM the sage urges his students to be vigilant over a daughter lest her misconduct make them "the malicious talk of the city" (דִּבַּת עִיר). Similarly, a person should follow suitable mourning customs "on account of malicious talk" (χάριν διαβολῆς, 38:17c G).[49] According to 28:9b G, a sinner's "enmity" (or "malicious talk," διαβολήν)[50] disrupts friendship. Hence, in 19:15a Ben Sira counsels his audience to warn a friend against any conduct that might engender "malicious talk" from an enemy. The friend is to be reproved so that he may avoid suffering from "malicious talk," true but unwelcome talk arising from his misbehavior.[51]

In 19:15b the sage warns against being gullible about reports of a friend's supposed misbehavior. Ben Sira's thought here is comparable to Qoh 7:21: "To all the words that people will say, do not give your

---

[47] The Hebrew term דִּבָּה may refer to an "evil report," talk that is true but unfavorable (Gen 37:2; Num 13:32; 14:36, 37; Sir 46:7 H^B). The cognate Greek verb διαβάλλω means "make a hostile accusation against [someone]," either with false and slanderous charges (4 Macc 4:1) or on the basis of the truth (Dan 3:8).

[48] Cf. Sir 41:14a; 41:16–42:8 (a twenty-three-line nonalphabetic acrostic); cf. Sanders, "Ben Sira's Ethics of Caution," 83–85.

[49] In 38:17, H^B reads דִּמְעָה ("tears") for דִּבָּה ("malicious talk").

[50] Note that S and L read "enmity"; see the brief discussion of 28:9 in the appendix. The cognate noun διάβολος has the meaning "enemy" in LXX Esth 7:4; 8:1.

[51] This interpretation agrees with the sense of דִּבָּה as "evil report" (Gen 37:2; Num 13:32; 14:36, 37; Sir 46:7), where the report is true but negative. It also corresponds to the normal explanatory meaning of כִּי (and γὰρ) as "for," "because." The more widely held interpretation of 19:15a sees διαβολή as a "slander" or "false accusation," which should therefore not be believed (19:15b); cf. Skehan and Di Lella, *Wisdom of Ben Sira,* 293; Segal, ספר בן־סירא השלם, 116. In this interpretation the verse is understood as follows: "Reprove a friend, though often there is slander, and [hence] do not believe every word." For the meaning "though" for כִּי, see Jer 14:12; Zech 8:6; Ps 37:24; compare also Joüon, 2:641 (§171b).

attention."[52] In warning the student against being so gullible as to believe everything said by others, Sir 19:15b seems also to draw on Prov 14:15a: "A simpleton will believe every word" (פֶּתִי יַאֲמִין לְכָל־דָּבָר).[53]

This wariness about believing what others say fits in with Ben Sira's "ethics of caution." The sage recommends this caution for a variety of human relationships, not just toward an enemy, but also toward a hated wife and toward a prince who holds long and testing conversations.[54] In 19:15b Ben Sira's warning against being gullible takes up the theme of 19:4a, the opening statement of 19:4–17: "One who quickly trusts is light-headed" (ὁ ταχὺ ἐμπιστεύων κοῦφος καρδίᾳ).[55]

Instead of opening with the expected command "reprove," Sir 19:16 digresses with a general statement that suggests two reasons for moderation in one's zeal to reprove a friend. Verse 16a is a reminder that some offenses may be unintentional, while verse 16b recalls that no one is guiltless (not even the person reproving).

Sirach 19:16a begins with "there is" (יֵשׁ = ἔστιν), a formula used to record an insight (often paradoxical or unexpected) from a general observation of the world and human behavior (cf. Prov 10:24; 12:18; 14:12; 16:25; 20:15). For instance, Prov 13:7 declares: "There is [יֵשׁ] one who pretends to be rich but has nothing, and [there is] one who pretends to be poor but has great wealth." A similar format occurs in Qoh 8:14: "There are [יֵשׁ] righteous people who get what the wicked deserve for their action, and there are [יֵשׁ] wicked people who get what the righteous deserve for their action." Such a format also has parallels in late Egyptian wisdom literature, such as P. Insinger 9.16–17: "There is he who has not been taught, yet he knows how to instruct another.

[52] Note that the following verse in Ben Sira (Sir 19:16) has a parallel in the thought of the preceding verse in Qoheleth (Qoh 7:20). Ben Sira may be aware of Qoheleth, though this is denied by F. J. Backhaus, "Qohelet und Sirach," *BN* 69 (1993): 32–55; and C. F. Whitley, *Koheleth: His Language and Thought* (BZAW 148; Berlin: de Gruyter, 1979), 122–46. See further J. Marböck, "Kohelet und Sirach: Eine vielschichtige Beziehung," in *Das Buch Kohelet: Studien zur Struktur, Geschichte, Rezeption und Theologie* (ed. L. Schwienhorst-Schönberger; BZAW 254; Berlin: de Gruyter, 1997), 275–301.

[53] Note also the advice of the prophet Micah: אַל־תַּאֲמִינוּ בְרֵעַ ("Do not believe a companion," Mic 7:5).

[54] Ben Sira advises caution toward an enemy in 12:10 H^{A} (cf. Prov 26:24–26; P. Insinger 12.8), toward a hated wife in Sir 7:26b H^{A}, and toward a prince in Sir 13:11b H^{A}, which warns: אל תַּאֲמֵן לְרֹב שׂיחו ("Do not believe his lengthy talk"); cf. Sanders, "Ben Sira's Ethics of Caution," 76–86.

[55] Behind this statement I suspect a Hebrew wordplay between קַל meaning "quick" (hence ταχύ, "quickly") and קַל in the sense of "light" (κοῦφος).

There is he who knows the instruction, yet he does not know how to live by it."[56]

Within Sir 19:20–20:31 there are twenty-four cola beginning ἔστιν (= יֵשׁ, "there is") or οὐκ ἔστιν (= אֵין, "there is not");[57] for instance, 20:6 H^C teaches: "There is [יֵשׁ] one who is silent without an answer, and there is [יֵשׁ] one who is silent because he has recognized the time." The same format also occurs in some of Ben Sira's friendship pericopes (6:8–10; 37:1).

The Hebrew verb "slip" (= "be tripped," *nipʿal* of תקל) denotes a physical fall in Sir 13:23 H^A and 32:20 H^BEF.[58] In 15:12, however, the causative of the verb (*hipʿil* of תקל) refers to a moral lapse: "Do not say, 'My transgression is from God,' ... lest you say, 'It was he who made me slip'" (15:11a, 12a H^AB). In the grandson's translation, the verb ὀλισθάνω ("slip") usually refers to a moral lapse (such as with the tongue, cf. 19:16b). For example, 14:1a G says, "Happy the man who did not slip [οὐκ ὠλίσθησεν] with his mouth,"[59] while 28:26a G urges care with the tongue: "Be careful, lest somehow you slip [ὀλίσθῃς] with it."

The phrase "not intentionally" means literally "from his heart" (מִלִּבּוֹ) in Hebrew (following S), whereas G reads "from the soul" (ἀπὸ ψυχῆς). The same Hebrew idiom occurs in Lam 3:33; although the destruction of Jerusalem appears to be God's punishment, "he has not willingly [מִלִּבּוֹ] caused affliction."

Just as Sir 19:16 connects the heart and the tongue, so too other sapiential texts point out the need to control both the tongue and the heart. Psalm 39 describes the psalmist's effort to avoid sinning with his tongue (39:1), an effort that caused his heart to grow hot within him (39:4). Ben Sira's prayer for self-control (Sir 22:27–23:6) takes up the thought of Ps 39 in praying for discipline of the tongue (22:27d) and of the heart (23:2b). Most similar to 19:16b is the sage's question in 22:27 G: "Who

---

[56] *AEL* 3:192. For other examples (usually in couplets), see P. Insinger 2.14–15; 5.3–4, 20–23; 7.13–14; 8.8–10; 11.13–14; 19.1–2; 21.3–4; 23.15–16; 32.22–24; Ankhsheshonq 26.3–7. Moreover, Ankhsheshonq 21.1–12 has a series of sayings beginning "There is no. . . ."

[57] Cf. Beentjes, "Full Wisdom Is Fear of the Lord," 37. For other examples of sayings with יֵשׁ ("there is"), see Sir 4:21; 10:30; 11:11–12, 18; 37:19–23.

[58] On the root תקל ("to trip"), see my exegesis of Sir 13:23d in ch 4.

[59] However, 14:1a H^A reads: אַשְׁרֵי אֱנוֹשׁ לֹא עֲצָבוֹ פִּיהוּ ("Happy the human being whose mouth has not caused him grief"). Compare also 4Q525 14 ii 26–27: "Be very careful against a slip of the tongue ... lest you be condemned by your (own) lips" (García Martínez, *Dead Sea Scrolls Translated,* 397). Besides verbal self-discipline, 4Q525 counsels a disciplined approach to eating and drinking, and the fragmentary text of 4Q525 25.4 seems to quote Sir 18:33; see Puech, *Qumran Cave 4.18,* 164–65.

[τίς] will place a guard upon my mouth and an effective seal on my lips, that I may not fall on account of them, and my tongue [γλῶσσα] may not destroy me?"

The concern about sin in Sir 19:16b already appears in the Levitical command to reprove a neighbor; Lev 19:17c says that by means of reproof "you will not incur guilt [or sin, חֵטְא] because of him." Sirach 19:16b implies that because everyone sometimes sins with the tongue and needs to be reproved, no one can claim moral superiority over a companion. In a balanced friendship, each friend will both give and receive reproof; indeed, this may be one aspect of the saying: "Iron sharpens iron, and one person sharpens the wits of another" (Prov 27:17 NRSV).

Ancient Israelite sapiential teaching often (as in Sir 19:16b) makes use of the rhetorical question מִי ("who?"), where the implied answer is "no one."[60] Sometimes, however, the question "who?" implies a more specific answer, "no one except God."[61]

Ben Sira has much to say on the sins of the tongue (5:9–6:1; 19:4–12; 20:16–26; 22:27–23:15; 28:8–26). A survey of his sayings on the subject will illustrate his outlook, which often connects the tongue with tripping and falling (cf. 14:1; 21:7; 28:26). At the heart of the sage's first discourse on the tongue (5:9–6:1) stands the aphorism of 5:13:

כָּבוֹד וְקָלוֹן בְּיַד בּוֹטֵא   וּלְשׁוֹן אָדָם מַפַּלְתּוֹ׃

Glory and dishonor are in the power of a speaker,
and the tongue of a human being is his downfall.[62]

So too, Sir 20:18a declares, ὀλίσθημα ἀπὸ ἐδάφους μᾶλλον ἢ ἀπὸ γλώσσης ("A slip due to the pavement rather than due to the tongue"),[63] while Sir 28:18 asserts: "Many have fallen by the mouth of the sword, but not like those having fallen on account of the tongue." In a similar fashion,

[60] E.g., Prov 30:4; Sir 10:29; 12:13; 14:5; 36:31; 42:25; 43:3; 46:3, 19.

[61] E.g., Job 38:5–6, 25, 28, 36–37, 41; 39:5; Sir 16:17, 20–22 H^A; 22:27 G; 23:2 G; cf. Isa 40:12–14; 41:2, 26.

[62] So H^A, but correcting ביוד to בְּיַד with H^C; for בּוֹטֵא as "speaker," see S. A comparable aphorism is present in the Egyptian Instruction of Any 7.9: "A man may be ruined by his tongue" (*AEL* 2:140).

[63] Compare Ankhsheshonq 10.7: "You may trip over your foot in the house of a great man; you should not trip over your tongue" (ibid., 3:167). Middendorp notes a parallel saying attributed to the third-century B.C.E. Stoic philosopher Zeno of Citium in Diogenes Laertius's *Lives of the Ancient Philosophers* 7.26: "Better to slip with the foot than with the tongue" (*Die Stellung Jesu ben Siras*, 20).

the macarism of 25:8 H^C teaches: אַשְׁרֵי שֶׁלֹּא נָפַל בַּלָּשׁוֹן ("Happy the one who has not fallen by the tongue"). The sage affirms the preeminence of the tongue succinctly in his list of the "four branches" (37:18a H^D) that grow up in the "heart" (or "mind"): "[They are] good and evil, and life and death—and ruling over them completely is the tongue" (37:18bc H^B).

The idea that all human beings have sinned, presumed in Sir 19:16b, is widespread in Israel's wisdom literature.[64] Thus, Qoh 7:20 declares: "There is no righteous human being on earth who will do good and will not sin" (וְלֹא יֶחֱטָא).[65] Similarly, using the same device of the rhetorical question as in Sir 19:16b, Prov 20:9 asks: "Who may say, 'I have purified my heart, I am clean from my sin'?"[66] In the New Testament, too, the Letter of James echoes these sapiential themes in its discussion of the tongue: "For we all stumble in many ways. If someone does not stumble in speech, he is a perfect man, able to restrain even his whole body" (Jas 3:2).[67]

In Sir 19:17a the sage returns to the thought of Lev 19:17–18; instead of bearing a grudge (Lev 19:18) and making angry threats (Lev 19:17), one should reprove a companion. Sirach 19:17a also makes use of the vocabulary of Prov 24:24–25:

> One who says to a wicked person, "You are righteous"—peoples will curse him, nations will be indignant at him [יִזְעָמוּהוּ];
> but for those who reprove [לַמּוֹכִיחִים] it will be pleasant, and upon them will come the blessing of prosperity.

In 19:17a Ben Sira has skillfully combined the thought and vocabulary of Lev 19:17–18 and Prov 24:24–25. While Lev 19:17–18 urges reproof instead of anger, Prov 24:24–25 says that failure to reprove will cause a reaction of indignation. Combining and adapting these ideas, Ben Sira

---

64 For a brief summary of Ben Sira's teaching on sin, see Skehan and Di Lella, *Wisdom of Ben Sira,* 81–83; R. E. Murphy, "Sin, Repentance, and Forgiveness in Sirach," in Egger-Wenzel and Krammer, *Der Einzelne und seine Gemeinschaft bei Ben Sira,* 261–70, esp. 262–65; Collins, *Jewish Wisdom in the Hellenistic Age,* 80–84.

65 For this idea cf. 1 Kgs 8:46; Pss 14:3; 53:4; 130:3; 143:2; Rom 3:23; 4 Ezra 6:35; 1QH 23.12; Aristotle, *[Rhet. Alex.]* 36 §1444a.

66 Cf. the similar question (expressing the rarity of virtue) in Sir 31:10cd H^B: "Who was able to turn aside but did not turn aside, or to do evil but was unwilling?"

67 On control of the tongue in the Letter of James, see W. R. Baker, *Personal Speech-Ethics in the Epistle of James* (WUNT 2/68; Tübingen: Mohr, 1995).

recommends the fearless honesty of unsentimental friendship: "Reprove a companion before you become indignant."[68]

Sirach 19:17b concludes the pericope by urging the student to "give place to the law of the Most High." The idiom נָתַן מָקוֹם ("give place"), found in a literal sense in Judg 20:36 ("yield ground"), often has a derived meaning in Ben Sira ("give an opportunity"). Thus, Sir 38:12a H^B advises: וְגַם לְרוֹ[פֵא תֵּ]ן מָקוֹם ("And also to the doc[tor gi]ve place"). Moreover, when urging generosity to someone poor, Sir 4:5 H^A explains: "You will not give him an opportunity to curse you" (לֹא תִתֵּן לוֹ מָקוֹם לְקַלֶּלְךָ)."[69]

The nuance of the "law of the Most High" (תּוֹרַת עֶלְיוֹן, equivalent to νόμος ὑψίστου) depends on the context in the sage's work.[70] In 23:23 G the phrase denotes the commandment against adultery (Exod 20:14; Lev 20:10; Deut 5:18; 22:22), while in 44:20 G it refers to God's commands to Abraham, especially the law of circumcision (Gen 17:9–14). In 41:4b H^B the "law of the Most High" that all must die appears to be an allusion to Gen 2:17. Hence it is reasonable to understand Sir 19:17b as a reference to another pentateuchal command, the law of reproof in Lev 19:17–18.[71] Indeed, a comparable allusion to Lev 19:17–18 seems to be present in Sir 28:7 G: "Remember the commandments, and do not be angry with your neighbor, and the covenant of the Most High, and overlook wrongdoing." Thus, Ben Sira teaches that instead of burning with anger, one should calmly reprove an erring friend in accordance with the provisions of Lev 19.

h. Summary

Both the Wisdom of Ben Sira and certain Qumran texts take seriously the injunction of Lev 19:17 to reprove a fellow Israelite for wrongdoing. However, whereas the Qumran texts (CD 9:2–8; 1QS 5:24–6.1; 4Q477)[72]

---

[68] My retroversion of Sir 19:17a follows Isa 66:14 G, where ἀπειλέω ("threaten") represents the verb זעם; cf. Kugel, "On Hidden Hatred," 48 n. 13.

[69] The text of G is somewhat different here; see Skehan and Di Lella, *Wisdom of Ben Sira,* 163. On the idiom in Sir 13:22d see the previous chapter above.

[70] On the phrase in Sir 9:15b G, see ch. 3 above. The same phrase in 38:34 G has a sapiential nuance; compare 9:14–15; 19:20; 21:11, which all connect wisdom with the law.

[71] So Skehan and Di Lella, *Wisdom of Ben Sira,* 294; and Schnabel, *Law and Wisdom from Ben Sira to Paul,* 46. However, Beentjes ("Full Wisdom Is Fear of the Lord," 33) understands the phrase as a reference to the whole law, in view of the following verse (19:20).

[72] CD 9.2–8 (from the Cairo Genizah) is almost completely preserved at Qumran in composite form (4Q270; 4Q269; 5Q12).

speak of reproof in a judicial context culminating in a community "chapter of faults," Ben Sira inculcates a private reproof in the context of friendship. The sage warns against excessive reproof, citing three reasons for moderation in this matter: the need to avoid being too gullible, the existence of unintentional offenses, and the fact that everyone commits verbal sins at one time or another. Nevertheless, he suggests that reproof according to the Torah prevents hidden resentments from harming one's friendships.

3. Sirach 27:16–21

The fifth part of the Wisdom of Ben Sira (24:1–32:13)[73] contains only one poem dedicated to the theme of friendship, namely, 27:16–21.[74] However, several other verses in 24:1–32:13 mention the topic briefly (25:1, 9; 28:9; 29:10; 30:3, 6). The second half of the present chapter will study 27:16–21, a didactic poem about the irrevocable harm done to friendship by betraying secrets. Since no Hebrew MS of the pericope is extant,[75] I offer a reconstructed text based on G and S; the textual notes will explain my retroversions.[76]

a. Delimitation

The concern of 27:16–21 with friendship distinguishes it from the surrounding material. In 25:13–28:7 φίλος ("friend") occurs only in 27:16b, 17a, while φιλία ("friendship") is present only in 27:18b.

Stylistic features also indicate that 27:16–21 is a separate unit. A prominent *inclusio* exists, whereby the first colon (27:16a) and the last colon (27:21b) both begin with a saying about "one who reveals a confidence."[77] A secondary inclusio is also present, since the loss of

---

[73] I consider that the sixth part of Ben Sira's book begins with the sapiential poem in 32:14–33:18; cf. Harvey, "Toward a Degree of Order," 52–54.

[74] On the pericope, see O. Kaiser, "Was ein Freund nicht tun darf," 107–22.

[75] Kaiser (ibid., 108–9) regards a gloss that follows 31:2ab H^B as the Hebrew original of 27:16. However, Skehan and Di Lella (*Wisdom of Ben Sira*, 315–16) point out that the bicolon "is closer ... to reflecting the content of 22:22 than that of 27:16." For the Hebrew text of the gloss, see my footnote on 41:18c in the appendix below.

[76] For this reconstruction Segal's text (ספר בן־סירא השלם, 167–68) has served as a useful model, although in a number of places I opt for different readings.

[77] In both cases G employs a participial expression: 27:16a opens with ὁ ἀποκαλύπτων μυστήρια, while 27:21b starts with ὁ δὲ ἀποκαλύψας μυστήρια; cf. Skehan and Di Lella, *Wisdom of Ben Sira*, 73 (for the secondary *inclusio*, see 358).

"faith" (πίστιν, 27:16a) is related to losing hope (verb ἀφήλπισεν, 27:21b).

Besides *inclusio,* the presence of opening and closing rhyme in my retroverted text also serves to delimit 27:16–21. There is opening rhyme between the second colon (לְנַפְשׁוֹ, 27:16b) and the third (עִמּוֹ, 27:17a), as well as internal rhyme within 27:16 (אֱמוּנָה, v. 16a, and יִמְצָא, v. 16b).[78] Closing internal rhyme exists within 27:21a (חֲבִישָׁה and מְרִיבָה), and there is a further rhyme with the final word of 27:21b (תִּקְוָה).

b. Retroverted Text of Sirach 27:16–21

I

16 מְגַלֶּה סוֹד[a] מְאַבֵּד[b] אֱמוּנָה   וְלֹא יִמְצָא אוֹהֵב לְנַפְשׁוֹ[c]׃
17 נַסֵּה[d] חָבֵר וְהֵאָמֵן עִמּוֹ   וְגִלִּיתָ[e] סוֹד אַל תִּרְדְּפֶנּוּ׃

II

18 כִּי כְּאִישׁ מְאַבֵּד אוֹיְבוֹ[f]   כֵּן אִבַּדְתָּ אַהֲבַת רֵעַ׃
19 וּכְעוֹף מִיָּדְךָ שִׁלַּחְתָּ   [g]כֵּן עָזַבְתָּ רֵעַ[g] וְלֹא תְצוּדֶנּוּ׃

III

20 אַל תִּרְדְּפֶנּוּ [h]כִּי הִתְרַחֵק[h]   כִּי[i] נָס כִּצְבִי[j] מִפַּח׃
21 כִּי [k]לְפֶצַע חֲבִישָׁה[k] וְרִצּוּי לִמְרִיבָה[l]   [m]וּמְגַלֵּה סוֹד אִבַּד תִּקְוָה[m]׃

c. Text-Critical Notes

My reconstruction represents an eclectic text based on G, S, and L.

16[a]. Singular as S; understood as collective by G and L.

16[b]. Participle with S; G uses aorist.

16[c]. So G and L; S presumes כְּנַפְשׁוֹ ("like himself"; cf. Sir 7:21; 37:2).

17[d]. So H[C];[79] cf. S. However, most MSS of G have στέρξον ("love," cf. L).[80]

---

[78] Both these rhymes occur in Segal's reconstruction (ספר בן־סירא השלם, 167).

[79] The last word on leaf VI (verso) of H[C] (= T–S 12.867) is נסה; see Beentjes, *Book of Ben Sira in Hebrew,* 99; as well as Di Lella, "Recently Identified Leaves," 166 (cf. photograph in tab. V). Di Lella suggests the word is the "beginning of another v., perhaps 38,10; see Ms B margin" (167). Since the word follows 36:31 in the anthological MS H[C], and since the edition of Schechter and Taylor (*Wisdom of Ben Sira,* 17) gives the word in the margin of H[B] at the start of 38:10 (where their text has נ[ו]ס, "flee"), the word could be understood as the emphatic imperative נֻסָה ("flee"), similar in form to קוּמָה ("arise," Num 10:35, cf. GKC §48k). However,

17[e]. So G and L, with "if" understood in the Hebrew protasis (as in Sir 6:7a H[A]; cf. 1:26 G). S has a third singular verb (S[M]: "he has revealed"; S[LW]: "he reveals").

18[f]. So most MSS of G (τὸν ἐχθρὸν αὐτοῦ, "his enemy"). Instead of אוֹיְבוֹ ("his enemy"), L presupposes אוֹהֲבוֹ ("his friend"). S has "his portion," from יְהָבוֹ ("his portion").[81] The reading of S, *mnth* ("his portion"), was seemingly corrupted into *myth* ("his dead person"), presumably the origin of τὸν νεκρὸν αὐτοῦ (G[157] and Ziegler's text: "his dead person") and *mortuum* [*suum*] (L[SX]: "[his] dead person").[82]

19[g–g]. S omits this phrase, found in G and L.

20[h–h]. S omits this phrase, which is present in G and L. The *hitpaʿel* verb (unattested in the MT) is found twice in Sir 13:10 H[A].

Smend (*Sirach, erklärt,* 340), Segal (ספר בן־סירא השלם, 243), and Skehan and Di Lella (*Wisdom of Ben Sira,* 440) read the word in the text of 38:10 as סוּר ("depart") and the marginal word as הָסֵר ("remove," cf. G and S). Furthermore, in his article דפים נוספים מתוך ספר בן־סירא (*Tarbiz* 29 [1959–1960]: 313–23, esp. 323), M. Z. Segal proposes that נסה in H[C] belongs to 37:27a, where H[B] reads נַס ("test"), but this proposal founders on the word's position in the middle of 37:27a (not at the start of the colon). After reviewing these two suggestions for the placement of the word (37:27a and 38:10a), P. C. Beentjes ("Hermeneutics in the Book of Ben Sira," *EstBib* 46 [1988]: 45–60, esp. 57) confesses perplexity in the matter. My suggestion is that נַסֵּה ("test") in H[C] is the first word of 27:17a; for the form, see GKC (Paradigm P, 528) and compare the vocalized *piʿel* imperative שַׁנֵּה ("change") in Sir 36:6 H[Bmg] (though the *qal* form "renew" fits the context better there). This suggestion depends on two considerations. First, the imperative in 27:17a corresponds precisely to the imperative form at the start of 27:17a S. Second, it fits in with the anthological series of verses in H[C]. Leaf VI of H[C] (Schirmann's second leaf) would then consist of the following verses: 26:2b–3, 13, 15–17; 36:27–31; 27:17a. It is characteristic of H[C] to disrupt the standard order of verses, as Beentjes's table shows ("Hermeneutics," 58). It is quite possible that H[C] would have quoted 27:17 (on friendship) as an introduction to the friendship passage in 37:1–6 (which immediately follows 36:27–31), just as 41:16 serves to introduce passages on shame (4:21; 20:22–23; 4:22–23, 30–31) in leaves I and II of H[C]. A section on friendship would fit the anthological theme of H[C]; cf. C. Camp, "Honor, Shame, and the Hermeneutics of Ben Sira's MS C," in Barré, ed., *Wisdom, You Are My Sister,* 157–71, esp. 160–61.

[80] The form נַסֵּה ("test") may have become orthographically corrupted at an early stage to כַּסֵּה ("cover," "conceal"); hence the reading στέξον ("cover up," "keep secret"; cf. 8:17b), suggested by Smend (*Sirach, hebräisch und deutsch,* 246). From στέξον may derive the reading of most MSS of G (στέρξον), as well as the variant στέναξον ("groan," G[L]).

[81] Hart, *Ecclesiasticus,* 169.

[82] So Skehan and Di Lella, *Wisdom of Ben Sira,* 354. Alternatively, τὸν νεκρὸν may perhaps be an inner-Greek dictation error for τὸν ἐχθρὸν.

20[i]. So S and L. G reads καὶ ("and").

20[j]. So G and S, but S adds "from a net, and like a bird" (an expansion based on Prov 6:5).[83]

21[k–k]. So S. G has "it is possible to bind up a wound."

21[l]. So S (cf. G); L has *maledicti* ("of a cursed person").

21[m–m]. So G; note that the verb אבד in the *piʿel* means "lose" in 27:21b (cf. Sir 41:2d), but "destroy" in 27:16a. S reads, "but to reveal a secret is despair"; L expands the reading of S.

d. Translation

I

16 One who reveals a confidence destroys faithfulness
and will not find a friend for himself.
17 Test a comrade—and remain faithful to him;
but if you have revealed a confidence, do not pursue him.

II

18 For like a person destroying his enemy,
so you have destroyed the friendship of a companion;
19 and as if you have released a bird from your hand,
so you have abandoned a companion and will not catch him.

III

20 Do not pursue him, for he has gone far away,
for he has escaped like a gazelle from a trap;
21 because for a wound there is binding-up, and for a quarrel there is reconciliation,
but one who reveals a confidence has lost hope.

e. Poetic Analysis

The poem consists of three stanzas (2 + 2 + 2 bicola).[84] The first stanza opens with "one who reveals a confidence" and ends with "do

[83] Cf. Kaiser, "Was ein Freund nicht tun darf," 115.

[84] So Peters, *Das Buch Jesus Sirach,* 224. The pattern of three stanzas in 27:16–21 (already foreshadowed by the numerical proverb in 26:28) continues with the threefold comparison in 27:18–20 and with the threefold phrase in 27:21. For the pattern of three in 6:5–17, see the poetic analysis of the pericope in ch. 2.

not pursue him." The second stanza consists of two parallel comparisons ("like/as if ... so ..."). The third stanza reverses the pattern of the first by beginning with "do not pursue him" and concluding with a colon starting "one who reveals a confidence."

The clearest poetic feature of 27:16–21 is its chiasm.

A: מְגַלֶּה סוֹד מְאַבֵּד אֱמוּנָה (v. 16a)
One who reveals a confidence destroys faithfulness.
B: אַל תִּרְדְּפֶנּוּ (v. 17b)
Do not pursue him.
C: כְּ ... כֵּן ... רֵעַ (v. 18)
Like ..., so ... a companion.
C: כְּ ... כֵּן ... רֵעַ (v. 19)
As if ..., so ... a companion.
B: אַל תִּרְדְּפֶנּוּ (v. 20a)
Do not pursue him.
A': מְגַלֶּה סוֹד אִבֵּד תִּקְוָה (v. 21b)
One who reveals a confidence has lost hope.

This chiastic pattern unifies the pericope and adds emphasis to its message.

i. Stanza 1: Warning against Revealing a Confidence (27:16–17). The opening bicolon exhibits alliteration, assonance, and rhyme. Alliteration of *m* exists in the series of words: מְגַלֶּה ... מְאַבֵּד אֱמוּנָה ... יִמְצָא. Verse 16a also has assonance between the two *piʿel* participles, מְגַלֶּה ("one who reveals") and מְאַבֵּד ("destroys"). In addition, the first bicolon exhibits internal rhyme between אֱמוּנָה ("faithfulness") and יִמְצָא ("will find"). Further rhyme is present between לְנַפְשׁוֹ ("for himself," v. 16b) and עִמּוֹ ("to him," v. 17a).

Repetition of two verbal roots and one noun also unites the two bicola, according to a chiastic pattern.

מְגַלֶּה סוֹד ... אֱמוּנָה
One who reveals a confidence ... faithfulness.
הֵאָמֵן ... וְגִלִּיתָ סוֹד
Remain faithful ... but [if] you have revealed a confidence.[85]

Several words in the first stanza create the structure for the rest of the poem. In accord with the poem's chiastic pattern, the last colon (27:21b)

[85] For a slightly different chiastic pattern in 27:16–17 G, see Skehan and Di Lella, *Wisdom of Ben Sira*, 71–72.

echoes the first colon (27:16a), while the concluding prohibition of the first stanza (27:17b) is identical with the opening phrase of the last stanza (27:20a). Furthermore, the pattern of verses 16–17 is taken up in verses 19–20.

> וְלֹא יִמְצָא ... אַל תִּרְדְּפֶנּוּ (vv. 16b, 17b)
> And he will not find.... Do not pursue him.
> וְלֹא תְצוּדֶנּוּ׃ אַל תִּרְדְּפֶנּוּ (vv. 19b, 20a)
> And you will not catch him. Do not pursue him.

ii. Stanza 2: The Effect of Revealing a Confidence (27:18–19). The second stanza exhibits alliteration, assonance, and rhyme. There is a sixfold alliteration of *k* in 27:18–19: כִּי כְּאִישׁ ... כֵּן ... וּכְעוֹף מִיָּדְךָ ... כֵּן. Moreover, Ben Sira creates assonance in 27:18 with the roots אבד ("destroy"), איב ("be an enemy"), and אהב ("be a friend"): מְאַבֵּד אוֹיְבוֹ ... אִבַּדְתָּ אַהֲבַת; note also the antithesis between "enemy" and "friendship." Furthermore, rhyme and assonance are present in the word series in 27:18b–19: אִבַּדְתָּ ... מִיָּדְךָ שִׁלַּחְתָּ ... עָזַבְתָּ.

The second stanza also makes use of simile: the two comparisons in 27:18–19 lead into a third comparison in 27:20b. In verse 19 the sage employs proverbial imagery from nature ("as if ... a bird"), just as in verse 20 he uses another such image ("like a gazelle").

iii. Stanza 3: The Irreparable Damage Done by Revealing a Confidence (27:20–21). Above we have seen how 27:20a begins with the very same phrase that concluded 27:17b, while 27:21b echoes 27:16a. Rhyme connects the second and third stanzas, since אַל תִּרְדְּפֶנּוּ ("do not pursue him," 27:20a) rhymes (and has assonance) with the final phrase of the second stanza, וְלֹא תְצוּדֶנּוּ ("and will not catch him," 27:19b). Further rhyme exists in the final bicolon with the series חֲבִישָׁה ("binding-up"), לְמְרִיבָה ("for a quarrel"), and תִּקְוָה ("hope"); there is also vowel assonance between חֲבִישָׁה and לְמְרִיבָה. Moreover, alliteration with *m* is present in 27:20b–21: מִפַּח ... לְמְרִיבָה וּמְגַלֶּה. Additional alliteration with *ṣ* occurs in verses 20b–21: צְבִי ... פֶּצַע ... רִצּוּי. Finally, as in the second stanza there is alliteration with *k* in verses 20–21a (note also the vowel assonance): כִּי ... כִּי ... כִּצְבִי ... כִּי.

f. Context

i. Sirach 27:16–28:7 within 24:1–32:13. The fifth part of Ben Sira's book, 24:1–32:13, consists of ten poems, including seven nonalphabetic acrostics.[86]

[86] This outline is adapted from Skehan and Di Lella, *Wisdom of Ben Sira,* xv. I consider that the wisdom poem on God's providence, 32:14–33:18, does not end

24:1–34: Praise of Wisdom[87]
25:1–11: Gifts That Bring Happiness
25:13–26:27: Wicked and Virtuous Women[88]
26:28–27:15: Hazards to Integrity[89]
27:16–28:7: Avoiding Wrath[90]
28:8–26: Quarreling and Evils of the Tongue
29:1–20: Loans, Alms, and Surety[91]
29:21–30:13: Domestic Life[92]
30:14–31:11: A Happy Life
31:12–32:13: Food, Wine, and Banquets

All of part 5 is about applying wisdom to domestic life and avoiding social relationships that would cause unhappiness.[93]

ii. Sirach 27:16–21 within 27:16–28:7. The friendship poem in 27:16–21 forms the opening portion of the twenty-three-line nonalphabetic acrostic in 27:16–28:7. The whole nonalphabetic acrostic, about how to maintain social relationships by avoiding wrath, seems to comprise four poems.[94]

part 5 (so Skehan and Di Lella, ibid.) but rather begins part 6; see further my discussion of the context of 37:1–6 in ch. 2 above. A somewhat different outline of 26:28–28:26 occurs in Krammer, "Die Auswirkungen des Verhaltens," 81–82.

[87] Including a twenty-two-line nonalphabetic acrostic, 24:3–17, 19–22; cf. Skehan and Di Lella, *Wisdom of Ben Sira,* 331.

[88] A nonalphabetic double acrostic of forty-six bicola. For another nonalphabetic double acrostic (of 44 bicola) see 22:27–23:27.

[89] On 26:28–28:26, see Krammer, "Die Auswirkungen des Verhaltens," 77–110; on 26:28–27:10, see P. C. Beentjes, "De getallenspreuk en zijn reikwijdte: Een pleidooi voor de literaire eenheid van Jesus Sirach 26:28–27:10," *Bijdr* 43 (1982): 383–89; on 27:3–10, see E. Pax, "Dialog und Selbstgespräch bei Sirach 27,3–10," *SBLFA* 20 (1970): 247–63.

[90] A twenty-three-line nonalphabetic acrostic; so also is 28:8–26. On 27:22–24 and 28:1–5, 22–23, see Krammer, "Die Auswirkungen des Verhaltens," 98–110.

[91] A further twenty-three-line nonalphabetic acrostic; cf. Skehan and Di Lella, *Wisdom of Ben Sira,* 74. On 29:1–20 see M. Gilbert, "Prêt, aumône et caution," in Egger-Wenzel and Krammer, eds., *Der Einzelne und seine Gemeinschaft bei Ben Sira,* 179–89.

[92] A twenty-two-line nonalphabetic acrostic; cf. Skehan and Di Lella, *Wisdom of Ben Sira,* 74. On 30:1–13, see Schrader, *Leiden und Gerechtigkeit,* 137–41.

[93] Compare W. Roth's comment that 25:1–33:15 contains "a mini-sociology of early Judaism"; see "Sirach: The First Graded Curriculum," *TBT* 29 (1991): 298–302 (quotation from p. 301).

[94] Cf. Skehan and Di Lella, *Wisdom of Ben Sira,* 357, 362–63. On Sir 27:25–29, see I. Krammer, "'Wer anderen eine Grube gräbt, fällt selbst hinein': Ben Sira als

27:16–21: Warning against Revealing Secrets
Inclusio: 27:16a, 21b (see poetic analysis above)
27:22–27: Warning against Mixing with Evildoers
Inclusio: 27:22b G^L: ὁ εἰδώς ("one who knows")
27:27b G: οὐ μὴ ἐπιγνῷ ("he will not know")
27:28–28:1: Warning against Vengefulness
Inclusio: 27:28b: ἡ ἐκδίκησις ("vengeance")
28:1a: ἐκδίκησιν ("vengeance")
28:2–7: Warning against Unforgiveness
Inclusio: 28:2a: ἄφες ἀδίκημα ("forgive wrongdoing")
28:7b: πάριδε ἄγνοιαν ("overlook ignorance")

An *inclusio* serves as an envelope for the whole nonalphabetic acrostic: while 27:18b G speaks of "a neighbor's friendship" (τὴν φιλίαν τοῦ πλησίον), 28:7a G urges, "Do not be wrathful to a neighbor" (μὴ μηνίσης τῷ πλησίον).[95] Moreover, the end of the whole poem is marked by the mention of death (28:6) and of the commandments (28:7).[96]

iii. Links between 27:16–21 and 27:8–15. According to G, verbal connections exist between 27:16–21 and the preceding short poem on virtue and sin (27:8–10), including use of the verb "pursue" (διώκω: 27:8a, 20a; cf. καταδιώκω: 27:17b) and the noun "bird" (πετεινόν: 27:9a, 19a). Thereafter, the poem on speech (27:11–15) exhibits a connection with 27:16–21, with the term λοιδορίας ("of an insult," 27:21a) echoing the word διαλοιδόρησις ("abusiveness," 27:15b).

iv. Links between 27:16–21 and 27:22–28:7. Links of vocabulary connect 27:16–21 with the subsequent material in the rest of the nonalphabetic acrostic (27:22–28:7). Words in common in the text of G include "keep away," "be away" (ἀφίστημι: 27:20a, 22b), "wound" (τραῦμα: 27:21a, 25b), "trap" (παγίς: 27:20b, 26b, 29a), and "neighbor" (πλησίον: 27:18b, 19b; 28:2a, 7a).[97]

Tradent eines bekannten Sprichwortes," in Egger-Wenzel and Krammer, eds., *Der Einzelne und seine Gemeinschaft bei Ben Sira*, 239–60, esp. 239–42.

[95] So the MSS of G; Ziegler substitutes an alternative form μηνιάσης.

[96] Ben Sira's poems ending with the mention of death (or the grave or worms) include 9:1–9; 11:7–28; 13:24–14:19; 18:30–19:3; 27:22–28:7. Poems that conclude by mentioning the commandments or the law include 6:18–37; 19:13–17; 27:22–28:7.

[97] In addition, several features in 27:16–21 G echo themes from 22:19–26 G. Besides the words "friend" (φίλος: 22:20, 21, 22 [bis], 25; 27:16, 17) and "friendship" (φιλία: 22:20; 27:18), terms that are in common include "secret" (μυστήριον:

g. Exegesis

i. Stanza 1: Warning against Revealing a Confidence (27:16–17). Ben Sira's warning against disclosing confidences is a commonplace of sapiential teaching, with relevance both to ordinary social relationships and to the professional life of civil servants. Comparable sentiments are present in the biblical book of Proverbs (e.g., 16:28; 20:19), in the Aramaic Wisdom of Ahiqar, and elsewhere in Ben Sira. Prov 11:13 teaches:

הוֹלֵךְ רָכִיל מְגַלֶּה־סּוֹד   וְנֶאֱמַן־רוּחַ מְכַסֶּה דָבָר׃

> One who goes about as a talebearer reveals a confidence,
> but one who is faithful in spirit conceals a matter.

In 27:16 Ben Sira has borrowed from Prov 11:13 both the phrase מְגַלֶּה סוֹד ("one who reveals a confidence")[98] and the root אמן (Prov 11:13: נֶאֱמַן־רוּחַ, "faithful in spirit"; Sir 27:16: אֱמוּנָה, "faithfulness"). Proverbs 25:9 also cautions against revealing secrets:

רִיבְךָ רִיב אֶת־רֵעֶךָ   וְסוֹד אַחֵר אַל־תְּגָל׃

> Argue your case with your companion,
> but do not reveal another's confidence.

In a similar fashion, Aramaic Ahiqar Saying 53 (line 141) advises: "Do not reveal your [secr]ets before your [frien]ds [(סתר)יך אל תגלי קדם (רח)מיך], lest your reputation with them be ruined." Likewise, Sir 22:22c declares: "One who reveals a confidence is a disgraceful person,"[99] while Sir 42:1

22:22; 27:16, 21), "faithfulness" (πίστις: 22:23; 27:16), "bird" (πετεινόν: 22:20; 27:19), "insult" (λοιδορία: 22:24; 27:21), "reconciliation" διαλλαγή: 22:22; 27:21), and "despair," "lose hope" (ἀφελπίζω: 22:21; 27:21).

[98] Cf. Kaiser, "Was ein Freund nicht tun darf," 119. The only occurrence of the phrase מְגַלֶּה סוֹד ("one who reveals a confidence") in the Hebrew MSS of Ben Sira is in 15:20cd H[AB]; but the couplet, absent from G, is a gloss (so Di Lella, *Hebrew Text of Sirach,* 133–34). The following Ahiqar quotation is from Lindenberger, *Aramaic Proverbs of Ahiqar,* 140.

[99] On Sir 22:22, see my text-critical notes in the next chapter. For the Essenes, too, keeping confidences was an important duty. In *Ag. Ap.* 2.207 Josephus asserts that the law "allows us to conceal nothing from our friends, for there is no friendship without absolute confidence; in the event of subsequent estrangement, it forbids the disclosure of secrets" (Thackeray et al., trans., *Josephus,* 1:377); he attributes this view to the Essenes in *J.W.* 2.141. A Qumran sapiential text also

H^M lists "exposing any matter of advice" as something deserving shame.[100]

The discretion that keeps confidences hidden accords with the silence of the wise person. In 5:11 H^A, for instance, Ben Sira declares: "Be quick to listen, but with patience return an answer." Similarly, in 20:7 H^C he teaches: "A wise person will be silent until the right time." Ultimately, this high valuation of silence echoes the outlook of earlier sapiential and gnomic literature. Amenemope 6.7–8, for example, states: "The truly silent, who keeps apart, he is like a tree grown in a meadow"; by contrast, Theognis 295 asserts: "To a talkative man silence is a sore burden."[101]

Ben Sira's counsel to "test" a companion (Sir 27:17a H^C, S) echoes his teaching in 6:7a[102] and also matches the advice in Egyptian sapiential texts (cf. Ptahhotep 33; P. Insinger 12.15). Once one has tested a companion and found him worthy of friendship, however, one should "remain faithful to him" (27:17a). Here the sage's teaching accords with the advice of Isocrates in *Demon.* 24: "Be slow to give your friendship, but when you have given it, strive to make it lasting."

Fidelity in friendship is an important virtue in Ben Sira's eyes; indeed, in 6:14–16 he thrice praises "a faithful friend" (אוֹהֵב אֱמוּנָה). In financial arrangements too, the sage insists on the need to keep faith with one's companion (29:3): στερέωσον λόγον καὶ πιστώθητι μετ' αὐτοῦ ("Confirm [your] word and keep faith with him"). The sage evidently considers it right to maintain fidelity, both in the matter of a loan (29:3) and within the context of friendship (27:17). By contrast, revealing a confidence is an act of infidelity that disrupts friendship and causes a friend to flee.

---

seems to reflect a concern for the keeping of secrets (though the reading is uncertain): "Into the hand of one who is stupid do not entrust a secret, for he will not keep private your affairs" (4Q424 1.6); see S. J. Tanzer, "4Q424," in Pfann et al., eds., *Qumran Cave 4.26: Cryptic Texts and Miscellanea, Part 1,* 333–46, quoting p. 337. In a similar fashion, Isocrates says in his oration *Demon.* 22: "Guard more faithfully the secret which is confided to you than the money which is entrusted to your care" (Norlin and van Hook, trans., *Isocrates,* 1:17).

[100] The verse in H^B speaks of "exposing any confidence [סוֹד] of advice." In 1:30c G, Ben Sira mentions the fear of having one's secrets revealed. Compare also P. Insinger 21.15: "He who reveals a secret matter, his house will burn" (*AEL* 3:202).

[101] Cf. *AEL* 2:151 (Amenemope); Edmonds, trans., *Elegy and Iambus,* 1:263 (Theognis).

[102] Already in 27:7 G the sage has advocated using discussion to test persons: "Before a conversation do not praise a man, for this is the test of human beings." The following quotation comes from Norlin and van Hook, trans., *Isocrates,* 1:19.

The first stanza ends with a prohibition, אַל תִּרְדְּפֶנּוּ ("Do not pursue him," 27:17b), for the damage brought about by a breach of confidence is irreparable. The second stanza will use poetic imagery to elaborate on this damage, before the third stanza returns to the same prohibition, "Do not pursue him" (27:20a).

ii. Stanza 2: The Effect of Revealing a Confidence (27:18–19). According to Ben Sira, destroying one's friendship with someone by revealing a confidence is a hostile action tantamount to killing an enemy. Here the sage uses a strong antithesis ("enemy" and "friendship") to highlight the negative effect of betraying a confidence. In 12:16 H[A] Ben Sira uses the word אוֹיֵב ("enemy") of a personal adversary, while elsewhere he employs the term for political foes (36:9 H[B]; 36:12 H[Bmg]; 46:1, 16 H[B]). Its synonym, שׂוֹנֵא ("enemy"), occurs in antithetical parallelism with אוֹהֵב ("friend") in the book of Proverbs (Prov 12:1; 13:24; 14:20; 27:6), and Ben Sira himself also plays on this contrast.[103]

In 27:19 the sage shifts from military imagery to an analogy from the world of hunting.[104] Verse 19 likens the former companion (whose confidence has been revealed) to a bird released from one's hand, never to return. At the same time, the imagery of the bird also suggests the swift movement of the secret that, once let out, can never be recaptured.

Ben Sira's imagery in 27:19 alludes to Prov 6:1–5, which warns against coming under the power of "your companion" (רֵעֶךָ, Prov 6:3) by guaranteeing his loan. Proverbs 6:5 urges:

הִנָּצֵל כִּצְבִי מִיָּד וּכְצִפּוֹר מִיַּד יָקוּשׁ׃

Save yourself like a gazelle from [his] hand,[105]
and like a bird from the hand of the fowler.

---

[103] Sir 6:1, 9, 13 H[A]; 12:8 H[A]; 33:6 H[EF]. There is also a contrast between שׂוֹנֵא ("enemy") and רֵעַ ("companion") in 12:9 H[A] and 20:23 H[C].

[104] For a comparison of hunting imagery in the Psalms and in ancient Near Eastern art, see O. Keel, *The Symbolism of the Biblical World: Ancient Near Eastern Iconography and the Book of Psalms* (New York: Seabury, 1978), 85–95.

[105] Perhaps the original phrase, shortened by homoioteleuton, was מִיַּד צַיָּד ("from the hand of the hunter"; cf. G and S). Aphorisms based on the behavior of animals were an important part of Israel's sapiential heritage (cf. Prov 6:6–8; 30:24–31; Job 12:7–9; Sir 13:17–19). Similarly, several animal proverbs occur in Aramaic Ahiqar (e.g., Sayings 7–11, 28, 35–36).

Ben Sira takes up the image of the bird in 27:19a and of the gazelle in 27:20b.[106] Whereas Proverbs urges the potential guarantor to escape from entering a pledge agreement as swiftly as a bird flies away from a fowler, Ben Sira states that a companion will be as quick as a bird in fleeing from a former friend who has revealed confidences.[107]

Here Ben Sira may also echo the Mesopotamian proverbial tradition, which compares spoken words to birds that fly away and can never be recaptured. Thus, Aramaic Ahiqar Saying 15 (line 98) warns: "Above all else, guard your mouth; and [as for] what you have h[eard], be discreet! For a word is a bird [צנפר הי מלה], and he who releases it [ומשלחה] is a f[ool]."[108] Just as Ahiqar notes that a bird flies away when released and a word (or saying) once spoken can never be recaptured, so too Ben Sira asserts that a friend whose secret has been disclosed will disappear and never return.[109]

Elsewhere, however, Ben Sira uses a bird as an image for a friend, as in 22:20: "One who throws a stone at a bird will scare it away, and one who disgraces a friend will make friendship vanish." In both 27:19 and 22:20 Ben Sira compares a friend to a bird that is scared off, either by a breach of confidentiality (27:19) or by insults (22:20).[110] A similar image, too, occurs in Theognis 1097–1100: "Now wing I my way like a bird [ὥστε πετεινόν] from the flaxen net, escaping an evil man by breaking the trammels; and as for thee, thou'st lost my friendship and wilt learn my shrewdness too late."

The saying of Sir 27:9a G also likens human beings to birds in their social relationships: "Birds will lodge with those that are like them." In the sage's thinking, betraying a confidence evidently means that one is not "like" one's friend and hence undeserving of his friendship.

---

[106] By inserting the "bird" alongside the "gazelle" in 27:20, S makes explicit the allusion to Prov 6:5.

[107] Just as Sir 27:19–20 alludes to Prov 6:5, so Sir 27:22–24 echoes Prov 6:12–19; cf. Skehan and Di Lella, *Wisdom of Ben Sira,* 362; Sanders, *Ben Sira and Demotic Wisdom,* 33–34.

[108] Lindenberger, *Aramaic Proverbs of Ahiqar,* 75; cf. Segal, ספר בן־סירא השלם, 170.

[109] Likewise, Qoh 10:20cd associates birds with the bringing of secret news: "A bird [עוֹף] of the sky may bring the message, and a winged creature may recount the matter." Such sayings involving birds form part of the traditional folk wisdom of many countries; compare the English expression: "A little bird told me."

[110] On the links between Sir 27:16–21 and 22:19–26, see the final note in the context section on this pericope; on Sir 22:20, see my exegesis in the next chapter. The following Theognis quotation comes from Edmonds, trans., *Elegy and Iambus,* 1:361.

Because the friend whose confidence has been broken has flown away like a bird, Ben Sira warns at the end of 27:19, "You will not catch him" (לֹא תְצוּדֶנּוּ).[111] The verb צוד ("hunt," "catch") refers to the catching of birds in Lam 3:52.

The hunting of birds is often mentioned in ancient Near Eastern literature or depicted in wall paintings and on monuments.[112] Biblical texts also employ imagery from bird hunting (e.g., Qoh 9:12; Ps 91:3).[113] Psalm 124:7 describes deliverance from mortal danger using the imagery of a bird escaping from a trap: נַפְשֵׁנוּ כְּצִפּוֹר נִמְלְטָה מִפַּח יוֹקְשִׁים ("Our life like a bird has escaped from the trap of fowlers").

Closer to the sage's text is Amos's series of questions (Amos 3:3–8), beginning with the mention of two friends walking together (Amos 3:3). In particular, Amos 3:5 asks: "Will a bird [צִפּוֹר] fall into a trap [פַּח] on the earth unless there is a snare for it?" Moreover, the two persons mentioned as meeting in 3:3 are seen to be God and the prophet: "The Lord Yahweh will not do anything unless he has revealed his confidence [גָּלָה סוֹדוֹ] to his servants the prophets" (Amos 3:7). Whereas Amos asserts that Yahweh reveals his secret to his friends (the prophets) as inevitably as a trap snares a bird (a positive image), Ben Sira declares that revealing the confidence of a friend causes him to escape like a bird (a negative image).

iii. Stanza 3: The Irreparable Damage Done by Revealing a Confidence (27:20–21). Having opened the third stanza with the prohibition that concluded the first ("Do not pursue him"), Ben Sira then uses the image of the gazelle to express the futility of trying to catch the betrayed friend. The verb "pursue" (רדף) occurs in the context of hunting in 1 Sam 26:20, where Saul's quest for David is compared to the stalking of a partridge. As in Sir 27:20, the verbal root נוס ("flee") often occurs in the MT (e.g., Lev 26:36; 2 Sam 24:13; 1 Kgs 20:20; Prov 28:1) as the counterpart of רדף ("pursue").

---

[111] Sirach 27:19 G has οὐ θηρεύσεις αὐτόν ("you will not catch him"); cf. Xenophon's use of the phrase "to hunt friends" (φίλους θηράσειν) in *Mem.* 3.11.7 (Marchant, trans., *Xenophon*, 243).

[112] In the Annals of Sennacherib, the Assyrian king says that he confined Hezekiah in Jerusalem "like a bird in a cage" (*ANET* 288). For pictures of bird hunting in ancient Egypt, see Keel, *Symbolism of the Biblical World*, 91–92.

[113] Proverbs 7:23b also uses bird imagery in referring to the man captivated by the wiles of the loose woman; his movement is "like the rushing of a bird into a snare" (כְּמַהֵר צִפּוֹר אֶל־פָּח). Sirach 11:30 compares the heart of a proud person to a "captured bird in a cage" (so H^A) or to a "hunting partridge in a basket" (so G); on the textual problems here, see Skehan and Di Lella, *Wisdom of Ben Sira*, 244.

In 27:20 Ben Sira notes that the betrayed friend has gone far away in order to escape from the trap of a disloyal comrade.[114] Whereas Sir 9:13a urges the student, "Keep far [רְחַק] from anyone empowered to kill," who is full of "traps" (פַּחִים, 9:13e), 27:20 says that the betrayed friend "has gone far away" (הִתְרַחֵק) in order to flee from the "trap" (פַּח) of the one who has revealed his secrets.

Just as 27:19a alludes to the bird image found in Prov 6:5b, so Sir 27:20b echoes the image of the gazelle in Prov 6:5a: "Save yourself like a gazelle" (כִּצְבִי). Although in ancient times the gazelle was hunted in Israel (Deut 12:22; 14:5; 1 Kgs 5:3), its speed was proverbial (cf. 2 Sam 2:18; 1 Chr 12:9).[115]

The final bicolon (27:21) of the last stanza contrasts the forgivable faults of wounding and disputing with the unforgivable offense of revealing a confidence. This verse exhibits several similarities with Sir 22:22, as a comparison will illustrate:

> Because for a wound there is binding-up, and for a quarrel there is reconciliation [רִצּוּי],
> but one who reveals a confidence [מְגַלֶּה סוֹד] has lost hope. (27:21)
>
> If you open your mouth against a friend,
> do not be terrified, for there is reconciliation [רִצּוּי].
> One who reveals a confidence [מְגַלֶּה סוֹד] is a disgraceful person,
> and a hidden blow will make friendship vanish. (22:22)[116]

Both texts agree that reconciliation is possible for a verbal dispute in someone's presence; 27:21a employs the term מְרִיבָה ("quarrel"), while 22:22a speaks of "opening one's mouth" against a friend. Both texts also agree that betraying secrets in someone's absence brings an end to the friendship; "one who reveals a confidence has lost hope" (27:21b) and is "a disgraceful person" (22:22c).[117] Whereas a verbal "wound" (פֶּצַע =

[114] In *Mem.* 3.11.8–10 Xenophon employs the comparable imagery of "nets" (δίκτυα) for catching friends; see Marchant, trans., *Xenophon,* 245.

[115] Isaiah 13:14 speaks of the day of Yahweh against Babylon that will cause the people to flee like gazelles: "And one shall be like a gazelle [כִּצְבִי] driven out, . . . and each one will flee [יָנוּסוּ] to his land." An Egyptian text, P. Lansing 3.8, speaks of "the desert antelope that lives by running" (*AEL* 2:169).

[116] The above text of 22:22 partly follows S; see the text-critical notes in ch. 6.

[117] For Ben Sira, what makes a dispute unforgivable is the betrayal of the person behind his back (22:22cd; 27:21b), whereas a face-to-face disagreement can be healed (27:21a). Thus, the parallelism in 22:22cd is synonymous, while in 27:21ab it is antithetical.

τραῦμα in 27:21a G) in a person's presence can be bandaged and healed,[118] a "hidden blow" (מַכַּת סֵתֶר, equivalent to "treacherous blow," πλήγη δολίας in 22:22d G) in the person's absence is unforgivable.[119]

Sirach 27:21a twice describes the same reality: the first time is figurative, employing medical imagery (לְפֶצַע חֲבִישָׁה: "for a wound there is binding-up"), while the second is realistic, explaining the previous imagery (רִצּוּי לִמְרִיבָה: "for a quarrel there is reconciliation"). In the MT the verb חבשׁ ("bind up") sometimes denotes bandaging up a broken limb (Isa 30:26; Ezek 30:21; 34:4, 16) or a brokenhearted person (Isa 61:1; Ps 147:3), while at other times the sense is general, speaking of God's healing action (Hos 6:1; Job 5:18). In Isa 1:6 the *puʿal* verb is specifically applied to a "wound" (פֶּצַע). Moreover, Sir 11:29b H^A speaks of the "wounds" caused by a person who betrays the confidences of others: "How many are the wounds of the talebearer [פִּצְעֵי רוֹכֵל]!"

Ben Sira believes that reconciliation is possible in the case of a quarrel, and hence he urges his students, "Forgive your neighbor's wrongdoing" (28:2a G). Although the term רִצּוּי ("reconciliation," "appeasement") does not occur in the MT,[120] the equivalent Greek noun διαλλαγή ("reconciliation") occurs here and in Sir 22:22. While the word מְרִיבָה ("quarrel, dispute") appears in Gen 13:8 and Num 27:14,[121] a synonym, רִיב ("dispute"), often occurs in the MT (e.g., Hos 4:1; Mic 6:2; Prov 15:18) and in Ben Sira (e.g., 6:9; 11:9; 35:25).

The concluding statement in 27:21b underscores the serious consequences of revealing a confidence: the betrayer has "lost [or destroyed] hope" (אִבַּד תִּקְוָה). The same idiom occurs in 41:2d, where it is connected with the question of different attitudes toward death.[122] Thus, 27:16–21 is

---

[118] Indeed, a faithful friend may sometimes need to inflict a "wound" (פֶּצַע) for a good purpose (Prov 27:6).

[119] In the MT פֶּצַע ("wound") and מַכָּה ("blow") are virtually synonymous (see Isa 1:6; Prov 20:30), while in the LXX the words τραῦμα ("wound") and πληγή ("blow") occur together in Isa 1:6.

[120] However, the *piʿel* of רצה ("placate," "appease") occurs in Job 20:10 and the *hitpaʿel* ("reconcile oneself") in 1 Sam 29:4. Note that nouns of a similar form to רִצּוּי ("reconciliation") occur in biblical Hebrew, such as שִׁקּוּי ("drink": Prov 3:8) and שִׁלּוּם ("payment," "recompense": Mic 7:3); see GKC §84bi. In Ben Sira the noun נִסּוּי or נִיסּוּי ("testing") occurs in 33:1 H^BEF; 44:20 H^B.

[121] In addition, Meribah (מְרִיבָה) designates the place where the Israelites disputed with God and put him to the test (Exod 17:7; Num 20:13).

[122] H^B reads אִבַּד תִּקְוָה (lit., "perishing with respect to hope"), whereas H^M has אָבוּד תִּקְוָה (lit., "perished with respect to hope"). On 41:2d see Reiterer, "Deutung und Wertung des Todes durch Ben Sira," 220–21. For a similar idiom, see Prov 11:7.

another of Ben Sira's pericopes that end with some kind of reference to death (27:21b).[123]

Many biblical writers speak generally of a "hope" of deliverance from enemies (e.g., Zech 9:12; Ps 9:19; Lam 3:29) or "hope" (or lack of hope) in the face of death (e.g., Job 7:6; 14:7; Prov 11:7; Sir 7:17; 38:21; 41:2). Ben Sira also uses "hope" (תִּקְוָה) to refer to an earthly expectation (11:22; 16:22) or "outcome" (7:13; 12:1). Both the earthly and the mortal aspects of "hope" underlie the use of the term in 27:21b. In the sage's view, revealing a secret has not only destroyed any earthly expectation of good from the friendship, but also brought the betrayer closer to the realm of death, where there is no hope.

h. Summary

Sirach 27:16–21 aims to inculcate the keeping of confidences by pointing out the damage done by revealing secrets: such breaches of confidence drive friends away irrevocably. The sage emphasizes the delicate nature of friendship using animal imagery (birds and gazelles). Even the wounds caused by quarrels can be healed, whereas revealing secrets puts an end to all friendship.

4. Conclusion

Both pericopes treated in this chapter, drawn from the central segment of Ben Sira's book, consider how to preserve friendship. The teaching of 19:13–17 is positive: when faced with a friend's misbehavior, one needs to offer reproof, so that the friend may change. By way of contrast, the advice of 27:16–21 is negative: one should not betray the confidence of a friend, or else the friendship may quickly vanish.

Whereas 19:13–17 concerns the right use of speech (for reproof), 27:16–21 is about the misuse of speech (in revealing secrets). In the central portion of the book, several other discussions of the use of the tongue occur (19:4–12; 20:5–8, 16–20, 24–31; 23:7–15; 28:12–26), as well as the sage's prayer for discipline in his speech (22:27–23:1).

While anger leads to breaches of God's commandments, reproof enables one to keep God's law (19:17). Whereas betraying secrets causes the loss of fidelity and hope in a friendship (27:16, 21), keeping

---

[123] Cf. 7:17 (ending 7:1–17); 7:36 (ending 7:18–36); 9:9 (ending 9:1–9); 11:28 (ending 11:7–28); 14:19 (ending 13:24–14:19); 19:3 (ending 18:30–19:3); 28:6 (ending 27:22–28:7); 39:11 G (ending 39:1–11); 44:14 (ending 44:1–15). Compare also 4:10 in H^A but not in G (ending 3:30–4:10).

confidences strengthens faithfulness and encourages hope. In these two pericopes, then, Ben Sira shows how a wise person is able to maintain friendships through proper use of the tongue.

6

Sirach 22:19–26

1. Introduction

This chapter discusses Ben Sira's longest friendship pericope from the central portion of his book (22:19–26).[1] Sirach 22:19–26 is the most problematic of the pericopes on friendship, not least because of its serious textual difficulties. G diverges widely from S; for example, S contains two bicola (22:20cd, 26bd) absent from G. Conscious of the integrity of these different textual traditions, I have based my reconstruction of the Hebrew text of Sir 22:19–26 largely on G, while the text-critical notes will indicate the divergent readings of S.

In addition to the ancient versions of the pericope, a Cairo Genizah MS (H^{3053}) preserves a medieval Hebrew rhymed poem based on Sir 22:22cd–23:9b.[2] This prosodic work exhibits some echoes of a Hebrew text of Sir 22:22cd, 24–26, though the date of its composition is unclear.[3] Whereas Ben Sira uses rhyme occasionally,[4] the later author has introduced rhyme into every line or couplet. Because the medieval poem extensively

---

[1] See J. Marböck, "Gefährdung und Bewährung: Kontexte zur Freundschaftsperikope Sir 22,19–26," in Reiterer, ed., *Freundschaft bei Ben Sira,* 87–106.

[2] I use the notation H^{3053} to designate MS Adler 3053, one of the Genizah MSS housed at the Library of the Jewish Theological Seminary of America in New York. For the text of H^{3053} see J. Marcus, "The Newly Discovered Original Hebrew of Ben Sira (Ecclesiasticus xxxii, 16–xxxiv, 1): The Fifth Manuscript and a Prosodic Version of Ben Sira (Ecclesiasticus xxii, 22–xxiii, 9)," *JQR* 21 (1930–1931): 223–40. A transcription of the poem appears on p. 238, facing a photograph of the manuscript. For comparison with the ancient versions of Ben Sira, Marcus added the relevant text of S and contributed a retroversion from G with explanatory footnotes (238–40).

[3] The MS dates from around the eleventh century C.E., although the poem could be older. In its free rhythmic form and use of end-rhyme, the poem has affinities to the *silluk.* See further B. Hrushovski, "Hebrew Prosody" (*EncJud* 13.1195–1239), esp. the section on "The Classical Piyyut" (cols. 1203–11).

[4] E.g., 6:11ab, 37cd; 7:17ab, 18ab; 9:16ab; 13:1ab, 23abcd, 24ab; 44:3abcd, 4abcd.

reworks the thought of Ben Sira, its testimony to the sage's original text is at best oblique.

For comparison, I give below the section of the poem based on Sir 22:22cd, 24–26, followed by a translation.[5]

22cd הוֹצָאַת סוֹד חֶרְפָּה גְדוֹלָה   וּמַכַּת סֵתֶר [תָּ]בִיא קְלָלָה׃
24 לִפְנֵי אֵשׁ תִּימֲרוֹת עָשָׁן   וְלִפְנֵי שְׁפַךְ דָּם צָרָה תֶּעְשַׁן׃
25 מַסְתִּיר סוֹדוֹ לֹא יֵבוֹשׁ   וּמַטְמִין דִּבָּה רָעָתוֹ יִכְבּוֹשׁ׃
26ab וְ[אִ]ם גִּלָּה לְךָ רֵעֲךָ סוֹדוֹ   אַל תְּגַלֵּהוּ׃
26cd פֶּן תְּהִי כְּנָבָל בְּהוֹצִיאוֹ   וְיִזָּהֵר מִמְּךָ שׁוֹמְעֵהוּ׃

22cd The disclosure of a confidence is a great disgrace,
and a hidden blow will bring a curse.
24 Columns of smoke precede fire,
and distress will smoke before the shedding of blood.
25 One who hides his confidence will not be ashamed,
and one who buries malicious talk will conquer his evil.
26ab And if your companion has revealed to you his confidence,
do not reveal it,
26cd Lest you become like a fool by disclosing it,
and one who hears it will be wary of you.

2. Delimitation

Sirach 22:19–26, a pericope united by literary features, is delimited from its context by the subject of friendship. Between 21:1 and 26:27 the word φίλος ("friend") occurs only in 22:19–26 G (vv. 20, 21, 22 [bis], 25).

The surrounding material treats foolish and undisciplined behavior. Preceding 22:19–26 is a long poem on folly (21:22–22:18), marked off by the term μωρός ("fool," "foolish") in the opening and closing bicola (21:22a; 22:18c). Following 22:19–26 is a nonalphabetic double acrostic of forty-four bicola (22:27–23:27), concerning control of the tongue and of physical desires. Thus, external factors confirm the internal indications that 22:19–26 is a distinct pericope.[6]

[5] To facilitate comparison, I provide Tiberian (Masoretic) vocalization (except for final pause), although this MS is vocalized according to the Babylonian system. Note that H^{3053} lacks any equivalent to Sir 22:23.

[6] Cf. Marböck, "Gefährdung und Bewährung," 87–88.

3. Retroverted Text of Sirach 22:19–26

I

19 מַכֵּה[a] עַיִן יוֹרִיד דִּמְעָה   וּמַכֵּה[a] לֵב [b]יוֹצִיא עַצֶּבֶת[b]:
20 מַשְׁלִיךְ אֶבֶן בְּעוֹף יַחֲרִידֶנּוּ   וּמְחָרֵף[c] אוֹהֵב יַעֲבִיר אַהֲבָה[d]:
21 עַל אוֹהֵב אִם תִּשְׁלֹף חֶרֶב   אַל תִּתְיָאֵשׁ כִּי יֵשׁ תְּשׁוּבָה[e]:
22 עַל אוֹהֵב אִם תִּפְתַּח פֶּה   אַל תִּפְחַד כִּי יֵשׁ רִצּוּי:
בֶּן[f] חֶרְפָּה[g] [h]מְגַלֵּה סוֹד[h]   וּמַכַּת סֵתֶר [i]תַּעֲבִיר אַהֲבָה[i]:
24 לִפְנֵי אֵשׁ [j]תִּימֲרוֹת עָשָׁן[j]   וְלִפְנֵי [k]שֶׁפֶךְ דָּם[k] דִּבָּה:

II

23 סְמֹךְ[l] רֵעֲךָ בְּדַלּוּתוֹ   לְמַעַן תִּחַד[m] בְּטוֹבָתוֹ:
בְּעֵת צָרָה הֵאָמֵן עִמּוֹ   לְמַעַן תִּנְחַל בְּנַחֲלָתוֹ[n]:
25 [o]כִּי יָמוּךְ אוֹהַבְךָ אַל תְּבִישֶׁנּוּ[o]   וּמִפָּנָיו [p]אַל תִּסָּתֵר[p]:
26 [q]וְאִם תַּשִּׂיגֶנּוּ רָעָה בִּגְלָלְךָ[q]   [r]כָּל הַשּׁוֹמֵעַ יִזָּהֵר מִמְּךָ[r]:

4. Text-Critical Notes

My reconstruction of the Hebrew original of Sir 22:19–26 draws mainly on G, with some attention to S.[7] Although 22:24 appears after 22:23 in G and S, I have placed it after 22:22 for the sake of the sense.[8]

19[a]. So most MSS of G; to vary the participle in verse 19a, G^{L} (except for G^{248}) employs ὁ ὀρύσσων, "one who gives a dig to." In both cola of verse 19, S presupposes מַכַּת, "a blow."

19[b–b]. So G with the present tense. S has "causes friendship to pass away," from verse 22d.

20[c]. So G. S reads "one who cheats."

20[d]. After verse 20b S adds an extra bicolon: "Do not be fickle toward your friend, but if you are fickle, do not suppose that you have friendship with him."

21[e]. So G, L. S reads "a way out."

22[f]. So S: "son." G reads πλὴν, "except."

[7] For text-critical notes on the ancient versions of 22:19–26, see Marböck, "Gefährdung und Bewährung," 89–90 (Greek), 98–100 (Syriac), and 100–102 (Latin).

[8] Thus Skehan and Di Lella, *Wisdom of Ben Sira,* 315–16; cf. Smend, *Sirach erklärt,* 202; Box and Oesterley, "Sirach," 392. Other examples exist where verses have been switched in the course of textual transmission; for instance, in H^{A} 12:1 precedes 11:34, while in H^{EF} (but not H^{B}) 32:24 comes before 33:1.

22[g]. After ὀνειδισμοῦ, "insult," G adds καὶ ὑπερηφανίας, "and pride," a gloss that is lacking in S and that overloads the colon; L adds a further noun, *convicio*, "taunting."[9]

22[h–h]. So S. G reads μυστηρίου ἀποκαλύψεως, "the revealing of a secret."

22[i–i]. So S with a participle. G paraphrases: "in the case of these things every friend will flee."

24[j–j]. So H^{3053}; compare Joel 3:3. S reads "smoke billows up" (cf. Joel 3:3 S), while G has "there is vapor of a furnace and smoke," presupposing תִּימְרוֹת כִּבְשָׁן וְעָשָׁן.

24[k–k]. So S^{ALW} (cf. H^{3053}); S^{M} reads the participle: "one who sheds blood" (= שֹׁפֵךְ דָּם). G has αἱμάτων (= דָּמִים, "blood"); the plural represents the Hebrew idiom for blood that has been shed.

23[l]. So S. G paraphrases: "acquire fidelity with."

23[m]. Reading εὐφρανθῇς, "you may rejoice," with most MSS of G. Instead of תִּחַד, "you may rejoice," S presupposes תֵּחַד, "you may be united." G^{B} (= Ziegler) paraphrases: ὁμοῦ πλησθῇς, "you may be filled together."

23[n]. After verse 23d the Lucianic witnesses add a gloss (absent in GI, S, and L) based on 10:23 and 11:2: "For one should never despise the appearance[10] [of someone], nor is a rich person lacking sense remarkable."

25[o–o]. So S. G has, "To shelter a friend I shall not be ashamed" (cf. Sir 6:14a); note that Sir 22:25–26 G appears to be influenced by 6:12–14 G.

25[p–p]. So S. G reads, "I shall not be hidden" (= לֹא אֶסָּתֵר, as in Job 13:20); cf. Sir 6:12b.

26[q–q]. Cf. G: "And if evil happens to me on account of him."[11] However, S presupposes a different reading: "If your comrade reveals to you a secret, do not disclose it"; possibly it misread בִּגְלָלְךָ, "on account of you," as גִּלְּךָ, "he has revealed to you," and רָעָה, "evil," as רֵעֲךָ, "your companion."

---

[9] In 22:22cd the textual problems affect the interpretation. The text of G here is open to doubt because verse 22c is overloaded (Smend, *Sirach, erklärt*, 201), whereas S presents a smoother text (Marböck, "Gefährdung und Bewährung," 91).

[10] Or "limited situation"; cf. Marböck, "Gefährdung und Bewährung," 95 n. 16; Wagner, *Die Septuaginta-Hapaxlegomena im Buch Jesus Sirach*, 343.

[11] In 22:26 the sense demands a change of person from G; cf. Skehan and Di Lella, *Wisdom of Ben Sira*, 315. The first-person reference in 22:25–26 G seems to have arisen by analogy with the first-person prayer in 22:27–23:6; cf. Marböck, "Gefährdung und Bewährung," 88. However, the first-person references in 22:25–26 G are taken as original by J. Liesen, "Strategical Self-References in Ben Sira," in Calduch-Benages and Vermeylen, eds., *Treasures of Wisdom*, 63–74, esp. 71–72.

26[r–r]. Cf. G: "Everyone who hears will guard himself from him." S has: "Lest everyone who hears you will be wary of you, and will consider you as a wicked person" (cf. 19:9 S).

5. Translation

I

19 One who strikes the eye will make tears descend,
    and one who strikes the heart will elicit pain.
20 One who throws a stone at a bird will scare it away,
    and one who disgraces a friend will make friendship vanish.
21 If you draw a sword against a friend,
    do not despair, for there is a way back.
22 If you open your mouth against a friend,
    do not be terrified, for there is reconciliation.
One who reveals a confidence is a disgraceful person,
    and a hidden blow will make friendship vanish.
24 Columns of smoke precede fire,
    and malicious talk precedes the shedding of blood.

II

23 Support your companion in his poverty,
    so that you may rejoice in his prosperity.
At a time of distress remain faithful to him,
    so that you may be an heir in his inheritance.
25 If your friend becomes impoverished, do not put him to shame,
    and do not hide yourself from his presence.
26 But if evil happens to him on account of you,
    everyone who hears will be wary of you.

6. Poetic Analysis

Sirach 22:19–26 consists of two stanzas: the first stanza (three couplets: vv. 19–20; 21–22b; 22cd, 24) discusses insensitive behavior that destroys friendship, while the second (two couplets: vv. 23; 25–26) speaks of preserving friendship with an impoverished friend. The first stanza is united by a triple *inclusio* between its first and last couplets.

22:19ab: מַכֵּה ("one who strikes," bis); 22:22d: מַכַּת ("a blow")
22:20b: מְחָרֵף ("one who disgraces"); 22:22c: חֶרְפָּה ("disgrace")
22:20b: יַעֲבִיר אַהֲבָה; 22:22d: תַּעֲבִיר אַהֲבָה ("will make friendship vanish")

In my reconstruction the second stanza is marked off by rhyme in all four cola of its first couplet (22:23abcd) and the last two cola of its second couplet (22:26ab).

a. Stanza 1: Destroying Friendship by Insensitive Behavior (22:19–22, 24)

The opening couplet of the first stanza (22:19–20) consists of two aphoristic bicola; in each case the example in the first colon introduces a lesson in the second. Poetic features also unify 22:19–20, since each colon begins with a participle starting with *m*, and rhyme exists between the first colon of 22:19 and the second colon of 22:20 (v. 19a: דִּמְעָה, "tears"; v. 20b: אַהֲבָה, "friendship"). In my reconstruction the opening bicolon (22:19) exhibits alliteration and assonance, which are evident when its two cola are juxtaposed ("one who strikes" + [part of body] + [*hipʿil* verb] + [feminine noun]):

מַכֵּה עַיִן יוֹרִיד דִּמְעָה
וּמַכֵּה לֵב יוֹצִיא עַצֶּבֶת

The second bicolon (22:20) contains further alliteration (v. 20a: מַשְׁלִיךְ, "one who throws"; v. 20b: מְחָרֵף, "one who disgraces"), as well as assonance (v. 20a: יַחֲרִידֶנּוּ, "will scare it away"; v. 20b: מְחָרֵף, "one who disgraces").

The second couplet (22:21–22ab) forms the center of the stanza, with parallel prescriptions on how to behave after acting "against a friend" (עַל אוֹהֵב). Verse 21 adds alliteration by repeating *t* and *š* in the word-series: תַּשְׁלִךְ ... תִּתְיָאֵשׁ ... יֵשׁ תְּשׁוּבָה. Alliteration and assonance are also evident between אִם תִּפְתַּח ("if you open," v. 22a) and אַל תִּפְחַד ("do not be terrified," v. 22b).

The third couplet (22:22cd, 24) describes kinds of talk that ruin a friendship. The phrase in 22:22d, תַּעֲבִיר אַהֲבָה ("will make friendship vanish"), echoes the same idiom at the close of 22:20b. The proverb in 22:24 exhibits anaphoric repetition: both cola begin with לִפְנֵי (lit., "before").[12] In addition, 22:24a evidences alliteration of *š* (אֵשׁ, "fire," and עָשָׁן, "smoke"), while 22:24b displays alliteration with *d* (דָּם, "blood," and דִּבָּה, "malicious talk"). The last word of verse 24b (דִּבָּה, "malicious

[12] In Sir 32:10 H[B] the sage also juxtaposes two cola beginning with לִפְנֵי ("before"): "Before hail lightning will shine out, and before a contrite person favor will shine out."

talk") rhymes with the final word of the previous bicolon (אַהֲבָה, "friendship," v. 22d).

As a whole, the first stanza exhibits chiastic features:

A (22:19ab): מַכֵּה ... וּמַכֵּה
B (22:20b): יַעֲבִיר אַהֲבָה
C (22:21ab): עַל אוֹהֵב אִם ... אַל ... כִּי יֵשׁ ...
C (22:22ab): עַל אוֹהֵב אִם ... אַל ... כִּי יֵשׁ ...
B (22:22d): תַּעֲבִיר אַהֲבָה
A' (22:24ab): לִפְנֵי ... וְלִפְנֵי

b. Stanza 2: Supporting a Friend in his Poverty (22:23, 25–26)

The couplet (22:23) that opens the second stanza exhibits a fourfold rhyme: בְּדַלּוּתוֹ ("in his poverty," v. 23a); בְּטוֹבָתוֹ ("in his prosperity," v. 23b); עִמּוֹ ("to him," v. 23c); בְּנַחֲלָתוֹ ("in his inheritance," v. 23d); note also that each colon in verse 23 has a word beginning with *b*. The antithesis between "his poverty" and "his prosperity" (22:23ab) matches the contrast between "distress" and "his inheritance" (22:23cd). Indeed, verses 23b and 23d share a common structure.

... so that you may rejoice in his prosperity (22:23b)
... so that you may be an heir in his inheritance (22:23d)

By contrast, verses 23a and 23c form an a:b::b':a' chiastic pattern:

Support your companion : in his poverty ::
At a time of distress : remain faithful to him.

Verse 23cd also exhibits alliteration, with נ occurring four times and other letters three times (ל, מ, ע, ת).

The final couplet (22:25–26), warning against neglect of a needy friend, also employs alliteration, assonance, and rhyme. There is alliteration and assonance between אַל תְּבִישֶׁנּוּ ("do not put him to shame," v. 25a) and אִם תַּשִּׂיגֶנּוּ ("if ... happens to him," v. 26a). The final bicolon exhibits rhyme, which serves to mark the end of the pericope: בִּגְלָלְךָ ("on account of you," v. 26a) and מִמְּךָ ("of you," v. 26b).

7. Context

a. Context of Sirach 22:19–26 within 14:20–23:27

Sirach 22:19–26 occurs near the end of Ben Sira's fourth part (14:20–23:27), which consists of a theological segment (14:20–18:14) and an ethical segment (18:15–23:27). While discussing the context of Sir

19:13–17 in the previous chapter, I already outlined the structure of 18:15–23:27. Just as throughout 18:15–23:27 the sage often contrasts wise and foolish talk, so too the use of speech is a theme of 22:19–26, since its first stanza mentions a verbal offense (22:22a), revealing confidences (22:22c), and malicious talk (22:24b).

b. Relationship with 21:22–22:18

While the preceding pericope (21:22–22:18) discusses folly of various kinds,[13] 22:19–26 describes foolish behavior that can put an end to friendship, namely, negative speech (the first stanza) and a refusal to help a friend (the second stanza). Whereas 22:13bc G admonishes, "Do not go to a person lacking understanding; be on guard against him," 22:26b warns that others will be on guard against someone who has failed to help a friend ("everyone who hears will be wary of you").[14] In a comparable fashion, the theme of shame, occurring in 22:3–5, recurs in 22:19–26, which speaks of disgrace (22:20b, 22c), calumnious talk (22:24b), and shame (22:25a). Finally, the thrice-mentioned "heart" (or "mind": καρδία) in 22:16–18 G serves as a *mot crochet* with "heart" (καρδίαν = לֵב) in 22:19b.[15]

c. Relationship with 22:27–23:27

Just as the first stanza of Sir 22:19–26 (= vv. 19–22, 24) concerns harmful words, so 22:27–23:27 treats self-control in matters of speech (22:27–23:1; 23:7–15).[16] In particular, the sage's warning against evil talk (22:22, 24) anticipates his prayer that begins in 22:27: "Who will place a guard over my mouth?"

8. Exegesis

a. Stanza 1: Destroying Friendship by Insensitive Behavior (22:19–22, 24)

In order to emphasize the delicate nature of human friendship, Ben Sira opens the poem with two comparisons from the natural world (the

---

[13] Sirach 21:22–22:18 G employs the word μωρός ("fool") nine times. For a discussion of 21:22–22:18, see Desečar, *La sabiduría y la necedad*, 44–74; on 22:9–15, see Di Lella, "Sirach 22:9–15: 'The Life of a Fool Is Worse Than Death.'"

[14] Both 22:13 G and 22:26 G use the verb φυλάσσομαι ("be on guard").

[15] So Marböck ("Gefährdung und Bewährung," 88), who also notes that διαλύω ("dissolve") occurs in 22:16b, 20b G.

[16] The noun στόμα ("mouth") occurs in 22:22, 27 G. Other parallel motifs include the "eye" (ὀφθαλμόν, 22:19; ὀφθαλμοί, 23:19) and "insult" or "disgrace" (ὀνειδίζων, 22:20; ὄνειδος, 23:26). On Sir 22:27–23:27, see Beentjes, "Sirach 22:27–23:6 in zijn context."

eye [22:19] and a bird [22:20]). The first bicolon (22:19) compares the sensitivity of the human eye to the delicacy of the heart in friendship. Just as by its tears an eye indicates that it has been injured, so too a human heart wounded in friendship displays its feelings of hurt (sometimes also with tears).[17]

Elsewhere in his book Ben Sira mentions the "tears" (דִּמְעָה) caused by injustice (35:18) or grief (38:16). Speaking of the plight of the poor widow, the sage exclaims: "Do not tears [דִּמְעָה, collective] descend upon her cheek?" (35:18 H[B]). In his advice on mourning for the dead, he counsels: "My child, over the dead make tears [דִּמְעָה] flow" (38:16 H[B]).

According to 22:19a the cause of the tears is "one who strikes the eye" (מַכֵּה עַיִן). Here Ben Sira echoes an ordinance of the Exodus Covenant Code. Exodus 21:26 specifies: "And if a person strikes the eye of his servant [וְכִי־יַכֶּה אִישׁ אֶת־עֵין עַבְדּוֹ] or the eye of his maidservant and destroys it, he shall let him go free in exchange for his eye." The Covenant Code stipulates that the destruction of the servant's eye as a result of the slaveowner's blow puts an end to the master-slave relationship. Similarly, Ben Sira uses the analogy of a blow to the eye (22:19a) when speaking of an emotional wound that puts an end to the relationship of friendship (22:19b).

The phrase מַכֵּה לֵב ("one who strikes the heart," 22:19b) refers to a person who hurts one's feelings by an act of unkindness or betrayal.[18] The same idea appears in the misogynistic statement of 25:13 H[C].

כָּל מַכָּה וְלֹא כְמַכַּת לֵב   כָּל רָעָה וְלֹא כְרָעַת אִשָּׁה

Any blow but not like a blow to the heart;
any evil but not like the evil of a woman![19]

In 25:13 the sage parallels a physical blow with an emotional blow (v. 13a) and physical suffering with the emotional suffering that can be

[17] Perhaps the saying derives from a traditional riddle: "What kind of blow causes the most weeping?" (Answer: "a blow to the heart.") In the book of Tobit it is not so much the blinding of his eyes (Tob 2:10) as the emotional wound of his wife's mockery (2:14) that causes Tobit to weep (3:1) and to pray for death (3:6). On the ancient Hebrew conception of weeping, see T. Collins, "The Physiology of Tears in the Old Testament," *CBQ* 33 (1971): 18–38, 185–97.

[18] A different nuance appears in the cognate phrase in 1 Sam 24:6 and 2 Sam 24:10: וַיַּךְ לֵב־דָּוִד אֹתוֹ ("and David's heart [= conscience] smote him").

[19] See Segal, ספר בן־סירא השלם, 155, for the completion of the lacunae in H[C]. The parallelism implies that רָעַת אִשָּׁה ("the evil of a woman") should be understood as "the distress caused by a wife." On 25:13–14, see Trenchard, *Ben Sira's View of Women*, 67–71.

caused by a wife (v. 13b); similarly, in 22:19 he parallels a physical blow (v. 19a) with an emotional wound (v. 19b).

A related saying in *b. Šabb.* 11a contains a kind of numerical proverb (similar to the 3 + 1 pattern of Sir 26:5–6): "Any sickness, but not sickness of the bowels; any pain, but not the pain of the heart [כְּאֵב לֵב]; any ache, but not the aching of the head; any evil, but not an evil woman."[20] A comparable statement occurs in 25:23ab G: "A downcast heart and a sullen face and a blow to the heart [πληγὴ καρδίας] [come from] a wicked wife." Whereas Sir 22:19 uses the pair "eye-heart,"[21] Sir 25:23 employs the series "heart-face-heart," while the rabbinic aphorism utilizes the triad "bowels-heart-head."

In 22:19b Ben Sira's grandson employs the noun αἴσθησις in the sense "feeling" or "pain," as in Jdt 16:17.[22] Although the Greek noun can mean "knowledge" or "discernment" as well as "pain," the context here demands the latter meaning.[23] Sirach 36:25 H^{B} connects the noun עַצֶּבֶת ("pain") with the "heart": "A deceitful heart will cause pain" (עַצֶּבֶת). Similarly, Prov 15:13 asserts that "by pain of heart [בְּעַצְּבַת־לֵב] the spirit is stricken."

The second bicolon of the first stanza (Sir 22:20ab) uses the image of a bird to express the fragility of friendship; a friend may be scared off as easily as a bird. Likewise, Sir 27:19–20 utilizes the imagery of a bird and a gazelle (both creatures that are easily frightened away) to convey the vulnerability of friendship.[24] In 22:20a, too, the bird flying away is an image of broken friendship, whereas in 27:9a G the same creature serves to depict friends gathering together: "Birds will lodge with those that are like them."

---

[20] Cited in A. E. Cowley and A. Neubauer, *The Original Hebrew of a Portion of Ecclesiasticus* (Oxford: Clarendon, 1897), xxiv.

[21] For other instances of "eyes" and "heart" in parallel, see, e.g., Prov 4:21; 21:4; 23:33; Sir 14:3 H^{A}; 43:18 H^{BM}. For a full discussion of this parallel word-pair, see W. G. E. Watson, *Traditional Techniques in Classical Hebrew Verse* (JSOTSup 170; Sheffield: Sheffield Academic Press, 1994), 284–92.

[22] Cf. Marböck, "Gefährdung und Bewährung," 92 n. 10. Judith 16:17 says that the hostile nations shall forever weep "in pain" (ἐν αἰσθήσει), while the same Greek phrase also means "painfully" in 1 Esdr 1:22 (24).

[23] Though LXX Proverbs nineteen times translates דַּעַת ("knowledge") with αἴσθησις (e.g., Prov 15:14; 18:15), Ben Sira's grandson never uses this rendering of דַּעַת but instead employs γνῶσις ("knowledge": 3:25 G^{OL}), σύνεσις ("perception": 5:10; 37:22, 23), or ἐπιστήμη ("understanding": 38:3). According to G. B. Caird the grandson was not acquainted with LXX Proverbs; see "Ben Sira and the Dating of the Septuagint," in *Studia Evangelica 7* (ed. E. A. Livingstone; TU 126; Berlin: Akademie Verlag, 1982), 95–100, esp. 100.

[24] See my exegesis of 27:19–20 in the previous chapter.

The throwing of stones (Sir 22:20a) indicates hostility (cf. Prov 26:27; 2 Sam 16:6); indeed, David actually caused a fatal wound to Goliath by slinging a stone (1 Sam 17:49–50). In this stanza Ben Sira draws a parallel between throwing stones (Sir 22:20) and wounding someone (22:19). The same parallel appears in Sir 27:25 G: "The one who throws a stone upward throws it upon his own head, and a treacherous blow will open up wounds."

The first couplet concludes by making the lesson explicit: "One who disgraces a friend will make friendship vanish" (Sir 22:20b). Similarly, in 41:22cd H^M the sage warns his audience to be ashamed:

מֵאֹהֵב עַל דִּבְרֵי חֶסֶד   וּמֵאַחַר מַתָּת חָרֵף

Before a friend concerning reproachful words,
and of insulting after giving a gift.[25]

The second couplet of 22:19–26 is an encouragement to maintain hope even if one has drawn a sword (22:21) or opened one's mouth (22:22ab) against a friend. Whereas "opening one's mouth" (v. 22a) appears anticlimactic after the hyperbolic act of "drawing a sword" (v. 21a), Ben Sira deliberately employs this juxtaposition for dramatic effect. Verse 21 speaks of an occasion when the sage thinks friendship can be mended, namely, a fit of temper that leads one to draw a sword.[26] Whereas 1 Sam 17:51 describes David drawing the sword to kill the hostile Goliath,[27] the tragedy of Sir 22:21 is that one draws the sword against a friend. Contrary to what one might expect, Ben Sira asserts that such a rash act (perhaps in response to a friend's negative remarks or deeds) is not irreparable.

In such circumstances the sage counsels: "Do not despair" (אַל תִּתְיָאֵשׁ). The same phrase occurs in *m. ʾAbot* 1:7, where it refers to a despairing attitude because of the evil in the world. The reason for Ben Sira's

---

[25] An alternative vocalization of 41:22d H^M yields the sense: "and before a stranger of giving reproach"; cf. Harrington, *Wisdom Texts from Qumran,* 96. However, H^B preserves a text closer to G:

מֵאוֹהֵב עַל [דִּבְ]רֵי חֶרְפָּה   וּמֵאַחֲרֵי מַתָּת אַל תִּנְאַץ

Before a friend concerning insulting [wo]rds,
and after giving a gift do not be contemptuous.

[26] Compare Aramaic Ahiqar Saying 31 (line 113): "A sword [חרב] stirs up quiet waters between good neighbors [רעין טבן]" (Lindenberger, *Aramaic Proverbs of Ahiqar,* 100).

[27] Similarly, Sir 37:5 speaks of a good friend fighting against one's foes.

encouragement to hope here is the possibility of a "way back" (22:21b). Similarly, 17:24 G connects a "way back" with hope: "Yet to the repentant he [= God] gave a way back [ἐπάνοδον], and he encouraged those abandoning endurance." The "way back" (תְּשׁוּבָה) is presumably apologizing to one's friend for the misdeed; indeed, the noun תְּשׁוּבָה can also mean "repentance" or "conversion" in postbiblical Hebrew.[28]

The whole of 22:21 serves as an ironic contrast to 22:22cd. Although drawing a sword seems to be the worst possible thing one can do against a friend, Ben Sira asserts that as an impulsive overt act against one's friend, it can be forgiven. The sage implies that such an extreme act is, ironically, not as harmful as revealing a confidence (22:22c) or inflicting a hidden blow (22:22d)—acts that are not impulsive but fully calculated, and all the more deplorable since they destroy friendship.[29]

Sirach 22:22 discusses occasions when friendship can and cannot be repaired. Whereas friendship can be healed after an offensive remark (22:22ab), revealing a confidence and injuring someone behind his back cause irreparable damage (22:22cd). While one can mend the harm created by offenses committed in a private conversation with a friend (22:22ab), the evil caused by publicly humiliating a friend in his absence cannot be undone (22:22cd). Hence, within a social system based on honor and shame, the dishonor done to a friend (22:22cd) makes the friendship break down irretrievably.[30]

Whereas 22:21a speaks of a physical threat with a sword (חֶרֶב), 22:22a mentions an attack with the mouth (פֶּה). Ancient Israelite literature (especially the Psalter) often compares verbal attacks to an assault with swords or spears or arrows.[31] Ben Sira asserts that if one has made a verbal attack, reconciliation is actually possible. Whereas the idiom "open one's mouth"

---

[28] This derived meaning is not attested in the MT or the extant Hebrew MSS of Ben Sira but appears in certain nonbiblical Hebrew texts (e.g., CD 19.16; *m. ʾAbot* 4:13).

[29] For this interpretation I am indebted to Professor Di Lella. Elsewhere Ben Sira employs comparable ironic hyperbole, such as in 19:10–11 G:

You have heard a story—let it die with you;
  take courage—it will not tear you apart.
On account of a story a fool will be in as much labor
  as is a woman giving birth on account of her baby.

[30] Compare Camp's assertion: "The concepts of honor and shame constitute an essential part of Ben Sira's ideological matrix" ("Honor, Shame, and the Hermeneutics of Ben Sira's MS C," in Barré, ed., *Wisdom, You Are My Sister,* 157).

[31] See, e.g., Pss 57:5; 59:8; 64:4. Note that the second Servant Song in Deutero-Isaiah says: "He made my mouth like a sharp sword" (Isa 49:2). Hebrew also speaks idiomatically of "the mouth [= edge] of the sword" (פִּי־חֶרֶב, e.g., Job 1:15).

(פָּתַח פֶּה) can simply mean "speak,"[32] here the context shows that the phrase refers to negative speech, such as an angry retort or a hostile remark.

Sirach 22:22b opens with the injunction אַל תִּפְחַד ("Do not be terrified"), a phrase that Ben Sira uses twice elsewhere in the context of death. Sirach 41:3a H[M] urges, "Do not be terrified of death, the decree for you," while Sir 9:13 H[A] promises that if you keep far from someone authorized to kill, "you will not be terrified of the terrors of death." In the case of a hostile or angry word (22:22ab), the sage teaches that there is no need to fear, because such talk does not necessarily mean the death of the friendship; there is the possibility of reconciliation.[33]

The disgrace of revealing a confidence (22:22c) is a frequent theme of Ben Sira (6:9; 27:16–21; 42:1).[34] Just as 22:22c declares that "one who reveals a confidence is a disgraceful person" (בֶּן חֶרְפָּה)," so 6:9 speaks of the former friend who "will expose a dispute to your disgrace" (חֶרְפָּתְךָ). Similarly, 5:14 H[A] states: "For the thief shame was created, and evil disgrace [= חֶרְפָּה רָעָה] for the two-faced person."[35]

Sirach 22:22d speaks of the damage done to friendship by a "hidden blow" (מַכַּת סֵתֶר). The parallelism of verse 22cd suggests that the revealing of the confidence in 22c is the "hidden blow" cited in 22d. Here Ben Sira adapts an idiom from the list of curses in Deut 27:15–26. While Deut 27:24 outlaws a physical attack on a neighbor—אָרוּר מַכֵּה רֵעֵהוּ בַּסָּתֶר ("Cursed is one who strikes his companion in secret")—Sir 22:22d alludes to an assault on a person's character. A related saying occurs in Sir 27:25 G: "A treacherous blow [πληγὴ δολία] will open up wounds."[36]

---

[32] See, e.g., Isa 53:7; Ps 39:10; Prov 24:7; cf. Sir 24:2 G. An inceptive meaning ("begin to speak") is appropriate in Dan 10:16; Sir 51:25 H[B], and perhaps also in Sir 22:22.

[33] On "reconciliation" (= רִצּוּי = διαλλαγή) see my exegesis of Sir 27:21a in the previous chapter. Note the sage's realistic and practical view of friendship, wherein reconciliation is possible (22:22ab; 27:21a). Theognis 325–328 also asserts that angry words, though harmful to friendship, are natural to human beings and hence must be forgiven: "If a man grow always angry with a friend's offence, they will never be friends and at peace: for offences against men are natural to mortals" (Edmonds, trans., *Elegy and Iambus*, 1:267).

[34] Aramaic Ahiqar Saying 53 also asserts that the betrayal of secrets causes dishonor; see further my exegesis of 27:16 in the previous chapter, as well as J. J. Pilch, "Secrecy in the Mediterranean World: An Anthropological Perspective," *BTB* 24 (1994): 151–57.

[35] Where H[A] reads חרפה רעהו, I read חֶרְפָּה רָעָה ("evil disgrace") with G and S.

[36] Smend (*Sirach, erklärt*, 201) observes that πληγὴ δολία ("a treacherous blow") is equivalent to מַכַּת סֵתֶר ("a hidden blow") in Sir 22:22d.

The mention of "malicious talk" (דִּבָּה, 22:24b) develops the reference to "a disgraceful person" (22:22c) who perpetrates a slanderous "hidden blow" (22:22d).[37] The comparison of 22:24 is like the English saying: "No smoke without fire." Just as smoke precedes the flames when one lights a fire with green or damp wood,[38] so "malicious talk" is often the prelude to fighting and bloodshed. Hence, to prevent bloodshed one must avoid speaking maliciously about one's friend.

A proverb similar to Sir 22:24 appears in Ankhsheshonq 22.21–23: "Do not insult a common man. When insult occurs beating occurs. When beating occurs killing occurs."[39] The sayings of both Ankhsheshonq and Ben Sira see bloodshed as the consequence of insults. Likewise, 27:15 G cautions: "A quarrel of the arrogant means bloodshed, and their abusiveness is something distressing to hear."

In Ben Sira's poetry "fire" (אֵשׁ) often has a negative connotation. In 3:30 H^A "fire" (אֵשׁ) represents "sin" (חַטָּאת), just as "water" corresponds to "almsgiving." The same kind of symbolism occurs also in 15:16, where the two options are "fire and water" (אֵשׁ וָמַיִם, H^A), equivalent (in reverse) to the choice between "life and death" (15:17). In 22:24 too, "fire" symbolizes death caused by "the shedding of blood" (שְׁפַךְ דָּם).

The imagery of 22:24 derives largely from Joel 3:3: "And I will place portents in the heavens and on the earth, blood and fire and columns of smoke" (דָּם וָאֵשׁ וְתִימֲרוֹת עָשָׁן).[40] Whereas in Joel these signs indicate God's punishment of the wicked, in Sir 22:24 they are the result of the sinful folly of human beings.

In his warning that the "shedding of blood" (שְׁפַךְ דָּם) is the result of "malicious talk" (דִּבָּה), Ben Sira may be echoing Ezek 22 and 1 Sam 25. After condemning the ruling class of Jerusalem for causing bloodshed (Ezek 22:6), Ezekiel links bloodshed with slander: "In you [Jerusalem] were those who slander for the purpose of shedding blood" (לְמַעַן שְׁפָךְ־דָּם; Ezek 22:9). In the story of Nabal and Abigail (1 Sam 25),[41] Nabal's rudeness

---

[37] On דִּבָּה, see my exegesis of Sir 19:15a in the previous chapter. Fuß notes that 22:24b is connected semantically with 22:22c ("Tradition und Komposition," 144). In view of this link I have moved verse 24 before verse 23.

[38] Compare the proverbial saying in Luke 23:31: "If people do these things with the green wood, what is to happen with the dry?" The death of Jesus may be seen as an example of how malicious talk can precede the shedding of blood.

[39] *AEL* 3:176.

[40] The verb שׁפך ("pour out," "shed") also occurs in Joel 3:2, while the phrase תִּימֲרוֹת עָשָׁן ("columns of smoke") appears in Cant 3:6.

[41] Note that in Sir 6:5–17 the sage alludes several times to 1 Sam 25; see ch. 2 above.

would have caused David's troops to kill, unless Abigail had urged moderation: "And this will not become for you a cause of stumbling or a mental obstacle for my lord, to have shed blood [לִשְׁפָּךְ־דָּם] needlessly" (1 Sam 25:31). Seeing the warning signs of impending conflict, Abigail wisely intervened to prevent bloodshed.

As a teacher of wise conduct, Ben Sira warns against various occasions or persons that might cause bloodshed.[42] Thus, the sage counsels caution in dealings with an angry person, because "in his eyes bloodshed [דָּמִים] is something trifling" (8:16 H^A^).[43] Moreover, the sage warns against associating with an enemy; despite his friendly words, "if he has found an occasion, he will not have enough of blood" (דָּם; 12:16 H^A^).

As in 22:24, Ben Sira parallels fire and bloodshed when discussing the backbiter in 11:32 H^A^: "From a spark he will multiply burning coals, and a worthless person will lie in wait for blood." Likewise, 28:11 G parallels fire and blood: "A hasty dispute kindles a fire [πῦρ], and a hasty quarrel sheds blood [αἷμα]."

In 22:24 the first stanza reaches its culmination. Hitherto, Ben Sira has portrayed a series of violent attacks: striking the heart (22:19b), drawing a sword (22:21a),[44] and a hidden blow (22:22d). Now, with its mention of "the shedding of blood," 22:24 serves as a forceful climax for the stanza, illustrating the worst result of malicious talk against a friend.

b. Stanza 2: Supporting a Friend in His Poverty (22:23, 25–26)

In the second stanza the sage leaves behind the violent imagery of stanza 1 in order to speak of the value of fidelity in friendship. In 22:23 Ben Sira offers a utilitarian motivation for being faithful in friendship: one will be able to share in the friend's subsequent prosperity. This advice accords with the sage's eudaemonistic approach to life, whereby he regards ethical action as leading to success and unethical activity as leading to failure.[45] Such a philosophy, though it may appear venal,

---

[42] By referring to the "sword" in 22:21a, Ben Sira has prepared the reader for the mention of "bloodshed" in 22:24b.

[43] Furthermore, in 9:9 H^A^ he advises against dining with a married woman, lest "you decline to the pit in bloodshed" (בְּדָמִים). The "bloodshed" here is the punishment meted out either by the jealous husband (Box and Oesterley, "Sirach," 1:347) or by the legal authorities according to Lev 20:10 and Deut 22:22 (Skehan and Di Lella, *Wisdom of Ben Sira,* 219).

[44] In 22:21a Ben Sira makes his point ironically, by comparison with 22:22cd.

[45] On the sage's eudaemonism, see briefly Sanders, "Ben Sira's Ethics of Caution," 79–80; Collins, *Jewish Wisdom in the Hellenistic Age,* 75–76; Hengel, *Judaism and Hellenism,* 1:142–43. For instance, Sir 7:32 H^A^ assumes that a divine

expresses the belief that God rewards good actions and repays evil.[46] In fact, Ben Sira derives his brand of eudaemonism largely from the Deuteronomic scheme of retribution; those who obey God receive the blessings of "prosperity" (טוֹבָה, Sir 22:23b; cf. Deut 28:11; 30:9), as well as an "inheritance" (נַחֲלָה, Sir 22:23d; cf. Deut 15:4; 26:1).[47]

The verb סְמַךְ("support") may refer to financial assistance or emotional support. In 51:7 H^B the participial form סוֹמֵךְ ("supporter") occurs in parallel to עוֹזֵר ("helper"), while 13:21 H^A employs the same verb סמךְ to describe the support that a stumbling rich person receives from a companion.

Sirach 22:23ab creates an antithesis between "poverty" (דַלּוּת) and "prosperity" (טוֹבָה), just as 22:23cd contrasts a "time of distress" (עֵת צָרָה) with an "inheritance" (נַחֲלָה). Similarly, speaking of his pious predecessors in 44:11 H^{BM}, Ben Sira places "their prosperity" (טוּבָם) in parallel with "their inheritance" (נַחֲלָתָם). The sage's insistence on fidelity to one's friend (22:23) contrasts with his earlier depiction of the fickle friend who is present "in your prosperity" (בְּטוֹבָתְךָ: 6:11 H^A) but who disappears "on a day of distress" (בְּיוֹם צָרָה: 6:8 H^A).

By means of the verb חדה ("rejoice")[48] and the noun טוֹבָה ("prosperity," "good"), 22:23b alludes to the story of Moses' friendship with Jethro. Whereas Jethro had formerly assisted Moses in his "time of distress" when he had fled from Pharaoh (cf. Exod 2:15–22), after the exodus Jethro was glad because through Moses the Israelites had been successfully delivered from Egypt: "And Jethro rejoiced [וַיִּחַדְּ] over all the good [הַטּוֹבָה] that Yahweh had done to Israel" (Exod 18:9). Similarly, Sir

blessing comes to the generous person: "Also to a needy person extend your hand, in order that your blessing be complete." Like the author of Prov 1–4, Ben Sira motivates his students by noting that right behavior can bring benefits, such as wisdom (Sir 51:25 H^B; cf. Prov 2:10) and a long life (Sir 1:12; cf. Prov 3:16a), as well as financial reward (Sir 51:28; Prov 3:16b).

[46] This belief in divine retribution is fundamental for Ben Sira; cf. Sir 1:12–13; 2:10; 7:1–3; 12:6; 15:13; 17:22–23; 35:13, 24; 41:8–9; 51:28. See further Di Lella, "Conservative and Progressive Theology," 143–46; and Dommershausen, "Zum Vergeltungsdenken des Ben Sira."

[47] Wishing to soften the materialistic motivation of 22:23, the Lucianic text of G adds a comment more favorable to poverty: "For one should never despise the appearance [of someone], nor is a rich person lacking sense remarkable."

[48] Smend (*Sirach, erklärt*, 202) notes the possible ambiguity of the verbal form תחד (22:23b). I read תִּחַדְּ ("you may rejoice," from the root חדה, "rejoice") with most MSS of G; likewise Segal, ספר בן־סירא השלם, 134. However, the reading of S (lit., "you may share") understands the verb as תֵּחַד ("you may be united," from the root יחד, "be united").

22:23ab advises: "Support your companion in his poverty, so that you may rejoice [תִּחַד] in his prosperity [בְּטוֹבָתוֹ]." Thus, Jethro's friendship with Moses serves as a paradigm for Ben Sira's teaching; because Jethro had supported Moses in his time of need, he was able to rejoice in his subsequent success.

The sage's advice in Sir 22:23ab agrees with the Egyptian proverb in Ankhsheshonq 17.18: "If you have grown up with a man and are faring well with him, do not abandon him when he fares badly."[49] However, the worldly wise Theognis warns against hoping in the future kindness of an afflicted friend: "Never make friends with a man in exile, Cyrnus, with an eye to the future, for when he is come home he becometh quite another man" (Theognis 333–334).

Sirach 22:23cd develops the sentiment of the previous bicolon. Parallel to בְּדַלּוּתוֹ ("in his poverty") stands בְּעֵת צָרָה (= ἐν καιρῷ θλίψεως = "at a time of distress"). Both 6:8 and 37:4 employ similar phrases to describe times of difficulty when the false friend disappears.[50] By contrast, 22:23c urges fidelity to one's chosen friend precisely at such times. Moreover, 40:24 G speaks of the assistance given by kinsfolk and helpers in times of need: "Brothers and help are for a time of distress [εἰς καιρὸν θλίψεως], but more than both almsgiving will rescue."[51]

The command to remain faithful to one's friend in his time of need (22:23c) exemplifies the high value that Ben Sira places on fidelity within friendship (cf. 6:14–16). A similar counsel regarding friendship occurs in 27:17a: "Test a comrade—and remain faithful to him."[52] A comparable saying appears in Theognis 1083–1084, describing the fidelity of the good person: "So true is it that the good man, though he change his disposition, must for evermore keep it steadfast to his friend."

---

49 *AEL* 3:172. According to Xenophon (*Mem.* 2.5.1), Socrates began one of his teachings when he "noticed that one of his companions was neglecting a poverty-stricken friend" (see Marchant, trans., *Xenophon,* 125). On the duty of reciprocal financial help expected in Greek friendship, see Konstan, *Friendship in the Classical World,* 78–82. The following Theognis quotation comes from Edmonds, trans., *Elegy and Iambus,* 1:269.

50 As equivalent of the phrase בְּעֵת צוּקָה ("at a time of stress," 37:4 H[BD]), G uses the exact phrase (ἐν καιρῷ θλίψεως = "at a time of distress") found in 22:23c G. Sirach 6:8 H[A] employs a synonymous idiom, בְּיוֹם צָרָה ("on a day of distress"), which G translates literally with ἐν ἡμέρᾳ θλίψεως.

51 H[B] partially preserves this saying (a free combination of Prov 17:17 and Prov 11:4), including the word צָרָה ("distress"; cf. Prov 17:17). The point of Sir 40:24 is that giving alms is even more beneficial for one's destiny than having helpful relatives.

52 See further my discussion of Sir 27:17 in the previous chapter. The following quotation comes from Edmonds, trans., *Elegy and Iambus,* 1:359.

The prescriptions of 22:23 may echo the Jubilee Year legislation in Lev 25. Behind the verse may lie the thought of the impoverished friend recovering his inherited property in the Jubilee Year (Lev 25:41).[53] Moreover, the call to "remain faithful" (הֵאָמֵן) toward a needy friend (Sir 22:23c) may allude to the command to offer charity to a poor relative: "You shall hold him fast" (וְהֶחֱזַקְתָּ בּוֹ, Lev 25:35; cf. Sir 29:1b). Sirach 29:1–3 G gives similar directions concerning care for an indigent neighbor.

> One who performs mercy lends to a companion,
> and one who holds [him] steadfastly with his hand keeps the commandments.
> Lend to a companion at the time of his need,
> and pay[54] a companion back again at the time.
> Confirm [your] word[55] and keep faith with him,
> and at all times you will find what you need.

The command to keep faith with the impoverished friend (29:3) parallels 22:23c, which counsels faithful support of such a person.

As the motivation for staying faithful toward the needy friend, Ben Sira holds out the possibility "that you may be an heir in his inheritance" (22:23d). Inheritance (22:23d) is of particular concern to Ben Sira because of his respect for tradition and because his outlook has no place for an afterlife. In 33:24 H^E he advises: "On the day of death [i.e., not beforehand] distribute [הַנְחֵל] an inheritance." The inheritance of the priesthood is different from that of the rest of society, for Sir 45:22 H^B says of Aaron's offspring: "Among the people's land he does not inherit, and in their midst he does not divide an inheritance [נַחֲלָה], because Yahweh is his portion and his inheritance."[56] The prescription of 22:23 thus implies that

[53] A stronger echo of the Jubilee Year law occurs in Sir 22:25. Although around 198 B.C.E. Antiochus III permitted Jerusalem to be governed "according to the ancestral laws" (Josephus, *Ant.* 12.3.3 §142), evidence is lacking that the Jubilee Year was ever practiced in Ben Sira's lifetime. For the sage, however, its stipulations may have served as an analogy revealing the demands of social justice. It is also possible that the plea to regard a servant as a "brother" in Sir 33:31 may echo Lev 25:46.

[54] In Lev 25:51–52 ἀποδίδωμι renders הֵשִׁיב ("pay back"). On Sir 29:1–7, see Gilbert, "Prêt, aumône et caution," esp. 179–81.

[55] Compare the phrase לְקַיֵּם כָּל־דָּבָר ("to confirm every word") concerning the generous redemption given by Boaz to Ruth (Ruth 4:7). Note that the גֹּאֵל ("one who redeems") is also mentioned in Lev 25:25.

[56] On the text here, see Skehan and Di Lella, *Wisdom of Ben Sira,* 508; cf. Segal, ספר בן־סירא השלם, 312.

the sage's students are not from priestly families and hence are able to share in a friend's inheritance.

In 22:25 Ben Sira avers that it is no shame to associate with a poor friend. Indeed, the sage urges his students not to add to the disgrace of a friend already experiencing the shameful condition of poverty. The opening phrase of 22:25a (preserved in S) echoes the language of Lev 25 on the Jubilee Year.[57] In particular, Lev 25:25, 35, 39 all begin with the phrase כִּי יָמוּךְ אָחִיךָ ("if your relative becomes impoverished"). Leviticus 25:35–36 urges one to support such a person.

> If your relative becomes impoverished and his hand shakes before you, you shall hold him fast; as an immigrant or a sojourner he shall live with you. Do not take from him interest or usury, but you are to fear God, while your relative lives with you.

The concern for an impoverished fellow Israelite found in Lev 25:35–36 is also echoed in Sir 29:2a G, "Lend to a companion at the time of his need," and in 29:10a G, "Waste money for the sake of a brother or a friend." Similarly, 29:14 G declares: "A good man will be a guarantor for his companion, but the one who has lost a sense of shame will abandon him."

Our discussion of 22:20b, 22c has already noted the importance of the polarity of honor and shame in Ben Sira's worldview. In 22:25a the sage urges his students not to add further humiliation to an impoverished friend by turning away from him.[58] Ben Sira's respect for the poor appears also in 10:22 H^B: "Immigrant, foreigner, alien, and pauper—their glory is the fear of Yahweh."

As a sign of concern for an impoverished friend, Ben Sira advises: "Do not hide yourself from his presence." Hiding from a troubled friend is a characteristic of false friendship, as noted in Sir 6:12: "When you are humbled he will turn against you, and from your presence he will hide himself" (מִפָּנֶיךָ יִסָּתֵר).

---

[57] Some of the Qumran documents exhibit interest in the Jubilee Year, either for calendrical reasons (Jubilees) or from an ethical viewpoint (11QMelch, which quotes Lev 25:9, 13 and Isa 61:1); cf. P. J. Kobelski, *Melchizedek and Melchireša*[c] (CBQMS 10; Washington, D.C.: Catholic Biblical Association of America, 1981), 49. A concern for social justice appears in 11QMelch 2.6–7, which describes Melchizedek's activity in the final age: "He will proclaim liberty for them, to free them from [the debt] of all their iniquities. And this will [happen] in the first week of the jubilee which follows the ni[ne] jubilees" (García Martínez, *Dead Sea Scrolls Translated,* 139–40).

[58] Similarly, Sir 8:6 H^A counsels: "Do not put an elderly person to shame." On Sir 22:25–26, see Krammer, "Scham im Zusammenhang mit Freundschaft," 191–93.

Sirach 22:26 warns about the social consequences for one "if evil happens" to the impoverished friend because of one's neglect of him. The phrase אִם תַּשִּׂיגֶנּוּ רָעָה (lit., "if evil overtakes him") uses an idiom found twice in MS H^A of Ben Sira (6:12 [where G and S differ] and 12:5). Just as Sir 7:1 H^C offers the advice אַל תַּעַשׂ רַע [וְאַל] יַשִּׂיגְךָ רַע ("Do no evil, and evil will not happen to you"), so Sir 22:26 suggests that helping a friend will enable one to avoid the ignominy of social disgrace.

The warning in 22:26 depends on public opinion for its effectiveness: a person who has refused to help an impoverished friend will be shunned in society. Elsewhere, Ben Sira invokes the same fear of public disgrace to discourage gossip (19:7–9). Sirach 19:7 S warns: "Never repeat a saying, and no one will reproach you." Elaborating on this point (derived from Prov 25:9–10), Sir 19:8–9 G says:

> Against friend or enemy do not recount it,
>   and unless it is sin for you, do not reveal it;
> for he has heard you and became on guard against you,
>   and in time he will hate you.

In the juxtaposition of the concepts of "hearing" (the verb שׁמע) and "being wary" (the *nipʿal* of זהר), Sir 22:26b (like 19:9) parallels Ezek 33:3–5. The divine message to Ezekiel employs the image of the sentinel:

> If he sees the sword coming against the land, and he blows on the horn and he warns [וְהִזְהִיר] the people, and the hearer hears [וְשָׁמַע הַשֹּׁמֵעַ] the sound of the horn and does not become wary [וְלֹא נִזְהָר] and the sword has come and taken him, his blood shall be upon his own head.... But one who did become wary [וְהוּא נִזְהָר] will have saved his life.

Just as Ben Sira encourages his students to learn with whom to associate by observing their conduct, so too he assumes that others in society watch the conduct of people and learn from what they see. Hence, he warns his students to be vigilant in their behavior.

The advice to be wary occurs frequently in Ben Sira's teaching (e.g., 6:13; 8:18–19; 12:10–12; 13:8–13). In 13:13 H^A, for instance, he counsels: "Be careful and wary [זָהִיר], and do not walk about with lawless persons." In 32:22, too, the second form of the saying in H^B reads: "Be wary [הִזָּהֵר] in your ways."[59] In 22:26b, however, the situation is somewhat different; instead of advising his students to be wary (13:13; 32:22), in 22:26b (as in

---

[59] In the first form of the saying in 32:22 H^B the verb is the synonym הִשָּׁמֵר ("be careful"), while 32:22 H^EF reads הֱיֵה זָהִיר ("be wary").

19:9) he states that others will be wary of them if they become known for refusing to help a needy friend.

9. Conclusion

Aside from its textual problems, Sir 22:19–26 is a thematically complex pericope, since it combines several messages about friendship. Whereas the first stanza focuses on sins of the tongue against a friend, the second concentrates on practical help for the friend at a time of need.

In the first stanza the opening couplet (22:19–20) employs imagery to speak of the fragility of friendship. Thereafter, the second and third couplets (22:21–22, 24) contrast offenses that may be pardoned (drawing a sword or saying something hostile) with unforgivable offenses (betraying a confidence and talking maliciously behind someone's back).

The second stanza (22:23, 25–26) urges support for a friend in his adversity; one should not despise him when he is impoverished, since he may later prosper. The final bicolon (22:26) asserts that one who refuses to help a needy friend will be an object of public contempt.

Ben Sira emphasizes his message by the use of three didactic illustrations: wounds to eyes, throwing stones at birds, and smoke preceding fire (22:19–20, 24). He also seems to allude to the legislation for the Jubilee Year (Lev 25) to inculcate an attitude of responsibility toward an impoverished friend (22:23, 25).

In summary, Ben Sira teaches in 22:19–26 that what destroys a friendship is emotional wounding (22:19b), abusive or malicious talk (22:20b, 24b), and also betraying confidences (22:22c). By way of contrast, what builds up a friendship is the hope of reconciliation (22:21b, 22b) and faithful support of a friend even in his poverty (22:23, 25).

7
Conclusion

1. Introduction

The theme of friendship in Ben Sira, which has only recently received any extended scholarly treatment, has formed the subject of this study. After surveying introductory questions such as Ben Sira's historical background, his book's problematic textual situation, and selected theological and ethical themes, I have examined the seven major friendship pericopes in detail. Besides providing exegesis of the passages, I have dealt with their textual problems, poetic features, and context within Ben Sira's book, as well as noting parallels from Greek and Egyptian literature.

This study reveals Ben Sira's use of themes found in other ancient writings. Basing his work on the foundation of Israel's Scriptures, Ben Sira develops ideas also found in Greek texts (especially Theognis) and Egyptian sapiential literature (particularly the prototype of P. Insinger). Either he knows such works (directly or indirectly), or else he is familiar at least with their thought-world. Such awareness of non-Israelite traditions, common elsewhere in Israel's sapiential heritage, may, in Ben Sira's case, reflect the influence of his foreign travels (Sir 34:12).

Nevertheless, although the sage is steeped in the traditions of Israel and the surrounding nations, he is not a slavish imitator. Rather, he forges a new synthesis, updating the truths of Israel's tradition for his contemporary audience in an increasingly hellenized society. He is not afraid to utilize insights found in foreign literature when these harmonize with Israel's faith. Since the book of Proverbs offers little specific guidance on how to form and maintain good friendships, Ben Sira expands traditional Israelite principles (such as caution and fidelity) using ideas also found in Greek and Egyptian writings. His originality lies not in the thoughts themselves but in his creative synthesis, whereby he brings ideas from diverse sources into harmony with Israel's faith, expressed through the leitmotif of the fear of God.

I now summarize the most significant aspects of the sage's teaching on friendship under four headings: the goodness of friendship, caution in friendship, faithfulness toward friends, and the fear of God as the most important quality in friendship.

2. The Goodness of Friendship[1]

One of the things delightful to Ben Sira is "the friendship of neighbors" (Sir 25:1c G); accordingly, he declares: "Happy is the one who finds a true friend" (25:9a L). Moreover, the sage includes friends (40:23) in his decalogue of good things (40:18–27), while Sir 6:15 declares that there is no weighing the benefit of a faithful friend.

Ben Sira's appreciation of friendship matches the Hellenistic esteem for φιλία, evident in Aristotle's remark: "The happy man requires friends" (*Eth. nic.* 9.9.3 §1169b).[2] Nevertheless, by his use of language Ben Sira takes care to root his friendship instructions within Israel's creation theology. Admittedly, the teaching that like is attracted to like is a commonplace of Greek literature.[3] In Sir 13:15, however, the sage formulates this idea using terminology from the Priestly tradition of Israel's primeval history: "All flesh will love its own kind, and every human being one resembling him." The fact that the terms employed (particularly "all flesh" and "kind") are reminiscent of Gen 1–11 suggests that friendship belongs to the natural order of God's good creation.[4] By contrast, a treacherous friend thwarts the purpose of his creation, so that the sage exclaims: "Alas, evil creature! Why were you formed, to fill the surface of the world with deceit?" (37:3).

Thus, in speaking of the goodness of friendship, Ben Sira combines Greek esteem for φιλία with Israel's theology of creation. This synthesis forms the foundation of the sage's teaching on friendship.

3. Caution in Friendship

The most prominent feature in Ben Sira's friendship teaching is his admonition to caution toward both potential and actual friends (6:7, 13). For instance, to inculcate discernment in the choice of friends, the sage observes: "Every friend says, 'I am a friend,' yet there is a 'friend' who is a friend in name only" (37:1).

---

[1] This concluding chapter echoes my earlier article "Friendship according to Ben Sira," in Egger-Wenzel and Krammer, eds., *Der Einzelne und seine Gemeinschaft bei Ben Sira,* 65–71. For a brief discussion of Sir 25:1, 9; 40:23, see the appendix below.

[2] Rackham, trans., *Nicomachean Ethics,* 559.

[3] E.g., Homer, *Od.* 17.217–218; Plato, *Symp.* 195b; Aristotle, *Rhet.* 1.11.25 §1371b; Aristotle, *Eth. nic.* 8.1.6 §1155a.

[4] The motif of the goodness of creation (cf. Gen 1:31) appears in Sir 39:16, 33; 42:22, 25.

Sirach 6:8–10 specifies the reason for such wariness, namely, that betrayal can easily occur: "There is a friend for a season.... There is a friend, turned into an enemy.... There is a friend, a table associate, but he will not be found on a day of adversity." A fair-weather friend remains close at a time of prosperity but disappears when adversity strikes (6:11).

Since the poor cannot offer material benefits, they tend to lack friends (Sir 13:21–23). In describing the unequal treatment of rich and poor, Sir 13:21–23 mirrors the insight of Prov 19:4: "Wealth will add many companions, but a pauper will be separated from his companions." Indeed, Ben Sira even asserts that friendship between rich and poor is no more possible than peace between wolves and lambs (13:17–19).

Ben Sira frequently cautions that friends may betray one in a time of need. Thus, 37:4 warns: "An evildoer is a 'friend' who gazes at the table, but at a time of stress he will stand aloof!" Similarly, the insight of 12:9 distills the wisdom of human experience: "In a person's prosperity, even an enemy is a companion, but in his adversity, even a companion will separate himself."[5] Ben Sira's warning that friends can disappear in a time of adversity echoes the experiences of Job and Jeremiah (Job 19:19; Jer 9:3; 20:10). Similar cautionary statements occur in Theognis 643–644; 697–698, as well as in P. Insinger 12.18.

Betrayal by a former friend can cause severe grief, as 37:2 acknowledges: "Is it not a sorrow reaching to death: a companion like oneself, turned into an adversary?" Such betrayal may inflict not only emotional wounds but also harm to a person's honorable name. Thus, Ben Sira warns that a former friend may expose a dispute, thereby bringing about one's disgrace (6:9). In the sage's outlook one should avoid disgrace, shame, and a bad name, just as one should seek to preserve one's name and honor. The embarrassing revelations of a quondam friend (6:9; 22:22cd) can, however, cause as much shame as one's own foolish conduct (4:20–22; 20:22–26) or one's undisciplined children (22:3–5; 41:5–7; 42:9–14).

To reduce the likelihood of a friend hurting or disgracing one, Ben Sira advises testing potential friends. Sirach 6:7 counsels: "You have acquired a friend—with testing acquire him, and do not hasten to rely on him" (cf. 27:17a). Just as wisdom teachers speak of the need for discernment when one confronts ambiguous human experiences (cf. Prov 14:12–13; 17:28; Sir 20:8–11; 36:23–24), so Ben Sira insists on the need for testing in order to discern real friends.

[5] For the text of 12:8–9, see the appendix.

The motif of testing potential friends reflects a common theme in Greek literature, as well as in Egyptian sapiential writing.[6] Ben Sira, however, adds a theological dimension by noting that God tests those who fear him (Sir 2:1; cf. 44:20) and that wisdom places tests in the path of those who seek her (4:17).[7]

It is not only toward potential friends, however, but also toward actual friends, that Ben Sira counsels a cautious attitude: "Be wary of your friends" (6:13). This advice matches his general caution, whereby one should not give control over one's life to "son or wife, friend or companion" (33:20). This wariness also accords with the outlook of Theognis (697–698), who laments being let down so often by his friends.

Such caution is all the more necessary, in Ben Sira's judgment, toward those who hold political power: "Keep far from anyone empowered to kill.... But if you have approached, commit no offense" (9:13; cf. 13:9–13). This cautious attitude toward the powerful is a regular feature of sapiential literature (cf. Prov 20:2; Sir 8:1–2; P. Insinger 3.14; 27.8).

Ben Sira's wariness leads him to suggest having only few friends: "Let those at peace with you be many, but the possessor of your confidence one in a thousand" (Sir 6:6). Such advice accords with sayings of Theognis (73–75) and Xenophon (*Mem.* 2.6.27). The phrase "one in a thousand" may be an echo of Qoh 7:28, which applies it to the rarity of a wise man; if so, Ben Sira implies that the one wise person out of a thousand should be chosen as a friend.

4. Faithfulness toward Friends

As an antidote to widespread faithlessness in friendship, Ben Sira inculcates fidelity toward one's friends. In a triple series Ben Sira describes a faithful friend as a strong shelter, beyond price, and a "bundle of the living" (6:14–16). Similarly, 9:10 compares an old friend to mature old wine, while 37:5 notes that a good friend will campaign on one's behalf.

Ben Sira often encourages his students to remain faithful to their friends, as in 22:23a: "Support your companion in his poverty." In addition, 37:6 counsels: "Do not forget an associate in the battle, and do not abandon him among your spoil." Sirach 7:18 states the corollary of such fidelity: "Do not exchange a friend for a price." Hence, 41:18c urges one to be ashamed before a partner and a companion if one has committed treachery.

---

[6] Such Greek texts include Theognis 125–126; Xenophon, *Mem.* 2.6.1. Egyptian texts include Ptahhotep 33; Ankhsheshonq 14.8; P. Insinger 11.23; 12.15.

[7] Cf. Irwin, "Fear of God," 557–59.

Ben Sira's emphasis on fidelity reflects the teaching of the book of Proverbs, which observes positively that "there is a friend sticking closer than a brother" (Prov 18:24), as well as asking negatively, "A faithful person who can find?" (Prov 20:6). Both Theognis and Xenophon speak specifically of faithful friends or comrades; whereas in a negative vein, Theognis notes the rarity of a faithful companion (Theognis 209; 415–416), Xenophon affirms positively the value of faithful friends in the setting of a royal court (*Cyr.* 8.7.13). For Ben Sira, however, fidelity in friendship has an additional theological dimension, since it reflects God's faithfulness (Deut 7:9; 32:4; cf. Sir 1:15; 37:15).

Faithfulness toward friends entails keeping confidences, a recurrent motif in Ben Sira (8:17; 22:22; 27:16–21; 42:1). For example, Sir 27:16 states: "One who reveals a confidence destroys faithfulness and will not find a friend for himself." This emphasis on the guarding of secrets echoes not only the book of Proverbs (11:13; 20:19; 25:9) but also Aramaic Ahiqar (Saying 53), as well as anticipating the Essene rule of life (Josephus, *Ag. Ap.* 2.207). Although one may need to reprove a friend for his faults (19:13–17) in accordance with the Torah (Lev 19:17), one should do so privately, instead of shamefully revealing the friend's faults to others (22:20, 22cd).

5. Fear of God

The fear of God is a major theme of Ben Sira, which he connects with friendship. Thus, the sage asserts that one who fears God will find a faithful friend (6:16). Moreover, his decalogues of macarisms and good things (25:7–11; 40:18–27), both of which list friendship among the blessings in life (25:9; 40:23), reach their climax in the fear of God, which is the best thing of all (25:10–11; 40:26–27).

Other motifs connected with the fear of God include the law and wisdom (cf. 19:20; 21:11). Hence, one's friends should be not only God-fearing (9:16) but also wise and observant of the law (9:14–15). A friendship guided by the law will allow for reproof (Sir 19:17; cf. Lev 19:17).

Ben Sira's emphasis on the fear of God echoes an earlier biblical theme characteristic of Deuteronomy, the Psalms, and Proverbs. While Theognis opens his poems with an invocation of the Greek gods (Theognis 1–18) and each section of P. Insinger concludes with a statement of fatalistic resignation to the deity,[8] Ben Sira brings his teaching on friendship into the sphere of his faith in Israel's God.

---

[8] E.g., P. Insinger 13.7: "The fate and fortune that come, it is the god who determines them" (*AEL* 3:195).

Furthermore, Ben Sira's whole view of friendship evidently has a theological rationale. Fundamentally, the goodness of friendship is rooted in the goodness of God's creation (Sir 39:16, 33; cf. Gen 1:31). Next, the need to test potential friends (Sir 6:7; 27:17) corresponds to the way God tests those who wish to serve him (2:1) and the way wisdom tests those who seek her (4:17). Again, Ben Sira's emphasis on fidelity in friendship (6:14–16; 27:17) is designed to enable human beings to mirror God's faithfulness (Deut 7:9; 32:4), since God created humanity in his image (Gen 1:27; Sir 17:3). Finally, the sage's insistence on the *fear* of God as the guiding principle of friendship (6:16; 9:16) is not made at the expense of the *love* of God, since (following Deut 10:12) he regards the two dispositions as different aspects of the same relationship with God (Sir 2:15–16). Thus, although the sage's friendship pericopes do not often mention God, they have a theological underpinning that relates his teachings on the topic to Israel's faith.

6. Conclusion

In an age when friendship was important, Ben Sira was not afraid to use any insight, whether from Israel's heritage or other traditions, to assist his students in making and keeping wise friendships. In our age friendship is no less important. While our modern circumstances differ from the social conditions of Ben Sira's time, much of his teaching has timeless value. Still relevant today is his teaching that the fear of God is the way to true happiness (1:12), an insight that applies in the realm of friendship as much as in other areas of life.

Appendix
Ben Sira's Incidental References to Friendship

Out of the forty-eight[1] instances of φίλος ("friend") in Ben Sira according to G^{B}, thirty appear in the seven pericopes examined in chapters 2–6 above. To round off my coverage of the topic, this appendix deals with the other eighteen occurrences of the word in the sage's book. Considerations of space allow only a brief discussion; it is beyond the scope of this appendix to give a full treatment of text-critical questions, poetic features, or the relation between each friendship reference and its overall context.

1. Statistical Tables

The following table lists Ben Sira's eighteen incidental references to φίλος, with comparisons to H (where extant) and S.[2]

Table 1: Eighteen occurrences of φίλος

Verse	*G*	*H*	*S*[3]
6:1a	φίλου	אוֹהֵב (H^{A})	*rḥmʾ*
7:12b	φίλῳ	רֵעַ וְחָבֵר (H^{A})	*rḥmʾ* … *ḥbrʾ*
7:18a	φίλον	אוֹהֵב (H^{A})	*rḥmʾ*
12:8a	ὁ φίλος	אוֹהֵב (H^{A})	*rḥmʾ*
12:9b	ὁ φίλος	רֵיעַ (H^{A})	*rḥmʾ*
14:13a	φίλῳ	לְאוֹהֵב (H^{A})	*lrḥmk*
19:8a	φίλῳ	————	*brḥmʾ*
20:16a	φίλος	————	**rḥmʾ*
20:23a	φίλῳ	רֵעֵהוּ (H^{C})	*ḥbrh*

[1] In Ben Sira φίλος occurs forty-six times in G^{A}, which lacks the word in 19:14a and 41:18c.

[2] Note also that outside the seven major pericopes φιλία ("friendship") occurs twice in G (9:8d; 25:1c).

[3] Throughout the appendix I have placed an asterisk by the plural forms in S.

28:9a	φίλους	————	*drḥm*[4]
29:10a	ἀδελφὸν	————	*ʾḥwk*
	καὶ φίλον		… *ḥbrk*
30:3b	φίλων	————	**rḥmwhy*
30:6b	τοῖς φίλοις	————	**lrḥmwhy* (30:6a)
33:6a	φίλος	אוֹהֵב (H^{EF})	**rḥmwhy*
33:20a	ἀδελφῷ	אֹהֵב (H^{E})	*ʾḥʾ*[5]
	καὶ φίλῳ	וָרֵעַ (H^{E})	*wrḥmʾ*
40:23a	φίλος	————	*rḥmʾ*
	καὶ ἑταῖρος	————	*wḥbrʾ*
41:18c	κοινωνοῦ	שׁוּתָּף (H^{BmgM})[6]	————
	καὶ φίλου	וָרֵעַ (H^{BM})	
41:22c	φίλων	אֹהֵב ($H^{M[B]}$)	————

Apart from the seven major friendship pericopes and the above-noted instances where G employs φίλος, there are ten other occurrences of אוֹהֵב in the Hebrew MSS of Ben Sira. Except for one gloss (31:2d H^{B}, absent from G and S), these occurrences are either textual errors (4x) or verbal usages (5x).

Table 2: Textual Errors Involving אוֹהֵב

Verse	*H*	*G*	*S*	*Emendation*
7:35a H^{A}	מֵאוֹהֵב	ἄρρωστον	**mrʿʾ*	כּוֹאֵב[7]
9:8d H^{A}	אֹהֲבֶיהָ	φιλία	*rḥmth*	אַהֲבָתָהּ[8]
33:6b H^{F}	אוֹהֵב	ἐπικαθημένου	*mn drḥm lh*	רוֹכֵב[9]
46:13a H^{B}	אוֹהֵב	ἠγαπημένος	*rḥym*	אָהוּב־[10]

[4] In 28:9a the reading of S ("who loves [contention]") suggests that the translator understood a verbal use of the participle אוֹהֵב.

[5] G and S presuppose אָח ("brother") here.

[6] The fragmentary text of H^{B} may point to חוֹבֵר ("associate") here. G^{A} omits 41:18c, while S leaves out 41:13–18 and 41:21–42:6.

[7] I emend 7:35a to read אַל תֵּשֶׁא לְבַקֵּר כּוֹאֵב ("do not forget to visit a sick person"; cf. G and S); see Segal, ספר בן־סירא השלם, 50. For כּוֹאֵב ("sick"), compare the cognate noun in Sir 30:17b H^{B}. Alternative emendations include the rare synonyms אוֹדֵב ("grieving"; cf. 1 Sam 2:33) or דוֹאֵב ("languishing"; cf. Sir 4:1b H^{A}).

[8] I read 9:8d: וְכֵן אַהֲבָתָהּ כְּאֵשׁ תְּלַהֵט ("and thus she will enkindle her love like a fire"; cf. S and G). An alternative reading is אֹהֲבֶיהָ ("her amours"; cf. Prov 7:18).

[9] This reading, presupposed by G, fits the context of 33:6b; cf. Minissale, *La versione greca del Siracide*, 167.

[10] So Segal, ספר בן־סירא השלם, 321.

Table 3: Verbal Usages of אוֹהֵב

Verse	*G*	*H*	*S*
3:26b H[A]	אוֹהֵב	ὁ ἀγαπῶν	*mn drḥm*
4:12a H[A]	אֹהֲבֶיהָ	ὁ ἀγαπῶν αὐτὴν	**rḥmyh*
31:5b H[B]	אוֹהֵב	ὁ ἀγαπῶν (31:5a)	*drḥm* (31:5a)
47:8c H[B]	אוֹהֵב	ἠγάπησεν (47:8d)	*rḥm*
47:22d H[B]	נֶכֶד	σπέρμα τοῦ	*zrʿʾ*
	[אוֹהֲ]בָיו	ἀγαπήσαντος αὐτὸν	**drḥmwhy* (47:22c)[11]

In the case of some of the above verbal usages (e.g., 4:12a; 47:22d), it is not possible to distinguish absolutely between "those who love her/him" and "her/his friends," since the meaning is so close. In the following survey, however, I leave aside all verbal usages of אוֹהֵב ("one who loves"), as well as its erroneous occurrences in the Hebrew MSS.

2. Survey

I will now survey Ben Sira's eighteen incidental references to φίλος, as listed in table 1 above. In 6:5–17; 9:10–16; and 37:1–6 three basic themes characterize the sage's outlook on friendship: caution toward potential friends (6:5–13; 9:11–13; 37:1–4), faithfulness to one's friends (6:14–17; 9:10; 37:5–6), and the fear of God as the guiding principle of friendship (6:16b; 9:14–16; cf. 37:12). Ben Sira's incidental references to friendship reflect one of these three themes or else the idea of the goodness of friendship.

a. The Goodness of Friendship (25:1; 25:9 L; 30:3; 40:23)

Ben Sira's appreciation of friendship combines his traditional Jewish theology of creation (cf. Sir 13:15–16) with the Hellenistic esteem for friendship.[12] Hence, the sage's decalogue of good things (40:18–27) includes friends (40:23 H[B]):[13]

---

[11] I reconstruct 47:22d: וְנֶכֶד אוֹהֲבָיו לֹא יַשְׁמִיד ("and he will not destroy the progeny of those who love him"; cf. S). Possibly, however, the original text read אוֹהֲבוֹ ("the one loving him"; cf. G), referring to David (cf. Sir 47:8cd).

[12] Compare Aristotle's dictum in *Eth. nic.* 9.9.3 §1169b: "The happy man requires friends" (Rackham, trans., *Nicomachean Ethics*, 559).

[13] I refer to Segal (ספר בן־סירא השלם, 271) for the completion of the lacuna on the basis of G.

[אוֹהֵב וְחָבֵר לְעֵ]ת יְנְהָגוּ וּמִשְּׁנֵיהֶם אִשָּׁה מַשְׂכֶּלֶת

[A friend and a comrade] will guide [for the ti]me,
but better than both of them is an insightful wife.[14]

Moreover, 25:1–11 offers a double appreciation of friendship.[15] Sirach 25:1c G explains that one of the three things delightful to him is "the friendship of neighbors" (φιλία τῶν πλησίον). The subsequent decalogue of macarisms (25:7–11) has the saying: "Happy is the one who finds a true friend" (25:9a L).[16] Furthermore, according to 30:3 G a father will be able to share with friends his joy over a disciplined son: "The one who teaches his son will make his enemy jealous, and before friends will rejoice over him."

b. Caution (12:8–9; 19:8; 20:16; 28:9; 33:6a, 20; 41:22)

In Sir 6:5–13; 9:11–13; and 37:1–4, the sage applies his ethics of caution to the realm of friendship. An observation encouraging caution toward potential friends appears in 12:8–9 H^{A}:[17]

---

[14] On Sir 40:23, see E. D. Reymond, "Sirach 40,18–27 As 'Ṭôb-Spruch,'" *Bib* 82 (2001): 84–92, esp. 87. Here I leave 40:20b out of consideration. Though S understands the phrase אַהֲבַת דּוֹדִים (40:20b H^{B}) to mean "the friendship of a friend" (cf. NRSV), its probable meaning is rather "sexual love"; compare M. H. Pope's comment on דּוֹדִים in Cant 5:1: "The plural of this word regularly means 'love,' as in Ezek 16:8; 23:17; Prov 7:18; and elsewhere in the Canticle: 1:2, 4; 4:10; 6:1; 7:13" (*Song of Songs* [AB 7C; Garden City, N.Y.: Doubleday, 1977], 508). G offers an allegorizing interpretation, "the love of wisdom."

[15] See F. V. Reiterer, "Gelungene Freundschaft als tragende Säule einer Gesellschaft: Exegetische Untersuchung von Sir 25,1–11," in Reiterer, ed., *Freundschaft bei Ben Sira*, 133–69, esp. 144–45 on Sir 25:1.

[16] The Latin verb *invenit* could also mean "has found." Although 25:9a S^{ALMW} has, "Happy is the person who has found mercy" (**raḥmēʾ*), Smend (*Sirach, erklärt*, 227) suggests reading instead "a friend" (*rāḥmāʾ*), which matches L better; cf. Reiterer, "Gelungene Freundschaft," 136. Sirach 25:9a G, however, reads, "Happy is the one who has found sense" (φρόνησιν), either confusing רֵעַ ("companion") with דֵּעַ ("knowledge") or introducing a sapiential interpretation. See also L. Schrader, *Verwandtschaft der Peschitta mit der (alt)lateinischen Übersetzung im Sirachbuch?* (BN Beihefte 11; Munich: Institut für Biblische Exegese, 1998), 39.

[17] On Sir 12:8–9, see Schrader, "Unzuverlässige Freundschaft und verläßliche Feindschaft," 23–39. In 12:9b I read יִבָּדֵל ("will separate himself") with G and S, whereas H^{A} has בּוֹדֵד ("is isolated"). With the thought of Sir 12:8–9, compare Theognis 299 and 697–698; see also Isocrates, *Demon.* 25: "As we try gold in the fire, so we come to know our friends when we are in misfortune" (Norlin and van Hook, trans., *Isocrates*, 1:19).

לֹא יִוָּדַע בְּטוֹבָה אוֹהֵב וְלֹא יְכוּסֶּה בְרָעָה שׂוֹנֵא:
בְּטוֹבַת אִישׁ גַּם שׂוֹנֵא רֵיעַ וּבְרָעָתוֹ גַּם רֵיעַ יִבָּדֵל:

A friend will not be recognized in prosperity,
but an enemy will not be concealed in adversity.
In a person's prosperity, even an enemy is a companion,
but in his adversity, even a companion will separate himself.

A similar warning against unsuitable friends occurs in 28:9 G^{SA}: "A sinful man will unsettle friends and will introduce enmity in the midst of those at peace."[18] Another warning against an undesirable friend appears in 33:6 H^{F}:

כְּסוּס מוּכָן אוֹהֵב שׂוֹנֵא תַּחַת כָּל רוֹכֵב יִצְהַל

Like a bridled horse is a hostile friend;
under every rider he will neigh.[19]

By contrast with the fruitful guidance obtainable from God's law (32:14–16), a hostile friend will refuse to accept guidance, symbolized by the bridle.

Caution is also at the heart of the injunctions of 19:8 and 33:20. Following the admonition against gossip in 19:7a G, "Never repeat a saying," 19:8a G teaches: "Against friend or enemy do not recount it";[20] here, "friend or enemy" serves as a merism for "everybody."[21] Moreover, by means of another merism[22] Sir 33:20 H^{E} emphasizes the need for caution in order to preserve one's independence:

---

[18] The noun διαβολή, usually meaning "slander" (or "malicious talk"), here seems to denote "enmity"; cf. Smend, *Sirach, erklärt*, 251. Sirach 28:9 S preserves a different form of this saying: "A wicked human being who loves contention sows enmity among brothers" (cf. Prov 6:19; 16:28).

[19] For the text of 33:6 H^{F} see Di Lella, "The Newly Discovered Sixth Manuscript," 237. In 33:6b I read רוֹכֵב (= ἐπικαθημένου, "rider"), where H^{F} repeats אוֹהֵב (as in 33:6a); cf. 30:8, where Ben Sira compares an unruly son to a restive colt. Both G and S understand 33:6 differently from H^{F}; cf. Segal, ספר בן־סירא השלם, 210; Skehan and Di Lella, *Wisdom of Ben Sira*, 396. On the horse, see Prov 21:31; Jer 5:8.

[20] Sirach 19:8a S reads the verb: "do not act treacherously." On Sir 19:8, see Kieweler, "Freundschaft und böse Nachrede," 70–71.

[21] For examples of polar opposites serving as merisms in the MT, see Watson, *Classical Hebrew Poetry*, 322–23.

[22] "Son or wife, friend or companion" is equivalent to "anyone at all."

בֵּן וְאִשָּׁה אֹהֵב וָרֵעַ אַל תַּמְשִׁיל בְּחַיֶּיךָ

Son or wife, friend or companion—
do not give them control over your life.[23]

In addition, Ben Sira advises the use of caution when speaking, since speech reveals whether the speaker is wise or foolish. For example, Sir 41:22c H^M^ advocates a true shame over the kind of speech that harms friendship: "[Be ashamed] before a friend concerning reproachful words" (מֵאֹהֵב עַל דִּבְרֵי חֶסֶד).[24] Moreover, the fool's words indicate his self-pity, which hampers him from giving friendship to others: "A fool will say, 'I have no friend,' and there is no gratitude for my good deeds" (20:16 G).

c. Faithfulness (6:1; 7:12, 18; 14:13; 20:23; 29:10; 30:6; 41:18)

The sage's emphasis on fidelity in friendship is evident in 7:18a H^A^, where friendship has a higher value than money: "Do not exchange a friend for a price" (אַל תָּמִיר אוֹהֵב בִּמְחִיר).[25] In 7:18–19 H^A^ the sage juxtaposes "friend" (אוֹהֵב) with "wife" (אִשָּׁה), as in 33:20 H^E^.[26]

Since faithfulness is an essential aspect of friendship, breaking promises (even out of shame) disrupts friendly relationships (20:23 H^C^):

יֵשׁ נִכְלָם וּמַבְטִיחַ רֵעֵהוּ וְקוֹנֵהוּ שׂוֹנֵא חִנָּם

There is one who is ashamed and makes promises to his companion
and needlessly acquires him as an enemy.[27]

---

[23] Or "in your lifetime." Both G and S presuppose אָח וָרֵעַ ("brother or companion"), perhaps the original reading; see P. C. Beentjes, "The Concept of 'Brother' in the Book of Ben Sira," in Calduch-Benages and Vermeylen, eds., *Treasures of Wisdom,* 75–89, esp. 84–85. For the phrase in H^E^, see Ps 88:19.

[24] Sirach 41:22c H^B^ reads ד[בְ]רֵי חֶרְפָּה ("insulting [wo]rds") instead of דִּבְרֵי חֶסֶד ("reproachful words"); cf. Skehan and Di Lella, *Wisdom of Ben Sira,* 479. On Sir 41:22c, see Krammer, "Scham im Zusammenhang mit Freundschaft," 197–98.

[25] Note the rhyme of תָּמִיר with בִּמְחִיר, continued in the last word of 7:18b, אוֹפִיר. For the sentiment of Sir 7:18a, compare Socrates' teaching as recorded by Xenophon (*Mem.* 2.5.1–5). On Sir 7:18, see Beentjes, "The Concept of 'Brother' in the Book of Ben Sira," 81–82.

[26] Similarly, in 36:26–37:6 the sage juxtaposes choice of a wife (36:26–31) with selection of a friend (37:1–6); on the context of 37:1–6 see further the discussion in ch. 2 above.

[27] For the text of 20:23 H^C^ see Di Lella, "The Recently Identified Leaves," 164; note the bicolon's a:b::b:a internal rhyme. On 20:21–23, see Krammer, "Scham im Zusammenhang mit Freundschaft," 188–91.

In other words, with empty promises a person acquires not a friend (cf. Sir 6:7) but an enemy instead.[28]

Fidelity also entails avoidance of unjust scheming against a friend (7:12 H^A; cf. S):

אַל תַּחֲרוֹשׁ חָמָס עַל אָח   וְכֵן עַל רֵעַ וְחָבֵר יַחְדָּו

Do not devise lawlessness against a brother,
or likewise against any companion or comrade.[29]

Similarly, 41:18c H^M speaks of the shamefulness of unfaithful behavior toward a friend: "[Be ashamed] before a partner and a companion concerning treachery" (מִשּׁוּתָּף וָרֵעַ עַל מַעַל).[30] Sirach 6:1a H^A puts the point simply: "Instead of a friend do not be an enemy."[31]

In addition to these negative admonitions, the sage speaks positively of the need to show kindness to friends. In view of the fact of death and the sage's lack of belief in an afterlife, he counsels his students: "Before you die be good to a friend" (14:13a H^A).[32] Similarly, in the context of admonitions to care for the poor, 29:10a G urges: "Waste money for the sake of a brother or a friend."

---

[28] Not only empty promises but also rash loans can turn a friendship into enmity. Such a lender may lose not only his money but also his former friend; by lending rashly, "he has needlessly acquired him as an enemy" (Sir 29:6d G).

[29] Sirach 7:12 G understands the verbal root חרשׁ in the sense "plow" and presupposes כַּחַשׁ ("lying") instead of חָמָס ("lawlessness").

[30] The damaged text of H^B at 41:18c seems to presuppose מֵחוֹבֵר ("before an associate") instead of מִשּׁוּתָּף ("before a partner"); see further Krammer, "Scham im Zusammenhang mit Freundschaft," 195–97. A gloss after 31:2ab, lacking in G and S but found in H^B, speaks of the harm of divulging secrets:

רֵעַ נֶאֱמָן תָּנִיד חֶרְפָּה   וּמַסְתִּיר סוֹד אוֹהֵב כְּנֶפֶשׁ

Insult will drive out a faithful companion,
but a friend like oneself hides a confidence.

Skehan and Di Lella (*Wisdom of Ben Sira,* 316) regard the bicolon as intrusive: "Most likely the line originated as a gloss on 22:22." However, Kaiser ("Was ein Freund nicht tun darf," 108–9) considers it to be the Hebrew form of Sir 27:16, although it differs somewhat from 27:16 G and S.

[31] On Sir 5:14–6:1, see Krammer, "Scham im Zusammenhang mit Freundschaft," 184–87. In its context, 6:1a is a warning against losing friends by being two-faced (cf. 5:14).

[32] Note the rhyme in the phrase הֵיטֵב לְאוֹהֵב ("be good to a friend"). For the sentiment, compare Ptahhotep 34–35: "Be generous as long as you live.... Don't be mean toward your friends" (*AEL* 1:72).

In a poem offering advice on the training of sons, Sir 30:6 G presupposes the filial duty of paying back a family friend's generosity; the father who has been a good disciplinarian will have confidence when he leaves his son his inheritance, because "toward enemies he will have left behind an avenger, and for friends one to repay kindness." Ben Sira's view is in accord with Creon's speech to his son in Sophocles' play *Antigone* 642–644:

> For 'tis the hope of parents they may rear
> A brood of sons submissive, keen to avenge
> Their father's wrongs, and count his friends their own.[33]

For both authors, family loyalty involves friendship to one's parents' friends and hostility to one's father's foes.

d. The Fear of God

The fear of God, which features in some of the sage's friendship pericopes (cf. 6:16; 9:16), provides the context for the mention of friendship in 40:18–27. We have already noted Ben Sira's saying in 40:23 H^B: "A friend and a comrade will guide for the time, but better than both of them is an insightful wife." The climax of the sage's decalogue of good things comes in 40:26 H^B: "Strength and vigor will make the heart rejoice, but better than both of them is the fear of God."[34] Thereby Ben Sira subsumes the goodness of friendship under the greatest good of all, which for him is the fear of God (cf. 40:27a).

Sirach 25:7–11 also places friendship within the context of the fear of God. While 25:9a L asserts, "Happy is the one who finds a true friend," the decalogue of macarisms concludes with the statement, "How great is the one who has found wisdom, but he is not superior to the one who fears the Lord" (25:10 G). Here too the goodness of friendship is ultimately of less significance for human happiness than the fear of the Lord. In the sage's outlook, reverence for God will both enable a person

---

[33] Storr, trans., *Sophocles,* 1:365. The idea that it was right to repay friends with friendship and enemies with hostility (mentioned in Sir 12:2–5 and Matt 5:43) was widespread in the ancient world; cf. Homer, *Od.* 6.184–185; Theognis 869–872; Xenophon, *Cyr.* 8.7.28; Solon 13.5; Isocrates, *Demon.* 26. See M. W. Blundell, *Helping Friends and Harming Enemies: A Study in Sophocles and Greek Ethics* (Cambridge: Cambridge University Press, 1989), 26–59; cf. J. P. Brown, *The Legacy of Iranian Imperialism and the Individual,* vol. 3 of *Israel and Hellas* (BZAW 299; Berlin: de Gruyter, 2001), 8–10.

[34] See Segal, ספר בן־סירא השלם, 271, for the above completion of the damaged text of 40:26 H^B.

to find friends (6:16b) and guarantee the truly moral nature of one's friendships (9:16).

3. Conclusion

Among Ben Sira's incidental references to friendship scattered throughout his book, one finds the three important themes of caution, faithfulness, and the fear of God that occur in the major friendship pericopes (cf. 6:5–17; 9:10–16; 37:1–6). A further theme, however, is the goodness of friendship, which appears particularly in the decalogue of macarisms (25:7–11) and the decalogue of good things (40:18–27). Significantly, both decalogues (like 6:5–17 and 9:10–16) conclude by mentioning the fear of God, which they regard as the greatest blessing of all. In this way Ben Sira brings us back to the thought of the first non-alphabetic acrostic of his book (1:11–30), which begins with the statement: "The fear of the Lord is glory and exultation, and joy and a crown of rejoicing" (1:11).

Bibliography

1. Texts and Versions of Ben Sira

a. Hebrew MSS of Ben Sira

Adler, E. N. "Some Missing Chapters of Ben Sira." *JQR* 12 (1899–1900): 466–80. [= 7:29–12:1 H^{A}]

Baillet, M., J. T. Milik, and R. de Vaux. Pp. 75–77 in *Les "petites grottes" de Qumrân*. DJD 3. Oxford: Clarendon, 1962. [small fragments of 6:14–15, 20–31 H^{2Q}]

Beentjes, P. C. *The Book of Ben Sira in Hebrew: A Text Edition of All Extant Hebrew Manuscripts and a Synopsis of All Parallel Hebrew Ben Sira Texts.* VTSup 68. Leiden: Brill, 1997.

Ben-Ḥayyim, Z., ed. *The Book of Ben Sira: Text, Concordance, and an Analysis of the Vocabulary.* Jerusalem: Academy of the Hebrew Language and Shrine of the Book, 1973.

Cowley, A. E., and A. Neubauer, eds. *The Original Hebrew of a Portion of Ecclesiasticus.* Oxford: Clarendon, 1897. [= 39:15–49:11 H^{B}]

Di Lella, A. A. "The Newly Discovered Sixth Manuscript of Ben Sira from the Cairo Geniza." *Bib* 69 (1988): 226–38. [= 25:8, 20–21 H^{C}; 31:24–32:7 H^{F}; 32:12–33:8 H^{F}]

———. "The Recently Identified Leaves of Sirach in Hebrew." *Bib* 45 (1964): 153–67. [= 10:19–11:10 H^{B}; 15:1–16:7 H^{B}; 3:14–18, 21–22 H^{C}; 4:21–23 H^{C}; 20:22–23 H^{C}; 26:2–3, 13, 15–17 H^{C}; 36:27–31 H^{C}; 41:16 H^{C}]

Facsimiles of the Fragments Hitherto Recovered of the Book of Ecclesiasticus in Hebrew. Oxford: Oxford University Press; Cambridge: Cambridge University Press, 1901.

Gaster, M. "A New Fragment of Ben Sira." *JQR* 12 (1899–1900): 688–702. [= 18:31–33 H^{C}; 19:1–3 H^{C}; 20:5–7, 13 H^{C}; 37:19, 22, 24, 26 H^{C}]

Lévi, I. "Fragments de deux nouveaux manuscrits hébreux de l'Ecclésiastique." *REJ* 40 (1900): 1–30. [= 6:18–19, 28, 35 H^{C}; 7:1–2, 4, 6, 17, 20–21, 23–25 H^{C}; 8:7 H^{C}; 36:29–38:1 H^{D}]

———. *The Hebrew Text of the Book of Ecclesiasticus.* SSS 3. Leiden: Brill, 1904.

Marcus, J. "The Newly Discovered Original Hebrew of Ben Sira (Ecclesiasticus xxxii,16–xxxiv,1): The Fifth Manuscript and a Prosodic Version of Ben Sira (Ecclesiasticus xxii, 22–xxiii,9)." *JQR* 21 (1930–1931): 223–40. Corrected reprint, Philadelphia: Dropsie College, 1931. [= 32:16–34:1 H^E]

Margoliouth, G. "The Original Hebrew of Ecclesiasticus XXXI.12–31, and XXXVI.22–XXXVII.26." *JQR* 12 (1899–1900): 1–33. [= 31:12–31 H^B; 36:24–37:26 H^B]

Peters, N. *Der jüngst wiederaufgefundene hebräische Text des Buches Ecclesiasticus untersucht, herausgegeben, übersetzt und mit kritischen Noten versehen.* Freiburg i.B.: Herder, 1902.

———. *Liber Jesu filii Sirach sive Ecclesiasticus hebraice.* Freiburg i.B.: Herder, 1905.

Sanders, J. A. Pp. 79–85 in *The Psalms Scroll of Qumrân Cave 11 (11QPs^a^).* DJD 4. Oxford: Clarendon, 1965. [= 51:13–20, 30 H^{11Q}]

Schechter, S. "A Further Fragment of Ben Sira." *JQR* 12 (1899–1900): 456–65. [= 4:23, 30–31 H^C; 5:4–7, 9–13 H^C; 25:8, 13, 17–24 H^C; 26:1–2 H^C; 36:24 H^C]

Schechter, S., and C. Taylor. *The Wisdom of Ben Sira: Portions of the Book Ecclesiasticus from Hebrew Manuscripts in the Cairo Genizah Collection Presented to the University of Cambridge by the Editors.* Cambridge: Cambridge University Press, 1899. [= 3:6–7:29 H^A; 11:34–16:26 H^A; 30:11–33:3 H^B; 35:11–36:26 H^B; 37:27–38:27 H^B; 49:12–51:30 H^B]

Segal, M. Z. "דפים נוספים מתוך ספר בן־סירא [*Dappîm nôsĕpîm mittôk sēper ben-Sîrāʾ*]." *Tarbiz* 29 (1959–1960): 313–23.

———. ספר בן־סירא השלם [*Sēper ben-Sîrāʾ haššālēm*]. 3d ed. Jerusalem: Bialik Institute, 1972.

Smend, R. *Die Weisheit des Jesus Sirach, hebräisch und deutsch.* Berlin: Reimer, 1906.

Vattioni, F. *Ecclesiastico: Testo ebraico con apparato critico e versioni greca, latina e siriaca.* Pubblicazioni del Seminario di Semitistica, Testi 1. Naples: Istituto Orientale di Napoli, 1968.

Yadin, Y. *The Ben Sira Scroll from Masada.* Jerusalem: Israel Exploration Society, 1965. [= 39:27–44:17 H^M]

———, revised by E. Qimron. "The Ben Sira Scroll from Masada." Pp. 151–231 in *Masada VI: The Yigael Yadin Excavations 1963–1965: Final Report.* Edited by S. Talmon. Jerusalem: Israel Exploration Society, 1999. [= 39:27–44:17 H^M]

b. Versions of Ben Sira

Biblia sacra iuxta latinam vulgatam versionem, 12: Sapientia Salomonis, Liber Hiesu filii Sirach. Rome: Typis Polyglottis Vaticanis, 1964. [= L]

Biblia sacra juxta versionem simplicem quae dicitur Pschitta. Pp. 204–55 in vol. 2. Beirut: Imprimerie Catholique, 1951. [= S^M]

Ceriani, A. M., ed. *Translatio Syra Pescitto Veteris Testamenti ex codice Ambrosiano sec. fere VI photolithographice edita.* 2 vols. Milan: Pogliani, 1876–1883. [= S^A]

Hart, J. H. A. *Ecclesiasticus: The Greek Text of Codex 248.* Cambridge: Cambridge University Press, 1909. [= G^{248}]

Lagarde, P. A. de. *Libri veteris testamenti apocryphi syriace.* Leipzig: Brockhaus; London: Williams & Norgate, 1861. [= S^L]

Swete, H. B. Pp. 644–754 of vol. 2 in *The Old Testament in Greek according to the Septuagint.* 3d ed. 3 vols. Cambridge: Cambridge University Press, 1907. [= G].

Thiele, W. *Vetus Latina: Die Reste der altlateinischen Bibel 11/2: Sirach (Ecclesiasticus).* Fascicles 1–7. Freiburg i.B.: Herder, 1987–1999. [= 1:1–19:28 L].

Walton, B. Vol. 4 of *Biblia sacra polyglotta.* 6 vols. London: Roycroft, 1657. [= S^W].

Ziegler, J., ed. *Sapientia Iesu Filii Sirach.* 2d ed. Septuaginta 12/2. Göttingen: Vandenhoeck & Ruprecht, 1980. [= G]

2. Secondary Literature on Ben Sira

Aitken, J. K. "Biblical Interpretation As Political Manifesto: Ben Sira in His Seleucid Setting." *JJS* 51 (2000): 191–208.

———. "Hebrew Study in Ben Sira's *Beth Midrash.*" Pp. 27–37 in *Hebrew Study from Ezra to Ben-Yehuda.* Edited by W. Horbury. Edinburgh: T&T Clark, 1999.

———. "Studies in the Hebrew and Greek Text of Ben Sira with Special Reference to the Future." Ph.D. diss., University of Cambridge, 1995.

Argall, R. A. *1 Enoch and Sirach: A Comparative Literary and Conceptual Analysis of the Themes of Revelation, Creation and Judgment.* SBLEJL 8. Atlanta: Scholars Press, 1995.

Backhaus, F. J. "Qohelet und Sirach." *BN* 69 (1993): 32–55.

Baldauf, B. "Arme und Armut im Buch Ben Sira: Eine philologisch-exegetische Untersuchung." M.Th. diss., University of Salzburg, 1983.

Barré, M. L., ed. *Wisdom, You Are My Sister: Studies in Honor of Roland E. Murphy, O. Carm., on the Occasion of His Eightieth Birthday.* CBQMS 29. Washington, D.C.: Catholic Biblical Association of America, 1997.

Baumgartner, W. "Die literarischen Gattungen in der Weisheit des Jesus Sirach." *ZAW* 34 (1914): 161–98.

Beentjes, P. C. "Ben Sira 5,1–8: A Rhetorical and Literary Analysis." Pp. 45–59 in *The Literary Analysis of Hebrew Texts.* Edited by E. G. L. Schrijver, N. A. van Uchelen, and I. E. Zwiep. Amsterdam: Juda Palache Institute, 1992.

———. "Canon and Scripture in the Book of Ben Sira (Jesus Sirach/Ecclesiasticus)." Pp. 591–605 in part 2 of vol. 1 of *Hebrew Bible, Old Testament: The History of Its Interpretation.* Edited by M. Saebø et al. Göttingen: Vandenhoeck & Ruprecht, 2000.

———. "Five Years of Ben Sira Research (1994–1998): An Annotated Bibliography." *Bijdr* 61 (2000): 76–88.

———. "'Full Wisdom Is Fear of the Lord,' Ben Sira 19,20–20,31: Context, Composition and Concept." *EstBib* 47 (1989): 27–45.

———. "De getallenspreuk en zijn reikwijdte: Een pleidooi voor de literaire eenheid van Jesus Sirach 26:28–27:10." *Bijdr* 43 (1982): 383–89.

———. "Hermeneutics in the Book of Ben Sira: Some Observations on the Hebrew Ms. C." *EstBib* 46 (1988): 45–59.

———. "'How Can a Jug Be Friends with a Kettle?' A Note on the Structure of Ben Sira Chapter 13." *BZ* 36 (1992): 87–93.

———. "Inverted Quotations in the Bible: A Neglected Stylistic Pattern." *Bib* 63 (1982): 506–23.

———. *Jesus Sirach en Tenach: Een onderzoek naar en een classificatie van parallellen, met bijzondere aandacht voor hun functie in Sirach 45:6–26.* Nieuwegein: privately published, 1981.

———. "'Ein Mensch ohne Freund ist wie eine linke Hand ohne die Rechte': Prolegomena zur Kommentierung der Freundschaftsperikope Sir 6,5–17." Pp. 1–18 in *Freundschaft bei Ben Sira: Beiträge des Symposions zu Ben Sira, Salzburg 1995.* Edited by F. V. Reiterer. BZAW 244. Berlin: de Gruyter, 1996.

———. "Sirach 22:27–23:6 in zijn context." *Bijdr* 39 (1978): 144–51.

———. "Some Misplaced Words in the Hebrew Manuscript C of the Book of Ben Sira." *Bib* 67 (1986): 397–401.

———, ed. *The Book of Ben Sira in Modern Research.* BZAW 255. Berlin: de Gruyter, 1997.

Begg, C. "Ben Sirach's Non-mention of Ezra." *BN* 42 (1988): 14–18.

Bohlen, R. *Die Ehrung der Eltern bei Ben Sira: Studien zur Motivation und Interpretation eines familienethischen Grundwertes in frühhellenistischer Zeit.* TThSt 51. Trier: Paulinus, 1991.

Böhmisch, F. "Die Textformen des Sirachbuches und ihre Zielgruppen." *PzB* 6 (1997): 87–122.

Botha, P. J. "The Ideology of Shame in the Wisdom of Ben Sira: Ecclesiasticus 41:14–42:8." *OTE* 9 (1996): 353–71.

———. "Through the Figure of a Woman Many Have Perished: Ben Sira's View of Women." *OTE* 9 (1996): 20–34.

Box, G. H., and W. O. E. Oesterley. "Sirach." Pp. 268–517 in vol. 1 of *Apocrypha and Pseudepigrapha of the Old Testament.* Edited by R. H. Charles. 2 vols. Oxford: Clarendon, 1913.

Breid, F. "Die Struktur der Gesellschaft im Buch Ben Sira." Ph. D. diss., University of Graz, 1971.

Bronznick, N. M. "An Unrecognized Denotation of the Verb *ḤSR* in Ben-Sira and Rabbinic Hebrew." *HAR* 9 (1985): 91–105.

Burkes, S. "Wisdom and Law: Choosing Life in Ben Sira and Baruch." *JSJ* 30 (1999): 253–76.

Burton, K. W. "Sirach and the Judaic Doctrine of Creation." Ph.D. diss., University of Glasgow, 1987.

Caird, G. B. "Ben Sira and the Dating of the Septuagint." Pp. 95–100 in *Studia Evangelica 7.* Edited by E. A. Livingstone. Berlin: Akademie, 1982.

Calduch-Benages, N. *En el crisol de la prueba: Estudio exegético de Sir 2,1–18.* Estella, Navarra: Verbo Divino, 1997.

———. "Elementos de inculturación helenista en el libro de Ben Sira: Los viajes." *EstBib* 54 (1996): 289–98.

———. "Il libro di Sirach: saggio di bibliografia recente (1984–1994)." *Ephemerides Liturgicae* 111 (1997): 419–33.

———. "La Sabiduría y la prueba en Sir 4,11–19." *EstBib* 49 (1991): 25–48.

———, and J. Vermeylen, eds. *Treasures of Wisdom: Studies in Ben Sira and the Book of Wisdom: Festschrift M. Gilbert.* BETL 143. Leuven: Peeters, 1999.

Camp, C. V. "Honor, Shame, and the Hermeneutics of Ben Sira's Ms C." Pp. 157–71 in *Wisdom, You Are My Sister: Studies in Honor of Roland E. Murphy, O. Carm., on the Occasion of His Eightieth Birthday.* CBQMS 29. Washington, D.C.: Catholic Biblical Association of America, 1997.

———. "Understanding a Patriarchy: Women in Second Century Jerusalem through the Eyes of Ben Sira." Pp. 1–39 in *"Women Like This": New Perspectives on Jewish Women in the Greco-Roman World.* Edited by A. J. Levine. SBLEJL 1. Atlanta: Scholars Press, 1991.

Caquot, A. "Le Siracide a-t-il parlé d'une 'espèce' humaine?" *RHPR* 62 (1982): 225–30.

Coggins, R. J. *Sirach.* Guides to Apocrypha and Pseudepigrapha. Sheffield: Sheffield Academic Press, 1998.

Corley, J. "Caution, Fidelity, and the Fear of God: Ben Sira's Teaching on Friendship in Sir 6:5–17." *EstBib* 54 (1996): 313–26.

———. "Rediscovering Sirach." *ScrB* 27 (1997): 2–7.

———. "Social Responsibility in Proverbs and Ben Sira." *ScrB* 30 (2000): 2–14.

Crenshaw, J. L. "The Primacy of Listening in Ben Sira's Pedagogy." Pp. 172–87 in *Wisdom, You Are My Sister: Studies in Honor of Roland E. Murphy, O. Carm., on the Occasion of His Eightieth Birthday.* CBQMS 29. Washington, D.C.: Catholic Biblical Association of America, 1997.

________. "The Problem of Theodicy in Sirach: On Human Bondage." *JBL* 94 (1975): 47–64.

Critchlow, J. "Exegetical and Topical Studies in the Greek Ecclesiasticus." M.A. diss., University of Manchester, 1978.

Delcor, M. "Ecclesiasticus or Sirach." Pp. 415–22 in vol. 2 of *The Cambridge History of Judaism.* Edited by W. D. Davies and L. Finkelstein. Cambridge: Cambridge University Press, 1989.

Desečar, A. J. "La necedad en Sirac 23,12–15." *SBFLA* 20 (1970): 264–72.

———. *La sabiduría y la necedad en Sirac 21–22.* Rome: Edizioni Francescane, 1970.

deSilva, D. A. "The Wisdom of Ben Sira: Honor, Shame, and the Maintenance of the Values of a Minority Culture." *CBQ* 58 (1996): 433–55.

Di Lella, A. A. "Conservative and Progressive Theology: Sirach and Wisdom." *CBQ* 28 (1966): 139–54.

———. "Fear of the Lord and Belief and Hope in the Lord amid Trials: Sirach 2:1–18." Pp. 188–204 in *Wisdom, You Are My Sister: Studies in Honor of Roland E. Murphy, O. Carm., on the Occasion of His Eightieth Birthday.* CBQMS 29. Washington, D.C.: Catholic Biblical Association of America, 1997.

———. "Fear of the Lord As Wisdom: Ben Sira 1,11–30." Pp. 113–33 in *The Book of Ben Sira in Modern Research.* Edited by P. C. Beentjes. BZAW 255. Berlin: de Gruyter, 1997.

———. *The Hebrew Text of Sirach: A Text-Critical and Historical Study.* Studies in Classical Literature 1. The Hague: Mouton, 1966.

———. "The Meaning of Wisdom in Ben Sira." Pp. 133–48 in *In Search of Wisdom: Essays in Memory of John G. Gammie.* Edited by L. G. Perdue et al. Louisville: Westminster/John Knox, 1993.

———. "The Search for Wisdom in Ben Sira." Pp. 185–96 in *The Psalms and Other Studies on the Old Testament Presented to Joseph I. Hunt.* Edited by J. C. Knight and L. A. Sinclair. Nashotah, Wisc.: Nashotah House Seminary, 1990.

———. "Sirach." Pp. 496–509 in *The New Jerome Biblical Commentary.* Edited by R. E. Brown et al. Englewood Cliffs, N.J.: Prentice-Hall, 1990.

———. "Sirach 10:19–11:6: Textual Criticism, Poetic Analysis, and Exegesis." Pp. 157–64 in *The Word of the Lord Shall Go Forth: Essays in Honor of David Noel Freedman.* Edited by C. L. Meyers and M. O'Connor. Winona Lake, Ind.: Eisenbrauns, 1982.

———. "Sirach 51:1–12: Poetic Structure and Analysis of Ben Sira's Psalm." *CBQ* 48 (1986): 395–407.

———. "Use and Abuse of the Tongue: Ben Sira 5,9–6,1." Pp. 33–48 in *"Jedes Ding hat seine Zeit…": Studien zur israelitischen und altorientalischen Weisheit: Diethelm Michel zum 65. Geburtstag.* Edited by E. Otto et al. BZAW 241. Berlin: de Gruyter, 1996.

———. "The Wisdom of Ben Sira: Resources and Recent Research." *CurBS* 4 (1996): 161–81.

———. "Women in the Wisdom of Ben Sira and the Book of Judith: A Study in Contrasts and Reversals." Pp. 39–52 in *Congress Volume: Paris, 1992.* Edited by J. A. Emerton. VTSup 61. Leiden: Brill, 1995.

Dommershausen, W. "Zum Vergeltungsdenken des Ben Sira." Pp. 37–43 in *Wort und Geschichte: Festschrift für Karl Elliger zum 70. Geburtstag.* Edited by H. Gese and H.-P. Rüger. AOAT 18. Kevelaer: Butzon & Bercker, 1973.

Duesberg, H., and P. Auvray, *Le livre de l'Ecclésiastique.* SBJ. Paris: Cerf, 1953.

Eberharter, A. *Das Buch Jesus Sirach oder Ecclesiasticus.* Die Heilige Schrift des Alten Testaments 6/5. Bonn: Hanstein, 1925.

Egger-Wenzel, R. "Der Gebrauch von תמם bei Ijob und Ben Sira: Ein Vergleich zweier Weisheitsbücher." Pp. 203–38 in *Freundschaft bei Ben Sira: Beiträge des Symposions zu Ben Sira, Salzburg 1995.* Edited by F. V. Reiterer. BZAW 244. Berlin: de Gruyter, 1996.

Egger-Wenzel, R., and I. Krammer, eds. *Der Einzelne und seine Gemeinschaft bei Ben Sira.* BZAW 270. Berlin: de Gruyter, 1998.

Faure, P. "Comme un fleuve qui irrigue: Ben Sira 24,30–34, I. Critique textuelle." *RB* 102 (1995): 5–27.

———. "La sagesse et le sage: Ben Sira 24,30–34, II. Exégèse." *RB* 103 (1996): 348–70.

Fuß, W. "Tradition und Komposition im Buche Jesus Sirach." Th.D. diss., University of Tübingen, 1962.

Gammie, J. G. "The Sage in Sirach." Pp. 355–72 in *The Sage in Israel and the Ancient Near East.* Edited by J. G. Gammie and L. G. Perdue. Winona Lake, Ind.: Eisenbrauns, 1990.

Gammie, J. G., and L. G. Perdue, eds. *The Sage in Israel and the Ancient Near East.* Winona Lake, Ind.: Eisenbrauns, 1990.

García Martínez, F. "Ben Sira: A Bibliography of Studies, 1965–1997." Pp. 233–52 in *Masada VI: The Yigael Yadin Excavations 1963–1965: Final Report.* Edited by S. Talmon. Jerusalem: Israel Exploration Society, 1999.

Gilbert, M. "Ben Sira et la femme." *RTL* 7 (1976): 426–42.

———. *Introduction au Livre de Ben Sira ou Siracide ou Ecclésiastique.* Rome: Pontifical Biblical Institute, 1989.

———. "Siracide." *DBSup* 12:1389–1437.

———. "Wisdom Literature." Pp. 283–324 in *Jewish Writings of the Second Temple Period: Apocrypha, Pseudepigrapha, Qumran Sectarian Writings, Philo, Josephus.* Edited by M. E. Stone. CRINT 2/2. Assen: Van Gorcum, 1984.

Goan, S. "Creation in Ben Sira." *MilS* 36 (1995): 75–85.

Hadot, J. *Penchant mauvais et volonté libre dans la sagesse de Ben Sira (L'Ecclésiastique).* Brussels: Presses Universitaires de Bruxelles, 1970.

Hamp, V. "Zukunft und Jenseits im Buche Sirach." Pp. 86–97 in *Alttestamentliche Studien: Friedrich Nötscher zum Sechzigsten Geburtstag, 19, Juli 1950, Gewidmet von Kollegen, Freunden und Schülern.* Edited by H. Junker and J. Botterweck. BBB 1. Bonn: Hanstein, 1950.

Harrington, D. J. "Sage Advice about Friendship." *TBT* 32 (1994): 79–83.

———. "Sirach Research since 1965: Progress and Questions." Pp. 164–76 in *Pursuing the Text: Studies in Honor of Ben Zion Wacholder on the Occasion of His Seventieth Birthday.* Edited by J. C. Reeves and J. Kampen. JSOTSup 184. Sheffield: JSOT Press, 1994.

Harvey, J. D. "Toward a Degree of Order in Ben Sira's Book." *ZAW* 105 (1993): 52–62.

Haspecker, J. *Gottesfurcht bei Jesus Sirach: Ihre religiöse Struktur und ihre literarische und doktrinäre Bedeutung.* AnBib 30. Rome: Pontifical Biblical Institute, 1967.

Hayward, C. T. R. "The New Jerusalem in the Wisdom of Jesus ben Sira." *SJOT* 6 (1992): 123–38.

———. "Sacrifice and World Order: Some Observations on Ben Sira's Attitude to the Temple Service." Pp. 22–34 in *Sacrifice and Redemption: Durham Essays in Theology.* Edited by S. W. Sykes. Cambridge: Cambridge University Press, 1991.

———. "Sirach and Wisdom's Dwelling Place." Pp. 31–46 in *Where Shall Wisdom Be Found?* Edited by S. C. Barton. Edinburgh: T&T Clark, 1999.

Herrmann, J. von. "A Stylistic and Poetic Study of Sirach 6:5–17." Unpublished seminar paper, Catholic University of America, Washington, D.C., 1990.

Hildesheim, R. *Bis daß ein Prophet aufstand wie Feuer.* TThSt 58. Trier: Paulinus, 1996.

Höffken, P. "Jesus Sirachs Darstellung der Interaktion des Königs Hiskija und des Propheten Jesaja (Sir 48:17–25)." *JSJ* 31 (2000): 162–75.

———. "Warum schwieg Jesus Sirach über Esra?" *ZAW* 87 (1975): 184–202.

Hoglund, K. G. "The Fool and the Wise in Dialogue." Pp. 161–80 in *The Listening Heart: Essays in Wisdom and the Psalms in Honor of Roland E. Murphy*. Edited by K. G. Hoglund. JSOTSup 58. Sheffield: JSOT Press, 1987.

Irwin, W. H. "Fear of God, the Analogy of Friendship and Ben Sira's Theodicy." *Bib* 76 (1995): 551–59.

Jolley, M. A. "The Function of Torah in Sirach (Wisdom Literature)." Ph.D. diss., Southern Baptist Theological Seminary, Louisville, 1993.

Jüngling, H. W., "Der Bauplan des Buches Jesus Sirach." Pp. 89–105 in *Den Armen eine frohe Botschaft*. Edited by J. Hainz et al. Frankfurt a.M.: Knecht, 1997.

Kaiser, O. *Gottes und der Menschen Weisheit*. BZAW 261. Berlin: de Gruyter, 1998.

———. *Der Mensch unter dem Schicksal*. BZAW 161. Berlin: de Gruyter, 1985.

———. "Was ein Freund nicht tun darf: Eine Auslegung von Sir 27,16–21." Pp. 107–22 in *Freundschaft bei Ben Sira: Beiträge des Symposions zu Ben Sira, Salzburg 1995*. Edited by F. V. Reiterer. BZAW 244. Berlin: de Gruyter, 1996.

Kearns, C. "The Expanded Text of Ecclesiasticus: Its Teaching on the Future Life As a Clue to Its Origin." S.S.D. diss., Pontifical Biblical Institute, Rome, 1951.

Kieweler, H.-V. *Ben Sira zwischen Judentum und Hellenismus: Eine Auseinandersetzung mit Th. Middendorp*. BEATAJ 30. Frankfurt a.M.: Lang, 1992.

———. "Freundschaft und böse Nachrede: Exegetische Anmerkungen zu Sir 19,6–19." Pp. 61–85 in *Freundschaft bei Ben Sira: Beiträge des Symposions zu Ben Sira, Salzburg 1995*. Edited by F. V. Reiterer. BZAW 244. Berlin: de Gruyter, 1996.

Krammer, I. "Die Auswirkungen des Verhaltens zum Mitmenschen auf die Beziehung zu Gott im Buch Ben Sira." Th.D. diss., University of Salzburg, 1997.

———. "Scham im Zusammenhang mit Freundschaft." Pp. 171–201 in *Freundschaft bei Ben Sira: Beiträge des Symposions zu Ben Sira, Salzburg 1995*. Edited by F. V. Reiterer. BZAW 244. Berlin: de Gruyter, 1996.

Krinetzki, G. "Die Freundschaftsperikope Sir 6,5–17 in traditionsgeschichtlicher Sicht." *BZ* 23 (1979): 212–33.

———. "Die Sprüche über das Reden und Schweigen in Sir 20 in traditionskritischer Sicht." Pp. 64–81 in *"Diener in eurer Mitte": Festschrift für Dr. Antonius Hofmann, Bischof von Passau zum 75. Geburtstag*. Edited by R. Beer et al. Passau: Universität Passau, 1984.

Lavoie, J. J. "Ben Sira le voyageur ou la difficile rencontre avec l'hellénisme." *ScEs* 52 (2000): 37–60.

Lee, T. R. *Studies in the Form of Sirach 44–50*. SBLDS 75. Atlanta: Scholars Press, 1986.

Lévi, I. *L'Ecclésiastique ou la Sagesse de Jésus, fils de Sira*. 2 vols. Paris: Leroux, 1898–1901.

———. "Notes sur les ch. VII.29–XII.1 de Ben Sira." *JQR* 13 (1900–1901): 1–17.

Levison, J. R. "Is Eve to Blame? A Contextual Analysis of Sirach 25:24." *CBQ* 47 (1985): 617–23.

———. *Portraits of Adam in Early Judaism: From Sirach to 2 Baruch*. JSPSup 1. Sheffield: JSOT Press, 1988.

Liesen, J. *Full of Praise: An Exegetical Study of Sir 39,12–35*. JSJSup 64. Leiden: Brill, 2000.

Mack, B. L. "Sirach (Ecclesiasticus)." Pp. 65–86 in vol. 2 of *The Books of the Bible*. Edited by B. W. Anderson. 2 vols. New York: Scribner's, 1989.

———. *Wisdom and the Hebrew Epic: Ben Sira's Hymn in Praise of the Fathers*. CSHJ. Chicago: University of Chicago Press, 1985.

Marböck, J. "Gefährdung und Bewährung: Kontexte zur Freundschaftsperikope Sir 22,19–26." Pp. 87–106 in *Freundschaft bei Ben Sira: Beiträge des Symposions zu Ben Sira, Salzburg 1995*. Edited by F. V. Reiterer. BZAW 244. Berlin: de Gruyter, 1996.

———. "Gerechtigkeit Gottes und Leben nach dem Sirachbuch." Pp. 21–52 in *Gerechtigkeit und Leben im hellenistischen Zeitalter: Symposium anläßlich des 75. Geburtstag von Otto Kaiser*. Edited by J. Jeremias. BZAW 296. Berlin: de Gruyter, 2001.

———. *Gottes Weisheit unter Uns*. Herders Biblische Studien 6. Freiburg i.B.: Herder, 1995.

———. "Kohelet und Sirach: Eine vielschichtige Beziehung." Pp. 275–301 in *Das Buch Kohelet: Studien zur Struktur, Geschichte, Rezeption und Theologie.* Edited by L. Schwienhorst-Schönberger. BZAW 254. Berlin: de Gruyter, 1997.

———. *Weisheit im Wandel: Untersuchungen zur Weisheitstheologie bei Ben Sira.* BBB 37. Bonn: Hanstein, 1971. Repr., BZAW 272, Berlin: de Gruyter, 1999.

Mattila, S. L. "Ben Sira and the Stoics: A Reexamination of the Evidence." *JBL* 119 (2000): 473–501.

McKechnie, P. "The Career of Joshua Ben Sira." *JTS* 51 (2000): 3–26.

Middendorp, T. *Die Stellung Jesu ben Siras zwischen Judentum und Hellenismus.* Leiden: Brill, 1973.

Milani, M. "La correlazione tra morte e vita in Ben Sira: Dimensione antropologica, cosmica e teologica dell'antitesi." S.S.D. diss., Pontifical Biblical Institute, Rome, 1995.

Minissale, A. *La versione greca del Siracide: Confronto con il testo ebraico alla luce dell'attività midrascica e del metodo targumico.* AnBib 133. Rome: Pontifical Biblical Institute, 1995.

Mulder, O. *Simon de hogepriester in Sirach 50.* Almelo: privately published, 2000.

Muraoka, T., and J. F. Elwolde, eds. *The Hebrew of the Dead Sea Scrolls and Ben Sira.* STDJ 26. Leiden: Brill, 1997.

Nelson, M. D. *The Syriac Version of the Wisdom of Ben Sira Compared to the Greek and Hebrew Materials.* SBLDS 107. Atlanta: Scholars Press, 1988.

Newsom, C. A. "The Sage in the Literature of Qumran: The Functions of the *Maśkîl.*" Pp. 373–82 in *The Sage in Israel and the Ancient Near East.* Edited by J. G. Gammie and L. G. Perdue. Winona Lake, Ind.: Eisenbrauns, 1990.

Okoye, J. I. *Speech in Ben Sira with Special Reference to 5,9–6,1.* European University Studies 23/535. Frankfurt a.M.: Lang, 1995.

Olyan, S. M. "Ben Sira's Relationship to the Priesthood." *HTR* 80 (1987): 261–86.

Owens, R. J. "The Early Syriac Text of Ben Sira in the Demonstrations of Aphrahat." *JSS* 34 (1989): 39–75.

Pax, E. "Dialog und Selbstgespräch bei Sirach 27,3–10." *SBFLA* 20 (1970): 247–63.

Penar, T. *Northwest Semitic Philology and the Hebrew Fragments of Ben Sira.* BibOr 28. Rome: Pontifical Biblical Institute, 1975.

Peters, N. *Das Buch Jesus Sirach oder Ecclesiasticus.* EHAT 25. Münster i.W.: Aschendorff, 1913.

Petraglio, R. "Figli e padri. Lettori, copisti e traduttori cristiani di Ben Sirac." Pp. 489–504 in *Letture cristiane dei Libri Sapienziali.* Studia Ephemeridis Augustinianum 37. Rome: Institutum Patristicum Augustinianum. 1992.

———. *Il libro che contamina le mani. Ben Sirac rilegge il libro e la storia d'Israele.* Theologia 4. Palermo: Augustinus, 1993.

Pilch, J. J. "Beat His Ribs While He Is Young (Sir 30:12): A Window on the Mediterranean World." *BTB* 23 (1993): 101–13.

Prato, G. L. *Il problema della teodicea in Ben Sira: Composizione dei contrari e richiamo alle origini.* AnBib 65. Rome: Pontifical Biblical Institute, 1975.

Prockter, L. J. "Alms and the Man: The Merits of Charity." *JNSL* 17 (1991): 69–80.

Puech, É. "4Q525 et les péricopes des Béatitudes en Ben Sira et Matthieu." *RB* 98 (1991): 80–106.

Reiterer, F. V. "Deutung und Wertung des Todes durch Ben Sira." Pp. 203–36 in *Die alttestamentliche Botschaft als Wegweisung: Festschrift für Heinz Reinelt.* Edited by J. Zmijewski. Stuttgart: Katholisches Bibelwerk, 1990.

———. "Gelungene Freundschaft als tragende Säule einer Gesellschaft: Exegetische Untersuchung von Sir 25,1–11." Pp. 133–69 in *Freundschaft bei Ben Sira: Beiträge des Symposions zu Ben Sira, Salzburg 1995.* Edited by F. V. Reiterer. BZAW 244. Berlin: de Gruyter, 1996.

———. "Markierte und nicht markierte direkte Objekte bei Ben Sira: Präliminaria zur Untersuchung der Hebraizität Siras anhand der Verben mit את-Verwendung." Pp. 359–78 in *Text, Methode und Grammatik: Wolfgang Richter zum 65. Geburtstag.* Edited by W. Gross et al. St. Ottilien: EOS, 1991.

———. "Die Stellung Ben Siras zur Arbeit." Pp. 257–89 in *Ein Gott, Eine Offenbarung: Beiträge zur biblischen Exegese, Theologie und Spiritualität: Festschrift für Notker Füglister, OSB, zum 60. Geburtstag.* Edited by F. V. Reiterer. Würzburg: Echter, 1991.

———. *"Urtext" und Übersetzungen: Sprachstudie über Sir 44,16–45,26 als Beitrag zur Siraforschung.* Arbeiten zu Text und Sprache im Alten Testament 12. St. Ottilien: EOS, 1980.

———. "Das Verhältnis Ijobs und Ben Siras." Pp. 405–29 in *The Book of Job*. Edited by W. A. M. Beuken. BETL 114. Leuven: Peeters, 1994.

———, ed. *Bibliographie zu Ben Sira*. BZAW 266. Berlin: de Gruyter, 1998.

———, ed. *Freundschaft bei Ben Sira: Beiträge des Symposions zu Ben Sira, Salzburg 1995*. BZAW 244. Berlin: de Gruyter, 1996.

Reymond, E. D. "Even unto a Spark. An Analysis of the Parallelistic Structure in the Wisdom of Ben Sira 40:11–44:15." Ph.D. diss., University of Chicago, 1999.

———. "Sirach 40,18–27 As '*Ṭôb*-spruch.'" *Bib* 82 (2001): 84–92.

Rickenbacher, O. *Weisheitsperikopen bei Ben Sira*. OBO 1. Freiburg i.d.S.: Universitätsverlag; Göttingen: Vandenhoeck & Ruprecht, 1973.

Rollston, C. A. "Ben Sira 38:24–39:11 and the Egyptian Satire of the Trades: A Reconsideration." *JBL* 120 (2001): 131–39.

Roth, W. "On the Gnomic-Discursive Wisdom of Jesus Ben Sirach." *Semeia* 17 (1980): 59–79.

———. "Sirach: The First Graded Curriculum." *TBT* 29 (1991): 298–302.

Rüger, H.-P. *Text und Textform im hebräischen Sirach: Untersuchungen zur Textgeschichte und Textkritik der hebräischen Sirachfragmente aus der Kairoer Geniza*. BZAW 112. Berlin: de Gruyter, 1970.

Ryssel, V. "Die Sprüche Jesus, des Sohnes Sirach." Pp. 230–475 in vol. 1 of *Die Apokryphen und Pseudepigraphen des Alten Testaments*. Edited by E. Kautzsch. 2 vols. Tübingen: Mohr, 1900.

Sanders, J. T. *Ben Sira and Demotic Wisdom*. SBLMS 28. Chico, Calif.: Scholars Press, 1983.

———. "Ben Sira's Ethics of Caution." *HUCA* 50 (1979): 73–106.

Saracino, F. "La sapienza e la vita: Sir 4,11–19." *RivB* 29 (1981): 257–72.

Sauer, G. "Freundschaft nach Ben Sira 37,1–6." Pp. 123–31 in *Freundschaft bei Ben Sira: Beiträge des Symposions zu Ben Sira, Salzburg 1995*. Edited by F. V. Reiterer. BZAW 244. Berlin: de Gruyter, 1996.

———. *Jesus Sirach (Ben Sira)*. JSHRZ 3/5. Gütersloh: Mohn, 1981.

———. *Jesus Sirach: Übersetzt und erklärt*. ATD Apokryphen 1. Göttingen: Vandenhoeck & Ruprecht, 2000.

Schechter, S. "A Glimpse of the Social Life of the Jews in the Age of Jesus the Son of Sirach." Pp. 55–101 in *Studies in Judaism, Second Series.* Philadelphia: Jewish Publication Society of America, 1908.

Schnabel, E. J. *Law and Wisdom from Ben Sira to Paul: A Tradition-Historical Enquiry into the Relation of Law, Wisdom, and Ethics.* WUNT 2/16. Tübingen: Mohr, 1985.

Schrader, L. *Leiden und Gerechtigkeit: Studien zu Theologie und Textgeschichte des Sirachbuches.* BBET 27. Frankfurt a.M.: Lang, 1994.

———. "Unzuverlässige Freundschaft und verläßliche Feindschaft: Überlegungen zu Sir 12,8–12." Pp. 19–59 in *Freundschaft bei Ben Sira: Beiträge des Symposions zu Ben Sira, Salzburg 1995.* Edited by F. V. Reiterer. BZAW 244. Berlin: de Gruyter, 1996.

———. *Verwandtschaft der Peschitta mit der (alt)lateinischen Übersetzung im Sirachbuch? Ein Beitrag zur Methodik textgeschichtlicher Forschung.* BN Beihefte 11. Munich: Institut für Biblische Exegese, 1998.

Selmer, C. "A Study of Ecclus. 12:10–19." *CBQ* 8 (1946): 306–14.

Sheppard, G. T. *Wisdom As a Hermeneutical Construct: A Study in the Sapientializing of the Old Testament.* BZAW 151. Berlin: de Gruyter, 1980.

Skehan, P. W. "Staves, Nails and Scribal Slips (Ben Sira 44:2–5)." *BASOR* 200 (1970): 66–71.

———. "Structures in Poems on Wisdom: Proverbs 8 and Sirach 24." *CBQ* 41 (1979): 365–79.

———. *Studies in Israelite Poetry and Wisdom.* CBQMS 1. Washington, D.C.: Catholic Biblical Association of America, 1971.

Skehan, P. W., and A. A. Di Lella. *The Wisdom of Ben Sira.* AB 39. New York: Doubleday, 1987.

Smend, R. *Die Weisheit des Jesus Sirach, erklärt.* Berlin: Reimer, 1906.

Snaith, J. G. "Ecclesiasticus: A Tract for the Times." Pp. 170–81 in *Wisdom in Ancient Israel: Essays in Honour of J. A. Emerton.* Edited by J. Day, R. P. Gordon, and H. G. M. Williamson. Cambridge: Cambridge University Press, 1995.

Söding, T. "Nächstenliebe bei Jesus Sirach: Eine Notiz zur weisheitlichen Ethik." *BZ* 42 (1998): 239–47.

Spicq, C. "L'Ecclésiastique." Pp. 529–841 in *La Sainte Bible 6.* Edited by L. Pirot and A. Clamer. Paris: Letouzey et Ané, 1951.

Stadelmann, H. *Ben Sira als Schriftgelehrter: Eine Untersuchung zum Berufsbild des vor-makkabäischen Sofer unter Berücksichtigung seines Verhältnisses zu Priester-, Propheten- und Weisheitslehrertum.* WUNT 2/6. Tübingen: Mohr, 1980.

Strotmann, A. "Das Buch Jesus Sirach." Pp. 428–40 in *Kompendium Feministischer Bibelauslegung.* Edited by L. Schottroff and M. T. Wacker. 2d ed. Gütersloh: Kaiser, 1999.

Trenchard, W. C. *Ben Sira's View of Women: A Literary Analysis.* BJS 38. Chico, Calif.: Scholars Press, 1982.

Wagner, C. *Die Septuaginta-Hapaxlegomena im Buch Jesus Sirach.* BZAW 282. Berlin: de Gruyter, 1999.

Weber, K. "Wisdom False and True (Sir 19,20–30)." *Bib* 77 (1996): 330–48.

Wicke-Reuter, U. *Göttliche Providenz und menschliche Verantwortung bei Ben Sira und in der Frühen Stoa.* BZAW 298. Berlin: de Gruyter, 2000.

Wieder, A. A. "Ben Sira and the Praises of Wine." *JQR* 61 (1970–1971): 155–66.

Williams, D. S. W. "The Date of Ecclesiasticus." *VT* 44 (1994): 563–66.

Winter, M. M. "Ben Sira in Syriac." Ph. D. diss., University of Fribourg, 1975.

———. "The Origins of Ben Sira in Syriac." *VT* 27 (1977): 237–53, 494–507.

Wischmeyer, O. *Die Kultur des Buches Jesus Sirach.* BZNW 77. Berlin: de Gruyter, 1995.

Wright, B. G. *No Small Difference: Sirach's Relationship to Its Hebrew Parent Text.* SBLSCS 26. Atlanta: Scholars Press, 1989.

Zapella, M. "Criteri antologici e questioni testuali del manoscritto ebraico C di Siracide." *RivB* 38 (1990): 273–300.

Ziegler, J. "Ursprüngliche Lesarten im griechischen Sirach." Pp. 461–87 in *Mélanges Eugène Tisserant, 1.* Studi e testi 231. Vatican City: Biblioteca Apostolica Vaticana, 1964.

———. "Zwei Beiträge zu Sirach." *BZ* 8 (1964): 277–84.

3. Other Literature on Biblical and Related Topics

a. Texts and Reference Works

Baumgarten, J. M., *Qumran Cave 4.13: The Damascus Document (4Q266–4Q273).* DJD 18. Oxford: Clarendon, 1996.

Colson, F. H., and G. H. Whitaker, trans. *Philo.* LCL. 10 vols. Cambridge, Mass.: Harvard University Press, 1929–1962.

Davies, G. I. *Ancient Hebrew Inscriptions.* Cambridge: Cambridge University Press, 1991.

García Martínez, F. *The Dead Sea Scrolls Translated.* Leiden: Brill, 1994.

Hartman, L. F., et al., eds. *Textual Notes on the New American Bible.* Paterson, N.J.: St. Anthony's Guild, n.d.

Hollander, H. W., and M. de Jonge, *The Testaments of the Twelve Patriarchs: A Commentary.* SVTP 8. Leiden: Brill, 1985.

Jacobsen, T. *The Harps That Once…: Sumerian Poetry in Translation.* New Haven, Conn.: Yale University Press, 1987.

Kottsieper, I. *Die Sprache der Ahiqarsprüche.* BZAW 194. Berlin: de Gruyter, 1990.

Kuhn, K. G. *Konkordanz zu den Qumrantexten.* Göttingen: Vandenhoeck & Ruprecht, 1960.

Lichtheim, M. *Late Egyptian Wisdom Literature in the International Context: A Study of Demotic Instructions.* OBO 52. Freiburg i.d.S.: Universitätsverlag; Göttingen: Vandenhoeck & Ruprecht, 1983.

Lindenberger, J. M. *The Aramaic Proverbs of Ahiqar.* Baltimore: Johns Hopkins University Press, 1983.

Lohse, E. *Die Texte aus Qumran: hebräisch und deutsch.* 2d ed. Munich: Kösel, 1971.

Milik, J. T., with M. Black. *The Books of Enoch: Aramaic Fragments of Qumrân Cave 4.* Oxford: Clarendon, 1976.

Pfann, S. J., et al., eds. *Qumran Cave 4.26: Cryptic Texts and Miscellanea, Part 1.* DJD 36. Oxford: Clarendon, 2000.

Puech, É. *Textes Hebreux (4Q521–4Q528, 4Q576–4Q579): Qumran Cave 4.18.* DJD 25. Oxford: Clarendon, 1998.

Strugnell, J., D. J. Harrington, and T. Elgvin. *Sapiential Texts, Part 2: Cave 4.24.* DJD 34. Oxford: Clarendon, 1999.

Thackeray, H. St. J., et al. *Josephus.* LCL. 10 vols. New York: Putnam; Cambridge, Mass.: Harvard University Press, 1926–1965.

van der Horst, P. W. *The Sentences of Pseudo-Phocylides.* SVTP 4. Leiden: Brill, 1978.

Viviano, B. T. *Study As Worship: Aboth and the New Testament.* SJLA 26. Leiden: Brill, 1978.

Walters, P. *The Text of the Septuagint.* Edited by D. W. Gooding. Cambridge: Cambridge University, 1973.

b. Biblical and Related Studies

Alonso Schökel, L. *A Manual of Hebrew Poetics.* SubBi 11. Rome: Pontifical Biblical Institute, 1988.

Archer, L. J. *Her Price Is Beyond Rubies: The Jewish Woman in Greco-Roman Palestine.* JSOTSup 60. Sheffield: JSOT Press, 1990.

Baker, W. R. *Personal Speech-Ethics in the Epistle of James.* WUNT 2/68. Tübingen: Mohr, 1995.

Barbiero, G. *L'Asino del Nemico.* AnBib 128. Rome: Pontifical Biblical Institute, 1991.

Beauchamp, P. *Création et séparation.* Paris: Aubier Montaigne, 1969.

Begg, C. "The Abigail Story (1 Samuel 25) according to Josephus." *EstBib* 54 (1996): 5–34.

———. "'Bread, Wine and Strong Drink' in Deut 29:5a." *Bijdr* 41 (1980): 266–75.

Bergant, D. *Israel's Wisdom Literature: A Liberation-Critical Reading.* Minneapolis: Fortress, 1997.

Berlin, A. *Zephaniah.* AB 25A. New York: Doubleday, 1994.

Bikerman, E. *Institutions des Séleucides.* Service des Antiquités: Bibliothèque archéologique et historique 26. Paris: Geuthner, 1938.

Boccaccini, G. *Middle Judaism: Jewish Thought 300 B.C.E. to 200 C.E.* Minneapolis: Fortress, 1991.

Braun, R. *Kohelet und die frühhellenistische Popularphilosophie.* BZAW 130. Berlin: de Gruyter, 1973.

Brown, J. P. *The Legacy of Iranian Imperialism and the Individual.* Vol. 3 of *Israel and Hellas.* BZAW 299. Berlin: de Gruyter, 2001.

Brown, R. E. *The Death of the Messiah.* 2 vols. New York: Doubleday, 1994.

Burke, D. G. *The Poetry of Baruch: A Reconstruction and Analysis of the Original Hebrew Text of Baruch 3:9–5:9.* SBLSCS 10. Chico, Calif.: Scholars Press, 1982.

Cohen, S. J. D. *From the Maccabees to the Mishnah.* LEC 7. Philadelphia: Westminster, 1987.

Collins, J. J. *Jewish Wisdom in the Hellenistic Age.* OTL. Louisville: Westminster/John Knox, 1997.

Collins, T. "The Physiology of Tears in the Old Testament." *CBQ* 33 (1971): 18–38, 185–97.

Crenshaw, J. L. *Ecclesiastes.* OTL. Philadelphia: Westminster, 1987.

———. "Education in Ancient Israel." *JBL* 104 (1985): 601–15.

———. *Old Testament Wisdom: An Introduction.* Atlanta: John Knox, 1981.

———. *Urgent Advice and Probing Questions: Collected Writings on Old Testament Wisdom.* Macon, Ga.: Mercer University Press, 1995.

Cross, F. M. "The Development of the Jewish Scripts." Pp. 133–202 in *The Bible and the Ancient Near East: Essays in Honor of William Foxwell Albright.* Edited by G. E. Wright. Garden City, N.Y.: Doubleday, 1961.

de la Potterie, I. *La Vérité dans Saint Jean, I.* AnBib 73. Rome: Pontifical Biblical Institute, 1977.

Dempsey, C. J. "The Gift of Wisdom and the Natural World." *TBT* 35 (1997): 147–51.

Derousseaux, L. *La Crainte de Dieu dans l'Ancien Testament.* LD 63. Paris: Cerf, 1970.

deSilva, D. A. *Despising Shame: Honor Discourse and Community Maintenance in the Epistle to the Hebrews.* SBLDS 152. Atlanta: Scholars Press, 1995.

Duesberg, H. *Les scribes inspirés: Introduction aux livres sapientiaux de la Bible.* 2 vols. Paris: Maredsous; Tournai: Desclée, 1966.

Duggan, M. *The Consuming Fire: A Christian Introduction to the Old Testament.* San Francisco: Ignatius, 1991.

Eißfeldt, O. *Der Beutel der Lebendigen.* Berlin: Akademie, 1960.

Eshel, E. "4Q477: The Rebukes by the Overseer." *JJS* 45 (1994): 111–22.

Feldman, L. H. *Jew and Gentile in the Ancient World.* Princeton, N.J.: Princeton University Press, 1993.

Fitzmyer, J. A. *The Gospel According to Luke.* AB 28, 28A. 2 vols. New York: Doubleday, 1981–1985.

Fletcher-Louis, C. H. T. "Wisdom Christology and the Partings of the Ways Between Judaism and Christianity." Pp. 52–68 in *Christian-Jewish Relations through the Centuries.* Edited by S. E. Porter and B. W. R. Pearson. JSNTSup 192. Sheffield: Sheffield Academic Press, 2000.

Gordis, R. "The Social Background of Wisdom Literature." *HUCA* 18 (1943–1944): 77–118.

Grabbe, L. L. "Jewish Historiography and Scripture in the Hellenistic Period." Pp. 129–55 in *Did Moses Speak Attic? Jewish Historiography and Scripture in the Hellenistic Period.* Edited by L. L. Grabbe. JSOTSup 317. Sheffield: Sheffield Academic Press, 2001.

———. *Judaism from Cyrus to Hadrian.* 2 vols. Minneapolis: Augsburg Fortress, 1992.

Greenberg, M. *Ezekiel 1–20.* AB 22. Garden City, N.Y.: Doubleday, 1983.

Harrington, D. J. *Invitation to the Apocrypha.* Grand Rapids, Mich.: Eerdmans, 1999.

———. "Two Early Jewish Approaches to Wisdom: Sirach and Qumran Sapiential Work A." *JSP* 16 (1997): 25–38.

————. *Wisdom Texts from Qumran.* New York: Routledge, 1996.

Hart, T. M. "Qoheleth Looks at Friendship." *TBT* 32 (1994): 74–78.

Hartman, L. F., and A. A. Di Lella. *The Book of Daniel.* AB 23. Garden City, N.Y.: Doubleday, 1978.

Hayward, C. T. R. *The Jewish Temple: A Non-biblical Sourcebook.* London: Routledge, 1996.

Hengel, M. *Judaism and Hellenism.* 2 vols. Philadelphia: Fortress, 1974.

Humbert, P. *Recherches sur les sources égyptiennes de la littérature sapientiale d'Israël.* Mémoires de l'Université de Neuchatel 7. Neuchatel: Secrétariat de l'Université, 1929.

Jackson, G. S. "Naomi, Ruth, and Orpah." *TBT* 32 (1994): 68–73.

Jagersma, H. A. *History of Israel from Alexander the Great to Bar Kochba.* Philadelphia: Fortress, 1986.

Jensen, J. *The Use of tôrâ by Isaiah.* CBQMS 3. Washington, D.C.: Catholic Biblical Association of America, 1973.

Kaiser, O. *Gottes und der Menschen Weisheit.* BZAW 261. Berlin: de Gruyter, 1998.

Keel, O. *The Symbolism of the Biblical World: Ancient Near Eastern Iconography and the Book of Psalms.* New York: Seabury, 1978.

Kobelski, P. J. *Melchizedek and Melchireša*ᶜ. CBQMS 10. Washington, D.C.: Catholic Biblical Association of America, 1981.

Kolarcik, M. *The Ambiguity of Death in the Book of Wisdom 1–6*. AnBib 127. Rome: Pontifical Biblical Institute, 1991.

Kosmala, H. "*Maśkîl*." *JANESCU* 5 (1973): 235–41.

Krašovec, J. *Antithetic Structure in Biblical Hebrew Poetry*. VTSup 35. Leiden: Brill, 1984.

Küchler, M. *Frühjüdische Weisheitstraditionen: Zum Fortgang weisheitlichen Denkens im Bereich des frühjüdischen Jahweglaubens*. OBO 26. Freiburg i.d.S.: Universitätsverlag; Göttingen: Vandenhoeck & Ruprecht, 1979.

Kugel, J. L. "On Hidden Hatred and Open Reproach: Early Exegesis of Leviticus 19:17." *HTR* 80 (1987): 43–61.

Kuntzmann, R., ed. *Ce Dieu Qui Vient: Etudes sur l'Ancien et le Nouveau Testament offertes au professeur Bernard Renaud à l'occasion de son soixante-cinquième anniversaire*. LD 159. Paris: Cerf, 1995.

Levenson, J. D. "1 Samuel 25 As Literature and As History." *CBQ* 40 (1978): 11–28.

Lindsay, D. R. *Josephus and Faith:* ΠΙΣΤΙΣ *and* ΠΙΣΤΕΥΕΙΝ *As Faith Terminology in the Writings of Flavius Josephus and in the New Testament*. AGJU 19. Leiden: Brill, 1993.

Luc, A. T. H. "The Meaning of ʾHB in the Hebrew Bible." Ph.D. diss., University of Wisconsin, Madison, 1982.

Marshall, P. *Enmity in Corinth*. WUNT 2/23. Tübingen: Mohr, 1987.

Mathys, H. P. *Liebe deinen Nächsten wie dich selbst: Untersuchungen zum alttestamentlichen Gebot der Nächstenliebe (Lev 19,18)*. OBO 71. Göttingen: Vandenhoeck & Ruprecht, 1986.

McCreesh, T. P. "Wisdom As Wife: Proverbs 31:10–31." *RB* 92 (1985): 25–46.

Mettinger, T. N. D. *Solomonic State Officials: A Study of the Civil Government Officials of the Israelite Monarchy*. ConBOT 5. Lund: Gleerup, 1971.

Mies, F., ed. *Toute la sagesse du monde: Hommage à Maurice Gilbert, S.J.: Pour le 65e anniversaire de l'exégète et du recteur*. Namur: Presses Universitaires de Namur, 1999.

Miller, P. D. "Animal Names As Designations in Ugaritic and Hebrew." *UF* 2 (1970): 177–86.

Mitchell, A. C. "'Greet the Friends by Name': New Testament Evidence for the Greco-Roman Topos on Friendship." Pp. 225–62 in *Greco-Roman Perspectives on Friendship.* Edited by J. T. Fitzgerald. SBLRBS 34. Atlanta: Scholars Press, 1997.

———. "The Social Function of Friendship in Acts 2:44–47 and 4:32–37." *JBL* 111 (1992): 255–72.

Moran, W. L. "The Ancient Near Eastern Background of the Love of God in Deuteronomy." *CBQ* 25 (1963): 77–87.

Murphy, R. E. *The Tree of Life: An Exploration of Biblical Wisdom Literature.* New York: Doubleday, 1990.

———. "*Yēṣer* in the Qumran Literature." *Bib* 39 (1958): 334–44.

Nel, P. J. *The Structure and Ethos of the Wisdom Admonitions in Proverbs.* BZAW 158. Berlin: de Gruyter, 1982.

Olivier, J. P. J. "Schools and Wisdom Literature." *JNSL* 4 (1975): 49–60.

Paeslack, M. "Zur Bedeutungsgeschichte der Wörter φιλεῖν 'lieben,' φιλία 'Liebe,' 'Freundschaft,' φίλος 'Freund' in der LXX und im NT." *ThViat* 5 (1953–1955): 51–142.

Peterson, E. "Der Gottesfreund: Beiträge zur Geschichte eines religiösen Terminus." *ZKG* 42 (1923): 161–202.

Pilch, J. J. "Secrecy in the Mediterranean World: An Anthropological Perspective." *BTB* 24 (1994): 151–57.

Pleins, J. D. "Poverty in the Social World of the Wise." *JSOT* 37 (1987): 61–78.

Pomykala, K. E. *The Davidic Dynasty Tradition in Early Judaism: Its History and Significance for Messianism.* SBLEJL 7. Atlanta: Scholars Press, 1995.

Pope, M. H. *Job.* AB 15. Garden City, N.Y.: Doubleday, 1965.

———. *Song of Songs.* AB 7C. Garden City, N.Y.: Doubleday, 1977.

Puech, É. *La croyance des Esséniens en la vie future: immortalité, résurrection, vie éternelle?* EBib 21. Paris: Gabalda, 1993.

Rad, G. von. *Wisdom in Israel.* London: SCM, 1972.

Reif, S. C. *A Jewish Archive from Old Cairo.* Richmond, Surrey: Curzon, 2000.

Schalit, A., ed. *The Hellenistic Age.* WHJP 6. New Brunswick, N.J.: Rutgers University Press, 1972.

Scherer, A. "Is the Selfish Man Wise? Considerations of Context in Proverbs 10.1–22.16 with Special Regard to Surety, Bribery and Friendship." *JSOT* 76 (1997): 59–70.

Schiffman, L. H. *Sectarian Law in the Dead Sea Scrolls.* BJS 33. Chico, Calif.: Scholars Press, 1983.

Schroer, S. *Die Weisheit hat ihr Haus gebaut: Studien zur Gestalt der Sophia in den biblischen Schriften.* Mainz: Grünewald, 1996.

Schürer, E. *The History of the Jewish People in the Age of Jesus Christ (175 B.C.–A.D. 135).* Revised by G. Vermes, F. Millar, and M. Goodman. 4 vols. Edinburgh: T&T Clark, 1973–1987.

Sterling, G. E. "The Bond of Humanity: Friendship in Philo of Alexandria." Pp. 203–23 in *Greco-Roman Perspectives on Friendship.* Edited by J. T. Fitzgerald. SBLRBS 34. Atlanta: Scholars Press, 1997.

Taylor, J. E. "Seleucid Rule in Palestine." Ph.D. diss., Duke University, Durham, N.C., 1979.

Tcherikover, V. *Hellenistic Civilization and the Jews.* Philadelphia: Jewish Publication Society of America, 1959.

Thomas, D. W. "*Kelebh,* 'Dog': Its Origins and Some Usages of It in the Old Testament." *VT* 10 (1960): 410–27.

Thompson, J. A. "The Significance of the Verb *Love* in the David-Jonathan Narratives in 1 Samuel." *VT* 24 (1974): 34–38.

Tiller, P. A. *A Commentary on the Animal Apocalypse of 1 Enoch.* SBLEJL 4. Atlanta: Scholars Press, 1993.

Ulrichsen, J. H. *Die Grundschrift der Testamente der Zwölf Patriarchen.* Uppsala: Almqvist & Wiksell, 1995.

VanderKam, J. C. *From Revelation to Canon.* JSJSup 62. Leiden: Brill, 2000.

———. *An Introduction to Early Judaism.* Grand Rapids, Mich.: Eerdmans, 2001.

Watson, W. G. E. *Classical Hebrew Poetry.* JSOTSup 26. Sheffield: JSOT Press, 1984.

———. *Traditional Techniques in Classical Hebrew Verse.* JSOTSup 170. Sheffield: Sheffield Academic Press, 1994.

Whitley, C. F. *Koheleth: His Language and Thought.* BZAW 148. Berlin: de Gruyter, 1979.

Whybray, R. N. *Wealth and Poverty in the Book of Proverbs.* JSOTSup 99. Sheffield: JSOT Press, 1990.

4. Greek and Latin Literature: Texts and Studies

Allinson, F. G., trans. *Menander: The Principal Fragments.* LCL. New York: Putnam, 1930.

Blundell, M. W. *Helping Friends and Harming Enemies: A Study in Sophocles and Greek Ethics.* Cambridge: Cambridge University Press, 1989.

Boardman, J., J. Griffin, and O. Murray, eds. *The Oxford History of the Classical World.* Oxford: Oxford University Press, 1986.

Bolotin, D. *Plato's Dialogue on Friendship: An Interpretation of the Lysis, With a New Translation.* Ithaca, N.Y.: Cornell University Press, 1979.

Chambry, E., trans. *Esope: Fables.* Paris: Les Belles Lettres, 1927.

Donlan, W. "*Pistos Philos Hetairos.*" Pp. 223–44 in *Theognis of Megara: Poetry and the Polis.* Edited by T. J. Figueira and G. Nagy. Baltimore: Johns Hopkins University Press, 1985.

Dugas, L. *L'amitié antique d'après les moeurs populaires et les théories des philosophes.* 2 vols. Paris: Alcan, 1894; rev. ed., 1914.

Edmonds, J. M., trans. *Elegy and Iambus.* LCL. 2 vols. New York: Putnam, 1931.

Engberg-Pedersen, T. "Plutarch to Prince Philopappus on How to Tell a Flatterer from a Friend." Pp. 61–79 in *Friendship, Flattery, and Frankness of Speech: Studies on Friendship in the New Testament World.* Edited by J. T. Fitzgerald. NovTSup 82. Leiden: Brill, 1996.

Evelyn-White, H. G., trans. *Hesiod, the Homeric Hymns and Homerica.* LCL. New York: Macmillan, 1914.

Falconer, W. A., trans. *Cicero: De Senectute, De Amicitia, De Divinatione.* LCL. New York: Putnam, 1923.

Figueira, T. J., and G. Nagy. *Theognis of Megara: Poetry and the Polis.* Baltimore: Johns Hopkins University Press, 1985.

Fiore, B. "The Theory and Practice of Friendship in Cicero." Pp. 59–76 in *Greco-Roman Perspectives on Friendship.* Edited by J. T. Fitzgerald. SBLRBS 34. Atlanta: Scholars Press, 1997.

Fitzgerald, J. T. "Friendship in the Greek World Prior to Aristotle." Pp. 13–34 in *Greco-Roman Perspectives on Friendship.* Edited by J. T. Fitzgerald. SBLRBS 34. Atlanta: Scholars Press, 1997.

———, ed. *Friendship, Flattery, and Frankness of Speech: Studies on Friendship in the New Testament World.* NovTSup 82. Leiden: Brill, 1996.

———, ed. *Greco-Roman Perspectives on Friendship.* SBLRBS 34. Atlanta: Scholars Press, 1997.

Fraisse, J. C. *Philia: la notion d'amitié dans la philosophie antique: essai sur un problème perdu et retrouvé.* Paris: Vrin, 1974.

Freese, J. H., trans. *Aristotle: The 'Art' of Rhetoric.* LCL. New York: Putnam, 1926.

Gerber, D. E., trans. *Greek Elegiac Poetry: From the Seventh to the Fifth Centuries B.C.* LCL. Cambridge, Mass.: Harvard University Press, 1999.

Glad, C. E. "Frank Speech, Flattery, and Friendship in Philodemus." Pp. 21–59 in *Friendship, Flattery, and Frankness of Speech: Studies on Friendship in the New Testament World.* Edited by J. T. Fitzgerald. NovTSup 82. Leiden: Brill, 1996.

Hummel, P. "*Philos/pistos:* étude d'un cas de complémentarité métrique." *Informations Grammaticales* 36 (1988): 17–19.

Kamtekar, R. "Friendship in Plato's Politics." Ph.D. diss., University of Chicago, 1995.

Konstan, D. *Friendship in the Classical World.* Cambridge: Cambridge University Press, 1997.

———. "Friendship, Frankness and Flattery." Pp. 7–19 in *Friendship, Flattery, and Frankness of Speech: Studies on Friendship in the New Testament World.* Edited by J. T. Fitzgerald. NovTSup 82. Leiden: Brill, 1996.

———. "Greek Friendship." *AJP* 117 (1996): 71–94.

Lamb, W. R. M., trans. *Plato: Lysis, Symposium, Gorgias.* LCL. New York: Putnam, 1925.

Mair, A. W., trans. *Oppian, Colluthus, Tryphiodorus.* LCL. New York: Putnam, 1928.

Marchant, E. C., trans. *Xenophon: Memorabilia and Oeconomicus.* LCL. New York: Putnam, 1923.

Miller, W., trans. *Xenophon: Cyropaedia.* LCL. 2 vols. New York: Macmillan, 1914.

Murray, A. T., trans. *Homer: The Iliad.* LCL. 2 vols. New York: Putnam, 1924–1925.

———, trans. *Homer: The Odyssey.* LCL. 2 vols. New York: Putnam, 1919.

Murray, O. "Life and Society in Classical Greece." Pp. 204–33 in *The Oxford History of the Classical World.* Edited by J. Boardman, J. Griffin, and O. Murray. Oxford: Oxford University Press, 1986.

Norlin, G., and L. van Hook, trans. *Isocrates.* LCL. 3 vols. New York: Putnam, 1928 (vols. 1–2); Cambridge, Mass: Harvard University Press, 1945 (vol. 3).

O'Neil, E. N. "Plutarch on Friendship." Pp. 105–22 in *Greco-Roman Perspectives on Friendship.* Edited by J. T. Fitzgerald. SBLRBS 34. Atlanta: Scholars Press, 1997.

Peck, A. L., and D. M. Balme, trans. *Aristotle: History of Animals.* LCL. 3 vols. Cambridge, Mass.: Harvard University Press, 1965–1991.

Pizzolato, L. F. *L'idea di amicizia nel mondo antico classico e cristiano.* Filosofia 238. Turin: Einaudi, 1993.

Price, A. W. *Love and Friendship in Plato and Aristotle.* Oxford: Clarendon, 1989.

Rackham, H., trans. *Aristotle: The Nicomachean Ethics.* LCL. New York: Putnam, 1926.

Rogers, B. B., trans. *Aristophanes.* LCL. 3 vols. New York: Putnam, 1924.

Sandys, J. E., trans. *The Odes of Pindar.* 2d ed. LCL. New York: Putnam, 1930.

Schmidt-Berger, U. "Philia: Typologie der Freundschaft und Verwandtschaft bei Euripides." Ph.D. diss., University of Tübingen, 1973.

Schollmeier, P. *Other Selves: Aristotle on Personal and Political Friendship.* Albany, N.Y.: State University of New York Press, 1994.

Schroeder, F. M. "Friendship in Aristotle and Some Peripatetic Philosophers." Pp. 35–57 in *Greco-Roman Perspectives on Friendship.* Edited by J. T. Fitzgerald. SBLRBS 34. Atlanta: Scholars Press, 1997.

Steinberger, J. *Begriff und Wesen der Freundschaft bei Aristoteles und Cicero.* Erlangen: privately published, 1955.

Stern-Gillet, S. *Aristotle's Philosophy of Friendship.* Albany, N.Y.: State University of New York Press, 1995.

Storr, F., trans. *Sophocles.* LCL. 2 vols. New York: Macmillan, 1913.

Tyler, J. "Philia and Echthra in Euripides." Ph.D. diss., Cornell University, Ithaca, N.Y., 1969.

Vince, J. H., trans. *Demosthenes.* LCL. New York: Putnam, 1930.

Way, A. S., trans. *Euripides.* LCL. 4 vols. New York: Macmillan, 1912.

5. Modern Works on Friendship

Argyle, M. *The Psychology of Interpersonal Behavior.* Harmondsworth: Penguin, 1967.

Badhwar, N. K. *Friendship: A Philosophical Reader.* Ithaca, N.Y.: Cornell University Press, 1993.

Bloom, A. *Love and Friendship.* New York: Simon & Schuster, 1993.

Blum, L. A. *Friendship, Altruism, and Morality.* London: Routledge & Kegan Paul, 1980.

Duck, S. *Friends, For Life: The Psychology of Close Relationships.* New York: St. Martin's, 1983.

Enright, D. J., and D. Rawlinson, *The Oxford Book of Friendship.* Oxford: Oxford University, 1991.

Leaman, O., ed. *Friendship East and West: Philosophical Perspectives.* Richmond, Surrey: Curzon, 1996.

McGuire, B. P. *Friendship and Community: The Monastic Experience 350–1250.* Cistercian Studies 95. Kalamazoo, Mich.: Cistercian Publications, 1988.

Meilaender, G. *Friendship, a Study in Theological Ethics.* Notre Dame, Ind.: University of Notre Dame Press, 1981.

Moltmann-Wendel, E. *Rediscovering Friendship.* London: SCM, 2000.

Pakaluk, M., ed. *Other Selves: Philosophers on Friendship.* Indianapolis: Hackett, 1991.

Rubin, L. B. *Just Friends: The Role of Friendship in Our Lives.* New York: Harper & Row, 1985.

Wadell, P. J. *Friendship and the Moral Life.* Notre Dame, Ind.: University of Notre Dame Press, 1989.

White, C. *Christian Friendship in the Fourth Century.* Cambridge: Cambridge University Press, 1992.

INDEX OF PRIMARY SOURCES

Hebrew Bible

Apocryphal/Deuterocanonical Books

Jewish Pseudepigrapha and Dead Sea Scrolls

New Testament and New Testament Pseudepigrapha

Josephus and Philo

Postbiblical Jewish Texts

Ancient Texts from Syria-Palestine

Ancient Mesopotamian Texts

Ancient Egyptian Texts

Classical Authors

INDEX OF MODERN AUTHORS

INDEX OF SUBJECTS